Negative Outcome in Psychotherapy and What To Do About It

Daniel T. Mays, Psy.D., is founder and director of the New Jersey Psychological Institute in Freehold, New Jersey, and a consultant neuropsychologist to the Carrier Foundation in Belle Mead, New Jersey. He holds a doctorate in clinical psychology from Rutgers University and a masters degree from Hahnemann Medical College. A diplomate of the American Academy of Behavioral Medicine, he is a licensed psychologist in the State of New Jersey. Dr. Mays is a member of the American Psychological Association; the New York Academy of Sciences; the New York Neuropsychology Group; the Association for the Advancement of Behavior Therapy; and the National Register of Health Service Providers in Psychology. He has served as an Editorial Consultant to *Psychotherapy Theory Research and Practice,* and has published in the areas of psychotherapy and neuropsychology.

Cyril M. Franks, Ph.D., is Professor of Psychology in the Graduate School of Applied and Professional Psychology at Rutgers University. He is cofounder and first president of the Association for Advancement of Behavior Therapy; founder and first editor (1970–1979) of the journal *Behavior Therapy;* senior author of the series *Annual Review of Behavior Therapy: Theory and Practice;* and founder and coeditor of the Springer Series on Behavior Therapy and Behavioral Medicine. Professor Franks received his Ph.D. from the University of London Institute of Psychiatry (Maudsley Hospital) in 1954. He also holds a B.Sc. from the University of Wales and an M.A. from the University of Minnesota. In addition to being editor-in-chief of the journal *Child and Family Behavior Therapy,* Dr. Franks is the author of some 300 articles and chapters, and the editor of numerous books in his field.

Negative Outcome in Psychotherapy and What To Do About It

Daniel T. Mays, Psy. D.
Cyril M. Franks, Ph.D.

Springer Publishing Company
New York

Springer Publishing Company, Inc.
536 Broadway
New York, New York 10012

85 86 87 88 89 / 10 9 8 7 6 5 4 3 2 1

Library of Congress Cataloging in Publication Data
Main entry under title:

Negative outcome in psychotherapy and what to do about it.

   Bibliography: p. Includes index.
   1. Psychotherapy—Complications and sequelae.   I. Mays, Daniel T.   II. Franks, Cyril
M.   [DNLM: 1. Psychotherapy.   2. Therapeutics—adverse effects. WM 420 N384]
RC480.5.N34   1985   616.89'14   84-26867
ISBN 0-8261-4030-0

Contents _____

Preface _____

The germination of this book occurred during a seminar I led at Rutgers University, which was attended by Daniel T. Mays. During the seminar, interest in the issue of negative outcome was provoked by an article written by A. E. Bergin for *Psychology Today* in 1975, about the potentially harmful effects of psychotherapy. As the seminar proceeded it became increasingly evident that the problems and issues needed more careful examination than Bergin suggested. Our reanalysis of Bergin's data led to interpretations which appeared in *Professional Psychology* in 1980, together with a reply by Bergin and a rebuttal by the two of us. These developments prompted an interest in a more intense examination of the entire problem, which culminated in the text of this book.

Bergin, "more than any other writer, . . . is responsible for bringing to professional attention the fact that some patients become worse rather than better over the course of psychotherapy" (Mays & Franks, 1980, p. 78). Therefore, we very much regret that Bergin's many prior commitments prevented his inclusion in this volume.

We are grateful for the secretarial, organizational, and other skills of Loraine Bernzweig and especially of Andrea B. Tubridy, and all of the New Jersey Psychological Institute, for assistance vital to the preparation of this text. Finally, we acknowledge with love and admiration the critical comments, encouragement, and support of our wives, Laura Mays and Violet Franks.

C.M.F.

Foreword _____

By considering potential negative outcome in our therapeutic work
with patients, our perspectives as therapists broaden to systematic or
ecological points of view. Unintended negative effects or side effects of
individual, family, group, or milieu therapies force us to use longer
time frames, multidimensional approaches to treatment evaluation,
and evaluation strategies that encompass the patient's larger social or
environmental network.

While discussion of negative outcome is novel in some quarters,
cases have been described for over two decades by clinical investigators
working with chronic schizophrenic patients and behavior therapy. For
example, it has been known for many years that vulnerable schizophrenics, indexed by their continuing florid symptoms, suffer an exacerbation of their disorder when they are introduced to total-push therapy in enthusiastic treatment and rehabilitation programs (Liberman,
1982; Liberman, Falloon, and Wallace, 1984). Behavior therapists have
often highlighted the unintended negative effects of treatment interventions with various types of patients (Sajwaj et al., 1972; Epstein et
al., 1974; Willems, 1974). For example, in token economies that do not
build in programming for generalization, patients may become token-
bound and unable to perform self-care and other tasks in aftercare
settings. Successful outcomes that are defined and linked in a single
treatment setting, whether on a psychiatric ward or in a psychotherapist's office, may handicap the patient elsewhere; treatment may have
a good outcome for the individual patient's self-fulfillment and symp-

tom remission, but lead to unintended negative effects on a spouse, child, or business partner. A longer time span for assessing outcome will help us recognize both positive and negative effects more clearly. For instance, a course of therapy may produce unwanted symptoms, maladjustment, and even disaffection of the patient with the therapist; however, on a longer view this may be seen as the start of a continuing trajectory of change that ultimately leads to a beneficial outcome. This process has been strikingly documented by Strauss (1984) in his longitudinal studies of psychotic patients undergoing long-term treatment.

We should be reminded that many effective treatments in medicine do have negative side effects which must be balanced in a benefit/ risk ratio to determine whether the drug or surgery should be administered. Similarly, in psychotherapy, it may be unrealistic to achieve total elimination of negative effects; instead, we need to better predict them, manage them when they occur, and balance the negative with the positive consequences of treatment. One approach to this would be to disavow the prevalent ideal endpoint in psychotherapy—to identify that treatment which, in the hands of a particular type of therapist, will produce the best outcome with a given type of patient—and instead to have our treatments guided by a flexible, multimodal strategy in which the patient and his or her ecological system are offered a variety of interventions depending upon their changing needs. Flexible therapeutic strategies that provide guidelines for clinical decision making have been articulated for depression and schizophrenia (Liberman, 1980; Liberman, Falloon, and Wallace, 1984).

The present volume represents a welcome movement in the direction of a more flexible and empirically guided use of psychotherapies.

R.P.L.

References

Epstein, L.H., Doke, L.A., Sajwaj, T.E., Sorrell, S. & Rimmer, B. (1974) Generality and side effects of overcorrection. *Journal of Applied Behavior Analysis*, 7, 385–390.

Liberman, R.P. (1980) Individualizing treatment strategies in depression. In L.P. Rehm (Ed.) Behavior therapy for depression. New York: Academic Press.

Liberman, R.P. (1982) Social factors in schizophrenia. In Grinspoon, L. (Ed.) *Psychiatry 1982 Annual Review*. Washington, DC: American Psychiatric Press, 97–111.

Liberman, R.P., Falloon, I.R.H., and Wallace, C.J. (1984) Drug-psychosocial interactions in the treatment of schizophrenia. In M. Mirabi (Ed.) The Chronically Mentally Ill: Research and Services. New York: SP Medical & Scientific Books.

Sajwaj, T.E., Twardose, S. & Burlee, M. (1972) Side effects of extinction procedures in a remedial preschool. *Journal of Applied Behavioral Analysis, 5*, 163–176.

Strauss, J.S. & Haber, H. (1981) Clinical questions and "real" research. *American Journal of Psychiatry, 138,* 1592–1597.

Willems, E.P. (1974) Behavioral technology and behavioral ecology. *Journal of Applied Behavioral Analysis, 7,* 151–166.

Contributors

Christopher R. Barbrack, Ph.D.
Princeton Center for Psycho-
therapy
Princeton, New Jersey

Harold R. Beech, Ph.D.
Professor of Clinical Psychology
The University Hospital of
South Manchester
Manchester, England

Donald Colson, Ph.D.
Director of Psychology
C. F. Menninger Hospital
Topeka, Kansas

Robert R. Dies, Ph.D.
Professor of Psychology
University of Maryland
College Park, Maryland

Michael G. Emerson, Ph.D.
Department of Psychology
University of Minnesota
Minneapolis, Minnesota

Hans J. Eysenck, Ph.D.
Department of Psychology
Institute of Psychiatry
London, England

Alan S. Gurman, Ph.D.
Professor and Director
Psychiatric Outpatient Clinic
Department of Psychiatry
University of Wisconsin Medical
School
Madison, Wisconsin

Suzanne W. Hadley, Ph.D.
Office of Extramural Project
Review
National Institute of Mental
Health
Rockville, Maryland

Steven D. Hollon, Ph.D.
Department of Psychology
University of Minnesota
Minneapolis, Minnesota

Robert Lynn Horne, M.D.
The Carrier Foundation
Belle Mead, New Jersey

Leonard Horwitz, Ph.D.
Chief of Clinical Psychology
The Menninger Foundation
Topeka, Kansas, and
Training Analyst
Topeka Institute for
  Psychoanalysis
Topeka, Kansas

Alan E. Kazdin, Ph.D.
Professor of Child Psychiatry
  and Psychology
Department of Psychiatry
Western Psychiatric Institute
  and Clinic
University of Pittsburgh School
  of Medicine
Pittsburgh, Pennsylvania

David P. Kniskern, Psy.D.
Associate Professor
Department of Psychiatry
University of Cincinnati College
  of Medicine
Cincinnati, Ohio

Lisa Lewis, Ph.D.
Staff Psychologist
The Menninger Foundation
Topeka, Kansas

Michael H. Stone, M.D.
Clinical Director and Professor
  of Psychiatry
University of Connecticut
  Health Center
Farmington, Connecticut

Hans H. Strupp, Ph.D.
Distinguished Professor
Department of Psychology
Vanderbilt University
Nashville, Tennessee

Patricia A. Teleska, M.A.
Graduate Student
Department of Psychology
University of Maryland
College Park, Maryland

Peggy Thoits, Ph.D.
Assistant Professor
Department of Sociology
Princeton University
Princeton, New Jersey

Margaret Vaughan, Ph.D.
Senior Lecturer in Clinical
  Psychology
The University of Manchester
Manchester, England

Negative Outcome in Psychotherapy and What To Do About It

Part I

Introduction

1

Negative Outcome: Historical Context and Definitional Issues

Daniel T. Mays and Cyril M. Franks

Introduction

The notion that psychotherapy can cause harm under certain circumstances is not new. This issue was and still is an outgrowth of controversy about the effectiveness of psychotherapy in general, and it is probably artificial to separate the two concerns. This caveat notwithstanding, there are good reasons for the specific focus upon negative outcome that is the main theme of this text. First, while much has been written about outcome research in general, *negative* outcome has received limited attention. Second, it cannot be assumed that the parameters related to positive outcome are identical to those that lead to negative outcome. Third, this issue has important ramifications for treatment. It is essential to examine the safety of a treatment approach as well as its effectiveness. Hence, the age-old dictum for health service providers: "Above all, do not harm."

Debate over the issue of negative outcome grew out of concern with the effectiveness of psychotherapy. Psychoanalysts and behavior therapists have long been engaged in cogent debate over the relative merits of their respective systems (Franks & Barbrack, 1983). Each lay claim to therapeutic superiority, and, in so doing, the entire area of the effectiveness of psychotherapy was opened for scrutiny. For the most part, these developments were constructive. They helped clarify the fundamental differences between the two systems and thereby sharpened thinking in both. In so doing concerns about the potentially harmful effects of all forms of therapy was generated. This forced more discerning therapists to examine more closely what they do.

With regard to negative outcome specifically, the impact is disappointing. This is due to several factors: First, as will be shown, the question was incorrectly posed from the start. Second, negative outcome research is more difficult to carry out than outcome research in general. Third, there has been and still is an understandable reluctance to cast colleagues in unfavorable lights. It is therefore quite understandable that the issue has not yet received the attention it merits.

Negative outcome was originally framed in terms of causality and restricted to those cases in which a decline in patient functioning is directly attributable to the therapy or the therapist. Since causality is intrinsically difficult to demonstrate, the entire issue stalled on the question of whether negative effects as defined exist at all. With the focus upon whether psychotherapy can or cannot be harmful, it is hardly surprising that negative outcome has not been explored within a total context which takes into account the many complexities involved. In particular, there has been an overemphasis upon the contribution of the therapist to negative outcome. Other potential sources of influence upon negative outcome, especially patient characteristics and extratherapeutic events, have been inadequately explored, largely because, by definition, these factors cannot produce negative effects.

Additionally, negative outcome has lagged behind other areas of outcome research for reasons peculiar to the field. For example, since patients who decline in functioning during therapy are a small subgroup of the patient population, it is hard to accumulate a sample size sufficient to permit a meaningful examination of contributing factors. Furthermore, for obvious reasons, it is not ethical to manipulate negative outcome experimentally. Thus, the major direct avenues to exploration of contributing factors are blocked.

The reluctance of professionals to publish research that casts their colleagues in an unfavorable light also contributes to the limited knowledge of negative outcome. For example, the publication of Ricks' "Supershrink" research (Ricks, 1974) was delayed for several years because of fear of the controversy it might engender (see Bergin & Lambert, 1978).

In somewhat oversimplified form, the essence of the negative out-come debate is as follows: One position, espoused by Bergin (1963, 1966, 1967, 1970, 1971, 1975; Bergin & Lambert, 1978; Lambert, Bergin, & Collins, 1977) is that psychotherapy, particularly the influence of the therapist, causes patients to become worse over the course of therapy. Others (particularly May, 1971; Rachman, 1973) refute this contention, insisting that there is no acceptable empirical evidence of negative out-come. It is our contention that negative outcome occurs in psycho-therapy, but that variables additional to therapist factors contribute to negative outcome: specifically certain patient factors and extrathera-peutic events.

Our present purposes are fourfold: (1) to generate a definition of negative outcome which takes into consideration factors beyond those contributed directly by the therapists themselves; (2) to bring some preliminary closure to the ongoing negative outcome debate; (3) to identify some of the specific contributing variables; and (4) to offer suggestions for research and treatment application. Each of the chapters that follow, written by a recognized expert in the topic under discussion, is selected to meet one or more of these purposes. To set the scene, it is necessary to resolve certain definitional discrepancies and present a chronological overview of developments in the area of negative outcome. The remainder of this chapter is devoted to these matters.

What to Call It When Patients Get Worse

Bergin (1963, 1966) coined the term *deterioration effect* to refer to what he called a "double-edged effect" observed in a number of studies show-ing greater change-score variance in experimental than in control groups. He took this as evidence that some of the therapy patients must be getting worse at a higher rate than those in the control group. Later, the term came to be applied to patient worsening as a result of psychotherapy. While Bergin suggests that deterioration implies an "impairment of vigor, resilience, or usefulness from a previously higher state" (Lambert et al., 1977, p. 454), he has not offered an explicit definition of "deterioration" and, in fact, suggests that "patient deterioration has not in the past nor can it presently be limited to a set definition" (Lambert et al., 1977 p. 454).

There are numerous problems with both Bergin's term and usage. The term *deterioration* has long been employed in psychiatry to suggest a "progressively increasing impairment in functioning," with the con-notation of "progressive loss of intellectual facilities" (Hinsie & Campbell, 1970, pp. 207, 193). But it is clear from the outcome research quoted by Bergin in support of the "deterioration hypothesis" that such usage is not what he means by the term. In practice, the term is applied to what are often superficial changes. For example, among the evidence presented as demonstrating a "deterioration effect" is a study by Wispe and Parloff (1965). APA psychologists who had received psychotherapy tended to decrease their rates of publication relative to psychologists who had not received psychotherapy. While pundits would understandably debate whether such an outcome is negative at all, it is hard to avoid the conclusion that this is hardly deterioration in the usual usage of the term.

Another objection to the term *deterioration* is that it does not give due consideration to the complex nature of change. One can experience negative change in one sphere of functioning and positive changes in another. For example, it is possible to become both less depressed and more anxious at the same time, or vice versa. Deterioration, connoting as it does a pervasive decline in functioning across the board, fails to accommodate the mixed outcomes which seem to be as much the rule as the exception in outcome research.

Bergin's suggestion that the meaning of "deterioration" should include a lack of significant improvement when such improvement is expected (Lambert et al., 1977) is also questionable. To do as Bergin suggests would be to distort the concept. One cannot assume *a priori* that the same factors which contribute to lack of change, even when expected, also contribute to negative outcome. Furthermore, lack of expected change can more readily be assessed by other means, such as comparing improvement rates between experimental and control groups.

Strupp and his co-workers suggest that the term *negative effect* replace *deterioration* (Strupp, Hadley, & Gomes-Schwartz, 1977) and define negative effect as

> a worsening of a patient's condition attributable to his having undergone psychotherapy. We further postulate that a negative effect must be relatively lasting, which excludes from consideration transient effects (e.g., temporary sadness or anxiety contingent upon separation from the therapist at termination) and random fluctuations due to momentary life stress and intercurrent events. Excluded also are instances in which psychotherapy produces no change in the patient. Thus, in order for us to speak of a negative effect in psychotherapy, there must be evidence of adverse changes in the patient's condition (in relation to his *status quo ante*) directly attributable to, or a function of, the character or quality of the therapeutic experience or intervention to which he has been exposed (pp. 91–92).

The rationale offered for this change in terminology by Strupp et al. is that the term *negative effect* appears to be a more accurate description of "therapy-induced changes for the worse." The term *negative effect* does avoid some of the misleading connotations of the term *deterioration*, and also seems more easily applied to a negative change in a specific area of functioning, taking into account the multivariant nature of change. However, both Strupp's and Bergin's definitions are generally restricted to therapy-induced negative changes. There appear to be two major problems with this facet of the above definition. First, such a definition implies a causal connection between the therapy and the decline in functioning. The review of the literature which follows illustrates the difficulties in establishing this causal connection. As Rachman and Wilson (1980) note,

> The fact that some patients experience deterioration during or after their participation in a course of psychotherapy cannot be taken to signify that the psychotherapy has caused the deterioration—any more than one can rashly presume that positive changes observed during and after psychotherapy are necessarily the result of that treatment. In both cases it is necessary to demonstrate that the positive or negative changes are greater than those which might be expected to have occurred in the absence of psychotherapy (p. 100).

In light of the difficulties imposed by the attempt to separate the therapist's contribution to a decline in a patient's functioning from other causes of such decline, it seems preferable to develop a definition of negative change which is independent of the causality question, and then to treat the causality question as an independent empirical issue. The failure to keep these questions distinct has contributed to at least some of the confusion in the discussion of negative changes. In actual usage, the data which have been presented in support of the therapist's contribution to negative outcomes are not restricted to those effects which have been demonstrated to be therapy-induced. A parallel difficulty applies to excluding life stressors and events as causal ingredients. The impact of life events has been attended to only sporadically in psychotherapy outcome research but, when looked for, an influence has usually been found (see Chapter 12).

All in all, some revisions of the above definition are needed. The term selected should be free from catastrophic connotations and should reflect the multivariant nature of change, so that in any given case one can speak of a negative outcome in one sphere of functioning while allowing for the possibility of positive outcomes in others. Instances in which the therapy produced no change should be excluded, as should transient effects. It is most important that all negative outcomes be included, whether attributable to the patient, to the therapist, or to events outside the therapy.

We propose, therefore, a modified definition, and offer Negative Outcome to distinguish usage consistent with the following definition from other usages:

> A Negative Outcome is a significant decline in one or more areas of a patient's functioning, between the onset of psycho- therapy and termination of therapy (and for controls, over an equivalent period of time), which persists for a substantial period of time beyond termination of therapy. The term Nega- tive Outcome is not restricted to those negative changes which are therapy-induced, and usage of the term does not therefore imply that the therapist is necessarily responsible for the nega- tive change.

To keep separate the distinction between (1) patients who improve over the course of psychotherapy only to decline between termination and the measurement of follow-up, and (2) patients who decline over the course of psychotherapy, Strupp and his co-workers (1977) distin- guish between a "relapse" and a "negative effect." Maintaining the distinction between a negative outcome and a relapse appears to sim- plify the task of sorting out the factors leading to negative change. This distinction should be retained.

Another area of confusion lies in the difference between treatment failure and negative outcome. Treatment failure is the more general category, and negative outcome is one facet of or possibility within this category. Treatment failure could encompass those cases of negative outcome, no change, or those in which progress is less than expected.

The Negative Outcome Literature: A Chronological Review

Current debate about negative outcome is profoundly influenced by how such concerns originated and by subsequent dialogue and evalua- tion. To appreciate the complex and often subtle issues raised in the chapters to follow, a historical perspective is helpful.

Although Freud suggested as early as 1910 that certain aspects of the therapist's behavior, which he termed countertransference, might exert a negative influence on the course and outcome of psy- choanalysis, such assertions were coupled with an anti-empirical bias which contributed to a lack of interest in controlled outcome research. Freud (1922) explicitly declined to compile "a statistical enumeration of our successes." "The strongest reason against it," he said, "lay in the recognition of the fact that in matters of therapy, humanity is in the highest degree irrational, so that there is no prospect of influencing it by reasonable arguments" (pp. 386–387). Given the influence of Freud's pronouncements, it is not surprising that empirical evidence of negative outcome did not emerge until the early 1950s.

The 1950s

It was not until 1951 that there was any empirical evidence of negative outcome (Powers & Witmer, 1951). These authors were among the first to point to evidence of deterioration, in the Cambridge-Somerville delinquency prevention study, later described as "one of the most devastatingly null of all outcome studies" (Malan, 1973). This evidence was ignored at the time.

In the following year, Eysenck's (1952) review stimulated much attention to outcome research in psychotherapy, as well as to possible negative outcome in therapy. Eysenck's examination of some 24 studies, covering over 8,000 cases, led to the conclusion that they

> fail to prove that psychotherapy, Freudian or otherwise, facilitates the recovery of neurotic patients. They show that roughly two-thirds of a group of neurotic patients will recover or improve to a marked extent within about two years of the onset of their illness, whether they are treated by means of psychotherapy or not (1952, p. 324).

In 1954, Rogers and Dymond edited a volume on the status of client-centered therapy in which the few passing references to negative outcome were overshadowed by other aspects of the report. The references to negative outcome include a statement that 24 percent of the treated clients declined in self-ideal correlation, and a notation of a "sharp decrease in the maturity of the behavior of those clients rated as unsuccessful" (p. 228). A similar trend was documented in Cartwright's (1956) analysis of data published by Barron and Leary in 1955. Cartwright noted evidence of greater variation in outcome among treated patients than among waiting list controls and commented that "some therapy patients deteriorated to a greater extent than did waiting list controls, while some therapy patients did improve significantly more than the controls" (p. 404). Neither paper prompted much concern with negative outcome at the time.

The 1960s

As dramatized by the first of three conferences on "Research in Psychotherapy" (Rubinstein & Parloff, 1959), the prevailing trend during this period was away from the analysis of outcome, toward an examination of the process of psychotherapy. Hoch and Zubin (1964) termed this trend the "flight from outcome into process." During the second conference, held in 1961, Betz (1962) described a therapist variable he had isolated in collaboration with Whitehorn in the treatment of schizophrenia. Betz reported having isolated two different types of therapists, designated "A" and "B" types, respectively. A-type therapists showed greater grasp of the personal meaning and motivation of the patient's behavior, were more personality-oriented instead of pathology-oriented, and tended to focus on the use of assets to a greater extent than did B-type therapists. Betz intimated that B-type therapists may promote "deterioration" among schizophrenics.

In the same year Truax (1961; see Truax, 1963) presented some preliminary data to a meeting of the University of Wisconsin psychotherapy research group suggesting that certain therapist characteristics were related to "deterioration" in schizophrenics. Therapists rated low on empathy, positive regard, and genuineness tend to make patients worse. This meeting, led by Rogers with Bergin among the participants, sparked interest in the negative outcome phenomenon.

The following year, Truax (1962; see Truax, 1963) again presented evidence for the harmful potential of psychotherapy among therapists offering low levels of empathy, positive regard, and genuineness. Bergin related evidence of "deterioration" to Eysenck's questioning of the effectiveness of psychotherapy and, based on controlled studies reporting null results, suggested that some therapists were making patients significantly worse. He took this as evidence that some therapists must be making patients significantly better. Bergin summarized six controlled studies which suggested evidence of "deterioration" in a portion of the patients receiving therapy (Bergin, 1963; Truax, 1963).

In the mid-sixties, Eysenck (1965, 1966) launched another attack on the effectiveness of psychoanalytic psychotherapy. This report considered six controlled studies of individual psychotherapy with neurotic patients. Only one was considered positive in outcome, and this one was regarded as methodologically inadequate. Eysenck's conclusion is interesting:

> . . . in the 1952 report, the main motive was one of stimulating better and more worthwhile research in this important but somewhat neglected field; there was an underlying belief that

while results to date had not disproved the null-hypothesis, improved methods of research would undoubtedly do so. Such a belief does not seem to be tenable any longer in this easy optimistic form, and it rather seems that psychologists and psychiatrists will have to acknowledge the fact that current psychotherapeutic procedures have not lived up to the hope which greeted their emergence fifty years ago (p. 40).

In the same volume, 18 discussants variously agreed and disagreed with Eysenck's position. The most significant critique was that of Kellner (1966, see Eysenck, 1966). He demonstrated biased treatment of therapy dropouts and, in addition, noted a number of studies (in which outcome significantly favored the experimental group) which Eysenck had neglected to mention. In reply, Eysenck suggested that, regardless of how interpreted, published studies failed to support psychoanalytic claims of effectiveness. If the existing studies are too poor to be taken seriously, then there is still no support for psychoanalytic claims. If adequate, they demonstrate its ineffectiveness. In explaining his intent, Eysenck states:

> I was not objecting so much to the failure of analysts to provide complete and unequivocal proof; I was objecting rather to the fact that no real effort was being made to provide such proof, to improve methods of investigation, or to devote more time and energy to this all-important problem. And I was objecting especially to the widespread practice of analysts to pretend that such proof was unnecessary or had already been furnished, and to continue making far-reaching claims for which there was simply no evidence worth looking at (p. 97).

In 1966, Bergin published a paper entitled "Some Implications of Psychotherapy Research for Therapeutic Practice," which seemed to be a response to Eysenck. In this paper he concluded that (1) untreated patients improve with the passage of time; (2) the client-centered approach is the only school of interview-oriented therapy consistently demonstrating favorable results; (3) in client-centered therapy, therapist characteristics such as warmth, empathy, and experience consistently correlate with improvement; (4) behavior therapy is effective, at least for certain symptoms; (5) certain kinds of patients are not helped by interview-oriented therapy; and (6) most forms of psychotherapy make patients worse as well as better, which accounts for the lack of difference in average improvement between treated patients and controls.

To support his latest conclusion Bergin produced seven studies, six of which had already been presented in 1964. He coined the term *deterioration effect* to describe his observation that, in a number of studies, while the average amount of change was only slightly better in experimental than in control groups, there was significantly higher variability in the experimental group. He suggested that this increase in variance resulted from psychotherapy causing patients to become both better and worse adjusted than comparable people not receiving treatment. Bergin took this "double-edged effect" to be evidence of the potency of psychotherapy. Bergin's 1966 article was reprinted in 1967 together with commentaries by Eysenck, Frank, Matarazzo, and Truax. Eysenck suggested that Bergin's argument was similar to advocating "a cure of the common cold on the grounds that while it kills some of the patients, others get well more quickly than they would have." With regard to the evidence of "deterioration," Eysenck comments, "I am not sure the evidence is as strong as it might be" (p. 152). Frank and Matarazzo found Bergin's evidence convincing. Truax stated conclusions similar to those of Bergin but in a more moderate form. Bergin's rejoiner was essentially a restatement of his original position.

The 1970s

Beginning in 1970, researchers began detailed examination of the research cited by Bergin in 1966. For example, in 1970, Braucht reviewed Bergin's seven studies and concluded that Bergin's research did not support his conclusion of a deterioration effect, "because of problems of criterion validity, lack of experimental control, inadequate experimental methodology and design" (p. 293). In his reply, Bergin (1970) shifted emphasis from the original proposition, that patients receiving psychotherapy experience a greater incidence of "deterioration" than comparable controls, to the more defensible proposition that some patients experience a decline in functioning over the course of therapy. Bergin referred to an abundance of evidence that "deterioration occurs during psychotherapy" (p. 300), and asserted that "the fact that some of the control groups in the studies reviewed are poor controls is irrelevant to the fact that deterioration occurs in the therapy groups" (p. 301). Bergin also alluded to additional studies which provided evidence of deterioration. These were eventually published in 1971 (see below). Bergin also reiterated his conclusion that the evidence of a "deterioration effect" demonstrates as well the evidence of an improvement effect ["to argue against deterioration is logically to argue that psychotherapy is ineffective or weak. To find data that it is indeed powerful is . . . a hopeful and not a negative sign" (p. 302)]. May (1971) reexamined the evidence presented by both Truax and Bergin in greater depth than had Braucht and concluded that "With the exception of one study of which the findings were equivocal, the conclusion that psychotherapy may induce a mixture of improvement and deterioration rests upon a flimsy and poorly controlled or weakly documented base" (p. 184).

The additional studies mentioned previously by Bergin were published again in the context of a reply to Eysenck's position concerning the effectiveness of psychotherapy. Briefly summarized, Bergin's criticisms of Eysenck's review pertain to (1) methodological problems with the studies themselves; (2) arithmetic errors made by Eysenck; (3) adopting a conservative position in reclassifying levels of improvement in studies whose categories differed from Eysenck's; (4) counting drop-outs as failures; (5) positive effects being counterbalanced by negative effects; and (6) unequal treatment of groups resulting in overstatement of spontaneous remission rates. Bergin also noted that, since untreated control groups receive substantial help, the comparison is actually between formal and informal treatment. With regard to negative outcome specifically, Bergin re-presented the seven 1966 studies along with 23 additional studies providing evidence of "deterioration" in psychotherapy. He estimated a 10 percent mean rate of "deterioration" among therapy cases and less than 5 percent for control cases.

In 1973, Rachman attacked both Bergin's spontaneous remission rate figures and his evidence for the deterioration effect. Rachman concluded that Bergin failed to demonstrate a cause–effect relationship between psychotherapy and "deterioration," labeling the evidence "scanty and incomplete." The same year, in the context of presenting the advantages of single and dual subject designs, Gottman (1973) provided a cogent analysis of the erroneous statistical assumptions underlying the Change-Score Variance Hypothesis which, in our view, nullifies this hypothesis as a valid argument to show the existence of negative outcome.

In 1977, Lambert, Bergin, and Collins presented nine studies relating to variance change, 31 additional treatment studies showing occurrences of "deterioration" in psychotherapy, plus eight additional studies showing "deterioration" in untreated groups of people. This review introduced 11 new therapy studies, bringing the total to 40, from which Bergin and his co-authors conclude that "the deterioration phenomenon is widespread" (p. 459). They abandoned previous attempts to estimate median deterioration rates, stating that such an estimate "would be nothing more than a conglomeration of diverse figures which would have very little predictive value" (p. 459). They also acknowledged Gottman's analysis of statistical flaws in their earlier change-score variance argument, in that "a treatment group can have a larger variance than a control group under quite varied circumstances" (p. 462).

The same year, Strupp, Hadley, and Gomes-Schwartz (1977) produced a significant volume on the problem of negative effects. Because many of the findings and views are addressed by Strupp and Hadley in Chapter 2, only a brief synopsis will be presented here. In the initial phase of the book, these authors address the empirical bases for concern with negative outcome and comment in some detail about problems of generalizability (how representative the patients and therapists in the studies are of patients and therapists in general), methodology, and design. After reviewing a sample of psychotherapy outcome studies alleged to provide evidence of therapy- or therapy-induced deterioration (Lambert et al., 1977), they concluded that "nearly all of the studies are marred by multiple flaws, both in selection of samples and [in] methodology" (p. 28). The authors then presented a commentary from 70 "experts" in the field of psychotherapy and concluded that the overwhelming majority of these experts consider the issue of negative effects to be "a significant problem requiring the attention and concern of practitioners and researchers alike" (p. 83). The book contains a lengthy tabulation of patient and therapist factors thought by these experts to contribute to negative effects. Finally, the authors present a "tripartite model" for evaluating therapy outcomes, emphasizing that "the problem of what constitutes a negative effect is inextricably interwoven with a definition of mental health" (p. 92). They identify three major interested parties involved in the evaluation of individual functioning: society (including the patient's significant others), the patient himself or herself, and the mental health professional. Then they examine how these particular vantage points of evaluation interact with the various aspects of patient change: adaptive behavior, sense of well-being, and inferred personality structure. This is an illuminating discussion, well worth reading in its original form by anyone involved in outcome research, evaluation, or treatment. In an appendix to the volume, Strupp and his co-workers present a brief synopsis of each psychotherapy study which Bergin had identified as relevant to negative outcome.

To help resolve some of the confusion surrounding negative outcome, Mays (1979) extracted four separate but interrelated propositions from the negative outcome debate:

1. Some patients experience negative outcome over the course of psychotherapy.
2. In general, patients receiving psychotherapy experience a greater incidence of negative outcome than do comparable no-treatment controls.
3. Psychotherapy causes negative outcome in a portion of patients receiving it.
4. The therapist is responsible for many of the negative outcomes which occur in psychotherapy.

Each study identified by Bergin as relevant to the issue of negative outcome was evaluated in detail with respect to the first two propositions. A study was considered to support proposition 1 if it validly demonstrates that a portion of the patients receiving psychotherapy treatment are worse at the end of treatment than prior to the start of treatment, regardless of the reason for the worsening. Strictly speaking, because of possible threats to internal validity, a control group is needed to demonstrate negative change. Nonetheless, Mays concluded that to apply such stringent requirements to these studies might unduly bias the evaluation in the direction of rejecting the possibility of negative outcome where it was in fact occurring. To balance the risks in both directions, it was decided that measurements of negative outcome would be considered as supporting proposition 1 provided that such measurements were conducted by an independent observer, or provided that a measurement from another source corroborated the first measurement, and provided that no other major confounds existed in the study. A limited support category was provided for those studies in which a valid finding of negative outcome pertained only to a delimited sphere of functioning, or where a finding was of limited generality.

A study was deemed to support proposition 2 if a legitimate comparison between an experimental and control group was possible, and a greater rate of negative outcome was found in the experimental group. A study was deemed to contradict proposition 2 if a legitimate comparison was possible, and a greater rate of negative outcome was found in the control group. When a comparison on some measures was contradicted by comparisons on other measures, a study was termed mixed. For both propositions, a study was deemed not relevant if a legitimate comparison was not possible because of major design flaws or insufficient data for a determination.

Rating the studies according to the criteria outlined above is somewhat arbitrary. For this reason inter-rater reliability was assessed by both Mays and an independent rater familiar with outcome research methodology. For each study, characteristics of the treatment, adequacy of control groups, and measurements of outcome were rated, and overall agreement achieved was 97.6 percent (Pearson product-moment correlation = .96).

The conclusions about these propositions are presented in tabular form (Table 1-1).

Of the 45 experimental groups available for comparison, 8 were deemed to support proposition 1, and 6 others as offering limited support. Two contradict the proposition, and 1 finding is mixed. The 2 findings contradicting proposition 1, and the third providing mixed evidence, are all studies of behavior therapy. Thus, for psychotherapy other than behavior therapy, the preponderance of evidence supports

Table 1-1   Distribution of Studies by Status Relative to Bergin's Propositions

	Proposition	
Status	One	Two
Supports proposition	8	0
Limited support, or support of limited generality	6	0
Contradicts proposition	2	6
Mixed support and contradiction	1	1
Not relevant to proposition	28	38
Totals	45[a]	45[a]

[a]Includes a separate counting of each experimental group in Category VII studies.

Reprinted from Mays, D.T. Negative effects in psychotherapy: Prevalence and causality reconsidered. Doctoral dissertation, Rutgers University, 1979, with permission.

the proposition that some patients decline in functioning over the course of treatment. As far as behavior therapy is concerned, the available evidence contradicts this proposition, but is insufficient to permit firm conclusions about negative outcome in behavior therapy.

Concerning proposition 2, no study was found to support the proposition and, in fact, six contradict it. One study found mixed support and contradiction. The author concluded that the preponderance of evidence contradicts Bergin's proposition that patients receiving psychotherapy suffer higher rates of negative effects than similar untreated patients.

As noted, the absence of evidence supporting proposition 2 substantially weakens the case for Bergin's proposition that psychotherapy causes negative outcome. Mays acknowledges the possibility that certain therapists are markedly successful in halting negative outcome, while other therapists cause negative outcome in patients who would not have declined without psychotherapy. Again as noted, further evidence is needed in order to support such a conclusion. Concerning whether the therapist is responsible for the preponderance of the negative outcome, Mays referred to data available in Truax and Mitchell (1971). He noted that, while some data do demonstrate a correlation between therapist behavior and negative outcome, the one adequately controlled study available showed greater decline in the control than the experimental group. This fact precluded the conclusion that the therapist causes the negative outcome in the studies quoted in Truax and Mitchell. Overall, Mays' 1979 contention was that the available evidence is insufficient to support the conclusion that the therapist is responsible for causing the preponderance of negative therapeutic outcome.

A reformulation of the Mays (1979) analysis was presented by Mays and Franks in 1980, with a reply from Bergin (1980) and rejoinder from Franks and Mays (1980). Studies bearing on the negative outcome question were categorized according to characteristics of treatment; adequacy of control groups, if any; and the outcome measurements employed. From their analysis, Mays and Franks concluded that few of the studies allow for meaningful comparisons between experimental and control groups. In studies permitting such comparisons, there is no significant evidence of greater negative outcome among the experimental groups. Given the evidence for greater decline among control as contrasted with therapy patients, these authors suggest the possibility that some patients who would have deteriorated without therapy are prevented from doing so, whereas others who would not have deteriorated do so because of the therapy. Another possibility is that certain patients manifest a deteriorating course with or without conventional psychotherapy. They urge investigation of each of these possibilities, to seek out characteristics associated with harm to specific types of patients.

Bergin's response is highly critical. Labeling the original article "a polemic rather than a critique," Bergin accused Mays and Franks of setting "impossible standards of proof," which he labels "methodolatry," producing "errors of both fact and interpretation," and resulting in "a caricature of the empirical status of deterioration effects." Bergin further accuses Mays and Franks of "establishing absolutistic and impractical standards regarding method, selecting illustrative studies that are inherently weak cases for the phenomena in question, dismissing strong evidence as irrelevant, and selecting bits of data from studies that support their view" (p. 99). Bergin also states that "more balanced critical reviews of this topic have been done by May (1971), Rachman (1973), and Strupp et al. (1977)" (p. 99).

Bergin's reply to our article seems misdirected. As noted in the rejoinder (Franks & Mays, 1980), our standards for methodology were anything but absolutistic and impractical since we identified three methodologically adequate studies that contradict Bergin's position. In his reply, Bergin confuses the issue of whether certain patients decline in functioning over the course of therapy with the question of whether they decline at a greater rate or with higher frequency than they might have without therapy (here again, the definition of negative effect as therapist-induced causes confusion). Again as noted in our rejoinder, we are arguing that there is no evidence of greater negative outcome in patients than in comparable untreated controls. We have always rejected, and continue to reject, the absurd position that no one ever declined in functioning over the course of psychotherapy.

Bergin's charge of selective bias is particularly puzzling, since, to demonstrate that Bergin has not offered a single psychotherapy outcome study (meeting minimal requirements for adequacy of design), we included every study he has presented as bearing on his conclusion that therapy causes negative outcome. Bergin also accuses us of failing to report the full facts in five of the studies. In our rejoinder, we quote from the original studies to demonstrate that our conclusions are consistent with the original data.

Finally, in regard to Bergin's statement that more balanced reviews have been published elsewhere, we believe that these "more balanced reviews" are entirely consistent with our findings. These may be summed up as follows: (1) "The conclusion that psychotherapy may induce a mixture of improvement and deterioration rests upon flimsy and poorly controlled or weakly documented base" (May, 1971); (2) [the evidence is] "scanty and incomplete" (Rachman, 1973); and (3) "nearly all of the studies are marred by multiple flaws, both in selection of samples and in methodology" (Strupp et al., 1977). In the words of Rachman and Wilson (1980)

> Franks and Mays offer a compelling rejoinder to Bergin's comments, reiterating their original point that ". . . if therapy causes deterioration, one would expect to find one adequate psychotherapy outcome study in which a higher rate of decline occurs among the treated patients. This study has yet to be found." Bergin's reply does little to force a revision of this verdict, despite the strength of his conviction (p. 102).

Summary

Factors leading to a limited impact of the negative outcome question upon clinical practice are elucidated and the purposes of the book delineated. These are (1) to generate a definition of negative outcome which leads to a meaningful consideration of the many factors involved; (2) to bring some closure to the ongoing negative outcome debate; (3) to identify and delineate some of the specific contributing variables; and (4) to offer suggestions for the application of this understanding to further research, and to the treatment situation.

Negative outcome is defined as:

> a significant decline in one or more areas of a patient's functioning, between the onset and termination of psychotherapy (and for controls, over an equivalent period of time), which persists for a substantial period of time beyond termination of therapy. The term Negative Outcome is not restricted to those negative changes which are therapy-induced, and usage of the

term does not therefore imply that the therapist is necessarily responsible for the negative change.

As a brief orientation to the chapters that follow, a chronological review of developments concerning negative outcome is presented. Our interpretation of the data is that, in psychotherapy other than behavior therapy, the preponderance of evidence supports the conclusion that some patients decline in functioning over the course of therapy. As far as behavior therapy is concerned, there is insufficient evidence available to permit a firm, generalizable conclusion. In those studies permitting a legitimate comparison to comparable untreated controls, psychotherapy patients appear to have lower rates of negative outcome than the untreated control subjects.

Debate over the issue of negative outcomes has proceeded in phases. At first there was little concern with or even recognition of the possibility of negative outcome. Beginning in the early 1960s, due largely to the efforts of Bergin, the issue received considerable attention, with most professionals accepting the conclusion that therapy patients experience higher rates of negative outcome than untreated controls. More recently, there has been growing acceptance of the above conclusions.

The fact that negative outcome rates are generally low, lower than those for untreated control subjects, is a basis neither for complacency nor apathy. It is time now to proceed toward greater understanding of the factors responsible for negative outcomes and what to do about them, and this is what this book is about.

2

Negative Effects and Their Determinants

Hans H. Strupp and Suzanne W. Hadley
Part of this material has been adapted from Strupp & Hadley (1976).

EDITORS' NOTE: *Strupp and Hadley, who originally defined the term* negative effect, *correctly apply the term to "patients getting worse as a function of the therapeutic influence," as opposed to the term "negative outcome" which pertains to a decline in functioning regardless of the cause. Therefore, no change has been made in their usage of this term. Note, however, that Strupp and Hadley at times apply the term* negative effect *to instances of patient worsening where there is little or no evidence that these changes were in fact "a function of the therapeutic influence."*

Considering the growing interest in psychoanalysis and behavior therapy and the increasing popularity of "innovative" therapies, it is surprising that the study of negative effects of psychotherapy was not systematically pursued until Bergin's (1963, 1966, 1970, 1971) provocative articles on the subject of what he termed "deterioration effects" in psychotherapy. (The term "negative effects" will be used in preference to "deterioration," because it seems to describe more accurately the problem of patients getting worse as a function of the therapeutic influence, as opposed to other factors possibly extraneous to psychotherapy.)

Practicing therapists, of course, have known for a long time that some patients fail to improve or actually seem to "get worse," even in prolonged psychotherapy. Other patients experience a recrudescence of their original difficulties following the termination of psychotherapy and find it necessary to return to therapy at a later time. Many thera-

This work was supported, in part, by Contract 278-75-0036 (ER) and Research Grant MH 20369 from the National Institute of Mental Health. Dr. Hadley is currently affiliated with the National Institute of Mental Health.

pists have worked with patients whose previous therapy experience was "incomplete" or disappointing. The term *negative therapeutic reaction* has been used to describe patients who apparently fail to benefit from psychotherapy or get worse; and a sizable literature on "countertransference" has sprung up since Freud introduced the term in 1910 (see Orr, 1954 for a summary).

Guided by a long-term interest in exploring the nature of the therapeutic action in psychotherapy, we undertook a focused investigation into the problem of negative effects. Specifically, we posed the following questions:

1. Is there a problem of negative effects of psychotherapy?
2. If so, what constitutes a negative effect, that is, by what criteria does one judge an individual to have become worse as a result of therapy?
3. What factors are prominently associated with or are responsible for negative effects?

As a part of this inquiry, we undertook a survey of expert clinicians, theoreticians, and researchers in the field of psychotherapy. Letters were sent to approximately 150 experts, spanning a wide range of theoretical orientations soliciting their opinions on the foregoing issues.

Approximately 70 persons responded to our request (see Strupp, Hadley & Gomes-Schwartz, 1977.). (A complete listing of these respondents appears in Table 2-1 on p. 22.) Their answers were often detailed and thoughtful, indicating a keen interest in the general subject of negative effects. Taken as a whole, the responses represent a spectrum of contemporary thinking of some of the best minds in the field of psychotherapy. The themes emerging from these responses, together with our own thinking and experience, are the subject of this chapter.

Is There a Problem of Negative Effects?

Among the experts in psychotherapy who responded to our letter, there was virtually unanimity that there is a real problem of negative effects in psychotherapy. The frequency of occurrence was judged as moderate by some, whereas others, for example, Spitzer, suggested that "negative effects in long-term outpatient psychotherapy are extremely common." On the other hand, there were some noteworthy dissents. One respondent felt that there is little evidence for negative

Table 2-1   Survey Respondents

D. Wilfred Abse, M.D.	Peter H. Knapp, M.D.
John M. Atthowe, Jr., Ph.D.	Heinz Kohut, M.D.
Ann Appelbaum, M.D.	Leonard Krasner, Ph.D
Stephen A. Appelbaum, Ph.D.	Robert J. Langs, M.D.
Aaron T. Beck, M.D.	Arnold A. Lazarus, Ph.D.
Leopold Bellak, M.D.	Robert P. Liberman, M.D.
Irving N. Berlin, M.D.	Morton A. Lieberman, Ph.D
Barbara J. Betz, M.D.	Lester Luborsky, Ph.D.
Irving Bieber, M.D., P.C.	Michael J. Mahoney, Ph.D.
Edward S. Bordin, Ph.D.	David Malan, M.D.
Pietro Castelnuovo-Tedesco, M.D.	Isaac Marks, M.D.
Jacob Cohen, Ph.D.	Judd Marmor, M.D.
Gerald C. Davison, Ph.D.	Joseph D. Matarazzo, Ph.D.
John Dollard, Ph.D.	Philip R. A. May, M.D.
Jarl E. Dyrud, M.D	Paul E. Meehl, Ph.D
Albert Ellis, Ph.D.	Neal E. Miller, Ph.D.
Jean Endicott, Ph.D.	John C. Nemiah, M.D.
George L. Engel, M.D.	Martin T. Orne, M.D., Ph.D.
O. Spurgeon English, M.D.	James O. Palmer, Ph.D.
Norman L. Farberow, Ph.D.	Gordon L. Paul, Ph.D.
C. B. Ferster, Ph.D.	George H. Pollock, M.D.
Rueben Fine, Ph.D., P.C.	Arthur J. Prange, Jr., M.D.
Donald W. Fiske, Ph.D.	S. Rachman, Ph.D.
Donald H. Ford, Ph.D.	John M. Rhoads, M.D.
Daniel X. Freedman, M.D.	Howard B. Roback, Ph.D.
Lawrence Friedman, M.D	Leon Salzman, M.D.
Sol L. Garfield, Ph.D.	Robert L. Spitzer, M.D.
Robert W. Goldberg, Ph.D.	Hans H. Strupp, Ph.D.
Israel Goldiamond, Ph.D.	Leonard P. Ullmann, Ph.D.
Louis A. Gottschalk, M.D.	Robert S. Wallerstein, M.D.
Ralph R. Greenson, M.D.	Irving B. Weiner, Ph.D.
Alan S. Gurman, Ph.D.	Walter Weintraub, M.D.
Michel Hersen, Ph.D.	Otto Allen Will, Jr., M.D.
Marc H. Hollender, M.D.	Lewis R. Wolberg, M.D.
Donald J. Holmes, M.D.	Joseph Wolpe, M.D.
Frederick H. Kanfer, Ph.D.	Benjamin Wolstein, Ph.D.
Otto F. Kernberg, M.D.	Irvin D. Yalom, M.D.
Jane W. Kessler, Ph.D.	Clifford Yorke, DPM
Donald Kiesler, Ph.D.	Joseph Zubin, Ph.D.

effects of therapy, noting that although most clinicians are able to cite experiences they have had with patients who appeared to deteriorate during treatment, he believes that there is no persuasive evidence that the negative effects which appeared were caused by the psychotherapy itself. Similarly, an operant-oriented expert expressed reservations about the reality of negative effects, stating that he himself does not think too seriously about negative effects in psychotherapy because "that idea gives the therapist more power and influence than he has."

The issue of negative effects as a result of psychotherapy is intimately related to the question of the potency of psychotherapy per se, as many of our respondents noted. Cohen, for example, stated that "we had better be able to speak of getting worse in psychotherapy," or else we cannot speak of a patient getting better. Will commented similarly that psychotherapy "cannot in any sense be 'neutral,' " while Prange noted that "if psychotherapy can't do harm it is the only therapy in medicine so blessed." There is a consensus that if it is possible for psychotherapy to produce beneficial effects, it must be capable, at least theoretically, of producing negative effects as well.

The foregoing consensus was qualified, however, in the sense that all of the experts proceeded to list various limitations, definitions, and conditions. Many elaborated on what a negative effect *is not*. Liberman noted that a negative effect is not the same as the temporary deterioration which is an inevitable part of some forms of psychotherapy. In a similar vein, Marks and a number of other respondents noted that we must distinguish between normal and expected regressions from psychotherapy which are temporary, and real or lasting negative effects.

Ford suggested that we must determine whether an observed negative effect is indeed the product of a therapeutic intervention or merely an event independent of that intervention which may coincide in time. He went on to discuss the time issue in general terms, noting that it is important to make decisions about the temporal proximity of a negative effect to the termination of therapy. Thus, the most clear-cut negative effects are "those that appear immediately in temporal relationship with the psychotherapy" (Gottschalk), although there can, in addition, be delayed adverse effects. Atthowe spoke of this issue in terms of short-term versus long-term goals of psychotherapy. In his opinion, it is fulfillment of long-term goals which is most critical for ultimate judgments of treatment outcome, but these goals may not be correlated with short-term measures.

Marks provided a concise but comprehensive definition of a negative effect as "a lasting deterioration in a patient directly attributable to therapy."

Multiple Perspectives on Psychotherapy Evaluation

Having dealt with the issue of negative effects in general terms, many respondents went on to consider conceptual issues relevant to the problem. Mahoney, speaking from the perspective of his interest in therapeutic ethics, urged that we examine the basic premises and the prime goals of therapy (e.g., Is it true that the "satisfaction" of the "customer" is the primary criterion by which therapy shall be evaluated?). Ford stressed that the identification of a negative effect from psychotherapy is basically a value judgment which depends heavily on the value reference of the person or persons making the judgment. A similar comment was made by Gurman, who noted that the judgment of a treatment's effects as positive or negative depends on the evaluative perspective chosen as most valid. It is thus incumbent upon researchers to evaluate therapy-related change in the patient from a variety of perspectives.

Krasner spoke of the growth in importance of the study of negative effects which, in his view, is related to the shift from the medical to the social-educational model of psychological functioning and psychotherapy. He added that the assessment of behavior changes resulting from psychotherapy must include an assessment of the consequences of those changes for the client, for the people in his life, and for the therapist: "Issues of negative effects must now be considered within this broader issue of values (what is good behavior for an individual and for society)."

Of course, discrepancies are likely to exist among judgments of outcome made from different perspectives, for example, those made by a therapist and those made by the patient (Weintraub). Judgments from these perspectives may include two kinds of negative effects: (1) those generally harmful to the patient and (2) those harmful to the attainment of the goals of therapy which "may or may not include harm to the patient." Weintraub cited as an example of the latter outcome the "transference cure." An identical effect may be viewed by the therapist as positive or negative depending on his strategies and goals in therapy. Further, in more general terms, effects may be viewed as positive or negative by others, depending on the impact of the patient's behavior upon them.

The latter issue is particularly salient in family therapy, in which assessments must include changes in the patient's relationships with others as well as changes in those significant others to whom the patient relates (Gurman). Speaking from her experience as a child therapist, Kessler cited examples illustrating this. Psychotherapy with children may create behavioral or loyalty conflicts with the parents; the latter, as a result of having a child in therapy, may come to feel alienated, helpless, or guilty over their performance as parents.

Abse gave a vivid clinical description of an adult patient who became hostile and sadistic toward his family, and whose therapy outcome he therefore considers definitely negative. Nonetheless, the patient was judged a therapeutic success by others who knew him, including some of Abse's colleagues, largely on the basis of his achievement in the business world. For Abse, this patient represented a clear-cut example of the discrepancies among evaluative perspectives, and he summarized the lesson learned from this patient as follows: "The identifiable psychiatric syndrome following intensive analytic work may be succeeded by personality malfunctioning vis-à-vis other people, though adapted to 'sick' aspects of our present society."

Divorce resulting from an individual's therapy experiences is one of the most clear-cut examples of the multiple perspectives issue. Ann Appelbaum described the dilemma which typically surrounds such situations and offered suggestions on how such outcomes should be evaluated.

> A person who has lived for some years as a conventionally good wife and mother at the price of suppressing her hatred for an unloving, emotionally limited and intellectually inferior husband, and who as the result of psychotherapy becomes aware of her own needs for love and stimulation, enters into an affair and eventually divorces her husband—is she "worse" or "better"? Would her children have been better off had she lived out the marriage at least until they grew up so as to provide them a stable home? I think the answer to this would depend on the kind of life the woman would be able to create for herself and her children after the divorce, and the extent to which her awareness and acceptance of her own emotional needs went hand in hand with a growing capacity for concern and a growing capacity to take into account the needs of others as well as of herself.

It is obvious from the foregoing examples that the issues we dealt with in our discussion of the tripartite model of therapeutic outcomes (Strupp & Hadley, 1977) are increasingly salient for therapists today. Numerous therapists agree that therapy outcomes cannot be evaluated in isolation, nor from a strictly intrapsychic perspective; and they rarely can be viewed as absolutely positive or negative. As noted earlier, a number of interested parties are demanding a voice in evaluating therapy outcome, and this is particularly true in the case of negative effects. Judgments of therapy outcome, whether positive or negative, will depend heavily on the perspective of the evaluator.

Assessing the Outcome of Psychotherapy

How then shall we measure therapy outcome in general, and negative effects in particular? Ford stressed the need for analytic precision and a sophisticated conceptual approach to the problem. He suggested that in the early stages of research one might "conceptually canvass and try to explicate the value frameworks within which such judgments might be made and to elaborate the alternatives."

Any judgment of therapy outcome obviously must be centered on the patient. Roback noted that the determination of a negative effect from psychotherapy requires initially a "comprehensive understanding of the patient," which leads to the question of the dimensions in which a patient shall be evaluated. Changes in target symptoms are commonly used as a measure of therapeutic effectiveness. Lieberman, for example, reported "numerous" instances of patients "doing worse" on the basis of an assessment of target problems. However, as Orne notes, evaluating a patient in terms of target symptoms may not be altogether appropriate to the study of negative effects since "the patient who gets worse does not usually do so in terms of target symptoms." As an alternative, reminiscent of Freud's maxim, Orne suggested that patients should be evaluated in terms of their ability to enjoy work, love, and play and to successfully cope with the usual stresses of life. Marks advocated a problem-oriented approach to the study of negative effects, noting that adequate evaluations of therapeutic effectiveness must specify the problems being treated and "the precise criteria for outcome during, at the end of, and subsequent to treatment."

Marks' stress on measures throughout the course of therapy was reiterated by Liberman, who suggested repeated and continuous measures of behavior and affect over the course of therapy. Hersen, stressing a single-case research strategy, urged repeated measurements of both targeted and nontargeted behaviors as essential for the identification of negative effects. With respect to the problem of identifying causative factors, Hersen suggested that only a functional analysis of therapy will enable us to draw conclusions about such factors. Thus, there emerges a consensus that measures of the effectiveness of psychotherapy must be made at repeated intervals.

Further, many respondents urged that psychotherapy be evaluated in a comprehensive, multifaceted sense. Will, for example, suggested that one must evaluate the overall effect of therapy on the patient's personality; it is conceivable that the effect of therapy on only one aspect of the personality might be judged as negative, while the overall judgment might be that therapy had led to a positive outcome.

Fiske suggested a multiple-criterion approach to the problem. Similarly, Atthowe urged that measurements be multidimensional, and Stephen Appelbaum proposed the use of an algebraic sum by which the overall effectiveness of therapy would be evaluated.

What Constitutes a Negative Effect?

Exacerbation of Presenting Symptoms

Gottschalk spoke of the "worsening" of presenting symptoms, and Rhoads described "the increase in symptoms corresponding to heightened resistance or defensiveness." Such exacerbations are particularly noteworthy if they result in hospitalization or institutionalization (Berlin). Other examples include "exacerbation of suffering" or the generalization of symptoms to new areas (Wolpe); decompensation in a patient who had previously exhibited equilibrium (Greenson, Weiner); or the development of a harsher superego and more rigid personality structure (Strupp). Specific indicators of exacerbated symptoms included the following:

- Depressive breakdown, severe regression, destructive acting out (Malan)
- Increased anxiety, hostility, self-downing, behavioral shirking, inhibition (Ellis)
- Paranoia (Will)
- Fixing of obsessional symptoms, exaggeration of somatic difficulties, extension of phobias (Salzman)
- Increased guilt or confusion, lowered self-confidence (Lazarus)
- Lower self-esteem, diminished capacity for delay and impulse control (Golberg)
- Worsening of phobias.

Appearance of New Symptoms

Rhoads noted that a negative effect may occur when a psychic disturbance is manifested in a less socially acceptable form than had been the case previously, for example, a shift from somatic complaints (which might elicit sympathy from others) to paranoia. Miller suggested that new symptoms may be due to substitution, that is, the classic case of a new symptom developing when another, which had fulfilled some imperative need, is blocked without a suitable available alternative.

Obviously, any of those listed above as instances of exacerbation could also arise as part of a novel symptom configuration. In addition, the following were mentioned as examples which might be judged as negative therapeutic results:

- The erosion of solid interpersonal relationships, and decreased ability to experience pleasure (Weintraub)
- Severe or fatal psychosomatic reactions (Ann Appelbaum)
- Withdrawal, regression, rage, dissociation
- Acting out (Marmor, May)
- Drug or alcohol abuse, criminal behavior (Gottschalk).

The most extreme manifestations of new symptomatology are suicide and psychotic breaks. Suicide was identified repeatedly as the most clear-cut example of a negative effect, particularly if the patient was not noticeably suicidal at the beginning of therapy (Greenson). Insensitive handling of patients with suicidal tendencies may provoke overt attempts at self-destruction. Knapp, for example, described the case of a therapist who refused to recognize the depth of his client's depression, interpreting her behavior as stubbornness. When she made her third serious suicide attempt and missed an appointment with the therapist, it was only at his supervisor's insistence that a visit was made to the home, where the woman was found in a deep stupor as the result of a barbiturate overdose.

Suicide, as Dyrud observed, is not necessarily a negative effect of psychotherapy, particularly with a suicide-prone patient, with whom one takes a calculated risk in attempting therapy. Farberow notes that when suicide does result from psychotherapy, it is most likely to occur as the result of a "burned out" syndrome in the therapist, due to the repeated and exhausting demands of seriously depressed and suicidal patients. This may become a particularly grave problem for formerly hospitalized patients who have alienated the hospital staff by their demanding behavior and thus may feel there is no haven to which they may return when suicidal urges recur, as they often do.

Psychotic breaks resulting from psychotherapy were also frequently mentioned as a clear-cut negative effect. Matarazzo noted that such an occurrence would most typically be due to ego disintegration brought on by therapy.

Misuse/Abuse of Therapy

Less obvious perhaps than the exacerbation of presenting symptoms or the appearance of new symptoms is a negative effect which was often mentioned and which we have chosen to term the patient's "misuse/abuse" of therapy. This phenomenon may take a number of forms. Will, for example, described the substitution of intellectualized insights for other obsessional thoughts in patients, as in a patient who appears to benefit from therapy in the sense of achieving and internalizing therapeutic insights, but who may in fact be merely substituting these insights for earlier obsessional thoughts.

Marmor identified a phenomenon observed in some patients which he described as "utilization of a psychotherapeutic experience . . . to rationalize feelings of smugness, superiority over others, or utilizing 'insights' to aggressively comment on other people's behavior." Many former patients exhibit this "symptom" as an undesirable by-product of some therapies. Even the mental health professional may be a "victim," as witness the example cited by Friedman of a professional in training who, after several years of analysis, "declared that she no longer found anything in common with people who weren't analyzed, or any pleasure in their company."

Psychological jargon may also be directed toward oneself, functioning as an " 'alibi' for certain actions or lack of action" (Endicott). More generally, for some patients therapy may become an end in itself. Ann Appelbaum put it this way: "Therapeutic work begins to assume priority over other tasks and goals . . . being a good patient comes to assume priority higher than that of living life to the fullest." Stephen Appelbaum described a similar phenomenon in which therapy becomes a substitute for action, thereby reinforcing passivity in the patient's life. Lazarus commented that such an outcome often results from therapists fostering patient dependency by teaching them to become preoccupied with intrapsychic phenomena instead of solving their problems.

Franz Alexander (Alexander & French, 1946) and others have noted previously, intensive psychotherapy carries with it a multiplicity of dangers, one of which is inadequate regard for the patient's intentionality or will. The analytic therapist's persistent search for unconscious determinants of behavior may stifle constructive action in the outside world, where therapy must come to fruition. Unless the therapist remains alert to this problem, the patient may, in Salzman's words, have an "endless and interminable therapeutic experience and fail to change while verbalizing insights and formulas of living."

Meehl described a similar phenomenon of patients becoming so focused on "wonders of their psyche and its internal connections" that they lose the willingness and disposition to examine their ethical and philosophical commitments. In Meehl's view, this examination of one's basic life commitments is essential to healthy living and the loss of this disposition is related to therapy's tendency to "downgrade the work of the intelligence and to classify almost any rational examination of either external reality or value commitments as being mere intellectualization."

Most of the foregoing abuses of psychotherapy are particularly likely to occur in the context of analytic or insight-oriented therapy. However, the most radical therapies have other drawbacks. Salzman voiced the opinion that participation in such organizations as est and marathon groups, particularly for excessive periods of time, encourages belief in the irrational as a comfort, by which the patient hopes to avoid more painful confrontation with the realities of life.

Undertaking Unrealistic Tasks or Goals

If, as a result of some aspect of the psychotherapeutic intervention, the patient feels constrained to undertake or pursue goals for which he is ill-equipped and which, therefore, place great strain on his psychological resources, a negative effect may result. Similarly, excessive stress may be experienced by the patient who feels called upon to act prematurely in the outside world.

Such situations may arise from a patient's intense wish to please the therapist (Ann Appelbaum), which in turn is related to excessive dependency on the therapist, discussed previously. It is also possible that some therapists may actively push individuals into facing challenges for which they are ill-prepared (Davison).

Stephen Appelbaum attributed this form of negative outcome to the value judgments which communicate an expectation that the patient must live up to some grand ideal. And he noted further that "it is not writ in stone that all people should conform to middle class values, and many patients would be well advised to stay out of them."

Similarly, Ellis discussed the increase of "irrational ideas" within the patient during the course of therapy—for example, one must be loved all the time, must do very well in all achievements (he is no good if he does poorly), or must have immediate gratification.

Whether such outcomes are due to a wish to please the therapist, or the inculcation of unachievable ideals, they often result in increased instances of failure, accompanied by guilt, anxiety, and pain.

Loss of Trust in Therapy and the Therapist

As a result of one or more of the foregoing adverse influences, or because of failure to change at all, a patient may come to experience a sense of disillusionment with therapy and the therapist.

This disillusionment may be manifested in various ways. One respondent, for example, discussed "wasting" the patient's resources when he is not helped by his therapy—resources which might have been better utilized by another therapist or in another form of therapy.

Yorke, with special reference to psychoanalysis, noted that "it is not so much a question of adverse response as a waste of time, skills, resources, [and] money" which constitutes negative effects in analysis. Moreover, a patient may become discouraged from seeking more effective forms of therapy—what Lazarus called "hardening in . . . negative attitudes toward future help."

A severe negative outcome is exemplified by a loss of confidence in the therapist, which generalizes (Rhoads) to disillusionment with any form of human relationship (Will).

Perhaps even more serious is the general loss of hope which a patient may experience as a result of not succeeding in therapy. Bieber spoke of this as a sense of "futility," and Davison added that this futility is all the more severe because of the initial hopes raised in any patient entering therapy. Meehl poignantly described this situation:

> When a patient finally comes to a point of seeking professional help for his functional incompetence or subjective distress, and goes and spills his guts to a psychotherapist and takes time and money to do it, it means, even among most intellectuals, a certain amount of ego threat, from having to admit his failure to cope on his own, and the whole business about labeling oneself as "mentally aberrant" and the like. Then, when the patient finds that, despite what he perceives as his own cooperative behavior in paying the fee and showing up and talking and so forth, he doesn't get better, this result is experienced by many people as a *nearly catastrophic removal of a background source of hope*, an "ace in the hole" that they had carried around (sometimes for years). . . .

What Factors Are Prominently Associated with Negative Effects in Psychotherapy?

In discussions of negative effects it is often difficult to identify what is cause and what is effect, and at times we may face a semantic problem. In psychoanalysis, for example, becoming dependent upon the therapist is seen as a sign of progress because it may facilitate resolution of the transference neurosis. Instead of "acting out" in the outside world, the patient now enacts his problems with the therapist, and if all goes well he may resolve them in this interaction. For complex reasons, however, the patient may come to cling tenaciously to the therapist and the therapy may become interminable. Is this the therapist's fault or are we dealing with a "negative therapeutic reaction"? These factors may interact, leading to further complications. While we are aware of these cause–effect complexities, we shall wherever possible attempt to relate negative effects to specific causative factors.

Inaccurate/Deficient Assessment

Earlier we noted that determination of the presence of negative effects requires an initial comprehensive understanding of the patient (Roback). Further, several correspondents stressed that "the best safeguard against adverse effects is a thorough diagnostic assessment" (Yorke).

Problems in this area may include either inadequate or erroneous assessments of the patient (Palmer). The consequence may be mismatching or misapplication of therapies to particular patients. Positing "mismatching" as a factor in negative effects presumes, of course, "that we know which therapies fit which problems" (Palmer), which is not always the case.

What should such an assessment include? The following specific assessment areas were mentioned by our respondents:

- Ego functions (Nemiah)
- A *general baseline*, including the patient's age and current tasks, diagnosis, state of his capacities, family history, and life situation (Freedman)
- Natural history of the patient's difficulties (Orne)
- "The functional value of the psychopathology . . . which kinds of symptoms serve useful needs in overall adjustment" (Orne).

Deficient or mistaken assessments may lead to a number of adverse developments. For example, the therapist may "probe more deeply than the patient is capable of tolerating, and hence . . . provoke untoward regressions" or else he may not "work intensively enough, and thus cheat the patient of the possibility of experiencing as much change for the better as he is capable of" (Ann Appelbaum). Bordin observed that certain temporary regressions may be expected during the course of therapy and that patients with minimal resources of strength will be able to weather these temporary periods of stress. Some patients, however, may lack these resources, and deficient assessments may fail to identify these vulnerabilities.

Goldberg discussed the prevailing trend away from diagnostic assessment, holding it responsible for an increased incidence in misdiagnosis. For example, the practice of treating hysteriform and overly ideational borderline schizophrenics as high ego strength neurotics is a flagrant mistake which has resulted from this incidence of misdiagnosis.

Therapist Variables

The therapist himself was one of the most often cited sources of negative effects in psychotherapy. Roback's statement is typical: "Most *prominent* factors leading to negative treatment effects are therapist variables." More specifically he implicated "poor clinical judgment." Similar views were expressed by Gottschalk and by Fiske, who observed that "any overall negative effect is due to the fallibility of the therapist." Fiske went on to say that even when the therapist himself is not directly contributing to negative effects in psychotherapy, he should be able to tell when the treatment or some other variable is producing negative effects. He should then be able and willing to take appropriate countermeasures.

Major therapist variables discussed fell into two broad categories, the first being deficiencies in training and skills, resulting in part from poor training facilities and "the development of delivery systems which do not require the maximum background in the biomedical and psychological sciences" on the part of practitioners (Salzman). Goldberg likewise noted deficiencies in training and supervision, which result in the delivery of inadequate professional services. Deficiencies in the therapist's skill may produce particularly severe negative effects in dealing with borderline patients, when, for example, the therapist stimulates the release of primitive aggression without quite knowing how to deal with it in psychotherapy. Such negative effects may be exacerbated by the therapist who masochistically participates in the patient's acting out.

Part of the problem with training in the mental health field, of course, is simply the relative lack of knowledge within the field itself. What is not known cannot be taught and, as Salzman observed, "The total picture of human behavior and its neurophysiological and biochemical correlates has yet to be established." Similarly, after laying the blame for negative effects at the doorstep of fallible therapists, Fiske noted that, "more charitably, negative effects are due to our limited knowledge about treating persons."

Several respondents observed that the contribution to negative effects in psychotherapy resides in what Bordin termed a *"complex* of ignorance and inappropriate personality." Engel suggested that negative effects may be caused by an ill-trained or incompetent person or by "one who abuses his position."

The second important variable which may contribute to negative effects is the therapist's personality. Incompatibility between patient's and therapist's personalities may contribute to negative effects in psychotherapy (Wolberg). Even more ominous are the problems posed by certain noxious personality traits in the therapist. Ellis identified three such characteristics: ignorance or stupidity, incompetence, and the "need to exploit the patient." Roback described therapists whose personalities have an adverse effect on therapy as "unable to utilize their intellect and acquired knowledge in therapeutically productive ways . . . [C]linical decisions are based on their own personality needs (although perhaps theoretically rationalized)." He listed "sadomasochism, voyeurism, and faddism" as examples of personality traits in the therapist which may have an adverse effect on therapy.

Additional deleterious personality attributes mentioned by respondents include:

- Coldness, obsessionalism—"anything goes as long as 'analyzing' is happening" (Ann Appelbaum)
- Excessive need to make people change (Ann Appelbaum)
- Excessive unconscious hostility, often disguised by diagnosing the patient as "borderline" or schizophrenic (Fine)
- Seductiveness, lack of interest or warmth (Marmor)
- Neglect, pessimism, sadism, absence of genuineness (Betz)
- Greed, narcissism, dearth of self-scrutiny (Greenson).

As we shall see, the variety of factors discussed here may adversely influence therapy in a number of ways, including deleterious effects on the relationship with the patient (English) and misuse of therapeutic techniques. It is also possible for a well-meaning therapist, with the unconscious motivation of enhancing his own personal and professional self-esteem, to inadvertently overemphasize his assets (Holmes). For the present, we note in passing Ann Appelbaum's general comment that pathology or deficient skills in the therapist may lead to inadequate recognition of transference manifestations, premature uncovering of unconscious conflicts without provision of concomitant support, or both.

Patient Qualities

Certain patient variables may, of course, also contribute to negative effects in therapy. Low or absent motivation—especially in patients who feel "sentenced to treatment"—strongly suggests a poor prognosis (Goldberg). As noted previously, patients with low ego strength or deficient psychic resources may be poor candidates for certain kinds of therapy and indeed may prove vulnerable to psychotic breaks as a result of the uncovering process. Adequate diagnosis at intake should provide better identification of high-risk patients before therapy is undertaken.

Adequate assessment might also help to identify patients with a masochistic character structure, which was identified by several respondents as a potential contributor to negative effects in therapy (Gottschalk). Such patients do not feel comfortable when functioning well. Other patients may experience guilt due merely to the fact that the therapist provides concern and understanding. Special psychotherapeutic techniques based on careful diagnostic assessment might forestall such negative outcomes.

Finally, it is important to note, as Castelnuovo-Tedesco observed, that some neurotic patients are "prone to disappointment and . . . have a special talent for seeking it (and finding it) even as they yearn for deliverance from it." Such patients inevitably may be disappointed with their experience in psychotherapy, regardless of what the therapist may do or say.

Misapplication and Deficiencies of Technique

Over and above any contribution made by the therapist's personality, negative effects may result from errors in technique. Lazarus, for example, described "seemingly responsible practitioners who never deviate from the specified ethical norms but who nevertheless harm rather than help many of the people who consult them." The implication here is that these apparently well-meaning individuals are nonetheless noxious to their patients because of the manner in which they apply therapeutic principles and techniques.

Numerous and varied examples of mistakes in the practice of therapy were cited. These statements appeared to be based on strong sentiments exemplified by Dyrud: "Negative effects must be linked to the therapist's error—either inappropriate technique or misapplication." Orne described as potentially deleterious the use of any technique which undercuts symptoms that function for the patient's adjustment in the absence of the development of alternative coping mechanisms. In a general sense, Greenson identified as a potential contributor to negative effects any therapy which "dehumanizes" the patient.

False Assumptions Concerning the Scope and Potency of Therapy. This is a fundamental issue, relating to the most basic premises therapists hold about themselves and their therapy. Problems may arise when the therapist entertains assumptions of omniscience (Salzman), or when he believes himself to be "God" (Davison). Therapy by its very nature can be "meddlesome" (Prange), that is, it may send a message to the patient, "you're not okay."

An additional problem is that therapy is not able to solve all ills. As Zubin noted, "The omnipotent view of therapy in being able to improve adjustment in general . . . is beyond the scope of therapeutic intervention today." The negative effect potential arises when the patient is simultaneously given messages of "you're not okay" coupled with "therapy can solve anything." Such a patient may come to entertain or perpetuate unrealistic expectations and goals for himself in therapy and when these are not achieved fall prey to disillusionment and loss of faith in therapy and therapists.

Problems with the Goals of Therapy. The problem most frequently mentioned relative to therapeutic goals concerned failure to discuss, describe, or even acknowledge the reality of goals per se (Weintraub, Freedman). Another respondent called attention to therapeutic goals that are too "abstract," as well as failure by therapist and patient to reach mutual agreement on the goals of therapy. Many of our respondents strongly expressed the view that "some sense of direction is necessary. The patient's realistic hopes need to be distinguished from his fantasies" (Goldberg).

Further problems may arise when the goals of therapy are not in the patient's best interest (Davison), as when the goal of therapy is directed toward "fusion" with others or requiring directives from others (Betz). The latter observed that although the achievement of such goals may provide some immediate gratification to the patient, it will in the long run have a negative effect, particularly in terms of perpetuating the patient's dependence.

Finally, problems may be created by a therapist who sets up goals which exceed the patient's capabilities or who fosters expectations of speedy progress beyond the patient's capabilities. Knapp related an example of a therapist who, acting out some of his own wishes, urged a divorce on his patient, with destructive consequences (including the development of alcoholism). Friedman described a patient for whom the imposition of the therapist's values had even graver consequences:

> The worst consequence I have personally seen was in a man with a process-type schizophrenia, who had seriously and continuously loosened associations, and very great difficulty keeping track of the elementary procedures of daily life. His expressed interest in becoming a physician was enthusiasti-

cally welcomed by a group psychotherapist who was culturally and ideologically sold on upward mobility, and who encouraged his group to challenge the patient to implement his
ambition, and simultaneously strip away his rationalizations
and ways of maintaining his self-esteem. He decompensated,
became catatonic and required hospitalization.

These patients exemplify a negative effect described earlier—the
emergence of guilt and lowered self-esteem (and for these particular
individuals, the development of serious psychiatric symptoms) as a
result of their being urged to attempt life tasks for which they were
ill-prepared.

Misplaced Focus of Therapy.   There was a consensus among respondents that there is a fundamental problem in determining whether
psychotherapy should focus primarily on the patient himself and his
inner workings, or be externally directed toward significant others and
toward society. Palmer stressed the environmental emphasis, faulting
psychotherapy which is devoted entirely to the inner man, for it is only
by awareness of environmental stresses that the patient will be helped
to evaluate these stresses realistically. Similarly, Atthowe saw a problem in therapy which fails "to involve the patient's environment in his
treatment"; he not only spoke of enlisting the cooperation of institutions and significant others in treating the patient, but also urged comprehensive treatment of the relevant social community systems.

Others argued against a form of "determinism" which presumes
that "the focus of difficulty lies with parents, society, others, and not
within the individual's own resistances to change" (Salzman). Meehl
took a similar tack, faulting therapy which focuses on "anything and
everything" instead of problem behaviors, such as drinking, procrasti-
nation, etc., which may have brought a person to psychotherapy.
Meehl put the case well:

> I have known quite a few people . . . who have spent many
> hours in intensive psychotherapy and who have in fact
> learned a good deal about themselves . . . who are still pretty
> ineffective or unhappy individuals, in large part because they
> are persisting in overt behavior of a destructive or ineffective
> kind. For such persons it would require some kind of massive
> brainwashing for them to stop feeling unethical or incompe-
> tent, for the simple reason that they are *in fact,* by any usual
> standards of ethics or of vocational, financial, family and sex-
> ual performance, doing things that are wrong, inept, or both.

The thrust of this argument is that one can spend a great deal of
time and energy in psychotherapy which will nonetheless remain rela-

tively ineffectual both in changing behavior and alleviating distress because the therapeutic focus is displaced from "behavior and will" (Salzman) to insights, interpretations, and the like. We shall presently deal with the problem of insight at greater length. For the present, we note that the kind of outcome described by Meehl may readily lead to the feelings of disillusionment and loss of hope identified previously as a particularly pervasive negative effect of psychotherapy.

Mismatch of Technique to the Patient. We have previously called attention to the need for adequate assessment and diagnosis, as well as problems which may result from failure to identify patient characteristics that militate against a positive therapeutic outcome. Inadequate assessment may also contribute to "mismatching" of therapy to the patient, with even greater potential for negative effects (Greenson).

Malan urged that patients be assigned to a form of psychotherapy appropriate to both the nature and the degree of their disturbance, particularly to "exclude from very deep-going psychotherapy those patients who have not the strength to bear it." More generally, he stated that "it is the failure to match therapy to the patient's disturbance that is most likely to lead to negative effects." Others affirmed that it is quite possible for therapy to have negative effects even when skillfully conducted, if it happens to be inappropriate for the particular patient in question (Engel).

What specifically are mismatches in psychology? What kinds of therapy may be actually harmful if applied to a particular kind of patient? Nemiah observed that psychoanalytically oriented insight therapy can be "actively harmful" when it is applied to either borderline patients, in which case it may promote regressive transference, angry acting out, or manipulation; or to patients with psychosomatic symptoms, where the focus on fantasies and feelings may be incomprehensible to the patient with the result that he may either give up therapy or show an exacerbated somatization. Knapp vividly described just such a situation:

> In the late 1940s we were just beginning to learn about the psychotherapy of patients with severe psychosomatic disease, particularly ulcerative colitis. We saw numerous instances of patients who were encouraged to express their emotions. They got enormously involved with therapists, poured out beautiful material, and became steadily worse. Several of them died.

Knapp went on to observe that soon thereafter there developed an awareness of such "ill-advised" interventions and the "need for sensitive supportive therapy with such sick individuals." In a similar vein, Garfield noted that a negative effect may occur when a therapist attempts to uncover repressed material which is very threatening to the patient and which he is uncapable of assimilating—a likely outcome when the patient is not sufficiently well integrated to handle the uncovering process.

Weintraub discussed problems that may accompany attacking the defenses of patients with particularly fragile egos and defense structures. Prange foresaw problems if the therapist allies himself with id mechanisms when this is inappropriate (as is true with many adolescents). With respect to behavior treatments, Davison discussed problems in aversion therapy. This form of therapy may be counterproductive with some homosexuals, by feeding into the patient's pathology and need for punishment.

Technical Rigidity in Therapy. Problems resulting from the mismatch of therapy to the patient may be exacerbated if the therapist adheres rigidly to a particular form of therapy (Palmer) or the theoretical prescriptions of one individual (Greenson). Most of the respondents who discussed rigidity of technique related it to the therapist's insecurity. Salzman, for example, observed that "when the therapist is rigid, inflexible, insecure, and essentially a technician following rules of procedure," the process of therapy itself may become "an obsessional ritual."

The consequences of therapeutic rigidity bode ill for the patient because his individual characteristics and needs may not be given sufficient consideration (Will). Excessive rigidity may also force the patient into submission to a preestablished procedure (Fine), or may encourage him to perform certain "standard" behaviors (aggressiveness, bluntness) which conform to the therapist's definition of mental health (Friedman). Additional problems may arise when a therapist's rigidity prevents him from shifting to other modes of treatment, even when it is clear that the original treatment of choice is inappropriate for the patient involved (Atthowe). One behavior therapist observed that in behavior therapy (as well as in all other forms), rigidity and strict adherence to technique restricts the therapist's ability to understand the patient and his problems, with potentially adverse consequences for the patient–therapist relationship and the therapeutic outcome.

Overly Intense Therapy. Any or all of the mistakes discussed here may be aggravated by therapy which is overly intense (e.g., "pushing too much" or getting too close to the patient when he is unable or unwilling to tolerate such proximity [Orne]). Paul spoke of "coming on too strong" to the patient, particularly in terms of overly specific advice or tasks. Garfield discussed the issue of intensity in terms of particularly fragile patients who may be pushed too hard to reveal themselves while being unable or unwilling to relax their defenses.

Misuse of Interpretations or Insight Therapy. Misuse of interpretations in psychotherapy was frequently mentioned as a factor contributing to negative effects. Generally, the problems related to misuse of interpretations appear to fall into two major categories. The first of these includes problems in focusing discussed earlier. Thus, therapy may fail to achieve a proper "balance between internal investigation and utilization of life resources for energy, pleasure, and integrity of function," which according to Freedman leads to the development of many "half persons" impaired in their real development and growth. The problem here is excessive diversion of critical personality resources and energies from growth into internal investigation. We have discussed this issue previously in terms of therapy becoming an end in itself.

Even more directly related to the issue of inappropriate focus in therapy are interpretations which are so "predominantly 'transference-centered' that they distort or minimize the impact of reality factors in the patient's life" (Marmor). Such interpretations may contribute to a pervasive denigration of the patient's sense of autonomy, responsibility, and self-esteem—a trend which in Salzman's view characterizes much of psychotherapy today. The reason given by this respondent is that much of psychoanalytic training and therapy still focuses on interpretation as the *key factor* in effecting change.

Malan noted in particular the potential for negative effects in the analyst's tendency to interpret apparent "getting better" as a "flight into health" to avoid continuing therapy. In Malan's opinion, such improvement may at times represent considerably more than merely a flight into health and "even if it is, a patient is sometimes able to make use of it as a point of growth. Keeping the patient in therapy may bring back his symptoms without the final outcome of resolving them."

Particularly severe problems may result from destructive interpretations or from critical interpretations made before genuine trust and rapport have developed between patient and therapist (Marmor). Dollard observed that the mere revelation of a patient's problems in the course of psychotherapy may increase his adjustment difficulties in everyday life. The problem may become especially acute, of course, with borderline or psychotic patients where the "ill-conceived utilization of uncovering or insight-oriented approaches" may have decidedly negative effects.

At a minimum, interpretations may arouse anxiety. As Wolpe noted, interpretations may convey an implicit message to the patient of "basic abnormality." At its most extreme, this may lead to an "excessively deep and terrifying awareness of the person's primitive longings and/or of the actual discrepancies between legitimate and instinctual needs and their likelihood of satisfaction in reality" (Ann Appelbaum).

These misuses of interpretations are particularly likely to have negative consequences when they are presented without adequate follow-up or opportunities for working through—in Bellak's terms, "analysis without sufficient synthesis." The proper use of interpretations requires skill in timing, tact, and "buffering." Failure to exercise these skills may result in a patient with a "battered self-concept" (Meehl).

Meehl also expressed the opinion that it is better sometimes for people not to know too much about themselves and their relationships to others: "I had never seen any really convincing theoretical argument which shows that it is *always* a good thing to 'have insight.' " Thus, even when the therapist is skillful and "uncovering" psychotherapy may be indicated in a particular case, the patient still may emerge from treatment with his self-concept further impaired. Since defects in self-esteem are almost a defining characteristic of patients in psychotherapy, such an outcome must be viewed as extremely unfortunate and clearly indicative of a negative effect.

Dependency-Fostering Techniques. Greenson observed that any form or aspect of therapy which makes the patient "an addict to therapy and the therapist" is undesirable. We have already observed that techniques which encourage interminable self-exploration to the exclusion of behavioral change and at the expense of the patient's intentionality may have these consequences. While the therapist may not actively encourage the patient's dependency, he may fail to take appropriate measures to counteract it—with equally unfortunate results (Hollender).

Problems in the Patient-Therapist Relationship

Negative effects in psychotherapy may arise from or become exacerbated by problems in the rapport between therapist and patient. In general, "too little" or "too much" rapport instead of an intermediate optimal level is implicated (Atthowe). The instance of poor rapport most often cited by our respondents was faulty handling of the manifestations of countertransference. Palmer reiterated the traditional view—a therapist should not underestimate his own reactions to a patient, but rather assess them honestly and deal with them constructively. The therapist must also be on guard against countertransference problems that extend beyond the patient to his environment—for example, to the parents of disturbed children (Berlin).

A major source of difficulty relating to the patient–therapist interaction was termed by Langs "interactional neurosis." He called for intensive study of both the conscious and unconscious interaction between patient and therapist to understand precisely how this neurosis develops and in what ways it may adversely affect the progress of psychotherapy. Luborsky similarly described the therapist's failure to recognize the patient's "conflictual relationship theme" and the more serious problem created if the therapist unwittingly "fits in" with the theme.

Hostile countertransference by the therapist toward the patient may assume a number of deleterious forms, including the following (Goldberg):

- Prevention of the establishment of a working alliance
- Lack of respect for the patient's pain
- Failure to allow the patient to experience choices
- Aggressive assault on the patient's defenses
- A disappointed attitude toward the patient and his progress.

For a variety of reasons—including hostile countertransference—some therapists may fail to maintain minimally necessary professional distance (Weintraub). Several respondents mentioned the therapist's exploitation, manifested as seductiveness, as the most blatant example of this problem. Therapists' sexual involvement with their patients is currently a "hot issue" in the news media and most recently has led to a number of lawsuits. The consequences of such liaisons are almost invariably negative, including occasional suicides. Rhoads, for example, described the case of a female patient who committed suicide at her psychiatrist's cabin following their sexual involvement and his subsequent rejection of her.

A number of respondents stressed the importance of making the patient–therapist relationship explicit in order to deal with developing problems and to forestall the development of difficulties.

Communication Problems

Fundamental problems which may contribute to or aggravate other negative effects, particularly those relating to the therapeutic relationship, pertain to difficulties in patient–therapist communication. Problems may arise if the therapist is unable to communicate his ideas clearly or fails to determine whether the patient is comprehending adequately what has been said (Bieber). On the patient's side there is great potential for problems when distortions, omissions, or falsifications in his communications to the therapist occur and go uncorrected (Roback). A particular problem with patient communications was noted by Berlin in his discussion of the nonverbal communication of disturbed children and the need for the therapist to understand and respond appropriately to those communications.

Problems Unique to Certain Forms of Therapy

Behavior Therapy. Behavior therapy has long been the target of criticism, particularly from proponents of other forms of therapy. Symptom substitution is one of the most often mentioned negative effects attributed to behavior therapy. From the psychoanalytic perspective, Abse noted that behavior therapy "has so many possibilities of negative effects, not the least being that some people best treated analytically are seduced along the lines of their resistance to change."

A major advantage of many of these techniques is their great potency for the rapid modification of behavior. This same advantage, however, simultaneously creates a greater potential for abuse. In a case described by Knapp, a woman with hysterical leg paralysis was "partly bullied, partly tricked" into walking by the use of a particularly crude and forceful form of behavior modification. The patient walked out of the hospital but returned that night with two arteries slashed in a major suicide attempt.

Even among the adherents of behavior therapy, there is a recognition of special problems that may result from this form of treatment. A general problem is increased behavioral feedback, which may at times lead to the reinforcement of inappropriate responses. When this happens, problem behaviors may actually show an increase during baseline or extinction periods before treatment is introduced. Further, when contingencies are reversed in order to demonstrate the efficacy of treatment in reducing negative behaviors, there will of necessity be an increase in these behaviors. Other problems may accompany hierarchical steps toward therapeutic goals which are too large or which are undertaken at too rapid a pace for the patient to achieve success (Liberman). Finally, one behavior therapist observed that the main contributor to negative effects in behavior therapy is failing to engage the patient in the "here and now"—suggesting concern with the *lack of relationship* during the strict technical application of behavior modification techniques.

Radical (Confrontational/Tactile) Therapies. Many of the more radical forms of therapy are relatively young, and thus there are few reliable data on their effects. However, some evidence is beginning to accumulate and a number of respondents indicated that they have questions or concerns about these therapies. Ellis, for example, minced no words in referring to certain "misleading and idiotic theories of psychotherapy."

Many of these therapies are group-based. Davison observed that with groups in general there is a danger of inadequate assessment and attention to the needs and vulnerabilities of individual members. Furthermore, there is the problem of charismatic group leaders whose potential for impact upon group members is great. Yalom, one of the few workers who has published evidence of negative effects associated with such group leaders (Lieberman, Yalom, & Miles, 1973), observed that there may be a further problem with time-limited groups or encounter groups in which the patient does not have sufficient time to work through issues of discomfort and distress confronting him at the time the group terminates.

Bellak referred to problems of "excessive awareness" brought about by some encounter groups as well as excessive repression due to "stupid value judgments" by the therapist and other group members. Similarly, another respondent noted problems of increased feelings of alienation or depression in some group members. In its extreme form, these negative effects may lead to decompensation of very disturbed individuals (Bieber).

Miscellaneous

Finally, respondents mentioned several general mistakes which, regardless of the context or form of therapy in which they occur, are clearly to be avoided. Among these are breaches in confidentiality (Weintraub); prolongation of therapy when an impasse is reached; refusal of the therapist to refer a patient to another therapist or another form of therapy if the present situation is not productive (Weintraub); and finally, labeling which becomes "either an excuse and/or a reason for repeated failure" (Lazarus).

Summary of Survey

It is clear that negative effects of psychotherapy are overwhelmingly regarded by experts in the field as a significant problem requiring the attention and concern of practitioners and researchers alike. The responses to our survey show that these experts are prepared to point the way for investigators by specifying criteria of negative effects and possible causative factors.

The traditional and relatively obvious identifying criterion of an increase in the number and/or the severity of problems was mentioned by most respondents. Many went on, however, to describe certain less obvious, but nonetheless real, indicators of negative effects including the patient's abuse or misuse of therapy; ill-fated attempts by the patient to overreach his capacities; and, as a result of any or all of these more specific, negative effects, disillusionment with the therapist or with therapy in general.

The list of factors which may conduce to negative effects in psychotherapy was lengthy. Deficiencies in assessment were described by many as one of the most fundamental contributory factors, leading to a variety of problems stemming from a failure to identify borderline patients and others for whom psychotherapy may pose serious risks.

A wide range of patient and therapist personality qualities was identified as problematical, along with the obvious but extraordinarily serious problem of deficiencies in the therapist's training. By far the greatest number of factors cited fell under the general heading of misapplications or deficiencies in techniques. In particular, the misuse of interpretations and insight therapy came in for severe criticism. At a minimum, the misuse of interpretations may promote an unhealthy imbalance in the patient's life, diverting his energies into the pursuit of insight as an end in and of itself. At its worst, the misuse of interpretations and faulty efforts to produce "insight" may be patently destructive of the patient's psychological well-being. (A complete listing of identifying criteria of negative effects and potential contributory factors mentioned by our respondents appears in Tables 2-2 and 2-3.)

Perhaps the most compelling finding of the survey was strong support of the need for systematic research into the problem of negative effects. There were repeated references to the issue as "important," "intriguing," and "exciting." A number of respondents expressed their pleasure at the fact that a systematic study of negative effects was underway and offered additional assistance and cooperation. Others indicated that they themselves had recently been thinking or writing about the problem of negative effects. The spirit of these experts was perhaps best summed up by Orne, who observed that "The issues . . . are as important as they are difficult. It certainly is time for someone to bite the bullet and seek to address the matters empirically. I wish you luck!"

The Vanderbilt Negative Indicators Scale (VNIS)

Based on the research carried out as part of the Vanderbilt Psychotherapy Research Project as well as our work in the area of negative effects (see Strupp, Hadley, & Gomes-Schwartz, 1977, which included the

Table 2-2. What Constitutes a Negative Effect?

Exacerbation of Presenting Symptoms

1. "Worsening"—increase in severity, pathology, etc.
2. *Generally,* may take form of (or be accompanied by):
   a. Exacerbation of suffering
   b. Decompensation
   c. Harsher superego or more rigid personality structure
3. *Specific* examples of symptom exacerbation:
   * Depressive breakdown
   * Severe regression
   * Increased self-downing
   * Increased behavioral shirking
   * Increased inhibition
   * Paranoia
   * Fixing of obsessional symptoms
   * Exaggeration of somatic difficulties
   * Extension of phobias
   * Increased guilt
   * Increased confusion
   * Lowered self-confidence
   * Lower self-esteem
   * Diminished capacity for delay and impulse control

Appearance of New Symptoms

1. *Generally,* may be observed when:
   a. Psychic disturbance is manifested in a less socially acceptable form than previously
   b. Symptom substitution where a symptom which had fulfilled an imperative need is blocked
2. *Specific* examples:
   * Erosion of solid interpersonal relationships
   * Decreased ability to experience pleasure
   * Severe or fatal psychosomatic reactions
   * Withdrawal
   * Rage
   * Dissociation
   * Drug/alcohol abuse
   * Criminal behavior
   * Suicide
   * Psychotic breaks

Patient Abuse or Misuse of Therapy

1. Substitution of intellectualized insights for other obsessional thoughts
2. Utilization of therapy to rationalize feelings of superiority or expressions of hostility toward other people
3. Therapy becomes an end in itself—a substitute for action
4. Fear of "intellectualization" prevents patients from examining their ethical and philosophical commitments

Table 2-2 (con't)

5. Participation in more radical therapies encourages belief in the irrational in order to avoid painful confrontations with realities of life
6. Sustained dependency on therapy or the therapist

Patient "Overreaching" Himself

1. Two forms:
   a. Undertaking life tasks (marriage, graduate school, etc.) which require resources beyond those of the patient
   b. Undertaking life tasks prematurely
2. May be related to:
   a. Intense wishes to please the therapist
   b. Inculcation of inachievable middle-class "ideals"
   c. Increased "irrational" ideas
3. May result in any or all of the following:
   a. Excessive strain on patient's psychological resources
   b. Failure at the task
   c. Guilt
   d. Self-contempt

Disillusionment with Therapy and/or the Therapist

1. May appear variously as:
   a. Wasting of patient's resources (time, skill, money) which might have been better expended elsewhere
   b. Hardening of attitudes toward other sources of help
   c. Loss of confidence in the therapist, possibly extending to any human relationship
   b. General loss of hope—all the more severe for initial raising of hopes which may have occurred at onset of therapy

survey previously described), we attempted to isolate "negative indicators" in early therapeutic interviews. The VNIS is built upon the general working assumption that the presence of an appreciable number of negative indicators in early interviews is predictive of poor therapy outcomes. We hypothesized that certain (1) patient variables, (2) therapist variables, (3) technique variables, and (4) patient-therapist interaction variables are conducive to such effects. Systematic efforts have been made to refine the scale and to determine the character, number, frequency, intensity, and combination of variables that are most highly predictive of poor therapy outcomes.

The VNIS is not intended to assess ingredients in the therapeutic interaction which are generally regarded as leading to *good* therapeutic outcomes nor is an attempt made to achieve a balance between "positive indicators" and "negative indicators." Instead, the focus is entirely upon identification of the latter. It is assumed that unless appropriate corrections in the therapeutic interaction are made or a different dyad is formed, the outcome of therapy will be poor, inconclusive, or negative.

Table 2-3. What Factors Are Associated with Negative Effects?

Inaccurate/Deficient Assessment

1. Assessment must include:
   a. Ego functions
   b. General baseline
      (i) age
      (ii) diagnosis
      (iii) state of capacities
      (iv) life situation
   c. Natural history of difficulties
   d. Functional value of psychopathology
2. Assessment deficiencies may lead to:
   a. Probing more deeply than the patient can tolerate
   b. Failing to work intensively enough—thus cheating the patient of experiencing as much change as he is capable of

Therapist Variables

1. Deficiencies in training or skills—related in part to limited knowledge within the field itself.
2. Personality factors:
   a. Need to exploit the patient
   b. Sadomasochism
   c. Voyeurism
   d. Faddism
   e. Coldness
   f. Obsessionalism
   g. Excessive need to make people change
   h. Excessive unconscious hostility
   i. Seductiveness
   j. Pessimism
   k. Absence of genuineness
   l. Greed
   m. Narcissism
   n. Dearth of self-scrutiny

Patient Qualities

1. Low or absent motivation
2. Low ego strength
3. Masochism—"feeling bad" because in some respects is doing well

Misapplications/Deficiencies of Technique

1. False assumptions concerning the scope and potency of therapy. Particularly, the assumption that therapy is all-powerful and the therapist is all-knowing.
2. Mistakes with therapeutic goals. (a) Failing to discuss or acknowledge reality of goals per se. (b) Failing to reach *mutual* agreement on goals. (c) Goals which are not in the patient's best interest. (d) Too demanding goals—or too rapid progress toward goals.
3. Misplaced focus. (a) Focus exclusively on "the inner man"—failure to in-

Table 2-3 (con't)

volve environment in treatment of the patient *or* to treat problem aspects of the environment. (b) Focusing on anything and everything except problem behaviors of the patient and his will to stop them.

4. Mismatch between therapy and the patient. Examples include: (a) Insight therapy applied to borderline or psychosomatic patients. (b) Attacking the defenses of fragile patients. (c) Therapist allying himself with id mechanisms when dealing with adolescents. (d) Aversion therapy which satisfies patient's "sick" need to be punished.

5. Technical rigidity. (a) Generally, considered to result from the therapist's insecurity. (b) May have any or all of the following adverse effects:
   (i) failure to take into account patient's individual needs
   (ii) forces patient to submit to preestablished procedure
   (iii) inability or unwillingness to shift mode of treatment
   (iv) decreased understanding and thoughtfulness

6. Overly intense therapy. (a) Getting too close to the patient. (b) Too specific advice or tasks. (c) Pushing the fragile patient to reveal himself.

7. Misuse of interpretation or insight therapy. May take form of:
   a. *Imbalance* between insights or interpretations and other processes of therapeutic change
      (i) diversion of patient's resources into pursuit of insights
      (ii) predominance of transference-centered interpretations to the exclusion of reality factors
   b. *Destruction interpretations*
      (i) at a minimum, may arouse anxiety through conveying message of "basic abnormality"
      (ii) adverse effects likely when insufficient follow-up, analysis without sufficient synthesis

8. *Dependency-fostering techniques.* Includes failure to recognize and head off development of overly intense dependency.

Problems with the Patient–Therapist Relationship

1. Too much or too little rapport

2. Countertransference (especially due to underestimating one's reactions to the patient) may have any or all of these effects:
   a. Prevention of working alliance
   b. Lack of respect for the patient's pain
   c. Failure to allow the patient to experience choices
   d. Aggressive assault on the patient's defenses
   e. Disappointed attitude toward the patient and his progress

3. Failure to maintain professional distance—especially sexual involvement with the patient

Communication Problems

1. *Therapist*—inability to communicate clearly *and* to determine whether patient is comprehending what was said

2. *Patient*—distortions, omissions, and falsifications in communications to the therapist

Table 2-3 (con't)

Problems Unique to Special Forms of Therapy
1. *Behavior therapy*
   a. Symptom substitution
   b. Reinforcement of inappropriate responses by behavioral feedback
   c. Increase in negative behaviors during baseline or extinction periods
   d. Too large or too rapid hierarchical steps toward therapy goals
   e. Failure to engage the patient in the here and now
2. *Radical therapies* (especially in group context)
   a. Inadequate assessment and attention to individuals
   b. Charismatic but destructive group leaders
   c. Time limitations may prevent some individuals from working through distress
   d. Excessive awareness
   e. "Stupid" value judgments
   f. Depression and feelings of alienation

Miscellaneous Problems Which May Occur in Any Form of Therapy
1. Breaches in confidentiality
2. Prolongation of therapy when an impasse is reached (refusal to refer patient elsewhere)
3. Labeling—especially when it becomes an excuse/reason for repeated failures

Background and Empirical Evidence

The item content of the VNIS was largely derived from the synthesis of contemporary professional views on the subject, presented earlier. Items also evolved from extensive clinical observations of therapy sessions from good and poor outcome cases in the Vanderbilt Psychotherapy Research Project (Strupp & Hadley, 1979; Strupp, 1980a, 1980b, 1980c, 1980d).

Gomes-Schwartz contributed the basic conception of the VNIS and obtained the first data regarding inter-rater reliability and the power of the instrument to distinguish good- and poor-outcome cases (Gomes-Schwartz, 1978).

Substantial developmental work on the original instrument and rating procedures has been undertaken by other members of the Vanderbilt Psychotherapy Research Team.* Inter-rater reliability and the power of the revised VNIS to predict good- and poor-outcome cases on the basis of early therapy sessions have been examined in a pilot study (Strupp et al., 1980). On the whole, these data indicated that satisfactory to good levels of inter-rater reliability can be achieved with the

---

*This team included Hans H. Strupp, Lois Keithly, Karla Moras, Stephanie Samples, Janet Sandell, and Gloria Waterhouse.

instrument. However, pilot work has suggested that rater characteristics (such as the degree to which raters share a theoretical orientation) can have a marked effect of the degree of interobserver consensus obtained. On the basis of a small sample of patients ($N = 10$), Strupp et al. (1980) also found preliminary evidence that the VNIS can differentiate between good- and poor-outcome cases as early as the third hour of therapy. In the most comprehensive study available to date, Sandell (1981) contributed further evidence corroborating the earlier findings.

Features of the VNIS

The current version of the VNIS consists of 42 items, all of which point to factors that singly or in combination are hypothesized to predict negative outcomes. Items are grouped into five broad sections. Four of these sections, "Patient Personal Qualities and Attitudes," "Therapist Personal Qualities and Attitudes," "Errors in Technique," and "Patient–Therapist Interaction," are consistent with prevailing conceptions of the major outcome-related dimensions of psychotherapy. The fifth section, "Global," contains items designed to tap general clinical impressions of therapy sessions that are hypothesized to predict negative outcomes. Each section of the VNIS is further divided into conceptually distinct categories of items.

A full description of the VNIS, together with rating procedures, is given in a manual (available from the senior author). In general, 15-minute segments or total sessions are rated by clinical judges. Audiovisual recordings are considered the preferred medium of presentation. Therapy sessions are subdivided into 7½ to 10 minute segments. Every item is considered for each segment, although numerical ratings are not made until the end of the entire segment. Acceptable levels of inter-rater reliability are most likely to be achieved by clinically sophisticated judges, well acquainted with the concepts, principles, and techniques of psychodynamic psychotherapy (for which the VNIS is probably most applicable). Clinical raters must undergo a period of training. All items are rated on a scale ranging from 0 (not present, that is, "within normal limits") to 5 (strong evidence that item is present).

In summary, the VNIS has shown promise as a reasonably reliable and valid instrument for assessing elements in psychotherapy interviews whose presence is predictive of unsatisfactory outcomes. Further work is clearly needed to answer such questions as the instrument's applicability to other forms of psychotherapy and the configuration of items that might be most detrimental to therapeutic progress. However, even at the present stage of development, the VNIS may serve a useful function in supervision, patient assignment, and determinations of whether a particular patient–therapist combination is a good (or poor) "match."*

Further Empirical Evidence and Concluding Comments

As part of the Vanderbilt Psychotherapy Project, several systematic comparisons between patient pairs treated by the same therapist were carried out (Strupp, 1980a, 1980b, 1980c, 1980d). In each comparison, one patient was a success and the second a failure case (measured by a set of criteria described in these articles). Detailed analyses of the patient–therapist interaction and related data led to consistent results which may be summarized as follows:

Given the "average expectable" atmosphere created by a person functioning in the therapeutic role, that is, a person who is basically empathic and benign, the key determinants of a particular therapeutic outcome are traceable to *characteristics of the patient:* If the patient is a person who by virtue of his past life experience is capable of human *relatedness* and therefore amenable to learning mediated within the context, the outcome, even though the individual may have suffered traumas, reverses, and other vicissitudes, is likely to be positive. If on the other hand his early life experiences have been so destructive that human relatedness has failed to acquire a markedly positive valence and elaborate neurotic and characterological malformations have created massive barriers to intimacy (and therefore to "therapeutic learning"), chances are that psychotherapy results either in failure or at best in very modest gains. Yet the therapist's ability to provide a nurturant environment and to curb counter-transference reactions undoubtedly plays an important part, as does his expertise in facilitating therapeutic learning (e.g., skills in eroding neurotic barriers against human relatedness). Thus, in the final analysis, the outcome of psychotherapy will be largely determined by the balance of these forces entering into and determining the patient–therapist interaction.

The preceding points place heavy emphases on the patient's character makeup, the nature and depth of his disturbance, and his ability

---

*The ability of untrained clinical observers to differentiate between good and poor "matches" is truly impressive. On several occasions, first-year graduate students were presented with 15-minute segments from the third interviews by the same therapist with two patients, one of whom was a "success" and the other a "failure" case. The vast majority of students had no difficulty in predicting correctly the eventual treatment outcome.

to become productively involved in psychotherapy. These criteria are essentially identical to those traditionally considered crucial in assessing a patient's suitability for psychoanalysis (Bachrach & Leaff, 1978). However, it is also important to stress that with most patients in our study, therapists employed a standard therapeutic approach structured along traditional psychoanalytic lines. In other words, therapists conducted therapy in terms of their predilections, and the patients were faced with the necessity of working within the therapist's framework. Some patients were able to do so; others were not. Does this mean that some patients are unsuitable for psychotherapy, or merely for psychotherapy of a certain kind? It is certainly plausible that failure patients should not be considered reasonable candidates for time-limited forms of dynamic psychotherapy. Indeed, workers like Malan (1976), Davanloo (1971), and Mann (1973) would undoubtedly rule them out. However, it is also possible that certain approaches, as yet poorly developed, might provide some form of therapeutic help for these difficult patients even when circumstances dictate time limitations. As is well known, the more "difficult" patients constitute a far larger segment of the total patient pool than the "easy" ones, and the challenge to the mental health professions is to provide more efficient and effective services to those individuals who have too long been neglected.

Further, one should not lose sight of the serious toll exacted by faulty patient–therapist matches. In the "success" cases there was a sense of mutual satisfaction, whereas in the opposites, termination was surrounded by feelings of profound frustration on the part of both participants. It is easy to see that any therapist would find a success patient a pleasure to work with. However, as therapists we have not adequately faced up to the negative reactions engendered in us by patients who bring to our offices the products of their unhappy life experiences.

Thus, major deterrants to the formation of a good working alliance are not only the patient's characterological distortions and maladaptive defenses but—at least equally important—the therapist's personal reactions. Traditionally these reactions have been considered under the heading of countertransference. It is becoming increasingly clear, however, that this conception is too narrow. The plain fact is that *any therapist—indeed any human being—cannot remain immune from negative (angry) reactions to the suppressed and repressed rage regularly encountered in patients with moderate to severe disturbances.* As soon as one enters the inner world of such a person through a therapeutic relationship, one is faced with the inescapable necessity of dealing with one's own response to the patient's tendency to make the therapist a partner in his difficulties via the transference. In the Vanderbilt Project, therapists—

even highly experienced ones and those who had undergone a personal analysis—tended to respond to such patients with counterhostility that not uncommonly took the form of coldness, distancing, and other forms of rejection. Needless to say, to the patient such responses become self-fulfilling prophecies leading to a dissolution of the therapeutic relationship, early termination, and poor outcome. In our study we failed to encounter a single instance in which a difficult patient's hostility and negativism were successfully confronted or resolved. Admittedly, this may be due to peculiarities of our therapist sample and the brevity of therapy; however, a more likely possibility is that therapists' negative responses to difficult patients are far more common and far more intractable than has been generally recognized. (For a similar conclusion, based on a review of the research literature, see Luborsky & Spence, 1978). Some years ago, Strupp adduced preliminary evidence on this topic through an anologue study (1960).

The material presented in this chapter clearly has far-reaching implications for the selection, training, and practice of psychotherapists. In recent years, the difficulties encountered by therapists in dealing with certain patients have been widely discussed with reference to narcissistic and borderline cases. The problems, however, are by no means restricted to the most severely disturbed patients. Nor are the difficulties isolated or transient. To be sure, greater self-understanding, self-acceptance, supervision, personal therapy, and the like may go a considerable distance in helping therapists cope with the vicissitudes of their craft. However, in the final analysis we are dealing with ubiquitous human tendencies that represent perhaps the single most important obstacle to successful psychotherapy, thus meriting much greater attention than they have been accorded (see, e.g., Vaillant, 1977, p. 371). We are referring to the human limitations of all therapists. The dilemma is that in order for therapists to function effectively they must be capable of immersing themselves and participating in their patients' inner struggles as they are played out in their interpersonal relations with significant persons, including the therapist. On the other hand, therapists can be helpful only if they can refrain from becoming too deeply involved. The dividing line is often fluid and potentially treacherous.

It has been said that all therapeutic failures are ultimately due to deficiencies in the therapist's empathy. As we have seen, the patient's character structure and developmental history set distinct limits to what any therapist can accomplish. It is equally clear, however, that empathy—and its concomitant, *understanding*—is the therapist's major tool. It informs, guides, and modulates his or her communications and keeps the therapy on course. That course, however, is importantly determined by a thorough grasp of the nature of the patient's struggle, the kind of help that is needed, and how it might best be provided. Toward this end, intensive and thorough training are the only known reliable guides. Empathy without training is at best of limited value in dealing with serious problems in living; "techniques" without empathy may be the most direct route to negative effects.

Thus, there seem to be only two major routes by which therapeutic outcomes can be improved and the two must coincide: We must select patients who are promising candidates for what psychotherapy has to offer (essentially, a good human relationship in which certain kinds of learning can be mediated) and therapists who are optimally equipped to work with such patients. In comparison to these factors, the third possibility, that of developing better "techniques," while certainly deserving further attention, pales in significance.

Part II

Negative Outcome and Therapeutic Modality

3

Negative Outcome in Psychotherapy and Psychoanalysis

Donald Colson, Lisa Lewis,
and Leonard Horwitz

This paper will deal with some failures in psychotherapy and psycho-analysis by examining a subsample of patients in The Menninger Foundation's Psychotherapy Research Project (PRP) who deteriorated during the course of their treatment or were judged to have deteriorated at treatment follow-up. To provide a context for our study of negative outcome in the PRP we will first review the clinical and research literature on negative outcome and then describe the major findings of the PRP.

Prior Literature

Though the majority of the studies which follow suffer from problems in design, collectively they provide some opportunity to understand the incidence and possible sources of negative therapeutic outcome. The incidence of negative outcome varies greatly both within and between studies, depending on the nature of the patient, the therapists sampled, outcome criteria, and the selection of raters (i.e., independent judges, the patient, or the therapist). In psychoanalysis the incidence ranges from 1 percent (Aronson & Weintraub, 1968) to 44 percent (for psychotic patients, Weber, Elinson, & Moss, 1965). The severity of the patient's psychopathology emerges as a strong contributing factor. The incidence of negative outcome in psychotherapy ranges from 1 percent (Rosenbaum, Friedlander, & Kaplan, 1956) to 14 percent (Sager, Riess, & Gundlach, 1964), with the probable causal factors being the interaction of severity of psychopathology and form of treatment (Fairweather et al., 1960), frequent changes in therapists (Feifel & Schwartz, 1963), the patient's sense that the therapist was bored, cold, or not understanding (Feifel & Schwartz, 1963; Paul, 1967; and Strupp, Wallach, & Wogan, 1964), and the patient's history of poor interpersonal relationships (Rosenbaum et al., 1956).

When one turns from empirical investigations to the clinical literature, several additional patient characteristics assume prominence, including masochism (Parkin, 1980; Valenstein, 1973), unconscious oedipal and pre-oedipal guilt (Kernberg, 1977; Modell, 1971), narcissistic envy (Rosenfeld, 1975), and an acquired or congenital imbalance of libidinal and aggressive instincts (Freud, 1937; Loewald, 1972). While most authors emphasize the pathological nature of these characteristics, a few explicitly focus on their adaptive and reparative meanings (Colson, 1981; Modell, 1971). Modell emphasizes that for many of such patients, improvement is viewed as necessarily hurtful and depriving of internal and external objects. Thus, the patient's decline in functioning or failure to improve in treatment would be viewed, in part, as an altruistic sacrifice of oneself to "goodness" in order to ensure that loved ones will not be deprived. Therapist factors believed to be significant in producing negative outcome are unrecognized countertransference reactions, particularly of a hostile nature; therapist deficiencies in personality, training, and skill (Strupp & Hadley, 1976); and failure to act and communicate in a fashion which conveys consistent regard for the integrity of the patient (Horner, 1980). The hypothesized treatment and technique factors include inaccurate or deficient assessment leading to misapplication of therapy (Strupp & Hadley, 1976), and failure to establish a consistent and proper working relationship (Strupp, 1980 a–d; Wolberg, 1977).

The Psychotherapy Research Project

The PRP was an intensive, naturalistic study of 42 patients in psychoanalytically oriented psychotherapy or psychoanalysis. All patients included were between the ages of 18 and 50, were anticipated to utilize psychotherapy as the primary or exclusive treatment modality, were not overtly psychotic, and evidenced no indication of organicity. Only 26 therapists were included because one therapist sometimes treated two research patients and in a few instances treated three. Seventeen of the 42 cases were hospitalized at some time during their treatment. The patients were studied at three intervals: immediately before beginning treatment, at termination, and at two-year follow-up. Neither patients nor therapists knew they had been selected for the study until treatment had terminated. Clinical materials pertaining to the case were studied independently by a research team. At the initial evaluation most patients routinely had psychiatric interviews, a social history, psychological tests, and a physical examination. At termination the patient was interviewed by the research team, psychological tests were readministered, and significant relatives were interviewed. Monthly progress notes and clinical summaries were examined, and the therapist and supervisor were interviewed. All of these sources of data were summarized in case reports categorized as patient variables, situational variables, and treatment and therapist variables.

The following are some of the major findings of the PRP as reported by Kernberg and his research colleagues (1972). A high level of patient ego strength is an indication of good prognosis for psychoanalysis, psychotherapy, and supportive psychotherapy. Kernberg notes that many of the patients who failed to profit from supportive psychotherapy manifested the form of primitive defenses associated with borderline personality organization, and that these characteristics interfered with the development of a working alliance.

One of the two major statistical analyses showed that high levels of quality of interpersonal relationships, anxiety tolerance, and motivation predicted good outcomes. While these three variables are highly related to levels of ego strength, an analysis of the interrelationship of these components revealed that (1) patients who were low on both ego strength and quality of interpersonal relations were the least improved with psychotherapy or psychoanalysis; (2) the higher the initial level of anxiety, the greater the global improvement and the higher the increase in ego strength at both termination and follow-up. Appelbaum's (1972) clinical analysis of the concept of motivation stresses the importance of differentiating the wish to get help, the wish to continue treatment, and the wish to change. Kernberg emphasizes a similar issue in differentiating a mature wish to change through a cooperative effort with the therapist from infantile and magical wishes to be taken care of by a powerful figure.

Data from the PRP strongly suggest that the therapist's skill and personality become increasingly important factors in treatment out-

come with the increasing severity of the patient's psychological disturbance. The more disturbed the patient, the less the treater can rely on
the prescribed methods of expressive psychoanalytic therapy or psychoanalysis, and the greater the need to be aware of the influence of
one's personality and specific countertransference reactions. Put simply, more disturbed patients make more stringent demands on the
therapist's patience, commitment, sense of security, and skills. In a
detailed examination of the impact of the therapist's personality and
level of competence on treatment outcome, Horwitz (1969) found, as
one might expect, that highly competent therapists are more likely to
convey warmth and acceptance toward the patient than therapists
rated low in competence. Also, therapists who rated high on competence showed more ability to be reflective and to defer quick action in
preference for thoughtfulness. Overall, highly competent therapists
showed a capacity to engage steadily over a long period of time in the
therapy process while maintaining empathic contact with the patient in
spite of a lack of immediate reward and, often enough, multiple reasons for frustration.

Horwitz (1974) in his description of the PRP clinical prediction
studies summarizes major findings bearing on curative factors. He emphasizes that the therapeutic alliance and the patient's internalization
of the alliance are significant for the successful cases regardless of
whether they were treated expressively or supportively. He describes
the negative transference as blocking internalization and thereby limit-
ing treatment gains. In general, he underscores that significant and
stable gains occurred for a number of "supportively" treated patients,
and contrasts this finding with the assumption held by some analytically oriented clinicians that lasting change must be achieved through
insight and so-called structural change in the ego.

One surprise of the PRP was that the major statistical analyses
found no significant relationship between outcome and an array of
environmental variables. However, Voth and Orth (1973), in their extensive clinical examination of environmental variables, found a correspondence between degree of disturbance and the extent of the patient's involvement with the environment. For many of the patients,
decreasing their involvement with the environment (responsibilities
and commitments) was accompanied by symptomatic improvement. It
seemed that patients who decreased their involvements, particularly
with the opposite sex, did so as a means of lessening tension or anxiety
and avoiding regressive pressures, and thereby achieved some improvement in their general psychological state and in symptomatology
at the cost of settling for a more narrow and limited life.

Method of Study for Negative Effects

We examine here a subsample of patients in the PRP who were judged to be worse either at the time of termination or at a two-year follow-up. When it is useful to refer to a comparison group, we will contrast these negative outcome cases with a subgroup of cases with the best treatment outcomes. These samples were selected as follows. At the time of the formal PRP data analysis, two senior clinicians on the research team made independent ratings of global change on a 5-point scale (from 1, worse, to 5, significantly improved with conflict resolution) for both termination and follow-up, and then reached a consensus rating. The 11 cases with consensus ratings of 1 at either of the two points in time constitute our negative-outcome group and the 10 cases rated 4 or 5 constitute the treatment-success group. The selection of negative-outcome cases by this method results in the following subsample: (1) 4 cases were worse at termination and follow-up; (2) 3 cases were unchanged at termination and worse at follow-up; (3) 1 case was a bit better at termination and worse at follow-up; (4) 3 cases were worse at termination and better at follow-up.

The Patients

Basic Characteristics

The reader is referred to Table 3-1 for a descriptive summary of information which will allow a contrast between the most and least successful cases. The age range in both groups is somewhat predetermined by patient preselection between the ages of 18 and 50 and, consequently, as might be expected, age does not seem to differentiate the groups. Although there is a greater number of men in the negative outcome group, our impression is that this is not a significant issue in itself, but is probably related to an issue of professional and academic achievement and the influence of such achievement upon diagnostic errors. With regard to educational and occupational level it seems, paradoxically, that the negative-outcome cases include a higher proportion of people at an advanced educational and professional level than in the sample of treatment successes. The resolution of this paradox is suggested in our detailed examination of the clinical write-ups, where we discovered that misdiagnoses in the direction of overestimating health were most consistent in the patients with high professional levels. For example, in the negative outcome cases, five of seven patients with high professional levels were initially judged to be considerably heal-

Table 3-1. Patient Characteristics

Variable	Negative Outcome (N = 11)	Success (N = 10)
Age	X = 34; range = 28–43	X = 33; range = 21–50
Sex	8 = male; 3 = female	5 = male; 5 = female
Marital status	8 = married (1 twice)	4 = married
		4 = remarried during Tx
	3 = single	2 = initially single and married during Tx
Children	5 = yes; 6 = no	4 = yes; 2 = no; 4 = had children during the course of Tx
Education/occupation	7 = high level of attainment	5 = high level of attainment
	4 = low level of attainment	5 = low level of attainment
Accuracy of diagnosis	7 patients were misdiagnosed, all in the direction of underestimating the severity of pathology; 5 of these patients had high-level educational/ occupational attainment.	2 patients were misdiagnosed, both in the direction of underestimating the severity of pathology; both patients had high-level educational/ occupational attainment.

thier than was subsequently found to be justified. Even in the successful sample there were only two glaring diagnostic errors, and in both
instances the patients had high-level professional standing (both were
university professors).

Given this misdiagnosis of level of psychological disturbance, we
reexamined the negative-outcome cases to determine contributions to
diagnostic errors. Our clinical examination of the cases led us to conclude that the negative-outcome group included primarily cases which
could be labeled borderline. However, they represented a broad range
of borderline conditions from character disturbances with prominent
borderline features, to patients (one in particular) who suffered severe
character pathology and intermittent but frequent affective turbulence
and distortions of reality at a psychotic level. In contrast, with the
successful cases there was a much broader range extending from borderline to neurotic levels of functioning. Four patients were in the
neurotic and mild character disturbance range. Five were in the range
of a more serious character pathology with two or three of these clearly
falling in the borderline range, and with one diagnosed as having
major bipolar affective disturbance with periodic psychotic episodes.
The Health–Sickness Scale had been completed for all cases at the
three assessment intervals, and there was a substantial difference between success and negative-outcome cases in the means of severity of
psychological disturbance. Since there were also a few borderline patients in the success group, we identify the types of borderline patients
which characterize the negative-outcome group.

Subtypes of Borderline Personality Organization

Our review of the clinical case descriptions of the negative-outcome
cases reveal several patient characteristics which tend to recur throughout this sample. In virtually all of them, the case materials described
prominent conflicts at a pregenital (oral) level which, translated in object relations terms, represents a search, frequently desperate and angry, for the satisfaction of intense and chronically thwarted needs.
Often enough, although these patients had achieved a reasonably high
level of academic or professional development, they had chronic difficulties establishing mature interpersonal relationships. The neediness
which they seemed unable to satisfy in the interpersonal realm reflected a chronic, driven hunger and was often expressed alloplastically
in a variety of basically self-defeating behaviors. These people searched
desperately, although in vain, for some semblance of satisfaction with
themselves and with life. With equal desperation they turned to maladaptive solutions or gratifications which actually prevented real satis-

faction of the needs involved. For example, a high number of the negative-outcome patients chronically abused drugs or alcohol compared with a considerably lower incidence in the successful group. As a result of conspicuous demandingness combined with self-sabotage, their life courses, particularly their relationships with others, tended to have the quality of a cumulative series of defeats and confirmations of their inability to obtain support, succor, and much needed aids to their profoundly disturbed self-esteem. This pattern of angry neediness and self-defeat seemed rooted in these patients' inability to tolerate the kind of closeness to others that is required to obtain interpersonal support and a sense of comfort. These features might be contrasted with the pattern more frequently encountered in the successful group. Here, even though several patients might also be classified as borderline, those borderline patients seemed less angry and showed more modulated, less self-defeating means of interacting with others. Although they clearly felt some degree of the pain and anger typical of the negative-outcome group, these affects and the behaviors stemming from them seemed better contained and generally less primitive. They were better able to delay acting quickly and were more receptive to deriving satisfaction from the treatment relationship. Consequently, they were not so driven and were more accessible to interventions, and to building a treatment alliance.

In addition to the alcohol and drug abuse, another feature of the negative-outcome group which expressed simultaneous neediness and self-defeat was a pattern of deviousness and dishonesty. A significant number of them consciously lied, withheld crucial information, or in other ways misled their treaters. Frequently they misrepresented substance abuse or other self-destructive behavior such as promiscuity. Their deception, itself part of a pattern of self-sabotage, precluded effective therapeutic work on the aspects of their lives most needing attention in order for treatment to have a chance of success. Seldom was the element of dishonesty clearly identified at the time of the initial examination.

In summary, the following pattern of features seem to emerge from our examination of the negative outcome cases. They were on the average more seriously disturbed than the successes but, in addition, an object-relations issue seemed involved. Their intense unsatisfied neediness, a pattern of responding to such needs with self-defeating behavior (frequently including alcohol or drug abuse), and the frequent occurrence of self-deception and dishonesty are all suggestive of a particularly self-destructive quality in the object-relations sphere. With many of the cases a masochistic binge of self-sabotage and self-destructiveness, once set in motion, was difficult and in some instances perhaps impossible to reverse. They consistently sought maladaptive solutions to conflict and dissatisfaction. Rather than attempting alterations in their behavior which could result in greater satisfaction with themselves and others, they misdirected their efforts into strategies which only temporarily reduced their needs. Insofar as such patients achieved higher level academic and professional standing, they presented difficult diagnostic problems and were frequently viewed at the time of the initial study as having less severe character problems than subsequent events demonstrated. Thus these patients tended to receive treatments which, at least at the outset, were mismatched in terms of the amount of support, containment, and structure required for a successful outcome.

The intensity of these patients' negative therapeutic reaction brings to mind a description of a particular relationship paradigm described by Modell (1971) and Colson (1981). These authors refer to a form of unconscious guilt, perhaps rooted in family dynamics, which is particularly prominent in some patients, probably a subsample of borderline patients. These people harbor a deep-seated unconscious conviction that they do not have a right to a better life and that success or acquisition of something good means that others will be depleted and destroyed. For such patients issues of envy are particularly intense and every potential for something better in their lives seems to exacerbate their worst pathological behavior. The ways in which such self-defeating patterns are intertwined with their closest interpersonal relationships (particularly family dynamics) will be clearer in our subsequent description of the environmental and situational variables.

The Family Context

Voth and Orth (1973), who wrote up the primary PRP findings of the Menninger study on the role of the environment, note that a significant number of patients improved in treatment as a result of withdrawal from particularly conflictual relationships and situations such as marriage or job. Such an adjustment, while ameliorating symptoms, can hardly be considered improvement, according to the criterion of living a full life.

In our study of the negative-outcome cases, one trend stands out above any other: significant people in the patient's life colluded to an extraordinary degree, either to sabotage treatment or to undermine opportunities for health. Of the 11 cases who failed to benefit from treatment, we found that for 10, one or another family member actively undermined the patient's growth as well as constructive use of psychotherapy. In contrast, in 7 of the treatment success cases, family were either absent or were largely supportive of the patient. The family were either clearly ambivalent or more openly disruptive in only 3 cases. In these 3 instances the lack of support, rather than being clearly destructive of the treatment process, consisted primarily of mixed messages to the patient about being in treatment. A few examples from the clinical write-ups about the family's role in treatment failures will illustrate the phenomena.

1. His illness was maintained by his wife by her willingness to accommodate extraordinarily to his pathology.

2. The patient's parents reacted to the patient in adulthood, as they had during childhood, by gratifying every whim, excusing every fault, and overlooking every antisocial act. His wife saw him as a spoiled naughty boy who needed love and understanding. He had license to regress and misbehave and would be shielded by others from the consequences.

3. The family endlessly tolerated the patient's disturbed behavior.

4. The wife was opposed to treatment, derogatory toward doctors in general, refused contact with the social worker, kept multiple lethal drugs available in the house (the patient abused drugs), humiliated and endlessly criticized the patient.

5. Husband was initially seen as passively devoted and compliant but his dependent need for the patient, fear of losing her, and worry about finances made his whole attitude toward her treatment much more negative than was originally taken into account.

6. Wife pressured the patient to leave the hospital against medical advice. Then several years later she stood by passively without efforts to intervene in his gradual deterioration and eventual suicide.

It seems then that the pattern of family involvement too often consisted of seemingly endless overindulgence and, occasionally, more direct encouragement of the patient's most pathological behavior. This encouraged a regression hostile-dependence on those particular family members, as well as irresponsible self-destructive behavior. The pattern was frequently inconsistent, with overindulgence alternating with harshly punitive and controlling stances toward the patient. Finally, when the family could no longer tolerate the patient's behavior, family members tended to turn away from the patient, sometimes becoming distant onlookers to the patient's deterioration and escalating self-destruction. A large number of these patients would have tried the tolerance and patience of the best intentioned and most psychologically stable. Voth and Orth were struck by the fact that the treatment failures seemed to have so fully duplicated the impasse around separation–individuation which the psychoanalytic literature describes as the hallmark of the borderline patient. The observation also fits with descriptions of a particular type of borderline patient: one who determinedly duplicates in his current relationships the separation–individuation impasses characteristic of the childhood family context. When these patients manage in one way or another to remove themselves from relationships which they have in part designed to maintain pathological modes of functioning, some degree of symptomatic relief is to be expected.

Another trend in the data, less consistent than the family issue referred to above, deserves mention. More frequently in the negative-outcome group, the patients began treatment only when crippling difficulties had become obstacles to their continued personal or professional survival (such as legal complications associated with deviant sexual practices or increasingly chronic alcohol or drug abuse, the consequences of which had come to permeate most areas of their lives). Consequently such patients, more often than those in the success group, were referred for treatment at the insistence of others. In the successful group 2 of the 10 patients began treatment at the insistence of others while in the negative group 6 of the 11 were referred under such circumstances. The following are examples:

1. The patient was threatened with suspension of his professional license unless he obtained treatment.
2. The patient came following a severe legal embroilment and his father played a crucial role in pressuring him into treatment.
3. The patient was referred by his professional school because of unethical behavior.
4. The parents strongly urged, insisted, that the patient obtain treatment.
5. The patient came for treatment at the urgent insistence of the parents because of increasingly severe alcoholism and inability to work.
6. The patient was referred by her physician because of a bewildering and incapacitating array of physical

problems and medical complaints which were intransigent and not attributable primarily to physical
illness.

How a patient came to therapy has implications for his motivation
to change, and also reflects a tendency, consistent with a self-destructive
lifestyle, to seek professional help only when problems are so severe
and relationships so disturbed that, for some, it would seem to require
little less than a miracle for the patient to resume a more constructive
and adaptive direction.

The Treatment and Therapists

Some Descriptive Variables

The therapists included eight psychiatrists and two psychologists in
the successful group and ten psychiatrists and one psychologist in the
negative-outcome group. There was no overlap of therapists between
these two groups. The therapists were relatively experienced clinicians
with an average of better than five years post-training experience.

In the negative-outcome group five of the patients were in psychoanalysis and six in psychotherapy, with an average period in treatment
of 33.2 months and a range from 4 to 96 months. In the success group,
six were in analysis and four in psychotherapy with an average treatment of 58.2 months and a range from 18 to 108 months. The slightly
greater proportion of successes who were in analysis and who stayed
in treatment longer fits with the relatively higher level of psychological
integrity and the greater patient–therapist collaboration achieved in
that group.

The necessity for hospitalization during psychotherapy seemed
little or no different for the two groups. However, there was a qualita-
tive difference between the groups in that generally there was a higher
level of collaboration between patients and hospital staff in the success
group. Finally, we concur with Horwitz (1974) that the therapists who
treated the successful patients have a bit higher level of overall clinical
skill than those in the negative-outcome group. It is quite clear that
aside from the general skill level, skill level as rated for the specific
negative-outcome cases was considerably below the skill level shown
in working with the successes (Table 3-2). In interpreting this finding
we should bear in mind that the majority of patients in the negative-
outcome group were adept in provoking the worst possible behavior
and judgment from a broad array of people, and that this disposition

Table 3-2. Therapist Characteristics

	Negative Outcome	Success
Therapist's professional affiliation	9 = psychiatry 1 = psychology	7 = psychiatry 2 = psychology
Years of experience[a]	X = 6 years Range = 1–14 years	X = 4.8 years Range = 2–14 years
General skill level[b]	X = 3.3 Range = 1.7–4.5	X = 3.7 Range = 1.9–5
Skill level in the case studied[b]	X = 2.2 Range = 1–4.3	X = 3.6 Range = 2–5

[a]Number of years of psychotherapy experience following completion of residency or postdoctoral training program.
[b]Rated on a 5-point scale with "1" representing the lowest skill rating. The rating was made by independent researchers.

was bound to be a factor influencing the adequacy of the therapist's performance.

The Therapeutic Alliance and Transference

One of the most clearly identifiable aspects of the treatment process for the negative-outcome group was the relative absence of cooperative and collaborative activity by the patient with the therapist. In this group conspicuous negative transference dispositions and a low level of collaboration were characteristic of nearly every case. In the treatment-success group the treatment of seven patients was characterized by far more stable positive attitudes toward the work. Two of the patients experienced periodic prolonged episodes of anger and negative affect storms in the transference but were able to eventually regain a collaborative stance. Only one patient, a man who characteristically shielded himself from emotion and commitment by enclosing himself in a kind of "narcissistic bubble" was consistently distant and evasive. For the negative-outcome cases the conspicuously uncooperative attitude which characterized treatment seemed based in part on the patient's perception of the treater as a person who should somehow cause the patient to feel better and have a better life without the patient's active work toward that end. The patients for the most part proceeded in therapy as though engaged in a struggle to extract such magical solutions from an ungiving and harsh therapist. The low level of the therapeutic alliance was manifested in two styles of participation (for some patients both styles were intermingled or alternated): In one stance the patient was distant and quite elusive, withholding conspicuous aspects of their daily lives from the treatment, thereby generally conveying a fearful, avoidant, and sometimes outright paranoid attitude. In these instances the treaters were frequently implicitly invited to function in a type of controlling or detective-like role, ferreting out the missing facts. The other style was to engage the therapist or analyst in a demanding, angry struggle, an intense form of psychotic or near psychotic transference which was therapeutically counterproductive.

The Therapist's Contribution

Therapists or analysts were often slow to recognize the negative-outcome patients' actual personal and treatment needs and to shift treatment approach accordingly, from tactics suitable to an expressive psychotherapy to a more highly structured and supportive approach. For several cases, from the clinical descriptions one can infer that the aura of thoroughness, and by implication of correctness, of the extensive initial evaluation process may have produced an inappropriate treatment orientation (since errors tended to be in the direction of overestimating health) which once undertaken was difficult to shift. The prevailing view of psychoanalysis as a long treatment in which signs of impatience are more culpable than waiting too long tended to introduce a similar force toward inertia. If, in addition, one considers the slightly less developed clinical skills of the therapists in the negative-outcome group, the problems of shifting perspectives and approaches with these very difficult patients is now more understandable.

   One other issue related to the "inertial drag" described above is the tendency for the therapists to be inconsistent and often blatantly remiss in attending to the patients' violations of basic aspects of the treatment contract. The therapists unwittingly tolerated behavior which should not have been tolerated if treatment was to have a chance of success. The reader may recall that this overtolerance of these patients' pathological behavior was one of the hallmarks of their family relations. Frequently the treatments were marked by inconsistent attendance, latenesses, delinquent payment of the bill, interminable contacts with the therapists at odd hours outside the treatment sessions, persistent verbal assaults on the treater, inconsistent use of medication, and a variety of other forms of "acting out" within and outside the treatment hours. In far too many instances the therapists patiently tolerated the continuation of such behavior, perhaps expecting in some instances that such behavior would yield to the "right" interpretations. In not one case did the treater insist that continuation of treatment would depend on an alteration in such behaviors. From our current perspective it would have been quite appropriate, and in some instances necessary, for the therapist to support treatment structures by putting the treatment itself on the line. This might consist, for example, on insistence that for treatment to continue the patient must have a realistic plan for paying his bill, that chronically inconsistent attendance or lateness are not acceptable, that severe drug or alcohol abuse would have to stop for treatment to have any chance of facilitating constructive changes in the patient's life, etc. The relative absence of such structure setting in a few instances was related to the therapists withholding commitment to the treatment process out of discouragement, anger, disappointment, or whatever. In one instance a patient was allowed to quit therapy prematurely because the therapist in an exasperated and frustrated state of mind was willing to be rid of him. It is possible as well that at the time these treatments were conducted (approximately 20 years ago), the knowledge about borderline pathology which we take for granted today (including the importance with such patients of firmly standing behind the basic treatment structure) was not as available. Tolerating the continuation of maladaptive behavior may have reinforced these patients in their magical assumption that their therapists should somehow inspire changes for the better without the patient's collaboration in the process, and in this way some therapists may have unwittingly colluded, like the family, to undermine the patient's maturation. Such tolerance, we might speculate, insofar as it allows reality, real responsibility, and the limits of acceptable behavior to become blurred and indistinct, would intensify the maladaptive aspects of regression and the potential for psychotic transference reaction. Once such a regression becomes established as the typical state of the treatment, it is extremely difficult for patient and therapist to find effective ways of resolving the consequent impasse or pathological enmeshment, or to dilute the intensity of the pathological aspects of the transference.

Summary and Synthesis

This chapter examines 11 cases from the Menninger Foundation Psychotherapy Research Project who experienced negative outcome in psychoanalytic psychotherapy or psychoanalysis, a group which we occasionally contrast with 10 of the most successful cases. We conclude that those who decline in functioning during treatment frequently have obtained relatively high educational levels, a factor which together with these patients' rather seductive "as if" personality orientation, led to diagnostic errors. They therefore tended to have a poor beginning in treatments not adequately matched to their level of psychological functioning. As one might expect, this group was on the average more seriously disturbed than the successes. All patients included in the negative outcome fell within a broadly defined borderline range. These patients, particularly after starting therapy, often engaged in a masochistic binge of self-sabotage. The consistency with which they sought maladaptive behavior solutions of their needs and conflicts (e.g., alcohol and drug abuse) reminds us of a dynamic described by Modell (1971). This consists of a deep-seated sense of unconscious guilt (taking the form of self-defeating behavior), and the conviction of such patients that they do not have a right to a better life and that success and maturation means that others will be depleted or destroyed. Thus every potential for something better in their lives (psychological treatment constituting one such unique potential) seems to exacerbate their worst pathology.

In our study of negative-outcome patients one environmental issue stands out, namely, an extraordinary degree of collusion by significant people in the patient's life to undermine healthy behavior. Too often family members engaged in an overindulgence and, occasionally, more direct encouragement of the patient's most pathological behavior, most particularly an encouragement of hostile dependence and irresponsible self-destructive action. When significant people in the patient's life finally could no longer tolerate such behavior, their reaction was to turn away from the patient, sometimes becoming distant onlookers to the patient's deterioration and escalating self-destruction.

One specific treatment variable emerging clearly from our clinical study is a relative absence of a cooperative and collaborative working alliance. The patients were prone to adopt either or both of two maladaptive stances in treatment. In one stance, the patients were elusive, frequently dishonest, and withheld conspicuous aspects of their lives from treatment; and in the other stance they became intensely engaged in an angry, demanding way, in a psychotic or near psychotic form of transference reaction from which they were unable to extricate themselves. Therapists tended to be slow to recognize the mismatch between the type of treatment and the patients' needs, and to shift treatment approaches. In addition, consistent with the pattern of family overindulgence of psychopathology, therapists were slow to attend to the patient's violations of the treatment contract, thereby unconsciously colluding with the patient's tendency to undermine his chances for using the therapy for growth. This issue raises difficult questions for therapists about how, particularly in the treatment with borderline patients, to deal with behaviors which when tolerated militate against treatment having a chance of success. Our opinion from examination of these cases is that failure to attend to lapses in the treatment contract, and to behaviors which should not be tolerated in treatment, contribute to the exacerbation of psychotic transference reactions. These findings challenge us to examine how and when one should make continuation of the treatment contingent on an alteration in certain patient behavior.

The act of beginning psychotherapy holds unique promise for patients by placing the focus on the patient's own needs and growth potential. In a certain type of borderline patient, this may strongly mobilize the unconscious guilt and self-destructiveness referred to above. The risk of overlooking this pattern is enhanced by a tendency of such patients to present themselves in a somewhat seductive "as if" fashion as being in better psychological condition than is actually the case. The therapist who fails to recognize both the severity of the patient's disturbance and this self-destructive pattern is likely to lapse into collusion with the patient, vascillating between passive overindulgence, rejecting prohibitions, and angry, frustrated withdrawal of investment in the treatment. Thereby, the therapist duplicates the borderline's impasse of being chronically stuck in a separation–individuation phase of development.

4

Negative Outcome in Behavior Therapy

Christopher R. Barbrack

Introduction

Owing largely to the editorial definition of negative outcome which temporarily sets aside the crucial element of causality, the material presented here highlights issues, raises questions, draws tentative conclusions, and offers recommendations in a way that departs somewhat from previous discussions. The first section of the chapter briefly reviews prevailing conclusions formulated by behavior therapists about the relationship between behavioral treatment and negative outcome. This is followed by a description of various factors that might function as barriers to the investigation of negative outcome in behavior therapy. The third section presents a selective review of several behavioral research programs/areas that have broken through many of these barriers, in an exemplary fashion. This information serves a dual purpose: (1) to examine negative outcome arising in concert with some of the best behavioral research currently available, and (2) to provide standards against which other behavioral studies which report negative outcome can be interpreted. A discussion of these studies comprises the fourth section. Finally, implications drawn from all of the foregoing material are set forth and discussed.

The View of Contemporary
Behavior Therapy
Toward Negative Outcome

While Bergin was by no means the first to raise the issue, his contention that some recipients of psychological treatment get worse (Bergin,
1963, 1966; Lambert, Bergin, & Collins, 1977) elicited several reactions
from advocates of behavior therapy. A review of treatment outcome
studies by Gurman and Kniskern (1978) concludes that only five
studies support the idea that therapy can cause a worsening in the
recipient's condition. This conclusion has attracted scrutiny and criticism from representatives of the behavioral camp.

Rachman and Wilson (1980) wrote a thorough and unmercifully
penetrating critique of the contention that some clients are actually
harmed by psychological treatment, and conclude by characterizing the
evidentiary basis for this idea as "scanty," and the idea itself as "woe-
fully incomplete" in terms of its explanatory value. Of course, the
Rachman–Wilson analysis pivots on the research conditions necessary
and sufficient for causal attributions. They endorse the issue of negative outcome as worthy of further research and correctly add that such
an endeavor would be influenced by the very same confounding factors that plague treatment outcome research in general. Mays (1979)
reached virtually the same conclusion after a comprehensive and rigorous reanalysis of Bergin's data.

Neither of these critiques deny that some recipients of psychological treatment get worse in conjunction with the implementation of that
treatment. In view of this fact, Mays makes it quite clear that the
"available evidence" (the ramifications of this frequently used phrase
are discussed in the next section) contradicts the notion that negative
outcome can be attributed to behavior therapy, a sentiment shared by
Rachman and Wilson and one which is not all that surprising in view
of the very small number of behaviorally oriented studies included in
Bergin's analysis. Mays and Franks (this volume) correctly conclude
that there is insufficient evidence to support Bergin's claims.

Suspending the causality issue for a moment, however, it seems
somewhat self-serving for behavior therapists to dismiss lightly the
Gurman–Kniskern analysis inasmuch as it is based upon 13 studies of
behavioral, marital, and family therapy, all of which present evidence of
negative outcomes. However flawed, this evidence should be viewed
with alarm and curiosity, conditions which hopefully would result in the
implementation of more carefully designed research studies and in dispassionate, nonproprietary interpretation of the ensuing results.

Beyond instigating the interest of several of the more prominent guardians of the standards of scientific rigor in clinical research and perhaps because of the centrality of the causality argument and the competent manner in which it was rebutted, Bergin's and Gurman & Kniskern's contentions about the connection between psychological treatment and negative outcome seem to have passed into oblivion. Perhaps this is best illustrated in the field of behavior therapy by the astounding lack of attention paid to deterioration effects in Foa and Emmelkamp's[1](1983) otherwise timely, comprehensive, and intellectually honest book devoted solely to the topic of treatment failures in behavior therapy. Hopefully, the present chapter will arouse attention, interest, and proactive empirical (rather than simply analytic and reactive) efforts on the part of the behavioral community toward the issue of negative outcome.

The question of whether and to what extent negative outcome occurs as a result of or in conjunction with behavior therapy is an important scientific, professional, social, and moral issue. One would have to search long and hard to find a professional psychologist of any theoretical persuasion who would not endorse this sentiment. Beyond socially desirable endorsements, however, contemporary behavior therapists have noted, examined, and publicly reported their treatment foibles and failures in a fashion unparalleled in the field of clinical psychology (Foa & Emmelkamp, 1983; Wilson, 1982). Given this state of affairs, it is startling to find answers bearing on the issue so scarce and unsatisfying. The unqualified position set forth in this chapter is that defensible, data-based responses to questions of negative outcome in behavior therapy cannot be formulated at the present time and that this state of affairs warrants immediate attention rather than complacency. In fairness to the intent of this book, reports of negative outcome which do appear from time to time in the behavioral literature are reviewed against the characteristics and findings of selected behavioral research that has successfully scaled many of the barriers that effectively block the production of high-quality outcome research in behavior therapy. This fragile evidence is included reluctantly and requires considerable circumspection. As will be shown, it offers little enlightenment and runs the risk of provoking hazardous speculation and self-serving conclusions about an issue that deserves and urgently demands rigorous scientific attention.

---

[1]I wish to express thanks to Edna Foa for allowing me to read *Treatment Failures in Behavior Therapy* prior to publication.

Journal Editorial Policies as Barriers to Investigation of Negative Outcomes

During the early stages of the development of behavior therapy, its advocates spent most of their energy demonstrating the efficacy (and superiority) of behavioral approaches to the treatment of psychological problems (Barlow, 1980; Hersen, 1981; Kazdin, 1979a). There was neither time nor inclination to explore and publicize those instances in which behavioral treatments either failed to result in expected outcomes, or worse, appeared to be associated with deterioration from pretreatment levels of functioning. In this intellectual climate, it is not implausible that contingencies under the control of editors of behavioral journals functioned to reinforce behaviors associated with overlooking, neglecting, glossing over, or otherwise disposing of data portraying behavioral treatments in a negative light. Proclamations regarding the unmitigated virtues of behavior therapy issued by its ardent and powerful advocates may have served to highlight these otherwise implicit rules governing publication, as well as to guide and instruct researchers regarding important versus trivial issues. In short, until recently, the failure of behavioral treatments has been aversive to many in the behavioral community. This state of affairs is not limited to behavior therapy. As Graziano and Bythell suggest,

> Failure is an event, and bound up with this event are our reactions to it. Our traditional response to failures is to reject them, to consign them . . . to the refuse heap where they are expected to decay and disappear into our tolerant environment like all our wastes and useless by-products. We tend not to "recycle" our failures and process what may be valuable in them; to examine conditions under which they occur so as to make appropriate adjustments in our procedures (1983).

While the behavior of some researchers may have been shaped directly by having manuscripts accepted or rejected based upon whether they supported the effectiveness of behavioral treatments, a more far-reaching effect may have been accomplished as a result of researchers observing or otherwise discerning implicit rules that pervasively govern the reinforcers they sought (e.g., published manuscripts are positively associated with promotion and tenure in academic settings). A study by Lancioni (1980) is subtly illustrative of this effect. In describing the behavioral treatment of the urine control problems of profoundly retarded, deaf-blind children, Lancioni noted the co-occurrence of bowel control in several of the subjects. Lancioni also noted that a punishment strategy "created great tension in the children" and played an ambiguous role in the success of the overall treatment. The so-called tension was not characterized, however, as an outcome. If it had been systematically observed and reported as a negative outcome, perhaps the article would have been rejected for publication.

There may be more than meets the eye in the situation which caused Gurman and Kniskern (1981) to rely on unpublished papers as the basis for studying negative outcome in behavioral marital therapy. Rachman and Wilson (1980) lament this state of affairs, contending that it limits the value of debating the negative outcome issue. Surprisingly, Rachman and Wilson do not even raise the question of why such data are not found in the behavioral literature. Eysenck (in press) attributes the high rejection rates reported by psychological journals to the poor quality of most research manuscripts submitted for publication. Undoubtedly, the quality of research plays some role in determining what is published. However, the contention that quality is the only factor or even the most important factor in this decision-making process is purely speculative. In fact, available evidence bearing on editorial practices raises very different possibilities. Uncertainty about the representativeness of research published in refereed journals is of paramount importance to behavior therapists who boast about being "scientific" and "data-based." To those interested in negative outcome, addressing the issue of editorial bias is at least as important as repetitive refutations of the negative outcome argument solely on the basis of experimental design imperfections found in published studies.

Mahoney (1977) conducted an investigation of the impact of variables on journal editorial review practices and found that behaviorally oriented reviewers in his sample exhibited significant biases against research reporting results contrary to expectations based upon the reviewers' theoretical inclinations. This finding raises profound and fundamental questions about the adequacy of data available to behavior therapists who formulate broad generalizations on topics ranging from therapeutic effectiveness to negative outcome (cf. Greenwald, 1975). It is difficult to imagine, and disturbing to speculate about, why Mahoney's findings have been ignored in influential texts on the evaluation of treatment effectiveness (e.g., Kazdin & Wilson, 1978; Rachman & Wilson, 1980).

Atkinson, Furlong, and Wampold (1982) demonstrate that studies reporting null results are rejected at a significantly higher rate than those reporting expected, statistically significant results. If the past forecasts the future, this study will probably generate as much lack of interest as Mahoney's work.

The practice of exempting editorial practices from empirical investigation raises serious questions about the "objectivity" of popular behavioral treatises on treatment effectiveness and casts suspicion on much of what has been written about behavior therapy outcome. It is not possible to predict the results of a study designed to investigate editorial decision making by varying null results, positive outcomes, negative outcome (i.e., deterioration effects), and combinations thereof. There is no reason to expect that significant editorial biases against negative outcome would not be found. Until this issue is carefully investigated, the possible relationship between behavioral treatment and negative outcome cannot be dismissed by "scientific" arguments that focus on published studies while ignoring factors that determine what is published.

Until more is known about how manuscripts are selected for publication and about the extent to which published materials accurately represent the population of studies in behavior therapy, caution must be exercised in concluding, as Rachman and Wilson (1980) appear to do, that negative outcome does not constitute a significant problem in contemporary behavior therapy.

If nothing else, the issues raised in this section should sensitize the reader to the inherent limitations of this chapter. Empirical evidence on the effects of behavior therapy, as well as compilations of and commentaries upon this evidence, may be substantially biased against negative outcome. This state of affairs limits how this problem can be treated. First, the view of negative outcome as insignificant in behavior therapy could be endorsed and the chapter could end here. Second, speculations about negative outcome could be advanced and clarified. Third, what little evidence there is that bears on negative outcome could be identified and discussed. As indicated earlier, the first option cannot be justified satisfactorily. Consequently, the second and third are pursued. If past practices predict future behavior, what is presented will be criticized for lack of evidence, and larger issues pertaining to factors affecting what is "allowed" to be evidence in behavior therapy will be ignored.

Theoretical Barriers to the Investigation of Negative Outcome

In one sense, negative outcome is relatively easy to explain on theoretical and empirical grounds. For example, studies employing reversal designs have shown time and again that undesirable, maladaptive behavior can be increased. Carried to an extreme, such methods could result in levels of functioning below those existing prior to treatment without posing theoretical problems for the behavior therapist. Work of this kind, however, represents a systematic, deliberate attempt to (temporarily) produce negative outcomes and, therefore, sheds no more than a dim light on negative outcome that occurs in spite of the best efforts of the behavior therapist to help promote change in a positive direction.

Attributions of negative outcome to the effects of adventitious reinforcement represent no more than *post hoc* speculations and fail to rule out alternative hypotheses pertaining to the connection between behavioral treatment and negative outcome. Instead, when faced with unanticipated, undesirable outcomes, behavior theory may have to be stretched beyond formulations based on reversal designs and reinforcement to explain their occurrence. If the premise that unintended negative outcome can occur as a result of behavioral treatment is theoretically inconceivable, it is difficult for the behavior therapist to "see" negative outcome, more difficult for him or her to publicly acknowledge it, and very improbable that he or she will pursue further research on negative outcome. Unintended negative outcome simply does not fit well with simplistic versions of behavior theory.

This issue has been addressed prominently but almost singlehandedly by Eysenck (1979a, 1982). While the bulk of his writing in this area is directed to the inadequacies of psychoanalytic and eclectic therapies, Eysenck's theoretical formulations are relevant to the issue of negative outcome in behavior therapy. Accepting the proposition that negative outcome does occur, although least frequently in conjunction with behavior therapy (Eysenck, 1964), Eysenck applies his Theory of Incubation to account for these unintended outcomes (see Chapter 13). Briefly, he proposes that repeated presentations of unreinforced conditioned stimuli (e.g., anxiety-provoking images) does not necessarily lead to extinction (e.g., elimination of anxiety), but may actually strengthen or enhance the CS-CR bond (e.g., image elicits more anxiety). This outcome would require the CR (e.g., anxiety) to act as a reinforcement for the CS, and is held to apply only to certain types of conditioning and to vary as a function of the time and duration of the CS exposure. To avoid strengthening the targeted CS-CR bond, the CR must be elevated above a critical point and held there for a specific length of time. Under such treatment conditions, extinction is predicted.

Turning the Theory of Incubation on behavior therapy, Eysenck argues that treatments such as flooding may be effective because they elevate CRs above the necessary critical point for relatively long periods of exposure to the unreinforced conditional stimulus. Moreover, and of particular relevance here, Eysenck maintains that some behavioral treatments, such as desensitization, might be predicted to result in a worsening of the client's condition. This would occur because, once aroused within the desensitization procedure, the unreinforced condition stimulus, according to standard clinical practice, is removed, leaving insufficient exposure time for the CR to diminish. A similar outcome would be predicted for clients receiving flooding or implosion treatments that are abruptly terminated (*in vivo* or imaginally) while in progress, once again resulting in insufficient exposure time for the unreinforced conditioned stimulus and a concomitant increase in the CS-CR bond.

The importance of theory for clinical research and practice is lucidly and cogently demonstrated by Yeaton and Sechrest (1981). In discussing the dimension of treatment strength, they speculate that clients exposed to weak therapy might be worse off than during the pretreatment period. Sharing no more than an appreciation for theory, Yeaton and Sechrest begin to formulate predictions that are startlingly similar to those of Eysenck. Interestingly, an appreciation for theory seems to make the prospect of negative outcome easier to accept.

The Theory of Incubation has been widely criticized within the behavioral camp (e.g., Levis, 1979), and it may well be inaccurate, incomplete, or superfluous. Reports in the behavioral literature do not provide clear support for its predictions (Levis & Malloy, 1982). Nevertheless, the Theory of Incubation succeeds in demonstrating how and why clients might manifest negative outcome in the course of receiving behavior therapy. This and similar theories (see Levis & Malloy, 1982), if more widely read and accepted, might help set the conditions for negative outcome in behavior therapy to be "seen," investigated, and reported more frequently.

Frameworks as Barriers to the Investigation of Negative Outcome

Over the last decade, the effectiveness of behavioral approaches has been demonstrated in an unparalleled fashion. Perhaps as a result, behaviors associated with noticing, mulling over, analyzing, and writing about failures associated with behavioral treatments are less aversive to its adherents and hence are more likely to be positively reinforced. The publication of *Failures in Behavior Therapy* by Foa and Emmelkamp (1983) and this chapter, *res ipsa loquitor*, lend support to this contention. The rhetoric of prominent contemporary behavior therapists relative to the broad domain of treatment failures also illustrates this change. For example, Rachman (1983) suggests that treatment failures facilitate the development of "fresh perspectives" on problems that have been more or less refractory to behavioral treatment, and goes on to suggest that behavior therapists can learn a great deal from certain classes of treatment failures. Emmelkamp and Foa (1983) characterize treatment failures as a "challenge" which may set the conditions to make improvement in knowledge and clinical practice of behavior therapy more likely.

Interestingly, in spite of these contemporary attitudes toward treatment failures in general, negative outcome continues to be largely ignored in behavioral research. Barlow (1980, 1981) has been virtually alone in raising this issue and in calling attention to the fact that the few published studies in the behavioral literature reporting negative outcome have not elicited further research any more than they have curtailed the widespread use of the techniques in question.

Perhaps this state of affairs is related to a poor fit between the event of a client becoming worse in conjunction with receiving behavior therapy and the conceptual frameworks employed by many behavior therapists. Emmelkamp and Foa (1983) correctly contend that treatment failures do not constitute a homogeneous group. Their delineation of four general types of treatment failure (refusal to follow through on treatment; dropping out of treatment; not responding to treatment; and relapse) does not take account of the possibility of negative outcome. Since negative outcome does not fit within their framework of treatment failure, that very few instances of such outcomes are documented in the 23 chapters of their book on treatment failures in behavior therapy is not surprising. If one's conceptual scheme of things does not allow for the occurrence of an event, it is unlikely such an event will be noticed and dealt with. This contention finds some support in the work of Kazdin (in press), who developed a conceptual framework that delineates different varieties of treatment failures, including deterioration as a category. Working within this framework, Kazdin refers to one study (Boren & Coleman, 1970) in which target behaviors deteriorated in conjunction with the implementation of a token program. Unless comprehensive frameworks are used to guide the research referred to in the previous section, knowledge about negative outcome will remain limited.

Conceptual Barriers to the
Investigation of Negative Outcome

Historically, advocates of behavior therapy have assiduously avoided using traits and other highly inferential constructions such as systems. This tradition has served to control tautological reasoning and to facilitate the production of knowledge by mandating clarity and parsimony. Moreover, it has had an adverse effect on the development of conceptual schemes able to take account of the complexities of human behavior, leading Wolpe (1981) to characterize contemporary behavior therapy as a collection of empirically supported techniques that are of limited value owing to their conceptual rootlessness. Whether this state of affairs stems from behavior therapists' unfortunate avoidance of (explicit) theories[2] or a myriad of other factors is beyond the scope of this chapter. Of relevance here, however, is that categories and subcategories of psychological disorders clearly exist and their use can bring about more sharply focused study of behavioral treatments. Risks of coalescing superficially similar clients into putatively homogeneous diagnostic groups must be avoided in favor of categorization developed by thorough empirical methods and guided by sound conceptual models. Wolpe's (1979) delineation of four distinct patterns of neurotic depression, each indicating a different approach to treatment, and a similar delineation of patients suffering from obsessive compulsive disorders formulated by Foa (1982), are exemplary. By their very nature, attempts to categorize and subcategorize psychological disorders imply, at the very least, the possibility of response clustering and covariation, thereby underlining the significance of these concepts in outcome research.

The concepts of response class and hierarchy, and response cluster and behavioral covariation, are not new. These concepts have the advantage of aiding the comprehension and investigation of complex and highly organized individual behavior. Yet the use of these concepts in the behavioral literature is *relatively* meager in contrast to the number of published studies that focus on one behavior or on a few unrelated behaviors (Stokes & Baer, 1977). The relative neglect of response cluster/covariation concepts has a number of implications bearing on the topic of negative outcome.

If it is true, as the response covariation concept would predict, that changing one behavior may have the effect of changing other behaviors, then any behavioral intervention that promotes change has the potential advantage of promoting more and different positive change than originally predicted, and runs the risk of producing unintended negative outcome as well. Conceiving of the coincidence of positive and negative therapeutic outcomes as symptom substitution is superfluous, contrary to the dictates of parsimony, and misleading. Since this issue has been the topic of many competently reasoned and

---

[2] I believe the general avoidance of personality theory in behavior therapy is not all that commendable or, for that matter, honest. In talking with many behavior therapists I find that they subscribe to implicit theoretical models of personality development and functioning. Since they have not been rigorously constructed, these implicit models are usually vague, inconsistent, and incomplete. Lazarus (1981) has done some pioneering work in this area, but his ideas about personality have not been explicated and developed.

thoroughly comprehensive behavioral analyses (see Kazdin, 1982), instead of engaging in polemical disputes with psychodynamic theorists, behavior therapists might derive greater benefit from examining the implications *for behavior therapy* of the positive/negative outcome phenomenon. As indicated, a prominent danger in the way behavior therapy research and practice are conducted is that positive/negative outcomes may, to some unknown degree, escape detection. The dual tragedy of this prospect is that benefits of behavior therapy are underestimated and, of particular significance to this chapter, negative outcomes go unrecognized. Lacking an explanatory theory, the behavior therapist cannot understand why negative outcome occurs, whereas lacking appropriate concepts and related methods, the behavior therapist runs the risk of failing to detect negative outcome altogether! Human beings are complex systems and the behaviors they issue are equally complex. Behavioral concepts and related methods do exist and can be used to understand and treat complex human problems.

The concept of *systems* is also centrally important to behavioral research, but it has not yet exerted a major impact on the manner in which outcome studies are designed and conducted. Systems exist at all levels from subatomic to cosmic (Miller, 1979). In addition to the individual, seen as a complex system (Barlow, 1980), behavior therapists are concerned with a variety of social systems ranging from marital and family constellations to communities and beyond (Franks, 1982). Investigating treatment outcomes at different system levels has recently attracted some attention, and conceptual shortcomings in this area are being eliminated rapidly. The question of whether therapeutic changes in one element of a system result in concomitant changes in other elements or subsystems, or in the nature of the system itself, is a legitimate one (Bandura, 1977). Even though the greater import of a so-called systems perspective may be related to the development of effective behavioral treatments and more durable behavioral change, it is also important in relation to the determination of treatment outcomes and, consequently, to the detection of conceptually remote and superficially unrelated negative outcome.

A major consequence of failing to take account of the complex organization of human behavior and of a social systems perspective is the tendency to conduct limited assessments and evaluations. In the extreme case, this would amount to the behavior therapist restricting assessment to a simplistic functional analysis of the presenting problem as a standard practice. Likewise, outcome evaluation would be limited to observed or reported changes in a target behavior. A more likely occurrence would involve the behavior therapist conducting a haphazard assessment, largely because probable correlates of most presenting problems are not known at the individual level or at the level of those systems within which the individual functions.

Aside from the kind of contributions represented in the work of Wahler (1975; Wahler, Berland, & Coe, 1979; Wahler & Fox, 1980), the most promising work in mapping the correlates of psychological problems is found in *DSM-III* (Nathan, 1980). Until more is known about response clusters and behavioral covariation, behavioral assessment and evaluation cannot reliably establish criteria for designing studies that will allow drawing firmer conclusions about the prevalence of negative outcomes. Even though there is some promising evidence regarding positive response covariation (e.g., Russo, Cataldo, & Cushing, 1981), to conclude that most unanticipated "side effects" in behavior therapy are positive is premature and without sufficient empirical support (Bitgood, Crowe, Suarez, & Peters, 1980). Unless behavior therapists appreciate the concepts of response cluster and behavioral covariation, it is unlikely that they will conduct broad-based inquiries based upon problem-specific multivariate problem identification and treatment evaluation procedures. Advocates of this approach to behavioral assessment (and treatment evaluation) are not in short supply (Cone, 1979; Hersen, 1981; Nelson, 1981), but thus far this aspiration has far and away outstripped progress in development and implementation of such procedures.

Further advances in the area of multivariate behavioral assessment might occur if behavior therapists continue to reexamine the utility of traits as organizing concepts for response clusters and behavioral covariation. Such inferred variables would be the sort accessible to therapist and client (Rimm & Masters, 1979) and, as such, do not threaten the integrity of fundamental principles of behavior therapy. Unfortunately, support for this effort has been more startling (e.g., Michel, 1978) than influential and widespread.

The same holds true for social systems, where little is known and myths abound. For example, predictions that positive changes in one member of a social system (e.g., marriage) often result in negative outcomes for other members or for the system itself (Title, 1973) have been largely debunked. In fact, the opposite is often found to occur (Brownell, 1982; Weisz & Bucher, 1980). However, in light of Gurman and Kniskern's review (1981), this issue is far from being resolved. Relationships between individuals and their surrounding subsystems must be delineated and clarified in order to inform behavior therapists where best to intervene and where to anticipate (via assessment and evaluation) positive or negative change.

Methodological Barriers to
Investigating Negative Outcome

Outcome evaluation in behavior therapy has been the subject of several books (e.g., Kazdin & Wilson, 1978; Rachman & Wilson, 1980), most of which address the shortcomings of extant research and set forth standards to be applied in designing and implementing more effective behavioral research and criteria for evaluating the meaning and merits of its results. Some of these texts even touch upon negative outcome or so-called deterioration effects, largely to redress the confusion stirred by Bergin's controversial work in this area. Since this material is readily available to the interested reader, it will not be repeated here. Instead, three methodological issues particularly relevant to the issue of negative outcome are discussed.

The first concerns the dimensions of dependent variables used in behavioral research. Undergraduate psychology students learn that responses can be gauged in terms of frequency, intensity, or duration. The necessity of matching the appropriate dimension to a target behavior has been discussed, but rules for doing so, if they can be called that, are largely notional. Progress has been made in training observers to rate dimensions of behavior in a reliable fashion. However, even here the use of recent technology (e.g., slow-motion videotaping) has raised questions about the value of some cherished behavioral formulations [e.g., behavioral incompatibility (Evans, 1982)]. If new technological methods give behavioral researchers a clearer look at what "really happens" and enable them to examine simultaneously occurring, multiple dimensions of target behaviors, the comprehensive accuracy of treatment outcome data may be increased. Current behavioral research using ordinary methods of observation (e.g., frequency checklists), particularly when applied in field-based settings, must overlook or otherwise lose considerable amounts of data. Whether this loss is of any consequence is an open question. The fact that it is an open question is an important conclusion. To illustrate, a positive outcome, expressed in terms of a decrease in frequency of a target behavior, may be accompanied by an increase in the intensity or duration of that same behavior. If such increases are above pretreatment levels, this finding might be considered a negative outcome (*vide infra*).

If data-gathering procedures used in behavioral research fail to take account of multiple dimensions of target and correlate behaviors, negative outcome again might go unnoticed. The information-processing implications of this statement are humbling for anyone who has conducted field-based behavioral research. This is not to demean the value of global measures and the use of static product data, but more fine-grained behavioral analyses will require the use of technology that is not widely available at the present time. Moreover, future availability of such technology may create other problems (e.g., reactivity) when used in field settings. The upshot continues the theme of this chapter: at the present time, the quality and scope of behavioral data reported in the majority of studies do not permit one to draw firm conclusions about negative outcomes. Use of new technology may enhance the quantity and scope of behavioral data but not without creating new problems bearing on the quality of evidence gathered in behavior therapy research.

A second important measurement issue revolves around the use of scales employing zero as an anchor point, that is, a client can score or be rated no lower than zero. This approach can never reveal negative outcomes whenever clients begin treatment with a zero rating (see, for example, Zitrin, Klein, & Woerner, 1978). Of course, the literature does not permit anything more than speculation on this point, but in certain studies, deterioration in a client's condition may be lumped in with zero treatment effects and then characterized as a "treatment failure" (*vide supra*), thus obscuring what is actually a negative outcome. The implication for behavioral research is to include scales of measurement that can take account of clients deteriorating from pretreatment levels of functioning.

Finally, a third important measurement issue concerns practices and procedures used to determine the nature and course of treatment outcomes after intervention is terminated. While a shortcoming in the entire field of outcome evaluation, this issue is particularly relevant to negative outcome. For example, "extinction bursts" have been frequently documented in the literature. If outcome measures are taken at such times or if treatment is terminated at this time, the incidence and degree of negative outcome might be misleadingly exaggerated. Simply to speculate that such undesirable effects would probably dissolve (Boren & Coleman, 1970; Pendergrass, 1972) is insufficient and unwarranted and may be dead wrong. The durability of treatment effects is also at issue here. Rightly so, the major interest of behavior therapists in this arena is to determine whether and under what conditions the positive effects of behavior therapy are maintained over time. In some cases, such effects "wash out" at some point after the termination of therapy, but the evidentiary basis for a firm conclusion on this issue is sparse and equivocal. When rigorous follow-up is conducted, some studies demonstrate maintenance of treatment effects over time (La Porte, McLellan, Erdlen, & Parente, 1981) while others (Fleishman, 1982; Mavissakalian & Barlow, 1981) provide indications of treatment effect "wash out" and even the emergence of negative outcome.

The exemplary follow-up conducted by Mathews, Gelder, and Johnson (1981) is instructive inasmuch as it illustrates the conceptual difficulties involved in an enterprise which is typically discussed in terms of practical problems. The Mathews group has conducted multiple long-term follow-up evaluations of treated agoraphobics. Their findings portray an irregular outcome pattern over time indicating that *when* treatment outcomes are measured at follow-up can exert substantial influence on conclusions about treatment outcome. Data gathered immediately upon the cessation of behavioral treatment are informative but fall far short of telling the whole story of therapy outcomes. Recipients of behavioral treatment continue to change after therapy, hopefully for the better. It is unlikely that this is true in every instance or in every aspect of clients' behavior. In some cases, clients' behavior may deteriorate below pretreatment levels, but not until some time after termination of treatment.

Consequently, while there is no compelling evidence that successful clients are worse off at follow-up, there are some indications that this may be the case. Investigation of this possibility requires the use of multiple long-term follow-ups in treatment outcome research. This requirement is particularly compelling for those aspiring to make more definitive statements about the relationship between behavioral treatments and negative outcome. Fortunately, Baum and Forehand (1981) and Mathews et al. (1981) provide excellent models to guide this kind of research.

The Lack of Appropriate Control Groups as Barriers to the Investigation of Negative Outcome

Research in contemporary behavior therapy is sophisticated, including use of traditional and innovative designs and statistical procedures to serve the purpose of experimental control. It has become increasingly apparent, however, that comparisons between treatment and no-treatment control groups, to the extent that niggling, persistent rival hypotheses (e.g., effects deriving from therapist attention or client's belief that treatment will be effective) cannot be ruled out in explaining observed changes, are less useful than previously believed. Kazdin and Wilcoxon (1976), Eysenck (in press), and others have argued that demonstrably credible placebo control groups are essential for less ambiguous interpretation of treatment outcome data. This requirement applies equally to the investigation of positive and negative outcomes. Placebo control groups have begun to appear more frequently in the behavioral literature but, at least with respect to studies reporting negative outcome, this condition has not been met often enough to generate useful information. In fact, if the credibility of any treatment varies from beginning to end as a function of the recipient's perceptions of treatment effectiveness (Kazdin, 1979a), maintaining the credibility of placebo treatment conditions may be roughly approximated but never fully achieved (Etringer, Cash, & Rimm, 1982).[3] Ethical issues may also prevail against the widespread use of placebo control groups if one takes seriously reports (Duncan & Laird, 1980; Parloff, 1982) suggesting that placebo control conditions may result in negative outcome. This possibility illustrates the perverse, but not uncommon, predicament of "solutions" creating problems in their own right. In any event, until the question of negative outcome is more thoroughly and competently investigated by means of carefully controlled studies, arguments on either side of the issue cannot progress beyond the rhetoric that constitutes much of what is currently written.

Uncontrolled Behavioral Treatment Variations as Barriers to the Investigation of Negative Outcome

Investigating the effects of any treatment requires an accurate, clear, and concise definition of that treatment. Formulating generalizations about the effectiveness of a particular type of treatment always requires some kind of aggregating process by which data generated from many applications of the particular treatment are consolidated such that general determinations about treatment effectiveness can be made. Whether this is a largely subjective (Eysenck, in press) or putatively objective (Smith, Glass, & Miller, 1980) process, aggregation and the conclusions based upon it make sense only to the extent that the particular treatment under consideration is applied relatively invariantly over its many and separate trials (Marks, 1982; Wilson, 1982). If behavioral treatment in one study bears little resemblance to behavioral treatment in another, then aggregating results across these studies becomes a tricky business more likely to generate controversy than clarification (Barbrack, in press; Rachman & Wilson, 1980; Wilson, in press).

---

[3]Unless, of course, one reconceptualized traditional comparative outcome studies such that one of the major treatments is considered to be a placebo control group. The credibility attributed to treatment by therapists and clients under such conditions might then be maximized.

A fundamental issue is whether the various conceptual foundations and clinical techniques set forth in the name of behavior therapy share enough in common to allow generalizations about such treatment effects as negative outcome. The current definition of behavior therapy endorsed by the Association for Advancement of Behavior Therapy is so very broad that it is unlikely that any meaningful generalizations can be made about behavior therapy as a whole. (See Franks, 1980; Franks & Barbrack, 1983, for a more extended discussion of this point.) The search for negative outcome in behavior therapy should be restricted to the effects of specific conceptualizations and techniques rather than determining whether negative outcome can be traced to some sort of homogeneous independent variable. A narrower definition of behavior therapy is not as essential in this regard, as are narrower generalizations about specific behavioral interventions and observed negative outcomes and painstaking monitoring of what is, in fact, implemented.

The fact that the application of a behavioral technique under rigorously controlled conditions does not result in apparent adverse effects is insufficient reason to conclude that the same technique, applied under a variety of unmonitored field conditions, functions in the same benign fashion. There is disturbing evidence in the literature indicating that field-based behavioral treatments are implemented in ways that deviate significantly from prescribed applications developed under laboratory conditions (Boruch & Gomez, 1977).

The reasons for this state of affairs are potentially numerous. First, as Wolpe (1981) contends, many behavior therapists may not be trained adequately. Second, even well-trained and professionally diligent behavior therapists tend to drift away from rigorous adherence to standard clinical procedures (Hersen, 1981). Third, there is evidence to suggest that behavior therapists do not even utilize standard behavioral techniques (Farkas, 1980; Kendall, Plous, & Kratochwill, 1981; Swan & MacDonald, 1978) and rely instead on a farrago of clinical procedures established on the basis of trial and error (Barlow, 1981).

Thus, it should not be surprising, and it is critically important to realize, that the practice of "behavior therapy" in field settings does not invariably yield the positive results obtained in laboratory settings (Fleishman, 1982).

In general, not enough is known about what actually goes on in field settings where behavior therapy is allegedly practiced. One might expect this state of affairs, especially in behavior therapy, to initiate a serious effort to monitor broad behavioral treatments and specific behavioral techniques *qua* independent variables. Recent evidence suggests, however, this is not the case even in research settings (Yeaton, 1982).

The upshot is clear enough. The best experimental circumstances generate numerous studies that are diverse enough to prohibit broad generalizations about the effectiveness of behavior therapy. Hence, the possibility of negative outcome occurring within the broad domain of behavior therapy cannot be dismissed out of hand on the basis of existing evidence. Perhaps more importantly, not enough is known about the effectiveness of behavioral treatment in field settings. Rationally, one cannot maintain that negative outcome does not occur in conjunction with the application of behavioral techniques in the field.

Disagreement over Significant Change as a Barrier to the Investigation of Negative Outcomes

The question of what constitutes significant change in behavior therapy has been the topic of ongoing discussion in the literature (Barlow, 1980; Garfield, 1981). Much of the earlier action in this interchange focused on the value of statistical analyses in outcome research and the relative merits of single subject and group experiments. Underlying this issue, however, is a more fundamental one which obtains regardless of whether statistical or visual and single subject or group methods are employed. It has to do with the size of the treatment effect. The problem is illustrated in the work of Smith, Glass, and Miller (1980). Among its many problems, this work, which undertakes to estimate the overall effectiveness of psychological treatments in general, uses a formula to generate the effect size (ES) of treatment. In analyzing the results of over 500 outcome studies, the authors conclude: (1) that the overall ES of psychotherapy is .85 and (2) that this is very commendable since it compares very favorably with ES's generated in other enterprises such as education. The speciousness of this conclusion has been described elsewhere (Barbrack, in press; Eysenck, in press; Wilson and Rachman, in press-a; in press-b); however, this approach and the controversy it stirred highlight problems involved with the interpretation of treatment effect size. Relative to the present topic, what treatment effect size is necessary to warrant the conclusion that a negative outcome indeed has occurred? How is a behavioral treatment resulting in multiple treatment outcomes [i.e., across behaviors (response covariation) and across dimensions of one behavior], some of which are positive and others negative, to be generally characterized in terms of effectiveness? The problem is a knotty one for individual studies and is immeasurably compounded when one aggregates negative outcomes (*vide supra*) for the purposes of determining the relative "dangerousness" of particular treatments for particular problems (see London & Klerman, 1982).

Negative Outcomes Viewed
in Relation to Exemplary
Behavioral Research

Reaching conclusions about the current status of effectiveness of behavioral techniques seems to be related to an epistemologic position which determines, among other things, how psychological problems are conceptualized and defined, what constitute acceptable data for indexing treatment outcomes, and what comes to be labeled as a significant (i.e., important) treatment effect. The epistemologic lens through which most contemporary behavior therapists view reality is shaped largely by values related to experimental methodology and empirical data. When viewed through this lens, there is little doubt that a very large number of behavioral techniques and a small but still significant number of behavioral treatment packages are effective in treating a wide variety of psychological problems. To conclude otherwise would require challenges to the fundamental philosophical underpinnings of behavior therapy. While such challenges are legitimate in their own right, the topic and general tone of this chapter militate against attacking or defending positions advocated by other approaches to psychological treatment. Instead, the goal of this section is to delineate characteristics of selected areas in behavior therapy research where many of the barriers described earlier have been overcome. Because so many advances have been documented in the recent history of behavior therapy, the material presented is idiosyncratically selective and illustrative rather than exhaustive. Consequently, much of what is commendable in the behavior therapy literature is not mentioned for reasons that those involved in such work will understand.

At the level of the individual client, anxiety-related disorders, which are prevalent and can be disabling (e.g., phobias and obsessions/compulsions), have elicited the attention of many behavioral researchers.[4] Recent developments in the treatment of anxiety-related disorders stem from several independent sources and, on the whole, represent a robust area in behavior therapy (Barlow & Wolf, 1981).

Rachman (1983), whose dedication and scholarly contributions in this area cannot be overestimated, recently characterized Foa's work (Foa & Emmelkamp, 1983) as exemplary. Developing treatment procedures along theoretical lines proposed by Lang (1969), Foa has not

---

[4]Even a casual familiarity with the literature in this area prompts the realization that these disorders are very complex and not the simple clinical problems for which behavioral treatment is grudgingly and almost singularly given due, but largely uninformed, credit by its opponents.

been satisfied with the relatively well-established exposure and response prevention techniques that have become virtually standard treatment for compulsive disorders. Her appreciation for and sensitivity to those instances in which such treatments have failed led her to develop a conceptual model which portrays many important mechanisms involved in compulsions and their treatment. These mechanisms include intra- and intersession habituation, and the model illuminates the role of depression in compulsive disorders. Rather than discounting the value of imaginal techniques in favor of *in vivo* techniques currently in vogue, Foa has explored the value of each in terms of the types of clients that can profit from one or the other. As indicated earlier, it is unfortunate that Foa's scheme of things does not seem to allow for negative outcome. Hence, while Foa's research (1983) suggests that a significant number of patients do not benefit from behavioral treatment, it fails to shed light on whether and to what extent negative outcome occurs in conjunction with the behavioral treatment of anxiety-related disorders.

Before leaving this area, the seminal contributions of Barlow (1980) warrant notice. In discussing the work of Marks (1971), Barlow employs an "estimate of expected failure to improve without treatment" developed by Agras, Chapin, and Oliveau (1972) to interpret Marks' findings. Against the benchmark of 57 percent as an expected level of failure-to-improve, Barlow demonstrates how Marks' reported failure-to-improve rate of 42 percent is interpreted differently than would be the case were this finding interpreted in isolation. Work of this kind represents a step in the direction of developing indices of spontaneous deterioration as standards against which outcome data can be interpreted. It is unfortunate and surprising that Barlow and Mavissakalian (1982) do not underline this or the entire issue of negative outcome as a primary focus for future research in the treatment of phobic disorders. Hopefully, more basic work, which takes account of spontaneous deterioration, will be carried out in the near future.

At a level encompassing concerns for individuals as well as for group and organizational dynamics, a monumental contribution to the behavior therapy literature and an exemplary approach to clinical outcome research is represented by the work of Paul and Lentz (1977) in which a token economy, formulated within the framework of social learning theory, was compared to milieu therapy in the treatment of hospitalized, chronically impaired mental patients. It is not possible to review adequately the many facets of this research program. This is perhaps for the best since reading the book in its entirety will richly repay those who take the time to do so.

The rigorousness of this research program makes its results particularly important since many confounding factors that are frequently found in such studies, making it virtually impossible to rule out rival hypotheses in explaining the observed results, are not present. Such results deserve added weight in any consideration of treatment effectiveness.

The results of this study indicate the following: (1) both treatments were effective; (2) the effectiveness of the token economy treatment was reflected in many more measures than was the effectiveness of the milieu therapy; (3) when deterioration occured in a patient's condition, it was documented (!); and (4) deterioration (i.e., a negative outcome) was associated more frequently and to a greater degree with the milieu therapy treatment. Hence, it might be contended that the token program significantly reduced potential negative outcome. Unfortunately, predictions could not be made regarding expected deterioration under no-treatment conditions. Consequently, one must either assume that untreated patients would manifest less deterioration than patients in either of the treatment groups or accept that the token program reduced potential deterioration effects. The same argument might be made for the milieu treatment but such a conclusion would be very difficult to defend. Conversely, since deterioration was observed in some token program recipients, the possibility that it was caused by the treatment cannot be ruled out definitively. Even if this were the case, the incidence of deterioration effects associated with the token program is minimal in a relative sense. The upshot, however, is that data from this exemplary study do not support the argument that behavioral treatment and negative outcome are causally associated.

The interested reader may wish to review work in the area of obesity conducted by Wilson (Dubbert & Wilson, 1983) and Brownell (Brownell & Stunkard, 1978, 1980; Brownell, Heckerman, Westlake, Hayes, & Monti, 1978), as well as the work of Maletsky (1980) in the behavioral treatment of exhibitionism, for additional illustrations of exemplary behavior therapy research and development. The general conclusion to be drawn is that, while some psychological problems remain refractory to behavioral treatment (see Rachman, in press), resulting in the so-called problem of treatment failure, there is very little to suggest that negative outcome occurs at all in behavior therapy.

To establish this conclusion more definitively, further research is essential. Standards to guide the conduct of such research are enumerated here and elsewhere (Rachman & Wilson, 1980). Exemplary research in behavior therapy has the following characteristics:

1. A long-term commitment by a relatively small group of investigators to planning, developing, implementing, monitoring, and evaluating *research programs*—a commitment to be maintained despite

substantial social and political obstacles and in the absence of a high rate of professional rewards.

2. Oddly enough, these same researchers are capable of adopting a critical, dispassionate attitude to a greater extent than they develop polemical advocacy positions and proprietary interest in the treatments in question. This is particularly noteworthy in view of the pressing human problems that confront them and the frequently misguided attacks to which they are exposed by advocates of opposing points of view.

3. These researchers exhibit what often amounts to an aversion for complacency regarding treatment effectiveness. This is expressed in varying ways, ranging from systematic fine tuning of largely effective treatments to wholesale abandonment of ideas and techniques that prove to be ineffective.

4. Treatments developed by these researchers are frequently based upon some theory or conceptual model, and empirical data are woven back into this foundation or give rise to new conceptual models. This is to say there is a reciprocal relationship between theory, research, and clinical practice.

5. Persistent attention is paid to maintaining the integrity of theoretically derived treatments, the technical adequacy of experimental design, and outcome evaluation procedures.

6. Clear, comprehensive descriptions of carefully delineated treatments are developed, and unanticipated deviations from the intended treatment are painstakingly documented.

7. Diligent attention is paid to the training of the implementors of behavioral treatments and monitoring is employed to check for subtle and not so subtle departures from the intended treatment.

8. Assessment and outcome evaluation receive rigorous attention and usually employ multivariate measures which do some justice to the complexity of the individual client while also taking account of some of the various systems levels which might be affected by or affect treatment outcomes. In many instances, outcome evaluations are formative and summative and include periodic short- and long-term follow-up. In most cases, clearly defined, so-

cially relevant criteria are used to index treatment
effectiveness.

9. There is usually some attempt to develop and use
    spontaneous remission rates as benchmarks for in-
    terpreting treatment outcomes (but in truth, it
    would be more honest to place this item under the
    heading of future aspiration rather than current
    accomplishment).

To be sure, behavioral researchers, entitled to some or most of
these accolades, are fewer than might be otherwise estimated on the
basis of the expanding literature in behavior therapy. Nonetheless, it
seems virtually certain that, if these professionals and their successors
turn their attention to the problem of negative outcome, much of the
uncertainty currently surrounding this topic would be replaced by a
solid body of more definitive information. In the meantime, however,
the standards already established by the work of these individuals can
be applied in evaluating the existing evidentiary basis bearing on negative outcome in behavior therapy.

Neglected Negative Outcome in
Behavior Therapy:
Results of 11 Studies

None of the studies described in this section has been taken into account in the critical commentaries of behavior therapists (Franks &
Mays, 1980; Mays, 1979; Mays & Franks, 1980; Rachman & Wilson,
1980) who have discredited Bergin's contention about the connection
between psychotherapy and negative outcomes. However, it is unlikely that adding them would modify the conclusions reached in these
reviews.

Most studies reporting negative outcome involve aversive stimulation, ignoring, or time-out with children manifesting a variety of severe
mental and emotional disturbances. There is also some evidence from
studies with adolescent and adult subjects exhibiting significantly less
severe impairments. Behavioral techniques in these studies include
punishment and positive reinforcement (monetary rewards, social contact, and tokens).

The language used in many of these studies is interesting insofar
as it characterizes unanticipated treatment results as "side effects,"
conveying a sense of secondary importance to negative outcomes. Rincover, Cook, Peoples, and Packard (1979) correctly point out that there

are only "effects" in behavioral intervention studies, the task of out-come evaluation being to use multiple measures to assess changes (positive, negative, intended, unintended) associated with the adminis-tration of behavioral treatments.

In an early study, Risley (1969) reported the results of the use of punishment with a six-year-old brain damaged, autistic youngster. Re-sponse covariation occurred in terms of the elimination of one target behavior being followed by the emergence of another target behavior. In the course of his discussion, Risley cogently discounts this sequence as an example of symptom substitution in the traditional sense and raises several important points pertaining to the possibility of condi-tioned suppression of a target behavior leading to the suppression of other (desirable) behaviors, the risk of learned associations between the caregiver's administration of punishment and the aversive stimulation experienced by the child, thereby rendering the caregiver's presence and attention more aversive and less (positively) reinforcing. Risley concludes by highlighting the positive nature of the primary "side effects," almost as if, in some relative way, this general conclusion eliminated or diminished the importance of the observed unintended negative outcomes.

Several years later, Epstein (1974) described the effects of overcor-rection on two schizophrenic youngsters. Similar to Risley, Epstein reported the occurrence of positive and negative "side effects" and speculated that the occurrence of one or both types of effects might be a function of the availability of appropriate behavioral alternatives in the individual's repertoire and the effects of reinforcement contingen-cies that are operating but not under the experimenter's control. Again, the importance of the negative outcome seemed to be diminished be-cause it occurred in concert with positive outcomes.

A frequently cited study reported by Kogel, Firestone, Kramme, and Dunlap (1974) showed that appropriate behavior increased when self-stimulating behavior was suppressed. One of the four youngsters in this study, however, exhibited an increase in self-stimulation that occurred coincidentally with punishment. A decrease in a desirable response was also observed.

Becker, Turner, and Sajwaj (1978) used a lemon juice treatment to eliminate the excessive vomiting of a three-year-old mentally retarded child. In this study both positive and negative "side effects" were observed. The latter disappeared upon follow-up, but the authors frankly admit being unable to explain this outcome. Rincover et al. (1979) used a treatment that involved removing sensory reinforcements to eliminate the inappropriate behavior of five severely retarded, autis-tic youngsters. The treatment was effective in four cases. In one instance, however, self-stimulation increased and appropriate behavior decreased. Sajwaj, Twardosz, and Burke (1972) used an ignoring technique to reduce a youngster's excessive conversation with his teacher. Positive and negative "side effects" were observed. The negative side effects in this case were decrease in appropriate behavior during group academic activities and increase in disruptiveness. Herbert et al. (1973) reported two studies conducted independently in different settings. The results indicate increases in deviant behavior and the appearance of new forms of deviant behavior in four out of six youngsters exposed to a behavioral treatment consisting of differential parent attention. The reversal design used in this study lends considerable support to a possible causal linkage between the treatment and the negative outcome. These findings are particularly significant since these are the types of behaviors that often result in the involvement of child behavior therapists and school psychologists, many of whom may advise the use of behavioral intervention involving ignoring of maladaptive behavior as a principal component.

The technique of time-out from reinforcement was studied by Pendergrass (1972) with two youngsters described as having very low IQ scores. Four target behaviors were observed and recorded. In one child, three of the four behaviors improved from pre- to posttest. For this youngster, one desirable behavior decreased whereas for the other youngsters, all four desirable behaviors showed a decline. In a disturbing fashion, Pendergrass seems to gloss over these negative outcomes, presuming that a longer period of extinction would result in a reversal of these undesirable outcomes!

Additional studies using similar behavioral techniques with similar subjects have reported similar outcome patterns (Tarplay & Schroeder, 1979; Wells, Forehand, Hickey, & Green, 1979).

The results of using behavioral techniques with adults, in this case so-called delinquent veterans, are reported by Boren and Coleman (1970). In this study a token program was used to promote socially appropriate behavior. Awarding tokens was effective in prompting the subjects to participate in an early morning running exercise and the addition of a modeling component was shown to add virtually nothing to the token system and was ineffective when used alone to promote participation. When a response cost component was added to increase attendance at a daily morning meeting, attendance dropped from a baseline rate of 30 percent absenteeism to 100 percent absenteeism after two days of intervention. The participants were also observed to manifest other negative behaviors including negative social coercion, rule infractions, fighting, and going AWOL. After one week, the response cost component was discontinued and the negative outcomes were reduced substantially (apparently back to baseline rates). Here again, this time in an adult sample, a punishment contingency is followed by unanticipated negative outcomes.

Eleven studies do not constitute an adequate basis for drawing conclusions about the relationships between certain behavioral techniques and negative outcomes exhibited by a small number of atypical youngsters and adults. The fragility of this evidence becomes even more apparent when the characteristics of these studies are compared to the exemplars described in the previous section. To their credit, these investigators were sensitive to the issue of response covariation and employed multiple measures to take account of it. At this point, it can only be concluded that future investigations of the relationship between behavior therapy and negative outcome should not overlook literature pertaining to the use of punishment and negative reinforcers with clinical populations manifesting relatively severe psychological problems.

Additional Evidence of Negative Outcome in Behavior Therapy: Results of Two Studies Using Positive Reinforcers

The long-term effects of a token program with youngsters ranging in age from 6 to 12 years was reported by Wasserman and Vogrin (1979). The focus of this investigation was on the effects of the intervention on undesirable nontarget behaviors that occurred concurrently with target behaviors. Data were gathered over a 150-day period and revealed an increase in desirable behavior and a concomitant increase in nontarget undesirable behaviors. The authors explain this finding in terms of response hierarchies and argue that an eliminated high-frequency behavior might be replaced and reinforced by a previously less frequent undesirable behavior.

A behavioral program conducted with behavior-problem adolescents by O'Donnell and his colleagues (Fo & O'Donnell, 1975; O'Donnell, Lydgate, & Fo, 1979) reports a variety of negative outcomes. The so-called buddy system involved making a monetary reward and contact with a buddy contingent on school attendance. While school attendance increased significantly in the group receiving treatment, a decrease in several other undesirable behaviors (fighting, failure to complete homework, returning home late, and not doing chores at home) was also noted (i.e., positive response covariation). Another important finding was the significantly lower arrest rate

(37.5%) in the treatment group compared to the control group (64%) during the year the project was conducted. In the first reported results, the only negative outcome involved the arrest rate of treatment group members who were never previously arrested (15.7%) being significantly higher than that of similar adolescents in the control group (7.2%). Another negative outcome was detected in a follow-up study with these groups which showed the arrest rate of those participating in the program for more than one year to be significantly higher than the arrest rate for control group members or for those participating in the program for only one year. The buddy system research has a number of excellent qualities including a relatively large sample size, use of a control group, multiple outcome measures, long-term follow-up, and dealing with a socially relevant problem exhibited in a population generally refractory to psychological intervention of any kind. Nevertheless, the design is flawed enough to preclude clear conclusions about the connection between the behavioral treatment and the observed negative outcomes.

Behavior-problem adolescents have been the object of considerable psychological intervention research. There are non-behavioral studies that have applied logical solutions to pressing social problems (e.g., potential for drug abuse) manifested by this age group which have resulted in unanticipated negative outcome, particularly among subjects with relatively good pretreatment histories (Blum, Garfield, Johnstone, & Magistad, 1978). These types of outcomes are counterintuitive and should at least alert well-meaning planners of psychosocial interventions to potential negative outcome. Again, while there are insufficient data in the behavior therapy literature to draw conclusions about such negative outcome, future research and reviews of research should be directed to work with adolescents who manifest or are considered at risk for developing severe behavior problems. This is an area of behavior therapy in which existing evidence of positive outcome does not far outweigh the admittedly meager and inconclusive bearing on potential negative outcome.

Implications of Negative Outcome Evidence in the Behavior Therapy Literature

The paucity of reported negative outcome and the ambiguous relationship of these outcomes to behavioral techniques give added credence to the contention that unanticipated adverse effects rarely occur in conjunction with behavioral treatment. Even when such effects are observed, it is virtually impossible to establish a causal linkage.

This, however, is no reason for complacency. As indicated in the second section of this chapter, there is considerable reason to doubt the contention that published reports are sufficiently representative of all behavioral research and some reason to question the comprehensive accuracy of what actually is published in the behavioral literature. Moreover, even if one were to accept the veracity and representativeness of such published reports, the issue of whether and to what extent negative outcome occurs in conjunction with the administration of behavioral treatments in actual clinical settings is unknown. Wilson's (1982) belief that behavior therapy research has had a decisive influence on clinical practice may be more of an aspiration than a documented reality. In another context, Wilson seems to agree when he states "subjective preference, personal habit, and community norms are likely to dictate the type of treatment a person will receive" (1982, p. 308). In regard to the practice of behavior therapy in clinical settings, Barlow (1980) and Hersen (1981) express similar sentiments, and evidence presented by Swann and MacDonald (1978) and Ford and Kendall (1979) raise serious questions about the extent to which laboratory tested behavioral techniques and behavioral methodologies are implemented as they were designed and intended by field-based behavior therapists.

Future Directions Regarding
the Question of Negative Outcomes

It is clear that the critical commentaries of Rachman and Wilson (1980), Mays and Franks (1980), and Franks and Mays (1980) are correct as far as they go, at least to the extent that the material presented thus far provides few compelling reasons to question their conclusions. All of them recognize that the imperfections that plague outcome research in behavior therapy apply equally to positive and negative outcome. Dedicated to the improvement of behavior therapy research, all of them agree on the importance of better investigations of negative outcome. Perhaps the difference lies in the importance and sense of urgency that are attached to this facet of outcome research in behavior therapy which, in turn, may be a manifestation of a difference in opinion about where the burden of proof is properly placed. Rather than rebutting claims that negative outcome occurs in behavior therapy, some of the abundant intellectual resources in the behavioral camp could be put to work on the experimental investigation of negative outcome. It is our responsibility to demonstrate that such outcome does not occur as a result of the application of behavioral techniques, instead of simply answering devastating claims to the contrary advanced by others. Rachman and Wilson (1980) delineate criteria for the improvement of outcome research in behavior therapy and, hopefully, the perspective developed in this chapter will serve to complement these excellent standards, and not simply be dismissed as "stale news."

Further, the previous section ends in a way which casts the question of negative outcome in behavior therapy in a very different light. This may be stated as follows: To what extent do therapeutic actions of *practicing* behavior therapists result in negative outcome? Since behavior therapists probably do not constitute a homogeneous group, the problem can be stated in another way: To what extent do behavioral techniques *employed in the field* result in negative outcome? Dealing with the issue of negative outcome on the basis of published evidence is difficult and inconclusive, creating an unacceptable state of affairs for behavior therapists who assume the burden of proof regarding negative outcome. Dealing with this issue on the basis of the unknown and somewhat suspect practices of field-based behavior therapists or from the vantage point of routine applications of behavioral techniques in the field would be a vastly more difficult task. [See Kazdin (1982b) for some promising guidelines in this area.]

If the evidence bearing on the original formulation of the problem of negative outcome is no reason for complacency in the behavioral camp, the lack of evidence bearing on the problem, as reformulated in the preceding paragraph, should arouse considerable concern which, hopefully, will translate into vigorous field-based investigation. Even if behavioral treatments are shown to be very effective and relatively inexpensive, even if they are shown to present the barest risk of negative outcome, there is absolutely no reason to assume that such treatments will be adopted and adhered to in the field. If nothing else, the aftermath of the Paul and Lentz (1977) work teaches that to expect otherwise is irrational. Once knowledge and skills are acquired, adherence becomes a primary problem for those concerned about the effects of behavior therapy *as delivered in the field on a routine basis*. Adherence problems are very complex, particularly when realistic social, political, legal, economic, and organizational factors are taken into account (Fishman, 1982). But adherence problems can be conceptualized and addressed from a behavioral perspective that extends beyond the important and necessary work of the traditional behavioral laboratory. Appreciation for this broader perspective may lead to the development of behavioral theories, models, concepts, and techniques that take account of such constraints in much the same way that experimental variables are dealt with in the laboratory. Perhaps teachers and supervisors of behavior therapists will begin to appreciate the importance of adherence to proscribed behavioral regimens as a problem falling in the domain of their knowledge and skill and, instead of a reason for despair, as an opportunity to meet their obligations to provide effective and appropriate treatments where it matters perhaps most of all, that is, in the burgeoning segment of our society seeking behavioral treatment and entitled to its full benefits. Widespread disillusionment with the scientist-practitioner model of training and practice in clinical psychology and undocumented criticisms of clinical training provided in schools of professional psychology may lead some to draw contrary conclusions. But if paraprofessionals can be taught to adhere to behavioral treatment regimens, there is sufficient reason to hold similar aspirations for students and practitioners of behavior therapy. Since adherence to techniques is a necessary condition for outcome evaluations in field settings, an increased portion of the available resources must be devoted first, to monitoring the field-based adherence behavior of behavior therapists, second, to the investigation and eventual modification of variables that affect adoption of and adherence to behavioral treatment regimens, and third, to the determination of the nature and extent of negative outcome. The specific problem of negative outcome will require further investigation under more tightly controlled conditions. The problem of negative outcome can be separated into two broad areas of concern, the clinical laboratory and the field settings. Whether negative outcome occurs in either context remains to be seen.

5

A Marital and Family Therapy Perspective on Deterioration in Psychotherapy

David P. Kniskern and Alan S. Gurman

Since marital and family therapy by definition involve the treatment of more than one individual, issues related to negative change in these therapy approaches are necessarily more complex than those involving the treatment of one individual. In addition to the worsening of individuals treated in marital-family therapy, worsening may occur in treated relationships, for example, the marriage, or even in untreated individuals and relationships. Moreover, worsening may occur at the level of the family-as-a-system. In this chapter, we will address the research evidence for the existence of this phenomenon in each of these categories, and will describe what is known about patient/family factors contributing to such outcomes, and what therapist and treatment factors seem to put couples and families at greater risk for deterioration. In addition, we will outline some conceptual issues relevant to the definition of deterioration in marital and family therapy and offer guidelines for the assessment and reporting of deterioration in such therapies. Finally, we will discuss some of the implications of these findings and conceptions for both marital-family therapists and individual therapists.

The histories of outcome research in psychotherapy in general and on specific therapeutic approaches seem to follow a roughly parallel pattern: initially, the focus of research is the demonstration of overall effectiveness of a method, followed by comparisons with untreated control groups of patients. Only when these steps have been accomplished, when treatment has been demonstrated to be of likely value, are the more specific questions of the mechanisms of change investigated, for instance, effectively practiced by whom? with whom? in what settings? according to what range, levels, and vantage points of assessment? It is still later, when some decreasingly crude empirical "handle" on such matters has been gotten, that researchers begin to ask whether, and under what conditions, treatment can worsen patients, and then in what ways.

Given that the various marital and family therapies are relatively new forms of psychotherapy (Gurman & Kniskern, 1981), it is understandable that the phenomenon of negative effects has only recently been discussed and that few outcome studies have systematically examined its occurrence (Gurman, 1973; Kniskern, 1975), despite the existence of several earlier clinical papers on the subject (Fisher & Mendell, 1959; Fox, 1968; Guttman, 1973; Hurvitz, 1967; Kohl, 1962). The first, and indeed, only comprehensive review of research related to negative change in marital-family therapy was not published until rather recently (Gurman & Kniskern, 1978). Even more surprising is that, despite the fact that over 30 reviews of research in the field have now appeared (Gurman & Kniskern, 1981b), the very phenomenon of deterioration in marital-family therapy is virtually never mentioned by the authors of these other critical reviews. Since very little research on the matter at hand has been published since the Gurman and Kniskern (1978) paper, and since nothing published in the period has significantly altered the trends we described at that time, we will first summarize briefly the empirical findings reported there. While continued study and discussion of the possible harmful effects of all types of psychotherapeutic intervention is called for, it is our view that the need for such investigation and scrutiny is currently nowhere more essential than in the field of family therapy, since this field has so persistently challenged the most basic epistemological premises of all approaches to individual psychotherapy (cf. Gurman & Kniskern, 1981a).

Factors Influencing Deterioration in Marital-Family Therapy

It is unfortunate that little empirical evidence exists about this clinically critical issue. We suspect, however, that many of the same variables associated with deterioration in various individual and group therapies described elsewhere in this volume are also salient in marital and family therapy (cf. Lambert et al., 1977; Strupp & Hadley, 1977).

Therapist variables appear to play a central role, indeed, as an aggregate, probably *the* central role, in the worsening which occurs in marital-family therapy. A particular therapist style appears to increase the probability of negative effects. This style is best described as one in which the therapist does relatively little to structure and guide early treatment sessions; uses frontal confrontations of highly affective material very early in therapy, rather than reflection of feeling; labels unconscious motivation early in therapy rather than stimulating interaction, gathering data, or giving support; or does not actively intervene to modulate interpersonal feedback in families in which one or more members have very low ego strength (Gurman & Kniskern, 1978). Such a therapist "style" is certainly reminiscent of the styles of therapist relating described in the research literatures of both group (Hartely, Roback, & Abramowitz, 1976; Liberman, Yalom, & Miles, 1973) and individual (Lambert et al., 1977; Strupp et al., 1977) therapy.

Even less is currently known about what patient and treatment variables influence the occurrence of negative effects in marital and family therapy. The available evidence does not demonstrate a relationship to severity or chronicity of the disorder alone. There is evidence pointing to the importance of the father's active involvement in treatment (Shapiro & Budman, 1973; Slipp, Ellis, & Kressel, 1974) with multigenerational cases, and, in the case of marital therapy, to the importance of the "other" spouse's involvement (Gurman & Kniskern, 1981b). In a related way, Wattie (1973) reported less improvement in couples when wives were more educated, implying that the probability of good treatment outcome is decreased the more threatened the husband feels. For perhaps the same reason, Wattie found that couples did better in short-term, time-limited therapy than in therapy which was open-ended. This possibility is supported by Ehrenkranz' (1967) finding that husbands in open-ended therapy, in contrast to their wives, were less active in sessions and were more oriented to the present than to the past.

Negative Effects of
Marital and Family Therapy

In 1978, we presented a summary and analysis of over 200 reports and studies related to marital-family therapy outcome (Gurman & Kniskern, 1978). These studies demonstrated an overall rate of improvement for marital-family therapy of 68 percent, with 30 percent no change and 2 percent of the couples worsening during treatment. As was noted in that article, many of the studies that were reviewed either did not include an outcome category of "worse," or combined the categories of "no change" and "worse," so that the rates of deterioration noted were biased against finding (or presenting) evidence of the phenomenon.

In those 36 studies that did allow for the possibility of the occurrence of negative effects, almost half (42%) presented reasonable or undeniable evidence of deterioration (see Table 5.1).

Patient change was rated on a large number of different criteria (e.g., self-concept, alcohol intake, delinquency recidivism, marital satisfaction), and from different rating sources (e.g., identified patient, objective measures, trained judges). Because of the heterogeneity of patient and family types, treatments, treatment settings, criteria, rating sources, and so on, it is not possible to derive from these data a really meaningful mean or modal figure. There is sufficient evidence, however, to conclude that deterioration does occur in marital and family therapy, and that the frequencies of both positive and negative effects of marital-family therapy exceed that of no treatment. It is worthy of note, however, that the data summarized in Table 5-1 suggests that 5 to 10 percent of patients as individuals, or of marital or family relationships, worsen as the result of marital and family therapy. This figure is surprisingly consistent with the frequencies of worsening reported for other modalities of psychotherapy (cf. Lambert et al., 1977; Strupp et al., 1977).

Negative Effects of Individual Psychotherapy on Couples and Families

Family therapy is an approach which inherently leads to concerns about clinical outcomes for persons beyond the identified patient and beyond those who are present in the consultation room at the time of both the initial assessment and later interviews. These considerations actively apply to all therapy, not simply family therapy, with a chief difference being that *the therapist treating only an individual can more easily remain unsure of the impact of individual intervention upon others who are significantly involved with the identified patient.*

A number of family therapists, using a systemic point of view, have argued that treatment can begin at any level, *including* that of the

Table 5-1. Summary of Reported Deterioration Rates in Studies of Nonbehavioral Marital and Family Therapy

Therapy Type/Setting	No. Studies Reporting Improvement Rates	No. Studies with "Worse" Category	No. Studies Reporting Deterioration	Percent Studies with "Worse" Category Reporting Deterioration	Deterioration Rate Across Studies with "Worse" Category (%)
Marital Therapy					
Conjoint	8	3 (37%)	1	22	2.7 (2/72)
Individual	7	5 (71%)	4	80	11.6 (27/233)
Group	15	7 (47%)	4	57	16.6 (17/102)
Concurrent/collaborative	6	4 (67%)	1	25	3.3 (11/332)
Total	36	19 (5.3%)	10	53	7.7 (57/739)
Family Therapy					
Inpatient	10	2 (20%)	0	0	0 (0/17)
Outpatient	26	13 (50%)	4	29	2.1 (10/477)
Day hospital	3	2 (67%)	1	50	7.3 (7/96)
Total	39	17 (44%)	5	29	2.8 (17/580)
Grand Total	75	36 (48%)	15	42	5.4 (74/1337)

From Gurman, A.S. and Kniskern, D.P. (1978). Reprinted with permission.

individual, and yet remain conceptually that of a "family therapy" orientation. At a theoretical level, it seems unreasonable to expect that individual change would reverberate automatically into the rest of the family system, some influential theories notwithstanding (Gurman & Kniskern, 1981a). Families are never fully integrated, and the resonance of change beginning in an individual may or may not be transmitted to and experienced by other members of the family. Change in an individual as a result of individual therapy, then, might produce negative effects in other family members or relationships. Unfortunately, at this point in the development of the field of psychotherapy in general, it is not possible to predict the conditions under which this might occur.

It is unfortunate (and therefore, we believe, misleading with regard to the range of effects of individual psychotherapy) that it is not possible to discuss the effects of individual therapy on other family members and relationships from an empirical perspective. The reason is straightforward: it is rare, indeed, almost unheard of, for psychotherapy researchers to collect data on the effects that treatment produces on the "significant family others" of the individually treated person. Indeed, a random check of any serious published studies of the outcomes of individual psychotherapy is guaranteed to yield a modal figure of zero that include such data.

Again referring to Table 5-1, however, one can see how much more commonly deterioration is found from individual therapy approaches to marital problems (11.0%) than in treatments which include both spouses (5.6%). Therapists and researchers reporting these studies considered this individual therapy approach a variant of marital therapy, that is, "individual therapy for marital problems," but in simple operational terms, it is more accurate to describe these treatments as "individual therapy." It is very important to note that, in almost all of these studies, there was no bias against "individual marital therapy" by virtue of a disproportionate representation of patients whose spouses had refused conjoint therapy. In almost all of these studies, patients entered individual therapy either on the basis of random assignment to this treatment or on the basis of therapists' recommendations for "individual therapy of marital problems."

One must remember that these cases of deterioration include, in different studies, not only the worsening of the patient but, at times, also a *worsening of the relationship when the treated patient "improved."* Most individual therapists suggest, or imply by their behavior, that as an individual patient changes for the better, this leads to increased happiness and better functioning in other family members, or, at least, to no change in other family members. This traditional, linear causal view suggests that if an individual is symptomatic, for example, depressed or anxious, such symptomatology reflects that person's "individual" problems. The clinical literature, however, is filled with examples and anecdotes of how such "individual" symptomatic behavior is used (not wittingly, of course) by other family members to stabilize and enhance their feelings and functioning, or when such symptomatic behavior in one family member helps another avoid the emergence of other symptomatic behavior.

A dramatic example of how an "individual" intervention can have dramatic effects on other family members was reported by Marshall and Neill (1977). They studied the effects of successful ileal bypass surgery on the spouses and the marital relationships of patients. This surgical procedure, used only in the most extreme cases of obesity, when successful, produces a rapid and extreme weight loss in the patient. Marshall and Neill reported that the rapid loss of weight tended to destabilize the sexual relationships of many of the couples, and produced a high incidence of both heterosexual and homosexual acting out and divorce. The rapid weight loss seemed to open up latent sexual conflicts or to create a new and unfamiliar sexual context with which neither spouse was able to cope effectively.

Less dramatic but more frequently occurring problems stemming from the treatment of one spouse (most commonly the wife) have been described by Hurvitz (1967). Hurvitz described eight types of problems frequently encountered in such an approach:

1. The transference complicates the basic relationship between the spouses.
2. The transference may create or complicate the specifically sexual problems between the spouses.
3. The relationship problems that the spouses have may become regarded as less amenable to solution.
4. The wife may regard the failure of her therapy as her husband's fault.
5. Therapy offers a setting in which she can disparage her husband and thereby reinforce her negative attitudes toward him.
6. The husband may begin to feel superfluous to his wife's therapy and unneeded in helping her to overcome her problems.
7. The wife's gain in therapy may make the husband feel inadequate.
8. The husband may resist the wife's efforts to impose a new interaction pattern upon their relationship.

Any of these problems may create conditions for the appearance of symptoms in the husband, or for an "iatrogenic divorce."

In a related vein, Gardner (1982), a psychoanalyst, has perceptively pointed out that the all-important "therapeutic alliance" in psychoanalytic psychotherapy suggests "an alliance *against* someone else," indeed, perhaps against everyone else! Gardner notes that the analysand/patient's experience is often, "of the four billion people in the world, I have chosen *you* to divulge all my innermost thoughts and feelings." The "mutual admiration society" which develops between patient and therapist in psychoanalytic psychotherapy, Gardner argues, is often destined to lead to major difficulties between the analysand/patient and his or her spouse.

We know of no study in which the effects of individual therapy on other individual family members has been investigated, despite the fact that many theories of psychopathology and treatment would predict the occurrence of negative effects (e.g., Framo, 1981; Skynner, 1981). It is common, in fact, for family therapists to assert that one family member cannot reliably or durably change without the family system changing. It is certainly the case that this situation does exist at times, for example, when an individual member's symptomatic behavior is highly functional in a relationship or system. There is meager empirical evidence, however, to suggest that such an outcome occurs with as high a probability as some influential family therapists have suggested. Indeed, those family therapists who would make this claim need to explain the generally positive effects of individual therapy (cf. Garfield & Bergin, 1978) on a wide variety of clinical problems. Since individual therapy does frequently benefit individuals, that is, produces desired changes, either these individuals' relationship systems did change, but such changes have not been documented because they have never been examined, or these systems did not change and did not need to change because they were not functionally involved in the individual patient's problems.

It is difficult for us to defend an offer of family therapy alone as the treatment for a problem for which there is available research evidence that shows that some particular individual therapy is reliably effective, or where psychotropic medication has shown to be beneficial. In these situations, it will be necessary for family therapy to demonstrate at least equal effectiveness on the patient's major symptoms, functioning, relapse rate, and so on, *or* to demonstrate additional changes beyond those accruing to the given individual treatment. These might include fewer problems in other family members, improvement in nonproblem areas of functioning of the patient, more rapid or durable improvement, greater cost effectiveness, and the like.

Another widely held belief among family therapists is that individual treatment, particularly medical treatment, reifies the illness and thus makes improvement more difficult (cf. Grunebaum & Chasin, 1978). While this may at some time be demonstrated to be the case, such an undocumented extremist position seems at this time to be motivated more by inter- and intraprofessional politics or the misguided notion that family systems theory would predict such a situation. Systems theory and family therapy can easily accommodate the fact that, at times, seeing an individual is the best treatment for the individual *and* his family, that, at times, such a treatment will require change in the system, and that, at times, it will not.

Assessment of Deterioration from a Marital-Family Perspective

For the family therapist, the assessment of change, whether positive or negative, has been more complicated than for the individual therapist because of the obvious need to assess change in more than one person. In addition to having more individuals to evaluate, the family therapist needs to assess the quality of dyadic relationships and multiperson systems. Finally, along with this increased number of loci for change is the increased number of potential perspectives from which change may be evaluated.

The need for *assessing this matrix of outcomes* (different loci x different perspectives) *should be recognized by individual therapists and therapy researchers as well as by family therapists and researchers.* We believe that such a matrix of change will be ecologically more representative of "true change" and will ultimately be of increased value to clinicians, theoreticians, and public policy makers.

Elsewhere (Gurman & Kniskern, 1978, 1981b), we have addressed the vexing problem of the ever-increasing number of individuals and relationships that can be potentially and meaningfully assessed, from a systemic perspective, as one shifts focus from an individual to larger systems for evaluation of both positive and negative therapeutic impact. Even in a small, two-generational, four-member unit, the number of dyads and triads to assess is clearly impractical for most researchers. We have proposed a model that we hope will provide clinically and conceptually relevant guidelines for the researcher to select subunits for assessment (see Table 5-2).

We have proposed that family units I, II, and III—the Identified Patient, the Marriage, and the Total System, which in some cases is equivalent to the Marriage—are the essential units for assessment in

Table 5-2. A Priority Sequence for Assessing Therapeutic Change in Couples and Families with Varying Constellations and in Varying Therapy Contexts

Familial Unit of Assessment	Family Therapy I: Child as Identified Patient		Family Therapy II: Parent(s) as Identified Patient	Marital Therapy: Spouse/Parents as Identified Patient	
	Family with More Than One Child	One-Child Family		Marriage with Child(ren)	Childless Marriage
I. Identified Patient (IP)	IP Child	IP Child	IP Parent	IP Spouse	IP Spouse
II. Marriage	Marriage	Marriage	Marriage	Marriage	Marriage
III. Total System	Family	Family	Family	Family	Family
IV. Same-Generation of IP: Individual	IP's Sibs		Non-IP Spouse	Non-IP Spouse	Non-IP Spouse
V. Cross-Generation of IP: Individual	Each Parent	Each Parent	Each Child	Each Child	
VI. Same Generation of IP: Relationship	IP Child and Non-IP Child(ren)		(Marriage)	(Marriage)	(Marriage)
VII. Cross-Generation of IP: Relationship	Parents & IP Child	Parents & IP Child	Child(ren) and IP Parent	Parents and Child(ren), i.e., Family	
	Parents and Non-IP Child(ren)	(Parents and IP Child)	Parents and IP Children and Non-IP Parent (as above)		

Note: Parentheses indicate that this familial unit has already been accounted for at an earlier level of assessment priority. Blank space indicates that this subunit of the family does not exist. From Gurman, A.S., & Kniskern, D.P. Family therapy outcome research: knowns and unknowns. In A.S. Gurman and D.P. Kniskern (Eds.), *Handbook of Family Therapy*. New York, Brunner/Mazel, 1981. Reprinted with permission.

any study of family therapy outcome. We have argued that these units represent the major clinically relevant levels of family system structure and organization.

At this time we are suggesting that these units also need to be assessed routinely even when the conceptual framework guiding treatment is other than family systems oriented. In fact, we see no reason to suggest a priority sequence for the assessment of deterioration. We believe, however, that such a sequence should ideally be altered empirically rather than by intuition and theory, as we have developed it. It is likely that particular types of deterioration will occur more frequently within families of particular types, diagnoses, or problems. As we increase our knowledge, we will be able to tailor our assessment to look for deterioration where it is most likely to occur, if it occurs at all. For example, research that demonstrated that the successful individual treatment of an adolescent in trouble with the courts was more likely to cause deterioration in his siblings than in the parent's marriage would suggest strongly that unit IV (IP sibs) in Table 5-2 should be raised in priority above unit II (the marriage) for future outcome evaluation with that population.

It is interesting to speculate that particular forms of treatment might be more likely to produce deterioration in different family members or relationships. This pattern, and the frequency of each type of deterioration, would be one way in which forms of treatment could be compared in effectiveness. The value-laden nature of comparisons such as that between the relative importance of marital dysfunction or depression in an individual may make researchers and clinicians hesitant. Deterioration in any individual or relationship is undesirable, but certain forms of deterioration may be more "desirable" than others. For example, we believe that worsening on a dyadic level is usually "better" than worsening on an individual level since the locus of distress remains, by definition, at an interactional level, rather than on a personal distress level. Distress in the marital dyad may be "worse" than distress in a child dyad, because functioning of the former dyad is more central to survival of the family system than any other dyad.

In addition, it is important to consider that deterioration in an individual or in a relationship may be an example of "process deterioration," that is, a worsening that is a mediating condition in a long-term process of improvement and re-equilibration. For example, a depressed man enters treatment, begins to feel increased self-esteem, and puts greater demands for intimacy on his spouse. This could lead to an increase in arguments, although eventually the marital bond might be strengthened. A marriage of this type might or might not be seen as deteriorating depending on the stage of the process at which assessment was made. In our view, it is likely that for some problems, "process deterioration" is unavoidable and, indeed, necessary, if therapy is to succeed in the long run.

Clinical Implications of Family Deterioration Evidence

The empirical findings related to deterioration in families as a consequence of individual or family therapy may lead to the conclusion that, as most family therapists have suggested for years, all therapy should begin with an assessment of the "identified patient" within his or her interpersonal context. In most cases, this would involve at least those individuals who live with the identified patient. After such an assessment, the therapist, in collaboration with the family, would choose the unit with which he/she will work. This unit, which Skynner (1981) calls the "minimum sufficient network" and which Stanton (1981) calls the "system of import," might be anything from an individual to a multigenerational extended family.

Even if therapy is conducted with only an individual, alliances may have been established with others that will reduce the likelihood of "sabotage" of treatment, or minimize the probability of untoward worsening of other individuals or relationships. For the researcher, beginning therapy with a large system can allow the evaluation of the pretreatment status of family members and thus allow the evaluation of change, both positive and negative, in these members. Given the data on worsening from the individual treatment of marital problems, the involvement of spouses and children may, in fact, be the only ethically responsible stance to take!

6

Negative Outcome in Group Psychotherapy

Robert R. Dies and Patricia A. Teleska

The group treatment setting offers a unique opportunity for therapy which differs from other forms of treatment, such as individual and family approaches (Dies, 1979). One implication of this perspective is that the group also provides a unique set of variables which may precipitate therapeutic casualties. Our goal in this chapter is to identify the principal areas in which clinicians have failed to be sufficiently sensitive to the unique properties of groups and may have inadvertently increased the potential of deleterious group outcomes.

Following Strupp et al. (1977), we interviewed 30 highly experienced group therapists who work in a variety of private practice, outpatient, and inpatient settings in the Washington, D.C., area. The purpose of the survey was to gather clinicians' general impressions of the major factors contributing to negative outcome in group treatments. We asked these clinicians to use a broad definition of contratherapeutic effects which was not limited to such extreme stereotypes as suicide and psychotic decompensation. We used the term *negative outcome* to mean that a group member actually became worse as a result of treatment as shown by an exacerbation of presenting symptoms, appearance of new symptoms, patient misuse of therapy (e.g., to rationalize maladaptive behavior), or disillusionment with treatment.

On the basis of this definition, the clinicians reported rates varying between 0 percent and 40 percent with an average incidence of just over 10 percent. These figures are quite consistent with other findings cited in the group literature (Bednar & Kaul, 1978; Hartley et al., 1976). We were less interested in the frequency of detrimental effects, however, than in the particular factors perceived as contributing to them. Since our survey was informal, we will not attempt to summarize the findings quantitatively. Instead, we will integrate the information into a broader discussion of the variables most often highlighted in the literature on negative outcome in group psychotherapy.

We agree with previous reviewers that negative outcome may indeed result from group treatments (Bednar & Kaul, 1978; Bednar & Lawlis, 1979; Hartley et al., 1976; Smith, 1975), and propose that it is feasible to identify the predominant reasons for its occurrence. We acknowledge that the empirical foundations for many of our recommendations have not been firmly established, but we believe that clinical reports and preliminary research findings are sufficiently conclusive to warrant our generalizations. It is not possible here to present a comprehensive set of guidelines for clinical practice. Rather, we have selected three major topics to illustrate some of the unique properties of groups and their possible relationship to negative outcomes: group curative factors; developmental stages and member roles; and leadership. Within each of these areas we offer specific suggestions for reducing negative effects that have been reported in the literature or by the clinicians we interviewed. Our focus is clearly upon groups established for psychotherapeutic change, but we also consider the literature on encounter groups and T-group methods when the findings have particular relevance to the clinical context. We have excluded information on specialized group formats, for instance, assertiveness training, theme-centered groups, and emphasize treatment groups which appear to be more broadly representative of actual clinical practice. We use the terms *patient* and *client* selectively to suit the type of group being discussed.

Curative Factors

Central Factors

There is a growing body of literature on the "curative factors" identified by Yalom (1975) in his popular text on group psychotherapy. Most readers will recognize the 12 curative factors: interpersonal input (feedback), catharsis, group cohesiveness, self-understanding, interpersonal

output (socializing skills), existential awareness, universality, instillation of hope, altruism, family reenactment, guidance, and identification. Several authors have investigated the value of Yalom's curative
factors in a variety of inpatient and outpatient settings (Butler & Fuhri-
man, 1980; Marcovitz & Smith, in press; Maxmen, 1973; Rohrbaugh &
Bartels, 1975). Despite discrepancies found in the relative importance
of the curative factors across group type, setting, and developmental
phase, research findings consistently demonstrate that five factors are
regarded as central to therapeutic change: interpersonal input, catharsis, group cohesiveness, self-understanding, and interpersonal output.
These factors emphasize the interpersonal processes inherent in group
treatments which are less evident in other models of therapy.

Conceptually, the association between these particular factors and
therapeutic change can be seen in Yalom's description of the components of the corrective emotional experience in group therapy. These
elements correspond, respectively, to the five curative factors of catharsis, group cohesiveness, interpersonal input, self-understanding, and
interpersonal output:

1. A strong expression of emotion which is interper-
    sonally directed and which represents a risk taking
    on the part of the patient.
2. A group supportive enough to permit this risk tak-
    ing.
3. Reality testing, which allows the patient to examine
    the incident with the aid of consensual validation
    from the other members.
4. A recognition of the inappropriateness of certain in-
    terpersonal feelings and behavior or of the inappro-
    priateness of certain avoided interpersonal behaviors.
5. The ultimate facilitation of the individual's ability to
    interact with others more deeply and honestly
    (Yalom, 1975, pp. 27–28).

At first glance, catharsis and self-understanding appear to be the
least unique of the curative factors since many forms of therapy attempt to stimulate strong emotional expression and to generate insight
of one form or another. Yalom has found, however, that it is the
special qualities of the group setting that makes these factors particularly powerful. He observes that catharsis is part of an interpersonal
process and that pure ventilation without the benefit of response from
significant others is rarely therapeutic. Similarly, regarding the factor of
self-understanding, Yalom's results indicate that the most relevant ex-

perience for most group members lies in their discovering the "positive areas of themselves—the ability to care for one another, to relate closely to others, to experience compassion" (p. 92). Kaul and Bednar (1978) call this unique group learning experience "reciprocal functioning," and suggest that it has at least three important psychological effects: (1) members' self-esteem may be enhanced by virtue of their contributing to the therapeutic process while taking from it; (2) the members' relationship with the therapist is modified as a consequence of the reciprocal sharing of roles; and (3) members are more likely to ascribe therapeutic gains to their own efforts.

There is little doubt that Yalom's other three curative factors of cohesiveness, interpersonal input, and interpersonal output are also unique in their importance in the group context. The close relationship established between the therapist and client in individual therapy is qualitatively dissimilar to the intimate relationship established within a group of peers. Furthermore, although individual therapy furnishes feedback to the patient, its impact is readily differentiated from the interpersonal input derived through consensual validation within a group. Finally, clients learn socializing skills in the individual therapy setting, but again the group provides unique opportunities for interpersonal output by more directly paralleling the reality outside of the treatment context.

Unfortunately, the process of systematically linking Yalom's curative factors to therapeutic outcome is barely underway, so the empirical literature stands virtually mute on the connection between these unique variables and negative effects. Careful extrapolation from related literature and reports of clinical observers, such as the mental health professionals we interviewed, may furnish important leads. Based on his own research, Yalom (1975) notes regarding catharsis that clients whose critical experiences in group treatment consisted "only of strong emotional expressions were not destined for a positive outcome; in fact, there was a slightly better chance that they would have a negative growth experience" (p. 84). The critical aspect of catharsis is the response of the other group members as well as of the therapist. If the client's strong emotional expression is met by silence, rebuff, or even counterattack, the client will rarely experience a positive effect. The clinicians in our survey cited numerous examples of ill-timed or inappropriate emotional expressions that left the guilty offender feeling abandoned, humiliated, or rejected by the group. The group leader can work to prevent these contratherapeutic effects by more adequately preparing clients before the group begins, by carefully monitoring intense emotional displays occurring early in the group sessions, and by having a more sophisticated understanding of the role of catharsis.

Unfortunately, many therapists push for strong emotional expression almost as an end in itself and fail to recognize that it is simply a means to an end. The goal is not just to produce intense emotional expression, but to make such expression part of a corrective emotional experience. Consequently, a group must have developed sufficiently so that its unique curative forces can be utilized constructively for individual member growth.

Obviously, in a cohesive group the anti-therapeutic effects would be less likely to occur. Abundant empirical evidence and ample clinical lore point to the importance of cohesiveness in the group therapeutic process. Yalom (1975) finds that one member's acceptance and understanding of another group member may carry greater power and meaning than acceptance by the therapist. Conversely, the failure to receive support and understanding from a group of peers can be devastating. In their review of the outcome literature over ten years ago, Bednar and Lawlis (1971) generalized that feelings of personal involvement, a group climate of support and unity, and the experience of acceptance by co-members play a crucial role in furnishing clients with the essential conditions to have a corrective emotional experience. A common theme running throughout the reports of negative outcomes by the clinicians we surveyed was the patient who for one reason or another was unable to develop a working alliance with co-members, who felt socially isolated and less well integrated into the group, or who did not allow a positive relationship to develop during treatment.

In their study of encounter groups, Lieberman, Yalom, and Miles (1973) discovered a high correlation between low cohesiveness and eventual dropping out from the group. The dropouts did not have a sense of belongingness and most often dropped out because they felt rejected or attacked by the group. Yalom (1975) summarizes a range of systematic studies showing that patients who prematurely terminate from group treatment demonstrate many problems related to the lack of cohesiveness. Among the major reasons for dropping out were group deviance, problems of intimacy, fear of emotional contagion, and complications arising from subgrouping, issues clearly related to Yalom's interpersonal input and output factors.

Yalom's (1975) third major factor, interpersonal input, refers primarily to the quality of feedback received by the group members. Most reviewers of the negative effects literature (Bednar & Kaul, 1978; Hartley et al., 1976) disparage feedback which focuses on negative personal attributes or is delivered in an overly confronting or hostile fashion. Such feedback is experienced by group members as attacking, rejecting, and destructive. The harmful effect of negative feedback is especially potent in the absence of a cohesive group climate. In this context the patient who is the target of the onslaught has nowhere to escape to. Despite the potential of harmful effects, however, the proper use of negative feedback may serve an important function in group therapy. The timing is crucial. Evidence suggests that highly critical feedback is less injurious after a solid foundation of trust has been established within the group. Several of the clinicians we interviewed recommended that the initial group culture should be built upon positive member experiences. One clinician said, for example, that the early patient self-disclosures should center around favorable content so that patients are afforded the opportunity for support from co-members. In agreement with this statement, Jacobs (1974) generalized that feedback sequenced from positive to negative was usually more constructive. Many group therapists underestimate the uniquely powerful effects of feedback in the group setting and may at times fail to moderate the feedback process effectively to optimize the curative forces in the group.

Yalom's fourth major curative factor, interpersonal output, is described as learning how to relate more effectively, that is, improvement in communication and problem-solving abilities, and in the capacity to trust and be more intimate with others. Clearly, patients who cannot benefit from the opportunities to improve their interpersonal skills through participation with co-members, or even worse those who recognize that they are deficient in relationship skills, are likely to become therapeutic casualties. Thus, not all patients come to experience themselves positively in the group setting. For some patients maladaptive interpersonal styles which have led them to seek therapy in the first place may unfortunately prove to be self-defeating in that context as well. One of our clinicians gave a poignant example of a client who felt insignificant, lonely, and a potential misfit prior to therapy, and whose group experience served only to reinforce that impression despite the good intentions of the therapist.

It is not entirely clear how Yalom's fifth main curative factor, self-understanding, can lead to negative effects. Self-understanding may not, of course, result from group participation, especially if the client terminates prematurely or plays a relatively inactive and uninvolved role during the group process. In these instances a client may feel disappointed or become disillusioned with treatment. This disappointment is more likely to occur if the client is not provided with a cognitive framework for understanding and does not attempt to work between sessions on issues raised in the group meetings (Lieberman et al., 1973).

Patient Selection and Preparation

There is widespread agreement in the literature that problems of premature termination and potential casualties in groups can be substantially reduced by careful patient selection and pre-group preparation. Hartley et al. (1976) cited the following member variables associated with negative group outcome: (1) unrealistically high expectations for solving problems, finding friendships, or having a mystical peak experience; (2) relatively low self-esteem; (3) misanthropic attitudes; (4) perception of self as low in interpersonal adequacy, high in interpersonal sensitivity, and having little opportunity to communicate with peers; and (5) a felt need for growth and change (p. 250). A majority of the clinicians we interviewed asserted that inadequate screening was a principal reason for negative group outcomes. They mentioned most of the variables highlighted in the published reports, but also stressed the importance of diagnostic considerations. Borderline, narcissistic, schizoid, and highly disturbed patients who were placed in group therapy too soon were most often cited by the clinicians as the potential group casualties. Problems relating to group therapeutic work with these patients have been discussed elsewhere (Kibel, 1980; Liff, 1979; Wong, 1980). It is not surprising that these particular patients experience difficulties with group treatment given the intense interpersonal issues confronting them from the outset. Despite the fact that the group setting poses a unique and complex set of interpersonal dynamics, clinicians have typically relied too heavily upon traditional, individually-oriented intake interviews to select their patients for group psychotherapy. Although current treatment emphasizes viewing psychopathology in interpersonal terms, behavioral and interpersonal measures are rarely used as bases for selecting patients for group treatment. This infrequency is particularly surprising given that the goal of changing interpersonal relationships is seen by many therapists and members as a major curative factor in group therapy (Woods & Melnick, 1979). To mollify the potential risks associated with patient selection, careful patient preparation for group therapy has been one of the popular recommendations (Hartley et al., 1976; Smith, 1975). In his contributions to the literature, Bednar has been especially sensitive to this issue; he concludes that clarifying patient role expectations, demonstrating desired patient behavior in group psychotherapy, and furnishing a framework that assists patients to anticipate and comprehend group process should be regarded as prerequisites for treatment (Bednar & Lawlis, 1971).

The clinicians we interviewed indicated that their own experiences over the years have led them to pay increasing attention to selection and preparation issues. Many of them devoted considerable time to working with patients before placing them in a group. For several clinicians this work meant a year of intensive individual therapy: others claimed that concurrent individual and group therapy was absolutely essential. A few clinicians, however, noted that concurrent therapy could be problematic for certain patients who might have difficulty sharing the therapist, or who, having lost the intensive one-to-one relationship, might feel abandoned by their therapist. Finally, other clinicians recommended careful follow-up with patients who drop out or who terminate. This suggestion has also been made by others (Bednar & Lawlis, 1971; Hartley et al., 1976).

Before closing this section on curative factors, it should be noted that Yalom's other factors certainly play an important role in group psychotherapy outcome and may represent relatively unique contributions not found in other therapy modalities. For example, universality and altruism do not have their parallels in individual therapy. Furthermore, the curative factors do not operate independently. Therapeutic change, for better or worse, may be a function of the particular constellation of curative processes and the range of beneficial events available to the client. Finally, some factors may be particularly important early in treatment (e.g., instillation of hope), others throughout the treatment process (e.g., cohesiveness), and still others mainly toward the end of therapy (e.g., existential awareness). In this light, the next section of this chapter will consider the implications of developmental phases in groups.

Group Stages and Member Roles

Group Stages

Every group is highly individualized by virtue of its unique composition and the divergent internal and external pressures influencing the group process. Nonetheless, a majority of clinicians would agree that groups generally face many similar issues in the course of their evolution such that recognizable patterns emerge in their development. The concepts employed to identify these phases may vary as a function of one's theoretical biases, yet the sequence of developmental milestones appears surprisingly stable (Beck, 1974). It is not necessary here to offer a comparative analysis of theories of group development. What is essential is the recognition that these developmental stages are unique to group treatments and that the group leader, and possibly the members, should be prepared for their appearance. Failure to acknowledge the significance of the natural development of treatment groups may heighten the likelihood of negative effects either by the leader's ill-timed interventions or by the group members' premature departures or other inappropriate behaviors.

In one recent model of group development, MacKenzie and Livesley (1981) propose that there are consistent rules guiding the sequential development of groups and that groups will not progress constructively until they have resolved earlier developmental hurdles. MacKenzie and Livesley offer a five-stage theory of group ontogeny.

The fundamental issue during the initial stage is *engagement*, the beginning sense of commitment to the group through personal sharing. Although the self-disclosures are comparatively superficial during this preliminary phase, they serve to demonstrate a sense of universality among members and pave the way toward a greater sense of cohesion. Too much interpersonal conflict, confrontation, or challenge at this point, or pressure toward highly intimate revelations, might prove to be too threatening to individual members and could, in fact, endanger the integrity of the group. Bednar, Melnick, and Kaul (1974) offer a developmental framework for initiating group psychotherapy which attempts to nullify these potential problems. They suggest that "lack of structure in early sessions not only fails to facilitate early group development but actually feeds client distortions, interpersonal fears, and subjective distress, which interfere with group development and contribute to premature client dropouts" (p. 31). The authors propose that levels of risk and responsibility most conducive to group development can be regulated by appropriate introduction of structure (Bednar & Kaul, 1978). Their recommendations are quite compatible with findings that too much ambiguity early in the group may be "an invitation to harmful interpersonal feedback which precipitates casualties" (Hartley et al., 1976, p. 251), and that lack of clarity about group norms may increase the chances of negative effects (Lieberman et al., 1973).

If the group has achieved some success by involving all the members in appropriate levels of personal sharing, and a sense of cooperation has been established, the group will be ready to move on to stage two, *differentiation*. At this point, the principal task is to deal with individual differences that exist among group members. MacKenzie and Livesley indicate that this stage often produces problems for the therapist and members alike because of the misunderstanding of the task facing the group, which is to explore personal differences in order to foster healthy differentiation, not simply to ventilate hostility and interpersonal frustration.

The inability of the therapist to moderate potentially volatile affects during this stage, or the failure of members to modulate their own emotionality, could result in group fragmentation or the loss of the more vulnerable group members. Another unique aspect of groups is that not only can members be harmed by the experience, but they in turn can harm one another. Entire groups may be seriously jeopardized, if not blatantly damaged, by the failure to follow sound principles of group composition. A review of the empirical and theoretical literature suggests that group composition has a significant effect on group process and outcome. Melnick and Woods (1976) argue for a support-plus-confrontation model, that is, "moderate diversity in group composition, recognizing that if either support or confrontation dominates the group culture, learning will not be facilitated. Too much ease or comfort in the group engenders complacency, while low cohesiveness coupled with high conflict engenders physical or psychological termination" (p. 507). A number of the clinicians we interviewed mentioned problems relating to group composition: they spoke of patients who were too aggressive or hostile, too anxious, too prone to act out their conflicts, and too demographically idiosyncratic.

Most stage theorists agree that the conflict-laden phase of group development is a natural characteristic of an evolving social system as members struggle with the potential loss of individuality in the face of pressures toward conformity with group norms (Beck, 1974; Bennis & Shepard, 1956; Tuckman, 1965). With a reasonably satisfactory resolution of this dilemma, however, the group can proceed with further exploration of individual members on a more personal and intimate level of sharing. For MacKenzie and Livesley this third stage is called *individuation* and leads to further appreciation of the complexity of individual members. Most likely to have acute difficulty with this stage are individuals who are particularly fearful of highly personal sharing, who cannot cope with potentially challenging or inconsistent feedback, or who cannot participate on an equal basis with co-members. Borderline and narcissistic patients, for example, may be unusually sensitive to pressure for more intimate self-disclosures. The clinicians we surveyed also mentioned paranoid, severely hypochondriacal, and socially isolated persons as likely to have difficulties with this stage. Even less disturbed patients, however, may balk at the threatening implications of demands for greater openness.

The continued mutual exploration of individual dynamics in the evolving social system almost inevitably results in an increased sense of *intimacy*, the fourth stage of MacKenzie and Livesley's model. The potential value of this stage rests in members exploring nonsexual aspects of intimate relationships and the meaning of genuine interpersonal commitment. Mackenzie and Livesley caution, however, that increased intimacy may also lead to irresponsible closeness, and occasionally to overt sexual relationships among group members. Such sexual acting out is apt to produce a stifling of open communication within the group meetings, or if the outside relationships come to an unsettled conclusion, they may result in actual fragmentation of the group.

The normal feelings of intimacy achieved in stage four must be worked through constructively to avoid disastrous consequences for group members and for the group. When intimacy is handled effectively, it leads to a greater sense of mutual respect and understanding, which MacKenzie and Livesley label as stage five, or *mutuality*. A high degree of trust is essential during this stage, because many of the personal issues shared earlier by group members will now be recycled to be explored more deeply and with a greater sense of commitment.

MacKenzie and Livesley declare that a person may terminate from the group at any point. For this reason they do not regard termination as one of their developmental stages. Upon leaving the group the individual member must cope with the painful sense of separation and loss. According to the authors, one danger is that patients may feel unable to cope without the group, and become resigned to the despair of their ultimate aloneness and responsibility for self. One clinician we interviewed observed that even at this late stage, negative group effects may occur if the client is not adequately prepared for termination.

Member Roles

Without question, individual members will contribute to the group's development in varied and highly complex ways and will experience the group positively or negatively depending upon their success in confronting the developmental tasks characterizing each stage. Beck (1974) has indicated that certain member roles serve either to facilitate or to hinder the group's progress toward the developmental challenges. She suggests that role differentiation among members is a natural evolution within groups that serves to provide the impetus to movement through the sequential steps of group development. Beck delineates four leadership roles assumed by group members; these functions are in addition to the role of designated or appointed leader. The emotional and task leaders represent roles which generally pose few difficulties for the group and its therapists. These roles may be played by different people at different times in a group's life. The emotional leader concentrates primarily upon interpersonal support, concern, and emotional involvement, whereas the task leader focuses on problem resolution and therapeutic work. The other two role functions, the scapegoat and defiant leaders, normally present greater conflicts for the rest of the group. MacKenzie (1981) explains that the scapegoat, by virtue of being out of synchrony with others, serves to confront the group with issues of acceptance or rejection. These people are frequently under attack by other group members, but this apparently helps the group to clarify and sharpen issues concerning its goals, adherence to norms, and competition. The defiant leader also generates negative reactions in relationship to certain issues, especially those centered on individual autonomy and compliance with group pressures, and this confrontation too may lead to valuable group discussions. Both Beck (1974) and MacKenzie (1981) thus state that even these seemingly undesirable roles serve a useful function which is keyed to the particular developmental task confronting the maturing social system.

If responded to properly, both the scapegoat and defiant leaders can play a constructive part in the overall progress of the group. Their unique and positive contribution, however, is seldom fully comprehended by many practicing group psychotherapists. MacKenzie, in a personal communication to the present authors, gave two illustrations of how membership roles may be poorly handled in the group context: (1) the group therapist who fails to moderate self-disclosure during the engagement phase of a group may allow a defiant member to blurt out too much too soon, and (2) the therapist may err by not supporting the scapegoat during stage two differentiation when that person is faced with the group's wrath. In both instances, a casualty may result. In one of the few studies related to this issue, Sampson (1972) reported preliminary evidence that leaders who are oriented more toward those group members whose behavior deviates from the group norms, for instance, scapegoats and defiant members, may be less effective than those therapists who focus upon members who fulfill the group's norms and values. Lieberman et al. (1973) offer a number of helpful recommendations for leaders to follow in working with group deviants.

Unfortunately, research on the interface between member roles and group phases, and the linkage of these phenomena to group outcome, is only now beginning to emerge. Research (Hartley et al., 1976) and clinical observation, including comments from the clinicians we interviewed, support the idea that individuals who assume scapegoat or defiant group roles are more likely to experience negative effects, but these findings are rarely coordinated with group stages.

With an increased understanding of the unique developmental properties of groups, and of the roles certain members may play at certain critical stages within the group, therapists should be more aware of group members' vulnerability to negative outcome and consequently better equipped to reduce the likelihood of contratherapeutic outcomes. It is regrettable that research evidence suggests that clinicians may not be sufficiently aware of individuals who are potential group casualties (Lieberman et al., 1973), much less of the unique properties of groups which contribute to the therapeutic deterioration. It is a common observation among highly experienced group psychotherapists that a major problem among their less seasoned colleagues is that they simply fail to understand the unique value of group therapy. They are either insensitive to group process or neglect to utilize the resources of the group effectively (Dies, 1980b). Lieberman et al. (1973) suggest that even highly experienced leaders may be unaware of the significant group forces promoting client change.

Leadership In Group Therapy

Leader Influence upon the Group

Based on his review of the literature, Lundgren (1979) concluded that leaders exert a distinctive influence upon group development, but he suggests that their role has been overemphasized. A number of authors confirm this perspective. Gurman and Gustafson (1976), for example, review evidence from a variety of studies showing that the strong support for the importance of the client–therapist relationship in individual therapy is not substantiated in the group therapy setting. They suggest that group psychotherapy may depart significantly from individual therapy in several ways: (1) the therapeutic strategy may systematically deemphasize the role of the group leader and stress the value of peer relations within the group; (2) even though the therapist may intend to emphasize his or her relationship with the group, the group may choose to underrate the leader; and (3) the group model may introduce dangers unlike those encountered in individual treatment, dangers which necessitate that the therapist be much more than empathic, warm, and genuine, that is, "the group may become quite vicious in its treatment of some members, or one or several of the members may show difficulties that are very frightening to the group. In these situations, the therapist must demonstrate rather forceful qualities if the group situation is to remain viable" (p. 1293). Dies (1977b) has also suggested that the group situation is different from individual therapy because the quality of the relationship established between a therapist and individual group members may vary within the same group, and across the sequential phases of group development. To illustrate, a leader-centered approach may be more efficacious early in a group's development, whereas a group-centered style may be more appropriate during later phases (Dies, 1977b; Goldstein, Heller, & Sechrest, 1966).

Other writers have also attempted to show that the relative influence of the group therapist has been exaggerated. Lundgren (1977) found that over 90 percent of the discussion within his groups dealt with members or intermember interaction, while less than 10 percent concerned the leader or leader–member interaction. Luke (1972) asked group members to rate the degree to which each participant and the leader influenced the development and maintenance of group norms, while Smith (1976) had members evaluate the major sources of influence on their own learning within the group. Both authors found that co-members were credited with the major proportion of the influence. Compared to other individuals within the group, the leader is typically perceived as most influential, but there is consensus that the group composition is just as powerful, if not more so (Smith, 1976). Lundgren (1979) concludes that leaders play a significant role in facilitating an open and supportive atmosphere within the group, but that it is the interaction among the group members that is the most direct mechanism of change in the therapeutic process. As we noted earlier, this is why careful attention to group composition is so essential (Melnich & Woods, 1976).

These comments about the comparative impact of the group therapist should not be misconstrued. None of these writers is saying that the therapist is unimportant. Rather, it is evident that the group treatment situation is a uniquely complicated one because the permutations of influence are more diverse than in the one-to-one context. Thus, there are leader–member direct effects as well as indirect influences manifested through either member–member effects or through observational learning. In the latter case, members witness, and are perhaps adversely affected by, leader–member or member–member interactions.

Leadership Styles

A wide variety of intervention styles may be effective in group psychotherapy (Dies, 1977b). Given the present state of our knowledge, however, it would be impossible to construct the ideal leadership style. Part of the confusion is that what is optimal in one setting or with certain group members may not be as ideal under a different set of circumstances. Although Gurman and Gustafson (1976) did not find uniform support for the critical importance of the therapist–client relationship in group psychotherapy, they did not eschew the value of its presence. Indeed, other writers have found that the therapist's liking for a client (Babad & Amir, 1978), client identification with the therapist (Peters, 1973), therapist affection (Reddy & Lipert, 1980), and client favorability of attitude toward the therapist are very important (Bolman, 1971;

Lundgren, 1973). In their classic study of encounter groups, Lieberman et al. (1973) found that high levels of leader caring were vital to positive group outcome. Many of the clinicians we interviewed agreed with this point. They often related therapist warmth, empathy, and support to positive therapeutic effects. Conversely, numerous clinicians also commented that a negative therapist–client relationship in group therapy was frequently the basis for therapeutic deterioration. They particularly implicated leaders who were highly confronting and aggressive. Such therapists not only fail to show warmth and consideration for group members, but also communicate through their active confrontational style a fundamental disrespect for their clients' needs. Dies (1976) found that when experienced group therapists were asked to furnish behavioral examples of "manipulative" and "facilitative" group therapist styles, the former were more often described as controlling, indiscriminately inflicting their techniques upon unprepared group members, more forceful and critical in their confrontations, and more secretive or deceptive. Hartley et al. (1976) indicated that manipulative leaders often imposed their values on group members and frequently neither recognized crumbling defenses nor allowed for individual differences. According to Lieberman et al. (1973), the majority of clients experiencing therapeutic harm mentioned attack by the leader as a major factor contributing to their therapeutic decline. In his evaluation of this investigation, Smith (1975) commented that had the highly aggressive leaders been eliminated, the casualty rate would have been reduced by more than half.

A second type of leadership style associated with negative outcome, the laissez-faire leader, represents a combination of low activity and low affection (Reddy & Lipert, 1980). Hartley et al. (1976) conclude that this leadership style diverts the responsibility for the direction of the group to the clients, and that casualties result when high levels of negative feedback are exchanged in the absence of protective norms. One implication of this style is that leaders who remain distant and aloof, or who refuse to provide guidance and structure, may be setting the stage for therapeutic deterioration (Dies, 1976). Cooper (1977) found that closed-incongruent and introverted-withdrawn leaders most often contributed to clients' negative outcomes.

So far, it seems that leaders who are low on affection and either high or low on activity are more likely to produce negative change. These conclusions are quite compatible with the findings of Lieberman et al. (1973), who found that leaders who exercised excessive degrees of control ("Managers"), who used impersonal, aggressive stimulation ("Impersonals"), or whose style provided limited therapeutic intervention ("Laissez-Faire"), were most likely to produce disappointing or even emotionally upsetting outcomes for their participants. Yet these authors also propose that the nature of therapist activity ought to be defined more precisely. They found that either too much or too little *"emotional stimulation"* or the *"executive function"* by the therapist was potentially harmful. Emotional stimulation referred to "leader behavior which emphasizes revealing feelings, challenging, confrontation, revelation of personal values, attitudes, beliefs, frequent participation as a member in the group, exhortation, and drawing attention to self" (p. 235). The executive function was "defined in terms of behaviors such as limit-setting, suggesting or setting rules, limits, norms, setting goals or directions of movement, managing time, sequencing, pacing, stopping, blocking, interceding, as well as such behaviors as inviting, eliciting, questioning, suggesting procedures for the group or a person" (p. 239).

On the other hand, structure in terms of *meaning attribution* was found to be highly conducive to positive outcome. Meaning attribution "involves cognitizing behavior—providing concepts for how to understand, explaining, clarifying, interpreting, and providing frameworks for how to change. Such leaders are perceived as 'interpreters of reality,' attaching meaning to a person or a group's behavior" (p. 238). Thus, high activity per se is not necessarily helpful or harmful. Therapists who were high on meaning attribution were more effective, whereas high (or low) levels of emotional stimulation and executive functioning were contratherapeutic. The type of structure or therapist activity that seems to be most beneficial in the group setting is that which adds meaning and significance to the group therapeutic enterprise. Perhaps this observation explains why pregroup structuring (Bednar & Kaul, 1978) has been so consistently linked to positive group process and outcome. Similarly, Schwartz, Harrow, Anderson, Feinstein, and Schwartz (1970) report that group members generally favor sessions in which there is a clear relationship between the therapeutic task structure and treatment goals. Yet there may also be individual differences in preference for structure. Researchers have found that structure which matches client expectations and interpersonal style is more likely to yield favorable outcome (Abramowitz, Abramowitz, Roback, & Jackson, 1974; Kilmann, 1974; McLachlan, 1972; Parloff & Dies, 1977).

In this chapter, however, we have been focusing primarily upon factors contributing to negative effects. It is probably safe to assume that a lack of appropriate structuring by the therapist will lead to client dissatisfaction, limited therapeutic progress, or even premature termination from treatment. Smith (1976) reported that influential group leaders were differentiated from noninfluential leaders by the fact that the former generated more tension within the group. Thus, a certain degree of challenge and structuring appears to be necessary (Lieberman et al., 1973). The clinicians we contacted often indicated that therapists who were unwilling to confront difficult issues might well foster therapeutic deterioration. Many felt that the courage to deal with difficult clients in the group, to face potentially harmful group processes, and to stand up to powerful group forces were prerequisites for effective group therapy.

Common sense would suggest that group therapists should avoid extreme leadership styles. We have seen that either too much or too little emotional stimulation and executive functioning are potentially detrimental. Similarly, too much aggressive confrontation is also a high-risk style of intervention. The clinicians we interviewed cited a variety of extremes. For example, even the cognitive input by the therapist can be carried to excess. Quotes from some of the clinicians we interviewed reveal that group therapists may be "too verbal," "know-it-all," "sermonizing," and "heavy into causes." Such therapists were depicted as having a brand of therapy to sell, for example, est or other "pop psychology" approaches (Greenburg, 1977); they have *the* way to do things. They work from a script but "have no heart." One clinician indicated that he was currently treating several "victims" of these newer group approaches who did not survive the rigors of the method. Another extreme leadership behavior linked to negative group outcomes by several of the clinicians we interviewed was excessive self-disclosure, especially in those instances when therapists use the group to work through their own personal problems. We are reminded here of emotional stimulation as defined by Lieberman et al. (1973), and the indictment that leaders who are high on this dimension are too personally intrusive (Dies, 1977a).

Obviously, the clinical context in which one works is of critical importance. A confrontational style might be quite inappropriate in a private practice setting, because group members disperse after the session and return to their respective homes, which may or may not furnish the support needed following a particularly upsetting experience. Confrontation in an inpatient facility, however, may be less destructive because the patient has the opportunity to return to a cohesive ward environment in which others have shared the group experience and can understand the pain the patient is undergoing. Although a Synanon "hot seat" type of group might be effective in an inpatient context, the same leadership style can be hazardous with a group of outpatients (Lieberman et al., 1973). The group structure must suit the context.

Several of the clinicians we interviewed noted that difficulties in matching style to setting may contribute to therapeutic deterioration.

For example, while the inpatient community may provide a foundation of security for patients who have been stirred up by the group experience, it may also precipitate an exacerbation of the symptoms. A number of clinicians we interviewed reported that other patients may reinforce pathological patterns. One group practitioner who works in a prison setting observed that a patient's progress in group therapy may impede adapting to the prison social system and is apt to result in rejection by his peers. Other clinicians mentioned problems of confidentiality in which group members have difficulty maintaining the boundaries between group sessions and other more casual interactions they have outside of the group. These problems are amplified in the institutional setting. Staff members in an inpatient facility may also undermine the influence of group psychotherapy, particularly when a patient is exposed to varying and perhaps even contradictory pressures for change. For instance, the group therapist may strive to increase a patient's capacity to express angry feelings while an overworked and understaffed nursing team may block such expression. Other pressures within the institution may also be detrimental to the patient's welfare. In a hospital setting patients may face ridicule or social ostracism if they are not participating in group psychotherapy.

Administrative constraints in some treatment facilities may pose similar problems. One of the clinicians we surveyed, for example, reported that patients are referred to groups for economic reasons rather than considerations of patient need or psychological preparedness. Even for some private practitioners financial concerns or the need to maintain a group of adequate size may lead them to select patients for group treatment who might otherwise be excluded. Research has discovered that the reasons patients enter group therapy (e.g., voluntary versus involuntary) may influence the incidence of negative effects (Dies, 1978; Smith, 1975). Additionally, administrative pressures might unduly restrict effective group psychotherapy by setting time limits on patient tenure in groups. In such instances therapists who are not sufficiently sensitive to the importance of group developmental tasks may encourage active self-disclosure and critical feedback among group members and then be forced to terminate the group prematurely because of administrative mandates. Certain patients may end up feeling vulnerable, exposed, and without ample opportunity to work through their conflicts. In some inpatient settings, patients are not hospitalized long enough to receive adequate exposure to group psychotherapy. The subsequent sporadic nature of attendance may be disturbing to individual patients and to the integrity of the group. Therapist turnover might also be a problem in certain treatment settings (e.g., with residents in training), or there may be problems caused by group members being seen concurrently in treatment by a number of other staff members. Finally, one clinician we interviewed spoke of group therapists employed at public mental health agencies who, because of the public nature of their work setting, felt constantly on stage, were unable to relax, and became less effective as group leaders. On the other hand, several clinicians noted that conducting groups in private practice had inherent problems because the therapist is not exposed to a system of checks and balances by colleagues, which might encourage more careful therapeutic work.

Many of the 30 clinicians we contacted indicated that co-therapy is an effective procedure for improving clinical practice. Indeed, many of them argued that treatment with a co-leader was absolutely essential and provided one of the unique benefits of group psychotherapy. As advantages of co-therapy, they cited modeling, offsetting the other therapist's blind spots, validation of therapist feedback, more effective monitoring of group process, enrichment of the group experience, co-supervision, and emerging friendship between the therapists. Most of the clinicians we interviewed were quick to add, however, that the unique merits of co-therapy are highly contingent upon the quality of the relationship established between the co-leaders. They agreed that a conflicted or faltering co-therapy team might contribute to therapeutic deterioration. Unfortunately, only a few empirical investigations have been conducted which shed any light on this issue. Dies, Mallet, and Johnson (1979) found that co-leader openness was generally correlated with favorable group process and outcome, especially when the leaders concentrated on relationship factors. An exception to these results occured with co-leaders who were viewed as quite open with each other, but also manifesting unresolved conflict and disagreement within the sessions. Hurst, Stein, Korchin, and Soskin (1978) also found that self-expression was effective only when caring between co-leaders was present. Findings from Piper, Doan, Edwards, and Jones (1979) revealed that consistent co-therapy teams produced more effective process and outcome. The authors reasoned that patients from inconsistent teams were more confused about co-therapists' goals, and more anxious about the competition between the two therapists.

A majority of the clinicians we interviewed voiced a belief that adequate therapist training was imperative. Many stressed that co-therapists should have regular meetings to discuss relationship issues and that an outside consultant should participate in the process. Other forms of ongoing supervision and training were also mentioned by the clinicians. In fact, improved therapist training is undoubtedly the most common recommendation in the literature for preventing negative effects in group psychotherapy (Bednar & Kaul, 1978; Hartley et al.,

1976; Smith, 1975). Hartley and her colleagues emphasize special, intensive training programs for group psychotherapists, continuing education, and certification and licensure. One of the clinicians we contacted suggested that therapists should gather systematic information on their groups to generate more accurate impressions of their own effectiveness. This recommendation is quite consistent with guidelines established by the American Group Psychotherapy Association, which propose a standardized outcome measures battery for clinicians to use in their own practice (MacKenzie & Dies, 1981). Dies (1980a; 1980b) has offered a detailed set of suggestions for improving training in group psychotherapy, including a more efficient integration of instrumentation into the academic, observation, experiential, and supervisory components of training. It is important to recognize that training in group therapy is unique, not only because the particular training environments and individual participants differ from setting to setting, but also because the group experience is itself unique. "Special properties of groups which differentiate this treatment modality from all others must be understood, and training programs must be designed to emphasize this fact" (Dies, 1980b, p. 361).

Conclusions

A large number of clinicians are dissatisfied with the quality of group psychotherapy training they have received (Dies, 1974; 1980a; 1980b). Traditional training programs have relied upon supervisory models and educational experiences which are more appropriate for individual treatment, and as a consequence many group therapists are ill-prepared to understand the complexity and uniqueness of group approaches. Regrettably, these problems are not the exclusive domain of the novice. Research suggests that even highly experienced practitioners may not adequately comprehend the unique properties of group treatments (Kaul & Bednar, 1978; Lieberman et al., 1973).

Without a proper understanding of how group psychotherapy differs from other treatment modalities, clinicians continue to rely upon individually oriented selection criteria and seldom consider screening clients in terms of group composition, that is, clients are selected on the basis of diagnostic criteria rather than on judgments of the interpersonal compatibility within a specific group at a particular point in time. Additionally, clinicians often do not adequately prepare their clients for group treatments; therapists rarely help clients to anticipate potential difficulties related to emerging group roles and developmental phenomena, nor do they place their own role as therapist in proper perspective. Effective client preparation presumes that the group psychotherapist has a thorough understanding of the subtleties and complexities of group treatment. Obviously, clinicians who are not well trained or who do not fully comprehend the unique properties of group psychotherapy cannot be especially adept at preparing clients for this complicated and potentially powerful form of treatment.

A limited understanding of group psychotherapy may restrict the clinician's effectiveness in facilitating the curative forces operating within the group and in helping group members to overcome obstacles which are inevitable in the group's development. Clinicians who are not well versed in process will be confused concerning their own direct and indirect role in shaping the group culture. Group therapists must realize that although considerable influence and therapeutic potential are inherent in the leadership role, powerful group resources exist to complement and supplement their own interventions. In fact, the therapeutic forces within a group may be sufficiently robust to compensate for an ineffective group psychotherapist. This is not the ideal situation, but even the most skilled therapist must recognize these valuable group influences and realize that there are times when it is expedient to step aside and let the group do its work. On the other hand, there are also occasions when the group forces are contratherapeutic, and then it is imperative that the therapist intervene to prevent their injurious effects. Both the capacity to limit one's interventions in the face of positive group processes and the ability to confront harmful group pressures require confidence in one's own clinical skills. This confidence can be attained only through effective training.

The incidence of harmful group effects could be diminished if clinicians were more mindful of group process and more keenly aware of the changes their clients were experiencing during group treatment. Unfortunately, most practitioners rarely gather systematic information on the progress of their groups or on the clinical status of their group members. They rely mainly upon clinical judgment to assess the effects of group therapy, but as we attempted to show earlier, evidence indicates that clinicians are often quite insensitive to group process and client change.

Group psychotherapists have been criticized for their exclusive reliance upon clinical impressions and increasingly urged to devise more sophisticated methodologies for objective evaluation of their group treatments (MacKenzie & Dies, 1981). Considerable pressure is currently being exercised by lawmakers and governmental agencies that demand that psychotherapy, in order to be a reimbursable enterprise, must be proven to be safe, cost-efficient, and efficacious (Coche & Dies, 1981). Appeals for empirical validation of clinical interventions are widely heralded. Regrettably, the gulf between research and practice in group psychotherapy is substantial (Dies, 1979; Parloff & Dies, 1977). Nevertheless, this chasm could be bridged if clinicians would demonstrate a greater willingness to incorporate systematic methods for evaluating therapeutic group process and outcome (Coche & Dies, 1981; Dies, 1980b; MacKenzie & Dies, 1981). In this fashion, clinicians could not only heighten their acuity to the unique properties of group psychotherapy, but also potentially reduce the likelihood of deleterious group outcomes.

Summary

The purpose of this chapter is to identify a number of the unique properties of group psychotherapy which differentiate this treatment modality from other forms of therapy, and to demonstrate how the failure to understand these distinct characteristics may actually increase the potential of harmful group outcomes. Three major topics were presented to illustrate the unique qualities of group treatment: group curative factors; developmental stages and member roles; and leadership.

The five group curative factors (Yalom, 1975) which relate most consistently to therapeutic change are catharsis, group cohesiveness, interpersonal input (feedback), interpersonal output (socializing skills), and self-understanding. The critical aspect of catharsis is the response of other group participants. If a client's intense emotional expression is met by silence, rebuff, or disparagement, the client will seldom experience a positive effect, and may in fact become a therapeutic casualty. A sense of group cohesiveness and the experience of acceptance by co-members may protect most clients from experiencing harmful group results. Unfortunately, however, clients who do not feel integrated into the dominant group culture may terminate therapy prematurely or experience nonconstructive effects. These detrimental consequences may occur more often if the quality of interpersonal input exchanged among group members stresses undesirable personal attributes or is delivered in an overly confronting fashion. When feedback is too negative, the unique opportunities to learn socializing skills in the group setting may not materialize. Thus, certain clients may not benefit from the opportunity to improve their interpersonal output through interaction with co-members, or even worse they may recognize that they are deficient in the skills necessary to be an effective group member. This painful realization may block further self-understanding and lead to disillusionment with group treatment.

Although it is clear that every group is unique, substantial evidence indicates that recognizable patterns of development emerge across widely divergent groups. This chapter examines one recent model of group ontogeny (MacKenzie & Livesley, 1981) to show how the clinician's neglect of this distinct aspect of group treatment may contribute to unfortunate outcomes. Too much intragroup conflict or pressure toward highly personal disclosures during the initial stage of engagement, for example, might prove to be unduly threatening to individual members and could even endanger the integrity of the group. During the second and third stages of group development, members are concerned with differentiation and individuation, respectively, as they confront individual differences and struggle with the potential loss of individuality in the face of pressures toward conformity with group norms. If the interpersonal conflicts inherent in these stages of group development are not properly resolved, the effects could be damaging. Satisfactory resolution of the tasks characterizing these earlier developmental stages will move the group members toward a greater sense of intimacy typical of stage four. Harmful group outcomes may occur if the focus on intimacy leads to irresponsible closeness and sexual acting out among group members. When intimacy is addressed competently, however, the group advances to the fifth stage, mutuality, in which members explore personal problems more deeply. Several authors (Beck, 1974; MacKenzie, 1981) have proposed that certain members assume significant leadership roles during the group's evolution, roles which either facilitate or impede the progress of the group through the developmental sequence. The most troublesome roles are the defiant and scapegoat leaders who are usually judged critically even though these roles may serve a useful function within the overall patterning of group development. Members who assume these deviant roles are more likely to drop out abruptly or become injured by the group experience. At critical periods in a group's development, conflicts sparked by the emergence of these roles may increase the likelihood of negative group outcomes. Careful client screening for balanced group composition and proper structuring of the group may prevent some of the contratherapeutic results.

In the third section of this chapter we highlight the unique contribution of the group practitioner to therapeutic deterioration. Although the therapist's relative influence has been exaggerated compared to the importance of relationships established among group members, it is clear that particular intervention styles are potentially pernicious. Highly aggressive therapists, therapists who are distant and aloof, and therapists who refuse to provide guidance and direction have been most often implicated in the group treatment literature as contributing to therapeutic decline. Co-therapy and improved clinical training have been recommended to enhance the quality of group leadership in clinical practice. The importance of matching therapist style with client needs and with the general context of group treatment have also been stressed. Failure to recognize basic contextual differences may exacerbate the problem of unsuccessful group treatment.

We conclude the chapter by underscoring the need for rigorous training in group psychotherapy, and by proposing that group practice could be significantly improved if clinicians would gather more systematic and objective information on the impact of their therapeutic interventions.

Part III _____

Negative Outcome
and
Patient Population

7

Negative Outcome in Borderline States

Michael H. Stone

EDITOR'S NOTE: *This detailed account of Stone's personal experiences with the treatment of borderline patients graphically illustrates the difficulties and challenges involved in treating such individuals and we commend him for his candor. However, we regret the failure to include data bearing on the high rate of negative outcome among borderlines (relative to other patient groups) in at least certain forms of treatment. The interested reader is urged to consult Aronson and Weintraub (1968), Horwitz (1974), Weber, Elison, and Moss (1965), Endicott and Endicott (1963), and Voth and Orth (1973) for further evidence bearing on this important question. (See also Chapter 14.)*

Introduction

Psychotherapists, in speaking of their failures, can have little to boast of, apart from candor. For this reason, the literature of success (even when it has been spurious or short-lived success) would fill many a library. The literature of failure is scant.

This is not as it should be. What can I have learned, after all, from my successes? To the extent that my native sense of omnipotence had suggested to me that I could treat anyone for anything, the successes I may have had along the way would only have served to perpetuate this illusion. Success is seductive in this regard; failure is instructive. It is through failure that we learn which patients lie within the boundaries of treatability, which outside. In time, and by comparing experiences with one's colleagues, each therapist works out his private lexicon of treatable cases. No two will be identical. With respect to analytically oriented psychotherapy, one soon begins to appreciate that there are some patients who can be treated with good results—by any competent therapist. A few seem beyond help (not always because of the gravity of their symptoms so much as their indifference, or the negativism of their personality). And in between—a gray zone inhabited by patients, some of whom can be helped by you, but not by your colleagues; others, by some of your colleagues, but not by you. After some years of practice, most therapists will have integrated their experience in such a way that two correlations of relevance to our topic emerge as convincing, if not altogether valid. The first: the sicker the patient was at the outset, the less likely he will be to improve (cf. Strupp & Bergin, 1969), or the less rapid and dramatic will the improvement be, where there is any. The second: the sicker the patient at the outset, the smaller will be the percentage of therapists in any community who can work well with that patient, and effect whatever degree of improvement was potentially within him (Stone, 1971). I have noted in my own practice the relationship between probability of improvement and initial level of function: a higher proportion of neurotic patients (using Kernberg's structural criteria; *vide infra*) did well than was noted among the borderlines, who, in turn, outperformed those with psychotic structure (Stone, 1981).

Before further discussion of treatment failures within the borderline domain, it will be appropriate to define this domain in some detail, so that there will be harmony between the author's mental picture (of which patients would be included under this label) and the reader's.

The Borderline Realm Defined

There are a number of currently popular definitions of the term *borderline*. No one of these definitions is the "correct" one, so in discussing psychotherapeutic failures among "borderline" patients, there is no escape from the necessity of outlining the various criterion sets that currently enjoy the widest use.

1.   The borderline personality disorder of Gunderson (Gunderson & Singer, 1975; Gunderson & Kolb, 1978) defines a clinical syndrome, felt to be distinct from (overt) schizophrenia and from the psychoneuroses, characterized by good socialization (at least superficially), poor work achievement, impulsivity, predominantly rageful affect, chaotic and intense relationships—with a tendency to become severely depressed upon loss or threatened loss of the important other person, manipulative suicide gestures, minipsychotic episodes (paranoid and depressive; especially likely in the presence of alcohol or abuse of illicit drugs), and a tendency to perform well on the *structured* portion of the standard psychological test battery, in the face of primitive pyschotic-

like responses on the unstructured portions (notably, the Rorschach). Patients with clear-cut alchoholism, drug abuse, or sociopathy are excluded. Partly for this reason, the realm of Gunderson-borderline patients is comparatively small, though it may, according to its promulgator (Gunderson, 1981), embrace some 6 to 10% of the total population.

2. Kernberg's use of the term (Kernberg, 1967, 1977) derives from psychoanalytic sources, particularly those relating to object-relations and to a theory of mental structures; his definition is less phenomenological and more abstract than Gunderson's. Primarily the Kernberg criteria define a level of function or a level of personality organization; namely, that level which is sandwiched between the high level neurotic, in whom the sense of identity is well integrated and whose capacity to test reality is well preserved, and the low level psychotic, who is deficient in both these spheres. By definition, the borderline patient *can* test reality adequately, even in the more subtle realm of interpersonal relationships, but remains deficient with respect to identity integration. Certain nonspecific clinical signs also occur with regularity in borderline patients, as defined psychostructurally by Kernberg: impulsivity, a poor capacity for work or hobbies, and an inability to tolerate much stress.

In actual practice, most Gunderson-borderline patients will be borderline according to Kernberg's criteria; there will be a few exceptional cases, consisting of schizotypal (*vide infra*) persons who fulfill all the Gunderson criteria, but whose reality testing about interpersonal relationships is chronically poor: they exhibit psychotic structure as Kernberg defines it, while remaining borderline in Gunderson's system. But because many alcoholics, sociopaths, and the like show poor identity integration, they show a *borderline* structure and thus expand the ranks of "borderlines" (i.e., using Kernberg criteria) well beyond what could still be included within Gunderson criteria. Perhaps 10 to 14 percent of the population functions at the borderline level.

3. Derived in part from the Gunderson and Kernberg criteria and in part from Kety, Rosenthal, Wender, and Schulsinger's definition of the borderline schizophrenic (1968), the catalog of borderline "items" developed by Spitzer, Endicott, and Gibbon (1979) has now been incorporated into the *DSM-III* (1980). There one notes a division into two separate personality types: the schizotypal and the "borderline." The latter had been called "unstable" in the 1979 edition, and consists mainly of affective items (affective instability, self-damaging acts, chronic emptiness or boredom, intolerance of being alone, predominance of anger . . .). The schizotypal items, whose presence betokens the likelihood of a borderline schizophrenia, include odd communication, suspiciousness, magical thinking, social isolation, and ideas of reference.

Most patients who are "borderline" by the Gunderson or Kernberg criteria show a mixture of items from the schizotypal and unstable lists, especially the latter. Only about one patient in six will be a "pure" type, exhibiting the features of only one list (Spitzer et al., 1979; Stone, 1980b).

Almost all patients considered "borderline" by any system show disturbance in the sense of identity. Though this was placed in the "unstable" category, I find it more useful, as a rough and rapid index of borderline pathology, to diagnose a patient "borderline" if the identity-disturbance item is present, along with five other items from the two *DSM-III* lists (schizotypal and unstable/borderline) combined.

Comment

The patients referred to in this text, including those of the clinical vignettes, are borderline in Kernberg's structural system, unless otherwise indicated. One, for example, was a schizotypal borderline (in the *DSM-III* sense), but exhibited a psychotic structure.

Some General Observations on Psychotherapy Failures

The remarks that follow relate to the patients I have treated in private practice, and who remained for at least two months in psychotherapy.

The 145 patients in this category can be divided by psychostructural criteria into three levels of functioning: neurotic ($N = 75$); borderline ($N = 51$); and psychotic ($N = 19$). These evaluations refer to when each patient was seen initially in consultation, since some change in level occurred over time in a number of the borderline and psychotic patients.

I considered therapy to have failed in 39 instances (26.9% of the entire sample), consisting of 31 patients who were unimproved when treatment stopped (21.4%) and 8 who were distinctly worse (5.5%). Failure rate among the borderlines was fairly high: 21 out of 51 (41.2%), as against only 10 of the 72 neurotics (13.9%). The difference would appear to be significant ($\chi^2 = 12.61$; $p < 0.01$). Three neurotic patients were excluded from this reckoning because they were referred not for intensive psychotherapy but for management of medication. In the group with psychotic structure, failure-rate was the same as in the borderlines (8 of 19; 42.1%). Many of these who failed to improve quit therapy precipitously: this occurred in 7 out of 10 neurotic treatment failures, and in 15 of the 21 borderlines.

Those who were decidedly worse at the end of therapy were either borderline or psychotic in all but one of the eight instances. The one neurotic patient was an obsessive and mildly alcoholic man of 43 who had his first attack of bipolar manic-depressive psychosis two days before he insisted, against advice, on terminating his two years of twice weekly sessions. Of the four borderlines who ended up worse, two quit treatment and two (including Miss L. of the vignettes below) had to be hospitalized—one for panic; the other, for a suicide attempt.

The treatment-failure group required hospitalization in a few cases (one neurotic; two borderline; six psychotic patients). Two of the borderline treatment failures developed an agitated depression, requiring antidepressant medications and a shift toward supportive therapy. In the remainder of the borderlines, the main patient factor contributing to failure could be understood as relating to *personality* (as a term embracing both elements of temperament and of character; cf. Stone, 1980a). Personality emerges as a major factor in outcome and deserves special attention. In the following section this issue is addressed in some detail and illustrated with a number of clinical vignettes.

The Role of Personality Type

Retrospective assessment of negative outcomes in borderline patients leads inevitably to discussion of personality factors. Elsewhere I have expressed the view that patients suspected of functioning at the borderline level need to be evaluated along three diagnostic dimensions: constitutional type (e.g., relating to the degree of predisposition to a primary affective or to a schizophrenic illness), usual adaptational level (neurotic, borderline, psychotic), and personality type (Stone, 1980b). These dimensions are not completely separable, inasmuch as the formation of certain personality types seems itself favored by certain hereditary/constitutional factors. Patients with manic-depressive illness, and their close relatives, would appear to be a greater than average risk, for example, to develop, out of what may be understood as an inborn *temperament* (Kraepelin, 1921; Stone, 1980a), a depressive, a hypomanic, or an explosive "personality."

If one includes the personality disorders mentioned in the current diagnostic manual (*DSM-III*), along with several others used primarily within the psychoanalytic community, a catalog will emerge containing the following types: hysteric (histrionic), obsessive, depressive (or depressive/masochistic), phobic, infantile, passive (including passive-dependent and passive-aggressive), paranoid, narcissistic, schizoid, explosive, hypomanic, inadequate, and antisocial. The "irritable" temperament of Kraepelin has many features in common with explosive personality. Individual patients will of course rarely exhibit traits of only one of these personality types; they will ordinarily show predominantly the features of one, while making it clear that a variety of traits associated with several other types are also applicable. Although I can conceive of no particularly "correct" order in which the 13 personality types mentioned above can be placed, that is, with respect to some external validating criterion, I have suggested as a useful working hypothesis that the first 6 are generally associated with a good prognosis (especially in relation to a psychoanalytically oriented therapy). The latter 7 seem to be associated with a less favorable prognosis (Stone, 1981). The borderline patients in my private practice who had the best outcomes had, with few exceptions, predominant personality types from among the first 6 entries in the list above; those who did poorly were clustered, from the standpoint of personality type, among the latter 7 (paranoid, narcissistic . . .).

Even if it were confirmed through more rigorous studies that borderline patients with one of the seven personality types I have suspected of predicting a poor response to psychotherapy did in fact do poorly with psychotherapy, one important question would remain unanswered. What would the fate of these individuals have been had they been left alone or treated merely with a supportive technique at relatively infrequent intervals? Put another way, was intensive psychotherapy merely failing to effect improvements, or was it contributing actively to their becoming worse? I think it is hard, in the present state of the art, to generalize on these points, there being so many variables to keep in mind, combinable in so many ways. There come readily to mind certain borderline patients who seemed distinctly worse off for having been in intensive psychotherapy and others who showed no movement in either direction. Among the former, some might have done well with a different therapist using a similar technique. Failures of this sort must be laid at my doorstep as manifestations of countertransference problems affecting my—but not all therapists'—work with a particular patient. There would appear to exist untreatable patients, whose failure to improve cannot be readily ascribed to personality factors either in myself or in others undertaking the task. Among the latter—those who did not budge one way or another in therapy—are some who might have done better with a supportive approach but others whose motivation and flexibility were too meager to permit any significant improvement, regardless of the technique or of the personal characteristics of the therapist. Borderline patients in this last category, if one could have somehow spotted them in advance, should, if only for economic reasons, have been left alone. Of course few clinicians are blessed with such wisdom as to know—or cursed with such inhumanity as to tell—which patients should not be treated.

The clinical vignettes that follow, chosen from among the 20 borderline patients who, in my private practice over the past 16 years, did the worst, illustrate a number of the relevant variables concerning patient, therapist, and treatment method.

A Paranoid Patient with Features of "Irritable" Temperament

A single woman of 26 was referred for psychotherapy because of repetitive difficulties in making a lasting relationship with a man. Miss L. had been born in Scotland to a prostitute and (as far as could be determined) a medical student from a foreign country. Although she was occasionally visited by—and therefore had some knowledge of—her mother, she was raised in a succession of orphanages and foster homes. She suffered many indignities and brutalities in these places, no one of which was she able to call home for more than two years, until, at about 14, she ran away from the last orphanage, along with a boy of 16 whom she had met there. They survived as street gamins, living by their wits—which for the most part entailed begging and petty thievery. Picked up by the authorities for the latter at 16, she was sent to a reformatory, where she received some supplement to her skimpy and sporadic education, until she was released two years later. Somehow, she made a successful transition into conventional life at this point, having managed to learn the art of wigmaking. Within a few years, in fact, she had become a highly respected perruquier with her own shop—when, rather impulsively, she decided to come to America, primarily to start a new life that would be untainted by the wretchedness of her past.

She opened a shop here, which was already thriving by the time I first saw her in consultation. Intelligent, articulate, and highly motivated for help, she seemed at the time a suitable candidate for intensive psychotherapy. Borderline features consisted of the "unstable" type, with intense anxiety when alone, a pervasive sense of emptiness, lability of mood, and a volatility of temper, confined largely to her relationships with men. She tended to select for partners men who were possessive and physically abusive; those who were stable and tender she found "boring."

After a few months of twice-weekly sessions, she reported a number of dreams, whose quality was singularly grotesque or bleak. In one, the entire world had been devastated by nuclear holocaust, leaving her to wander about, alone and frightened, among the desert and rubble. In another, she visualized a volcano atop which was perched a toilet: mountains of excrement exploded from the volcano, inundating her and her surroundings. I made the interpretation that therapy was becoming threatening to her because it was forcing to come to the surface all the sordid and disturbing aspects of her past. Though she acknowledged the accuracy of this, it was scarcely comforting. At the very next session, in fact, she went into a psychotic rage, screaming, crying, and hurling things around the office. She had to be taken to the hospital, where she remained for several weeks under sedation. Afterwards, deciding that examining her life was too threatening a business, she returned to her profession and to her sadomasochistic relationships, stronger only in her determination not to risk further breakdown by too close a confrontation with an intolerable past.

Comment

One of the difficulties of this case arises as a paradoxical effect of Miss L.'s unexpected vocational success. Through it, she was lifted out of the demimonde of foundlings and petty criminals by whom she was at least accepted—even while aspiring to escape from this world of rejects into the world of ordinary people. After her "escape," she found herself an alien—among those who had behind them the experiences of warm family life, a secure sense both of belonging and of social station. A probing kind of psychotherapy could serve only to remind her the more forcibly of her outcast status. The Pandora's box of her psyche contained nothing but bitter memories of degradation, humiliation, deprivation, rejection, and shame, and in reaction to all of this, a smouldering rage ready to explode at any moment, scarcely covered over by her engaging facade. I worked with this patient when only a few years out of residency—at a time when my omnipotent fantasies about how much could be done for someone with this background had not yet been whittled down to more realistic proportions.

Though superficially sweet and self-effacing, she mistrusted everyone, particularly men. There was nothing about her first 20 years to provide her with any template for a trusting attitude. It was highly unlikely that she could experience any human interaction as genuinely loving and altruistic, let alone that exposure to such could challenge her paranoid defenses. She was actually safer, in the topsy-turvy world she perforce inhabited, in choosing sadistic lovers—for whose meanness and infidelity her whole life had been a preparation; with a good man, she would have been lost. As with other paranoid patients, she consistently misconstrued goodness as evil behind a mask, and went about (through jealous taunts, provocative gestures, and angry outbursts) extinguishing any decent impulses directed at her by her lovers, while eliciting from them, instead, the cruelty she so much detested, but expected. As I reflect back on this patient from a distance of some 15 years, I am not sure that even long-term hospitalization under the care of a dedicated and highly skilled therapist could have made serious inroads into the skewed pattern of a paranoid and borderline person who had never even for a moment been the recipient of the selfless love of another human being.

Another clue, had I been alert to it, to the bleakness of her prognosis (especially with respect to intensive psychotherapy) was the grotesqueness of her dreams. The repetitive images of world-devastation, as with dreams of self-mutilation and of the dreamer's own death, betoken not only borderline-level (or psychotic-level) pathology, but also a brittleness of personality not likely to be ameliorated by techniques currently available.

A Narcissistic Patient with Paranoid Features

A young woman of 20 had dropped out of college because of an outbreak of crippling symptoms that included panic episodes, crying spells, promiscuity, globus hystericus, and trichotillomania (hairpulling), along with several suicide and self-mutilative gestures, consisting of wrist scratching and burning her forearms with cigarettes. Hospitalization was required, and she was referred, during the time of my residency, to a unit that specialized in psychoanalytically oriented therapy of borderline patients.

She was attractive, came from a well-to-do home, behaved rather seductively—so that she always had about her a number of male admirers—but she had no real friends (nor did she form any friendships during the year she spent in the hospital). In fact she alienated most people because of her haughty manner and peremptoriness. It was rare that she did not seem to be seething with a scarcely concealed hostility and was particularly scornful and contemptuous toward the nursing staff. Although she fancied herself an artist, she spent little time at her easel and showed a lamentable want of discipline; what canvases she did complete seemed slapdash and grotesque. Yet she felt destined for greatness, and entertained the fantasy that one day she would have a show in a prominent gallery, where her father, absent from the family since her parents' divorce when she was four, would visit, be awestruck by her work and acclaim, and beg forgiveness for his years of neglect.

Her first therapist was able to work with her for only four months, since he was about to move to a different city. She professed to like him and was considered by the staff to have developed a good "therapeutic alliance" with him. When I took over her treatment, however, the most remarkable feature of the transitional phase was the complete omission of any spontaneous reference to my predecessor. Inquiries on my part as to whether she at times missed—or even had an occasional passing thought of—her former therapist met invariably with derision and denial. Meantime, I had become incorporated into her dreams and thoughts with an immediacy that was disconcerting for its very rapidity: how genuine could her feelings be toward a total stranger whom she professed to accept as protector, interpreter, and admirer, 24 hours after our first session?

She recalled dreams well, such that we were able to focus on one nearly every session. Thematically, they centered on envy and rejection. A vivid dream of being overrun by little green monsters typified the former. Her sense of being rejected, although experienced more in relation to her father than to her mother, was highlighted by a dream in which she saw herself as a baby in a crib; her mother stood nearby—naked, and with a penis that was as long as a boa, but was curved back, bypassing the baby, and inserting into mother's own mouth. Mother fed only herself, as it were, and not the patient. Although her scorn and contemptuousness seemed to have evolved partly as responses to the central feelings of rejection, they softened only to a slight degree as the interpretive work continued.

One tends to see each patient, in the beginning of therapy, more as a victim (of "bad parents," harsh circumstances, etc.) deserving of sympathy than as a perpetuator of his own misery (through unkind treatment of others, as an example). I remained in a purely sympathetic mode, blind to the ways in which she hurt other people's feelings, longer than her behavior would have warranted. Doubtless, her superficial appeal and her (at times genuine) grief over the emotional aridity of her early life kept me stalled in this attitude, well into the time I should have been confronting her about her outrageous behavior. The following incident helped bring my perception of her more into line with the reality of her character.

However unlikely it seemed that the realization of her fantasy concerning her father would affect a dramatic "cure" (she had by now spent too many years accumulating maladaptive social habits to have them unraveled in the course of one magical meeting), I did come to feel that it would be beneficial for her and her father to become reacquainted. The gamble seemed small. It was almost inconceivable that he could have been the monster she (with generous help from her mother) had portrayed him to be in her mind's eye; I reasoned that her coming to know him could only lead to a more realistic grasp of what he was like. Surely this would help detoxify the venomous view she so tightly held, according to which all men, beginning with her father, were selfish and unfeeling bastards. Space does not permit a detailed setting forth of all the negotiations, diplomacy, and salesmanship required in persuading her father to make the 400-mile trip to see her again, after a lapse of 16 years. But he did come. I met with him first and satisfied myself that he was a reasonable and affable, if somewhat passive and timorous, man, recognition of whose warmer qualities ought, by rights, to have led to some mellowing in his daughter's harsh and distorted beliefs. She put on her best outfit for the occasion, and seemed aglow with anticipation.

I then effected the reunion, remaining in the room (at her request) as a supportive figure for her, and was thus witness to the shocking scene that unfolded. Far from shedding any tears of happiness at the opportunity of seeing her father after so many years, she at once grew cold and hostile in his presence, unleashing a torrent of abusive language, in which she excoriated him for having deserted her and for "daring" to shower more attention on his two children by his second wife than he ever bestowed on her. Understandably horrified at this display, he got up and left, not without some pointed remarks, incidentally, about the level of my clinical acumen that had led me to insist on their meeting when she was in so negative a state.

As it developed, this incident was only the most glaring example of a particular trend in her personality, which had manifested itself in countless small ways in relation to people other than myself (such that I was correspondingly slow in taking seriously what some of the nurses and attendants had been telling me), but which began to exert itself, as the course of the therapy continued, in the transference situation as well. The trend I am alluding to might be labeled under the heading of pathological narcissism [as Kernberg (1975) has defined it]. Some of the features of this narcissism, as pertained to my patient, were manipulativeness, lack of empathy, a withering contempt for others, side by side with a strong sense of entitlement to whatever she imagined was "owing" her in the way of affection and supplies.

Whereas for months she was deemed not well enough to be outside the hospital for more than a few hours at a time, she improved to the level where she was allowed to attend classes during the day and to remain out overnight on occasion with her mother. It was at this point that many of the irritating qualities in her personality became as visible to me as they were to the rest of the hospital staff. She began to overstay on overnight pass, without informing anyone of her whereabouts or intentions. This provoked considerable consternation, and genuine worry besides. She would breeze in a few hours late, quite mystified at all the "fuss" she had stirred up. Similarly, she would skip a session with me without bothering to let me know by phone. Sometimes the missed appointment represented the acting out of some uncomfortable transference feeling, exploration of which she simply dodged by "getting caught in downtown traffic." But there were other times when the most important causative element in her inattention was mere rudeness. There were other signs of this, as when she would appear at the home of acquaintances at midnight, ring the bell, and then become quite taken aback at getting a cold reception.

Acting out of transference themes was particularly marked in this patient, whose impulsivity had always been a serious problem, quite apart from whether or not she was in psychotherapy. Her promiscuity reasserted itself once she was allowed off the hospital grounds; the men she picked were generally much older than herself, but also of a different social class, and were often quite brutal. Occasionally she would become involved briefly with a more suitable man, whom she would treat shabbily and drop after a few dates.

Two things were becoming clear to me in her treatment: the wildness of her behavior was incompatible with methodical explorations of transference and other issues within the context of an "expressive" psychotherapy. The material was too threatening; our touching on it only seemed to make the chaos worse. Also she was poorly motivated for an insight-oriented therapy. She kept asking for practical advice (about school, about work, about matters of everyday living), and ultimately I saw the wisdom (with the help of a supervisor and a consultant) of modifying my approach. In a sense we had been working at cross-purposes for a long time: I kept trying to "cure" her condition by making her aware of her psychodynamics; she was trying to learn the ropes of survival at her job and to extract from me carte blanche to behave as she pleased. During the last few months of our work I did offer her practical pointers of the sort she wanted—which was really all she could absorb from the therapeutic encounter that was in any way beneficial to her. Eventually she found a job with which she could support herself, but in a different city. I heard some years later that she was still there, living alone, working, and leading approximately the same sort of chaotic personal life, with many spasmodic and ungratifying relationships, as I had begun to witness when she reentered the outside world.

Comment

This patient appeared superficially to have many assets. She evoked stong feelings of sympathy from me in the beginning, because of her extreme loneliness and the pain of parental rejection she had for so many years suffered. But therapy left her largely untouched: she was neither better nor worse when she moved away. I think it is not enough to say that the emotional deprivation of her early years accounted for her resistance to efforts at helping her. It was not merely that she was "too damaged" to get better, though she was severely damaged. The critical factor here, not apparent to me at the outset, was her lack of any genuine concern for others. This was coupled with a severe mistrustfulness, especially where men were concerned, that defeated any chance of establishing a warm and supportive relationship with anyone. She made no friends, gravitating instead toward sado-masochistic dalliances with men who were at best inappropriate; at worst, dangerous. It is noteworthy that of the five patients with whom I worked in analytically oriented therapy during my residency, she is the only one who, over the years, failed ever to let me know—through a call or a letter—how she was getting along. Ironically, after 16 years of silence on her father's part, another 16 years have passed in which she has visited the same "silent treatment" on me.

One should not ascribe the poor result solely to the presence of narcissistic traits in a borderline patient, since some traits of this sort are prominent in many borderline patients, including those who make good recoveries. It is rather that—and here one must resort to a language that lies outside our standard manual of diagnosis—she alienated everyone: she was cold, deceitful, suspicious, unkind, and apt to turn against an erstwhile friend in the flash of a second and without provocation. As therapists we can sympathize with the hardships our patients have often endured as children, we can unravel their psychodynamics, we can hold up for their inspection the maladaptive patterns they now perpetuate, to their own distress. But what if a patient is uninterested in all this? And what power does the analysis of psychodynamics have to convert a borderline patient whose character is shabby, or abrasive, or malevolent, into someone who is considerate, empathic, and respectful of the rights of others? As I have come to discover over the years, very little. One could add that group therapy and behavior-modification techniques are also of little avail in effecting the kinds of characterological changes that would be needed here—especially in an unmotivated patient. We seem to have no specific method for making an unfriendly person friendly.

A Schizoid Patient with
Paranoid and
Narcissistic Features

It is not readily determinable in advance just which, among one's difficult patients, were the personal and which were the universal failures.
Sometimes the position one occupies in the sequence of therapists
consulted may provide a clue: if seven therapists fail with a particular
patient, the general untreatability of that person would seem clearly
established, say, to the sixth or seventh consultant, whereas the first or
second could not as yet have formed any firm conclusion. For them it
would have been much harder to distinguish personal reasons (*viz.*,
lack of "fit" between the two personalities) from suprapersonal reasons
(*viz.*, the patient has alienated every person with whom he has come in
contact, and is now repeating the process with me).

The patient in the following vignette represents one of the most
abysmal failures in my 16 years of practice. Yet he had frustrated the
efforts of so many colleagues before he came to me that I was able
to take defeat "philosophically"—that is, with an attitude of detachment, rather than of disillusionment about my skills as a
therapist.

Mr. R. was 23 when he saw me in consultation. He had been
referred by a Boston psychoanalyst, preeminent in his work with severely disturbed patients, who informed me, not without a sense of
relief, that this man was about to move to New York City to attend
graduate school. My colleague, the fourth psychiatrist with whom Mr.
R. had worked over the preceding 2½ years, informed me that Mr. R.
was ". . . the most devious, malicious and diabolical human being"
whom he had ever met. In view of my predecessor's reputation for
doing effective work with cases others considered untreatable, this was
an awesome remark. I accepted Mr. R. for intensive psychotherapy
with a sense of challenge, but also of curiosity. The air of hopelessness
surrounding this man made me feel entitled to pull out all of the stops
in my efforts to help him, and at the same time diminished my anxiety
about possibly failing, since many of "the best" had already failed
before me.

Mr. R. sought help ostensibly because of difficulty concentrating
on his studies. He was preoccupied with fears that a former friend
from his hometown might have turned against him in some (never
clearly defined) way, and might be stirring up some (also never clearly
defined) trouble, despite the two thousand miles that (assuming the
friend had stayed put) lay between them. Mr. R.'s guardedness made
it next to impossible to determine whether these notions about the

friend had the force of delusion or were more in the nature of an "over-valued idea" (cf. Hoch and Polatin, 1949; Kernberg, 1967). The degree to which he bristled if pressed on the matter left me with the impression that he showed a psychotic structure (in Kernberg's terminology), and was thus one of those schizotypal patients who are simultaneously "borderline" with respect to the schizophrenia spectrum but psychotic from the standpoint of object-relations theory.

Characterologically, he was intensely narcissistic: demanding (of advice, small favors, "direct help" with his problems), haughty, contemptuous, and self-centered. He was friendless now, and lived as an isolate on the fringe of campus. His paranoid tendencies were not confined to the old friend but were readily apparent in his assumptions and misperceptions about most other people, including, of course, myself and my predecessors in therapy.

Mr. R. quit treatment with me precipitously after about four months of twice-weekly sessions. What it was like to work with this man can be extrapolated from the following material, which derives from his next-to-last session.

MR. R.: D'ya mind turning on the air-conditioner: How can I talk in this airless room?! (Before I could make a move . . .) Never mind! *I'll* turn it on! (Pause). I don't think we can work together. I really don't. I'm very upset, and I don't wanna go into it. I thought I ran into P. (his old friend) in the street. Whoever it was, he didn't stop to say hello. I don't wanna think about it; it'll open up a can of beans I don't wanna be bothered with just now. You understand that? You understand what I'm *talking* about? Anyway, I'm upset a lot about that, and it's pushing me to do desperate things.

DR. S.: Such as?

MR. R.: Such as quitting here. Such as doing extremely foolish things with money—which I don't care to go into. *I'm sorry!* We're simply not going to get along. I have *more* conflicts here now than when I started seeing you. *You* might consider that constructive (spoken with consummate disdain) but *I* don't! I need a lot of guidance; the feeling someone is on my side. And I do *not* get that here! I shouldn't have to *force* someone to . . . So that's it! We just don't get on. You obviously consider this devious, haugh-

ty . . . that's *your* business. It dawned on me last
time how much I was crying out for approval in
some way—how much I wanted your encouragement and your friendship and your backing. Everything I always wanted and never got. I know that
sounds melodramatic, which I hate . . . so
cliché . . . but that's how it *is*. You can't help me. So
this is our last session. You're not my money's
worth, that's all! So! Having said that, that's *it!*
(Pause) I'm sorry you see this as imperiousness, ar-
rogance . . . I'm sorry you see it that way (speaking
more loudly and haughtily than ever) . . . your view
is totally wrong, totally off the wall . . . but I'm not
gonna waste what little energy I have trying to convince the likes of *you* otherwise . . . you've nothing
to offer me. You've been offering me nothing. You
realize that, don't you?!

DR. S.:   Because, as it turns out, you repudiate whatever
offer of help, in whatever form, I might give.

MR. R.:   (Animated) There's *nothing* to repudiate! You have
zero—a big goose-egg—to offer me, there's nothing
to repudiate. And genuinely . . . I genuinely do *not*
feel any deep-seated hostility towards you.

DR. S.:   What you're directing at me at the moment is just a
kind of superficial hostil—

MR. R.:   (Interrupting) No! I don't mean it that way! That is
not how I mean it. I have respect for you. I think
you're a nice guy. I think you have some problems
of your own . . . which is none of my business to go
into. I do not feel deep-seated hostility towards you,
or antagonism, or anything like *that*. You simply
don't have what I need. You can interpret that sexually, if you like. That's *your* business.

DR. S.:   You keep claiming hostility is the farthest thing from
your feelings toward me just now. What name *would*
you care to give to what you've been saying? And to
the tone?

MR. R.:   (Long pause.) So this is our *last time*. Got anything
more to say to me? *You* probably feel hostility toward me, and I'm sorry. (Voice quieter now.) You
probably don't like me and I'm sorry. Genuinely

sorry. Because I basically like you. But the fact is I'm getting nothing here. Nothing. I have more conflicts than ever. I just need someone who's *stronger*. Someone who's outwardly more—*something*. How do I know if you've even had experience with problems like mine? I can't afford to wait and see. I can't afford that *luxury!* I need help right *now*. Right now! And *you* don't give it to me.

DR. S.: Unless it's a matter of you systematically defeating any effort I might make to be of some help.

MR. R.: (Interrupts, yelling) I don't see any *evidence* of it!

DR. S.: All anyone could see here is the delight you take in reenacting the drama—one would think it would have grown tiresome by now—where you "suffer" at someone else's "neglect," but retaliate by telling him to buzz off . . .

MR. R.: No! You've got it all wrong!

DR. S.: . . . because you obviously relish this whole . . .

MR. R.: Relish what? What am I relishing?!

DR. S.: This whole act of . . .

MR. R.: (Interrupting) It's no *act!*

DR. S.: . . . turning the tables so the other person "suffers" and you are the triumphant one!

MR. R.: It's no *act!*

DR. S.: Call it what you will; it's happened with three . . . four other therapists over the past three years.

MR. R.: They at least *talked* to me. There was response. It's true I didn't get anywhere. But we're not getting anywhere either. I don't like to bring this up, because you might take it *personally*, and, uh, I *told* you I like you. I see a lot of sensitivity I haven't seen in the others, as quiet as you are. But that's not what I *need*. Not *now!* I need something *more*. I can't go out of here and flunk my exams or make stupid decisions . . . so I feel desperate. If you don't like me, things are pretty hopeless. I feel that way about life in general. It's a doctor's *job* to quiet the patient's symptoms immediately through drugs. Though I'm convinced I don't need any. There must have been *something* you could have done.

Comment

I have provided this lengthy abstract of our penultimate session because the material so clearly highlights not only the primitivity of Mr.
R.'s defenses (a quality shared by better-prognosis borderlines as well)
but also the insuperable obstacles he set up against any attempts to get
through these defenses. Devaluation, omnipotent control, and denial
are all very prominent. His empathic ability was seriously defective,
almost negligible. He constantly disavowed certain feelings that were
unacceptable to him; these he would repetitively see me as harboring
instead (this is the mechanism of projective identification). Like many
borderline patients, he tried desperately to "actualize" the transference: he was much more eager to convert me into a real "friend" (and,
I suspect, into a homosexual lover) than to explore the reasons for his
loneliness or even to share with me the keenness of his anguish at the
isolation and barrenness of his life.

His insistence that I didn't "like" him, and that I could therefore
not possibly help him, represents two gross misreadings of the reality
of our situation. To begin with it is not a precondition for being able to
help a patient that we "like" him; it is enough that we have respect,
compassion for his suffering, and a dedication to the task of helping.
And, in any case, I had an array of complex reactions to this man, as
would be inevitable under the circumstances. He evoked sympathy in
me (at the genuineness of his distress), but also despair (at his remarkable inability to get along with others even in the simplest encounters),
horror (over the intensity and pervasiveness of his contempt, hatred,
contumeliousness, etc.), admiration (at his having been, willy-nilly, a
museum-piece of his kind, at his "gutsiness" in persevering at school
despite his handicaps), and a measure of friendliness also (he was
articulate; we had certain similarities of background, shared interests,
etc.). As is true so commonly with paranoid persons, however, he
could not appreciate the range and subtlety of other people's feelings.
The world was black or white to him, and any threatening hints of
grayishness he immediately oversimplified into "black" or "white"—
the only two states his psychic machinery could recognize or deal with.
He could not listen to alternative views; he permitted no dialogue. This
left me with the two unhappy choices of either trying to confront his
paranoid defenses head on (with the usual result) or sitting in silence
until he became more "reasonable" (there was little indication that this
approach would have succeeded).

One could argue, armed with the wisdom of retrospect, that with
so demanding and paranoid a patient and one whose support system
was so fragile (no friends; relatives whom he had alienated), I should

have eschewed any attempt to do an insight-oriented therapy in the first place. But I remind myself that he was equally adroit and vehement in rejecting help from those of my predecessors who had used a more supportive approach. One often recommends switching gender in choosing a new therapist for a patient who has not improved, or gotten worse; there was evidence that meeting twice a week with a male therapist stirred up intolerable homosexual anxieties in this man that after a time forced him to flee. But in Mr. R., the need to defeat any potential helper semed so great that a female therapist would doubtless have found her efforts sabotaged as well. Mr. R. wished to see himself, since he could not compete very successfully in everyday life, as the world's most maligned person. A negative hero is still a hero. To this end he developed a malignant personality impervious to anything a therapist might have to offer.

An Infantile Patient
with Phobic Features

Mrs. N. was 24 when she was referred to me for analytically oriented psychotherapy. She had been having marital difficulties, and a colleague, who had been working with her husband, suggested she seek help as well. Mrs. N. had been married only a few months before our initial consultation, but had already begun to feel rejected by her husband. There were alternating periods of tearfulness and rageful outbursts at him—for the many hours in which he would be preoccupied with reading, watching television, or other activities that shut her out. In addition, he had become a devotee of an obscure religious cult, the proper performance of whose rites required his presence (so he insisted), for long stretches during the evening hours several times a week, at the home of a certain female member of this sect. Nothing sexual transpired there, according to the husband, but as a result of all these activities, nothing transpired sexually between him and his wife either—a situation that provoked considerable despair on her part and moments of intense jealousy as well.

Mrs. N. had suffered for years from an overwhelming fear of abandonment or of being alone. She was still very immature, clingingly dependent, and given to ruminating incessantly about dying—even though she was in the best of health. Her weight had fluctuated widely over the past several years, ever since she developed an eating disturbance consisting of alternating bulimia and induced vomiting. She had never had anorectic symptoms.

Mrs. N. had come from an intact family. Her upbringing had not been conspicuously traumatic. The middle of three children, she had apparently been comfortable, if somewhat shy and passive, as a young girl, until the birth of a brother when she was six. The changes in the family network this brought about were not easy to reconstruct, but in her experience of it, her father began to dote exclusively on his little son, and "turned away" from her. She felt her father was "lost" to her, from that time forward. Subsequently, bouts of severe separation anxiety occurred periodically, as when she would attempt to go to camp (but be unable to do so) or, later, to move away from the city where she grew up.

By her own admission, she had married her husband less out of love than out of a desperate need for security, and for surcease from loneliness. He was much older than she, a markedly schizoid and eccentric man, inattentive to her not so much out of want of affection as out of near total absorption in a strange inner world, of which his bizarre religious practices were but one manifestation.

Within the first month of therapy it became clear to me that my patient had been unwittingly using her husband as something of a foil for her own ambivalence. This of course is discernible in almost any intimate partnership, but was particularly striking in theirs. His indifference to sex, for example, shielded her from having to become cognizant of her own squeamishness in this area. Similarly, she professed to want children, but did so in a lukewarm and unconvincing way. Her husband, meanwhile, was dead set against having any—thus allowing her to revel in the notion of being a martyr, obliged to suppress her normal urges to the will of a sick, unsympathetic man. The marriage had already begun to founder because the bargain she struck—secret even to her conscious self—was that her husband would provide her his physical presence (alleviating her anxiety in being alone), but would have no other obligations (sex and babies would only have disrupted this symbiotic equilibrium in any case). He had already begun to fail her, however, in this one simple demand (not to leave her) through his ever more frequent cult sessions with the other woman. All this, as I say, became clear to me at the outset—but never to her. No amount of interpretive work, dream analysis, or joint meetings with the husband (of which there were several) served to enlighten her about the conflictual feelings with which she was struggling. She behaved as though she had some inchoate awareness of the likelihood that, were she to acknowledge what she had been so busy disavowing about the nature of her marriage, she would have had to dissolve it and leave her husband; as little as she asked of the relationship, he was offering her substantially less.

Mrs. N. had been working with reasonable success at her job as an editorial assistant, during the time we worked together. Partly on the strength of this, I had judged her as capable of becoming sufficiently autonomous that she could afford the emotional price that exploration of her marital conflict might exact from her: namely, she might seek divorce. It seemed possible, though less likely, that her husband would change enough, through his own treatment, as to become a more gratifying partner. As it turned out, Mrs. N. was too ill at ease about the prospect of losing what little security she had. Calculating that therapy posed more of a threat than remaining with the status quo, she quit treatment after four months.

Comment

The negative outcome in this case was a reflection of countertransference factors as well as of factors ascribable to the patient.

The example was also chosen because it illustrates the difficulties attendant upon therapists who strive to shake loose a phobic partnership. Two symbiotically attached people, whether parent–child or husband–wife, have a way of remaining united, however ungratifying and destructive the partnership may appear on the surface. This will be so, no matter what we may do on behalf of their consciously avowed (but unconsciously repudiated) wish for greater separation. If one or both partners are borderline, our task will be correspondingly more arduous than if both are healthier, since the borderline person's flexibility and range of options is narrower.

Patients with an infantile personality (cf. Kernberg, 1967) are usually better candidates for insight-oriented therapy than are paranoid or schizoid patients (Stone, 1981). Yet one should not be misled into thinking that all borderline patients with this personality configuration have good outcomes. Some, like Mrs. N., who are extremely dependent and not highly motivated for change will prove resistive to therapy.

My contribution to the negative outcome—in particular, to the premature breaking off of treatment—consisted (confining myself perforce to elements of which I am consciously in touch) of impatience and non-neutrality. In most situations of marital discord, a therapist can usually discover, even amidst howling protestations about the undiluted awfulness of the spouse, some cherished attribute, some hidden, and often enough, paradoxical, source of gratification that continues to bind one to the other. Where a borderline person is involved, these sources may be paradoxical indeed, as when a passive man complained bitterly about his shrewish wife—who nonetheless reminded him, at a less conscious level, of his ambivalently loved, hypercritical mother. A borderline woman, much given to jealousy, complaining about her husband's infidelity, but secretly enjoying (1) the resemblance between his escapades and those of her still ardently loved father and (2) the "justification" her husband's activity lent to her own (strong but unacknowledged) need to be unfaithful provides another example. With Mrs. N., I was unable to find any such sources of gratification, hidden, paradoxical, or otherwise, such as might preserve their fragile alliance, apart from the manner in which the husband's disinclination for sex and children dovetailed with hers. His personality and interaction with her answered, in other words, to the "sick" aspects of her nature. *Any* growth she might have achieved over the course of treatment would, or so it seemed to me, have caused their paths to diverge rather than come together. Since it is more complicated to be a parent than to be a lover, her sexual inhibitions might have become resolved ahead of her conflict about the demands of motherhood. But an improvement of this kind, in her, would have left her feeling more estranged than ever, unless (as seemed unlikely) her husband made corresponding changes in synchrony with her evolution.

I noticed myself becoming quite pessimistic, after two months of our work, about the prospect of her marriage improving substantially, and also about the prospect of her changing in any significant way. Since I tend to err on the side of perseverance in what others might conclude were hopeless cases, this reaction was uncharacteristic and puzzling. Although I did not let on how I felt, she must have sensed my appraisal of her situation and my discouragement. She was not highly motivated and showed little psychological-mindedness. Work that cannot produce change becomes drudgery. It was a relief to us both when she discontinued. Whereas the patients of the preceding vignettes would have proven difficult, I believe, for any therapist, Mrs. N. probably would have done better with someone less disposed to become impatient with her than I— someone perhaps with more modest expectations who would have been content to go at her pace. I cannot say what level of maturation she might have achieved in relation to such a therapist, because she did not seek one out. Instead she has remained, as I learned recently from the referring colleague, stalemated in the unfulfilling marriage. She still tries to control her husband through alternating poutiness and tantrums and is symptomatically neither better nor worse.

Discussion

The current definitions of borderline have much in common, but the technical language of each system tends to obscure certain characteristic features, for which the language of everyday life often provides a more meaningful vocabulary. Borderlines are described as impulsive, as poor in anxiety-tolerance or in sublimatory channeling (Kernberg, 1967), as manipulatively self-injurious (Gunderson & Singer, 1975), or unstable and intolerant of being alone (*DSM-III*). More simply put they are *chaotic*. Exceptions are to be found among the pure schizotypals, who live as marginal loners, not buffeted by strong emotions of either valence, but strangers to the pleasures most people are able to enjoy.

But to be chaotic is to be predisposed to a negative outcome in psychotherapy. This is so for many reasons. For its greatest efficacy, psychotherapy depends on certain ground rules: regularity of appointments, the capacity to defer gratification of many impulses, empathy, self-discipline (without which the pursuit of work, study, or hobbies is impossible), appropriate concern about one's condition and the ability to form a "therapeutic alliance," for which *trust* is the cornerstone. An ability to be emotional (subjective) and rational (objective) at the same time is also important. Borderline patients lack many or all of just these attributes. Commonly they are, for example, either so engulfed in a strong feeling as not to be able to think clearly about it, or so detached as think very clearly, but to no therapeutic purpose. In their oscillation between total subjectivity and total detachment (that caricatures objectivity), they spend precious few moments in the gray zone of feelingful reason where, alone, therapeutic progress can take place. Borderline patients also oscillate, as a rule, between negative and positive affects toward the important people in their lives (therapists included). They have inordinate difficulty, when enveloped in one feeling-state, (*viz.*, hatred, envy), in simultaneously recalling opposite-tinged feelings (love, admiration) harbored toward the same individual—even the day before, or (if that individual is the therapist) earlier in the same session. It is crucial to their treatment that borderline patients with this kind of "splitting" learn to unite these disparate elements of their personality—elements they have for so long been at pains to compartmentalize. Merely to recognize the need for such integration does not guarantee that the therapist will be able to effect it. Sometimes the forces in the patient that oppose integration will be too powerful; the therapist's skill and patience may go for naught. Socially unacceptable feelings are more difficult to contain for borderlines, who are so prone to acting out impulses of whatever kind; worse still, the unacceptable feelings are often experienced more intensely in them than in neurotics. As luck would have it, the borderline patient has little control over these feelings; the neurotic, who *needs* less control (over his comparatively attenuated feelings) has more self-control at his disposal. In the struggle against impulsivity some borderline patients will exhibit the mechanisms of *disavowal*, or of outright *denial*—either of which renders a crucial area of their psychic life temporarily (at times, permanently) off-limits to therapeutic exploration. A prim, middle-aged lawyer I once worked with, for example, was, within the context of a deteriorating marriage, in the grips of incestuous feelings toward his eight-year-old daughter. This was abundantly clear from his dreams. Once, I recall, he dreamed of seeing her lying on her back, in a suggestive pose, on the living room sofa, followed moments later by a general conflagration in which the whole house, and himself as well, were consumed by the flames. But interpretation of the material was too threatening. The subtlest suggestion on my part that he might have been preoccupied with such a conflict precipitated a state of panic—and a bout of alcoholism—which was brought under control only when a less disturbing reconstruction of this material was offered, a few days later, that allowed him to save face.

Urgency of feeling coupled with poor impulse control leads many borderline patients to act out the emotions experienced within the transference. Their need to "actualize" the transference—by converting the therapist into parent, friend, lover, enemy, and so on, may elicit countertransference feelings, and counterproductive behavior, from their therapists. Therapeutic neutrality is in general much harder to preserve vis-à-vis borderline patients than with their neurotic-level counterparts. Treatment is apt to be less "scientific," less methodical, than with neurotic patients. The borderline patient, whose deficits seem to harken back to a preverbal stage of development, are more convinced by action than by the spoken word. The therapist is being tested constantly; his humanity, his personal foibles constantly exposed. There are thus more opportunities for a negative outcome to result from countertransference difficulties than is true for work with neurotic patients. The papers of Searles (1979) and Giovacchini (1980) are particularly instructive in this regard.

Therapists should keep in mind that adults—and this would be more strikingly noticeable with borderlines than with neurotics—who have been (or have felt) deprived of love and attention during certain "critical periods" of childhood, when one is customarily showered with such affection, crave this affection with a hunger that is insatiable. What was lacking cannot be made up for in any direct way by the therapist. Instead, the therapist can only pursue the unenviable task of interesting the borderline patient in the paradoxical way he goes about alienating others, in his quest for the elusive cornucopia, through excessive demands, or through the rage and resentment toward all those who have failed, as fail they must, in meeting these demands. We must convert someone who wanted to get "better" by getting more to someone who gets better (more mature) through requiring less. No wonder we only succeed occasionally.

Summary

Of the 51 borderline patients I have worked with in private practice, the outcome of treatment could be considered negative in the 17 who showed no improvement or in the 4 who got worse. The figures do not inspire optimism. Instances of dramatic improvement were also noted, but these are not the subject matter of this chapter. In the absence of comparable data from other clinicians who do intensive psychotherapy with borderlines, I cannot say whether my experience departs to this side or that from average. It would be helpful if others would share their experience, in published material such as this, so that clinicians in the future have a better way to evaluate their own work. Detailed descriptions of one's patient sample would be in order, in any such exercise, because some therapists see more borderlines with antisocial or other low-prognosis tendencies, while others restrict their practice to those with better social assets, to name only two possible patient populations.

We have alluded, in the preceding pages, to a number of patient factors and therapist factors that may contribute to a negative outcome in analytically oriented therapy of a borderline patient. Countertransference factors in therapists include those specific to the individual patient (who may remind the therapist of an important figure from his own early experience) as well as nonspecific feeling states (of boredom, anger, erotic interest, disdain) evoked by the often exaggerated and inappropriate behavior of certain borderline patients (especially those given to projective identification and to the personalization of the treatment atmosphere).

The list of patient factors contributing to negative outcomes is long and may be thought of as variables, capable of being subsumed under several broad headings, each of which may be rated in accordance with its absence, presence, and intensity in any given borderline patient. Those at "high risk" for a poor outcome would perhaps be identified earlier in the course of treatment, through the application of this method.

The following list is not complete, but includes many of the significant variables. I have made no pretense of trying to rank their relative importance, which may not be the same for one case as for another.

1. Anhedonia
2. Bizarreness of symptoms (*viz.*, bulimia/vomiting; carving letters in one's skin; trichotillomania)
3. Lack of motivation; lack of concern about one's condition; lack of seriousness about treatment
4. Lack of humor; lack of perspective and distance concerning one's shortcomings

5. Lack of psychological-mindedness; tendency to externalize
6. Urgency of impulses; need for actualization of the transference; acting-out tendency; sensation-seeking (inordinate need for strong and changing stimuli)
7. Lack of empathy; lack of friendliness
8. Unpopularity of dominant feeling states (preoccupation with murder, vengeance, incest, abandonment of one's children)
9. Barrenness or precariousness of current life
10. Degree of deprivation or of brutalization, during early life
11. "Negative" (abrasive, obnoxious) personality type; predominant personality type is associated with poor prognosis (paranoid, explosive, antisocial, schizoid)
12. Predilection for illicit drugs or abuse of alcohol
13. Grandiosity

Psychotherapy with borderline patients is comparable in some respects to a tightrope act. When all goes well, the result is deceptively unspectacular, because, to the untrained observer, the walk seemed easy, almost casual; one forgets the hazard that attended each step of the way. When all does not go well, the result is often quite dramatic: one is faced not with mild and inconspicuous failure but with catastrophe. It therefore behooves the therapist, during the opening phases of such an enterprise, to assess the patient variables I have outlined as painstakingly as he can, and also to look candidly into himself, the better to evaluate what danger signals he may be able to spot from the countertransference side. In this way he may be able with greater accuracy to limit the choice of borderline patients with whom he will do intensive psychotherapy to those providing the greatest likelihood of a successful, or at least of a nonharmful, outcome and the least likelihood of a catastrophic outcome, whether in the form of acute psychosis, suicide, panic, or a painful or premature disruption of treatment.

8

Negative Outcome
in Anorexia Nervosa

Robert Lynn Horne

EDITOR'S NOTE: *Aside from data supporting a significant mortality rate both with no treatment and with psychoanalysis, Horne's analysis relies primarily upon small group and individual case reports showing negative outcome. These data, while suggestive of the high risk potential of the anorexic population, do not permit a more exhaustive analysis of the factors involved. Unfortunately, they are all that exist at this time. Nevertheless, the potential risk among anorexics should be evident from the fact that, aside from certain psychosomatic disorders and organic brain syndromes, this is the only psychiatric disorder which, in and of itself, carries a significant mortality rate.*

Controversies abound regarding the syndrome of anorexia nervosa: Diagnostic criteria, etiology, the value of differing treatment modalities, and the measurement of outcome have all been a focus of extensive debate among therapists who deal with the illness on a daily basis. All agree on only one point: Anorexia is a life-threatening illness whose natural history includes a mortality of 15 to 20 percent (Dally & Sargent, 1960; Halmi, Brodland, & Rigas, 1975; Kay & Leigh, 1954; Theander, 1970).

Anorexia nervosa, as defined by the *Diagnostic and Statistical Manual* (Third Edition) of the American Psychiatric Association, is an eating disorder which occurs primarily in females whose essential features are an intense fear of becoming obese, which does not diminish as weight

The author wishes to acknowledge the valuable contributions of Erica Bergstrom, Frederick J. Evans, Helen Pettinati, Joanne Rosenberg, and Julie Staats during the preparation of this chapter.

loss progresses; a disturbance of body image, for example, claiming to "feel fat" even when emaciated; significant weight loss (at least 25%); refusal to maintain a minimum normal body weight; and no known physical illness that would account for the weight loss. The Research Diagnostic Criteria of Feighner et al. (1972) also require an age of onset prior to 25, and two of the following six symptoms: amenorrhea, lanugo (soft downy hair), bradycardia (heart rate less than 60), periods of overactivity, episodes of bulimia, and vomiting (usually self-induced).

Criteria for negative outcome and the therapy of anorexia nervosa include death, whether by malnutrition, infection, or suicide; failure to maintain a body weight within a normal range; persistence of neuroendocrine abnormalities, most commonly indexed by amenorrhea; poor vocational, social, family, or sexual adjustment; and persistent preoccupation with food or unusual eating behaviors.

This chapter reviews the effects upon psychotherapy outcome of the stages of the natural course of the illness, different types of psychotherapeutic treatments, and patient characteristics. It will focus upon negative outcome as a result of these variables and possible alterations in treatment to prevent or minimize the negative effects of psychotherapy on patients with anorexia nervosa.

Natural Course

The natural course of anorexia nervosa can be divided into three stages (modified from Casper & Davis, 1977). The first or prodromal stage of the illness occurs prior to any weight loss and is usually associated with a traumatic or stressful external event. Such precipitating factors produce loss of self-esteem and increased self-consciousness about physical appearance. Amenorrhea begins in about one-third of the patients.

The second stage begins with the initial loss of weight and usually continues until over 25 percent of body weight has been lost. Patients take great pride in successfully reducing their food intake and seeing steady weight loss and frequent weighings. Initially overweight patients start to receive compliments about their weight loss; even those who are not overweight are reinforced by peers who notice the change in eating behavior and body shape. The patients begin to feel unique or special because they have so much willpower and can lose weight so effectively. They are in control, at least of *this* aspect of their lives. They develop an ability to suppress awareness of hunger, and most report that they feel full and bloated after eating minimal amounts of food. Rituals about food preparation and eating develop or intensify. At some point during this stage patients notice that they have a fear of becoming fat, and this steadily increases as weight decreases. Patients do not accurately perceive the size of their own bodies—they are just a little overweight and need to lose about five pounds regardless of how much weight they have lost. This may be due to right parietal lobe brain dysfunction. Sleep loss develops, restlessness and hyperactivity increase, and strenuous exercise is begun in a ritualistic fashion.

Massive denial exists during this second stage. "I'm not sick—there is absolutely nothing wrong with me and I don't need to see a doctor" is the characteristic attitude. Thus if parents or others insist that the anorexic get professional assistance for the problem, a family battle typically ensues. If psychotherapy begins at this point the likelihood of negative outcome is very high because the patient is not motivated to change.

In the third stage of anorexia nervosa the physiological concomitants of starvation begin to intrude on the denial. Symptoms such as weakness due to muscle atrophy or electrolyte imbalances, hypothermia and marked cold intolerance, normal hair falling out and soft downy hair emerging, and amenorrhea finally convince patients that something is wrong with their bodies even though they continue to insist that they are not yet thin. Eventually they realize that they no longer have that superb control over their weight and eating behavior. Patients then stop resisting the efforts of loved ones to have them seek professional help: They may even request it. Patients at this stage who are motivated to change have better outcomes in psychotherapy (Crisp, 1980).

Psychoanalytic Therapy

The classic psychoanalytic interpretation of anorexia nervosa is based on the theory that eating behavior and/or food is eroticized (Freud, 1918, 1959; Lehman, 1949). Grote and Meng (1934) were the first to report a patient with anorexia nervosa who was treated with psychoanalysis. They state that fantasies regarding parthenogenesis and the role of menstruation and conception were worked through. The physical and psychological symptoms of anorexia nervosa are reviewed in psychoanalytic theory as manifestations of inner conflict: The refusal to eat is due to fantasies of oral impregnation; the mouth represents conception, the gastrointestinal tract symbolizes the womb (Waller, Kaufman, & Deutsch, 1940); bulimia is conceptualized as a breakthrough of unconscious desires for gratification (Kaufman & Heiman, 1964); amenorrhea is both a symbol of pregnancy (Kaufman & Heiman, 1964) and a denial of femininity (Lorand, 1943).

Although psychoanalysis has been widely recommended for the

treatment of anorexia nervosa, this model has been criticized on the grounds of its theoretical formulations, methodology, and therapeutic efficacy. Many studies are based on the analysis of one to four patients, and there are usually no comparison or control patients. Authors frequently admit that there was no or very little change in their patients as a result of the analysis. Consistent changes would have supported the theoretical formulations. Such influential authors as Waller, Kaufman, and Deutsch (1940) have concluded on the basis of two case studies that no improvement can be hoped for until the patient is given or perhaps accepts insight. Neither of their patients attained this insight.

Follow-up studies of psychoanalytically treated patients (Blinder, Freeman, & Stunkard, 1970; Bruch, 1973; Dally, 1969; Farquharson & Hyland, 1966; Moldofsky & Garfinkel, 1974; Selvini, 1971) have proven such therapy to be singularly ineffective in altering anorexic behavior (Bruch, 1973). The mortality rate for the illness in patients treated by psychoanalysis is not significantly different from the mortality rates of 10 to 20 percent in untreated patients (Bruch, 1973).

Several suggestions have been made about how to alter the negative outcome of pyschoanalytic psychotherapy. In 1967, Thoma advocated psychoanalysis utilized alone. By 1977, he had changed his general attitude about handling patients with anorexia nervosa. He frequently applied nasogastric tube feeding with or without phenothiazine. Thus, he advocated utilizing physical and chemical techniques during the acute phase of the illness to overcome the potentially lethal loss of weight, and either simultaneously or after a weight gain, started psychoanalytic psychotherapy aimed at changing the patient's attitude.

Analysts who have adopted the principles of ego psychology have suggested several modifications of psychoanalytic theory, including shifting the focus from sexual drive disturbances to disorders in the mother–child relationship (Bruch, 1973; Ehrensing & Weitzman, 1970; Gifford, Murawski, & Pilot, 1970; Groen & Feldman-Toledano, 1966; Selvi, 1965; Sours, 1974; Story, 1976). Eissler (1943) was the first to stress the patient's extreme dependence on her mother and the resulting inhibition of the patient's ego development. A complete absence of physical affection in the patient's childhood was a significant factor, and helping the patient to be able to give and receive affection was very useful in the therapy.

Others have suggested that early maternal deprivation created a powerful ambivalence toward the mother, which results in angry rejection both of food as a maternal substitute and of the feminine role. Several clinicians have thus altered traditional psychoanalytic treatment to provide a warm and nurturant relationship to help patients deal with their vast anaclitic needs (Groen & Feldman-Toledano, 1966; Margolis & Jernberg, 1960; Meuyer & Weinroth, 1957). Mintz (1980) views the anorexia syndrome as a compromise in which the patient can defy the mother (and father) through illness and not receive the rejection that more flagrant rebellion would cause. He suggests that if this is ignored, psychoanalysis will produce no improvement.

Bruch (1973, 1977), Selvi (1965), Wilson (1980), and others have described a mother–child relationship in which the individual needs of the child are subverted to the mother's needs and expectations. Although as children they are frequently described by the family as perfect, as adolescents they suffer a "paralyzing underlying sense of ineffectiveness" (Bruch, 1978, p. X) in coping with life's problems, and engage in a "desperate struggle for a self-respecting identity" (Bruch, 1975, p.1). Both Bruch (1978) and Selvi (1965) advocate modifying traditional psychoanalysis to an investigative, noninterpretive approach which is directed toward correcting the disturbances in the body image and in interpersonal relationships.

Bruch states that her therapeutic interventions are successful, but recently she extensively consults on only 20 percent of the patients referred to her and accepts only one-third of these for extensive psychotherapy (1978). She has provided information on the long-term outcome of 40 highly selected cases (1973), but it is difficult to assess the contribution of her psychotherapy because the mode and length of treatment in each case are not sufficiently described.

Sterling (1970, 1978) has also emphasized the importance of the mother–child relationship in the origin, maintenance, and resolution of these difficulties. She suggested that the mother needed therapy in addition to the child if the outcome of the analysis was to be successful. The mother had to recognize and change her ambivalent and often rejecting attitudes toward the child.

Based on psychoanalytic research with the families of 30 anorexia nervosa patients, Wilson (1980) suggested changes in classic analysis to avoid unresponsiveness to therapy. First, after an evaluation of the family by the analyst who will see the adolescent, the parents are referred for psychotherapy with colleagues "to change their unhealthy relationship to their child." He believes that a therapist who tries to do both individual and family therapy will be mistrusted by the child—the therapist will be too closely identified with the judging parents. Also, he suggests that the couch not be used until later in therapy.

In summary, there is increasing agreement that there will be a negative outcome if traditional psychoanalysis is utilized alone for the treatment of anorexia nervosa. Recommended modifications in technique to alter outcome have included (1) utilizing behavioral techniques and pharmacology to obtain a weight gain prior to or concurrently with psychoanalysis; (2) shifting the focus of psychoanalysis from sexual drive disturbances to disorders in the mother–child relationship; (3) providing a warm nurturant relationship; (4) minimizing or eliminating interpretations, and focusing on the correction of disturbances in body image and interpersonal relationships; (5) having one or both parents enter therapy with another therapist.

Behavior Therapy

One of the most controversial aspects of the treatment of anorexia nervosa concerns the results of treatment by behavior therapy techniques. Most proponents utilize this approach during the initial phase of hospitalization to produce weight gain in severely ill, cachextic patients. Even the staunchest critics of behavioral techniques acknowledge its success in achieving this goal. In evaluating and comparing the literature on the outcome of behavior therapy, the following differences must be considered: Many different types of behavioral techniques have been utilized, including systematic desensitization, reciprocal inhibition, and operant techniques; patient sample sizes have varied from 1 to 30; length of follow-up has varied from none to 13 years.

Bachrach et al. (1965) were the first to report the use of operant conditioning with positive reinforcement to achieve improved eating behavior. Their patient was a 37-year-old woman who had lost 71 pounds from 118 to 47 by the time of admission. The treatment plan utilized included giving the patient a hospital room devoid of television, books, and magazines and depriving her of visits from relatives and the nursing and medical staff. The therapists sat with her at every meal and conversed only when she ate. Later, other forms of attention including visits from relatives and walks were made contingent on satisfactory eating behavior. As an unwanted side effect of the reinforcement schedule, the patient began to vomit when her weight reached 63 pounds. Reinforcement was then made contingent on weight gain rather than eating behavior and there was a resumption of weight gain, until the patient was discharged. After 13 years, this patient was leading a useful and satisfying life without bulimia.

Bhanji and Thompson (1974) carefully minimized contact of patients with hospital staff and offered no psychotherapy other than a behavioral program. When seven patients were followed up at a mean of 32 months after discharge, only one had a good overall adjustment.

They concluded that such behavioral techniques are probably best used simply as a means of rapid weight restoration at times of nutritional crisis.

One of the most vocal critics of behavioral techniques has been Bruch (1974). She has labeled behavior modification a dangerous method and brutal coercion. She reported three cases as examples of the harmful effects of behavior therapy.

A 19-year-old patient's weight dropped from 118 to 78 pounds in three years prior to hospitalization. A behavioral therapy produced a weight gain of 18 pounds in two months, but the patient became increasingly depressed and escaped from the hospital. She lost 26 pounds in the next year. Wolpe (1975) has suggested that perhaps a better behavioral approach to this patient would have been a combination of assertive training and systematic desensitization.

A second patient maintained her weight at 96 pounds from age 12 to 15 despite growing four inches taller. Hyperactivity, sleep disturbance, and a morbid fear of gaining weight then led to a loss of 27 pounds in six months. With a behavior modification program in a hospital, she regained 25 pounds in two months. Upon discharge she began binge eating followed by self-induced vomiting and lost six pounds within two weeks. She was readmitted to another hospital and treated with a behavioral program which included tube feedings. She gained another 16 pounds to 104 within three months but became seriously depressed and had suicidal thoughts. After discharge, she continued to binge and vomit and within a year her weight had dropped to 72 pounds. At this time the *patient* asked her parents to get professional help for her, instead of her parents taking her for help. Thus, the patient had passed from stage 2 to stage 3 of her illness (*vide supra,*) and was ready to accept treatment. Bruch told the patient that no meaningful therapeutic work could be done during a state of starvation and she would not work with her until she had regained at least ten pounds. The patient did so and maintained this weight. She was unusually responsive during the psychotherapy, changed her attitude and appearance, and planned to attend college. Nevertheless, the patient's weight remained 30 percent below her ideal body weight, leaving some question about the success of Bruch's treatment.

Bruch's third case was actually an example of negative outcome of all therapy tried over a seven year period, including psychoanalytic, behavioral, and family therapy. At age 13, with a weight of 94 pounds, the girl decided to restrict her food intake. Within a year she lost 22 pounds and was admitted to a hospital for psychoanalytic care. In one year she gained eight pounds and was discharged. In ten months she again lost 12 pounds and was readmitted to a hospital. Over the course of six months she lost another eight pounds to 60 before a behavioral program was instituted. It successfully produced a gain of 30 pounds in five months but she felt guilty about eating so much food. After discharge, family therapy replaced individual therapy. The patient reacted to this with a serious suicide attempt that required lengthy medical and surgical hospitalization. After discharge she returned to live with her parents, who allowed her to sleep all day and spend her nights eating and vomiting. No data were presented about this girl's progress after she began treatment with Bruch. Behavior therapy certainly did not produce a complete remission in this patient's illness, but in 3½ years after discharge the patient never lost 17 of the 30 pounds which she gained in the behavioral program.

Opponents of behavior therapy assert that the technique's greatest strength—its demonstrated superiority in producing weight gain—is also its greatest weakness. Potential negative outcomes include increased feelings of helplessness or hopelessness, despair of achieving autonomy, and the appearance of new symptoms including binge eating, vomiting, and severe depression.

In designing a behavioral program for a patient, the risk of increased feelings of helplessness can perhaps be avoided by allowing the patient to select her own food instead of the treatment team selecting the type and amount of food she must consume. The emergence of self-induced vomiting as a weight-losing device may be discouraged by rewarding weight gain instead of food eaten. Binge eating may be encouraged by any behavioral contract that rewards a patient for a daily weight gain of half a pound or more. A patient soon learns to effectively lose weight by gaining half a pound on one day to obtain privileges so that she can increase her activity level, severely restrict her food intake, and lose three-quarters of a pound or more the following day. A pattern of "one step forward and two steps back" can be discouraged by requiring a gain of half a pound or more over the *highest previously recorded weight* in order to obtain privileges.

Another factor in the reinforcement schedule can encourage binge eating. Agras and Werne (1977) have compared different schedules of positive reinforcement for weight gain. In one program privileges were given at 5-day intervals to allow for daily physiological variations in weight to occur without penalizing the patient unjustly (Halmi, Powers, & Cunningham, 1975). A second program reinforced patients for weight gain each day. At the end of 30 days, the overall weight gain for two groups of seven patients matched for age of onset was very similar (6.94 and 6.96 kg, respectively). However, the number of days of weight gain was significantly different and there was significantly less variation in weight gain for the daily group. The authors concluded that the more variable 5-day reinforcement interval is more like the eating behavior of many anorexics before treatment, namely restricted intake interrupted by episodes of bingeing. The more steady weight gain encouraged by the daily schedule may then be a better management technique, likely to encourage more normal eating habits. Indeed, a participant in a program which had a 7-day reinforcement schedule reported, "I had to gain two pounds by Monday morning, so I ate about 500 calories a day from Monday through Saturday, and then pigged out on Sunday. I usually made it."

In summary, behavioral techniques including operant conditioning with positive reinforcement are extremely effective in producing weight gain in patients with anorexia nervosa. However, weight gain is *not* synonymous with recovery. The risk of weight loss after discharge can be minimized by teaching the patient to maintain weight within a narrow range. The risk of producing bulimia and vomiting can be minimized by reinforcing daily weight gain instead of food consumption. Negative outcomes can be minimized by concurrent psychotherapy to assist a patient in developing a sense of inner control, improved self-esteem, increased self-confidence, a sense of independence, and a reduction in the fear of being fat.

Family Therapy

Because of the characteristically young age of onset of anorexia nervosa, it is perhaps not surprising that the majority of these patients are living at home with their parents when they present for treatment. Most clinicians agree that family interactions are important in the etiology and maintenance of anorexia. As early as 1888 Sir William Gull stated that it was essential for therapeutic success to separate a patient from her family. Venables (1930) stated that all patients should be hospitalized and forbidden to see their parents during the entire course of treatment. All nine of his patients were doing well at the time of follow-up and had not had any relapses.

Bruch (1973, 1978), Crisp, Harding, and McGuinness (1974), Minuchin, Rosman, and Baker (1978) and Wilson (1980) have all reported studies of the families of large series of anorexic patients. All have suggested that therapy *involving* the families can be useful, but they differ in their recommendations.

Minuchin and his colleagues have been the most ardent supporters of family therapy, without concurrent individual therapy, as the treatment of choice for anorexia nervosa. Indeed, they recently refused to see a single 35-year-old woman who was living in her own apartment unless her mother and married sister came to each therapy session.

Minuchin et al. (1978) conceptualize anorexia nervosa as an interpersonal rather than an individual problem and maintain that successful treatment must involve a restructuring of the dysfunctional family system as a whole. The family's perception of reality must be changed. The parents must view their child as a rebellious adolescent whose refusal to eat is an act of disobedience, not of illness. The refusal to eat is a voluntary act, oriented toward defeating the parents, rather than being an involuntary symptom. The anorexic patient is thus powerful, and a winner in her battle—not an incompetent, powerless, ineffective invalid, as she has frequently described herself. By creating "an expanded reality" the therapist can convey an expectation of change through alternative familial interactions.

Minuchin, Rosman, and Baker (1978) postulate that five types of family transactions are directly related to the appearance and maintenance of the anorexic symptom. Challenging and changing these patterns are essential for maintaining the weight gains produced by a short-term treatment program which includes outpatient contingency contracting or an inpatient behavioral management progam. The therapist must (1) challenge enmeshment which curtails autonomy, accommodation, and growth, without challenging the value of family togetherness; (2) challenge overprotection while supporting healthy coping behavior; (3) challenge conflict avoidance (which is sometimes confused with harmony) by creating boundaries that help the disagreeing family members to discuss and resolve the conflict; (4) challenge the rigidity of the anorexic family, which should be like the ebb and flow of water, and not that of stone, by increasing the intensity of his interventions until change occurs; and (5) challenge the involvement of the symptomatic child in detouring conflict between other family members, especially the parents.

They propose a "family therapy lunch session" which lasts two or three hours as an initial diagnostic and therapeutic technique. The therapist initially assumes therapeutic leadership, develops family trust, supports areas of competence of family members, and prepares the therapeutic system for the stress of the lunch. The emotionally charged mealtime situation provides the opportunity to further explore the dynamics of family interaction and to carry out interventions by deemphasizing eating or overfocusing on eating.

Rosman, Minuchin, Baker, and Liebman (1977) presented follow-up data on 53 patients who had been ill for a median of six months prior to treatment with this family therapy approach for a median duration of six months. The median age of patients was 14. They found

86% of the cases were recovered from both the medical and the psychosocial components of the illness after a median one-year follow-up (three months to four years).

Crisp, Harding, and McGuinness (1974) found that family members did not have a high degree of psychopathology at the time of hospitalization of the anorexic child. However, the level of parental neurosis increased significantly after the patient's recovery. They concluded that the family psychopathology and morbidity is displaced onto the anorexic patient until the designated patient regains normal weight. Other family members are then forced to deal with their own conflicts directly.

Crisp now tries to prevent this subsequent increase in parental psychopathology by meeting the parents before seeing the child. During the history taking he helps the parents to see themselves as being partially responsible for the healing process but not to blame for their child's illness. He encourages parents to elaborate on their own and their spouses' strengths and weaknesses and to honestly evaluate their marital relationship. Then, during the hospitalization, after the therapist has established a good rapport with the anorexic, family therapy begins with the parents and the patient. Occasionally other sisters and brothers are allowed to attend. The goals of the sessions are to allow a wider sharing of feelings and of experiences (particularly between mother and daughter) and to elucidate and change habitual pathological transactions within the family.

Wilson (1980) and Dally, Gomez, and Isaacs (1979) disagree with both Minuchin's and Crisp's approaches for dealing with previously unresponsive patients. They advocate that the parents be seen for therapy, without the anorexic being present, by a therapist not directly involved with the treatment of the child.

Bruch (1978) disagrees with them and believes that the family should be seen by the same doctor who is treating the patient. She states that it is important to work with the family of all anorexics, and points out that families characteristically deny that there are any problems in the family other than the anorexia. Also, there is a tendency for each family member to speak, not for himself or herself, but in the name of another member while modifying, correcting, or invalidating what the other person has said. In evaluating the reports of Minuchin's group, she says "this approach is successful in fairly young patients who are relatively healthy emotionally. In those with severe deficiencies in personality development, family therapy is an important and necessary adjunct—but the chief work needs to be done through individual psychotherapy."

One of the detailed case reports of Minuchin et al. (1978) seems to support Bruch's conclusions. After failing to respond to six months of individual psychotherapy and a brief hospitalization, 15-year-old Debra and her family entered family therapy for six months. However, in some of the sessions there was a need to see the parents alone for sex therapy and sometimes Debra was seen individually. At 3½ year follow-up, Debra's response to family therapy had been only "fair." She had a borderline body weight, problems with eating and occasional vomiting, and an unsatisfactory relationship with her peers. Later, at age 20, Debra made a suicidal gesture by swallowing an overdose of tranquilizers because of a frustrated love affair. After a one-week hospitalization, she entered individual psychotherapy for four months. The pattern of episodic binge eating which she developed in college in response to anxiety from her relationship with boys subsided during this last individual therapy.

In summary, family therapy is advocated to minimize negative outcomes in the treatment of anorexia nervosa. This is especially true if the patient is young or will be returning to the same family environment after the initial treatment. Various and sometimes conflicting modifications of family therapy have been suggested. These include utilizing a two or three hour "family therapy lunch session" as a diagnostic and initial therapeutic technique; adding individual inpatient or family outpatient behavioral contracts; having different therapists for the parental couple's therapy and the anorectic's individual therapy; having the same therapist see first the parents, second the child, and then the entire family; and having family therapy without any individual sessions. If family therapy is utilized as the sole treatment, there will sometimes be negative outcomes including treatment failures. When this occurs, individual psychotherapy of some type should be instituted.

Sexual Therapy

Anecdotal reports have claimed that anorexia nervosa patients are psychosexually immature and that their illness results from a failure to cope with problems of puberty or with guilt feelings about sexual feelings, desires, or behavior. In his classic description of "anorexia hysterique," Lasegue (1873) cited difficulties in heterosexual relationships as a precipitant of the illness. Freud (1902) wrote that "the nutritional neurosis parallel to melancholia is anorexia. The well known anorexia nervosa of girls seems to me a melancholia occurring when sexuality is undeveloped . . . Loss of appetite in sexual terms [is] loss of libido." Janet (1929) believed anorexia nervosa was due to sexual frustrations. Dally and Sargant (1966) considered the illness a consequence of a failure to cope with the problems of puberty, particularly conflicts over sexual feelings and behavior. Crisp (1967) stated that anorexia nervosa patients were sexually immature and that their parents conveyed an attitude that sexuality is bad. Thus, the illness is seen as a means of coping with the conflict between instilled values and the biological and social demands of puberty. He also believes that the loss of libido which accompanies the weight loss serves to reinforce the condition by reducing the anxiety associated with adult sexual feelings. Palazolli (1971) maintained that anorexia nervosa arises when a girl is unable to cope with the change of her childish body into that of a woman. Bruch (1974) describes her patients as resistant to learning about sexuality. Thus, many clinicians agree on the importance of sexuality in the development and maintenance of anorexia nervosa, but there have been few systematic investigations of the psychosexual histories of large series of anorexics and even fewer descriptions of specific treatment programs which deal directly with the sexual problems.

In a report of 30 cases, Rowland (1970) found that 57 percent of these patients believed that the onset of puberty or traumatic sexual events were directly related precipitating events for anorexia nervosa. Puberty seemed to be a precipitating factor in 40 percent, and first significant relationship with a boyfriend was a precipitating factor in 37 percent of Crisp's (1980) 102 cases. He also reported that 27 percent showed a definite avoidance of heterosexual contact even before illness onset.

Dally et al. (1979) have reported on the sexuality of 400 patients with anorexia nervosa seen over a 20-year period. They state that the libido of most patients before they develop anorexia nervosa is probably within normal limits. Once it is established, however, sexual feelings and interest diminish and usually disappear altogether. Only 15 percent of their patients age 15 or over have reported masturbating before developing anorexia nervosa and most of these stopped before they began to diet. Of those 19 or older, 50 percent had sexual intercourse before developing the illness. First sexual intercourse or other sexual difficulties were closely linked to refusal to eat in 13 percent of their patients ages 15 to 18 and in over 50 percent of those 19 or more.

Beumont, Abraham, and Simson (1981) report that 65 percent of their 31 female anorexia nervosa patients had a poor knowledge of sexual matters and 19 percent deliberately avoided reading sexual material. Sexual problems were reported by 42 percent as a major precipitant of their illness. Anxiety and guilt feelings about sexual activity, insistence by boyfriends that they have sexual intercourse, and parental disapproval of a boyfriend with whom they were having regular sexual contact were the most common problems cited by the patients.

An additional 16 percent of the patients said ongoing sexual problems were factors which maintained their anorexic behavior. Only 27 per-c•nt of their patients had a positive attitude toward menstruation. Others described it as dirty, messy, or a nuisance. There were signifi-cant differences among "dieters" and "vomiters or purgers" on several variables: A higher proportion of the vomiters or purgers had experi-enced sexual intercourse (88% vs. 33%), engaged in oral-genital sex (25% vs. 12%), and had more than one sexual partner (68% vs. 6%). Unfortunately, no data from a matched control group of young Aus-tralian women were presented.

Guile, Horne, and Dunston (1978) have reported the case of Kay, a 19-year-old girl, who had been unresponsive to family therapy, to pharmacotherapy with Thorazine 200 mg per day, to a behavior ther-apy program with bed rest and weekly contingencies, and to individual psychotherapy. In therapy sessions Kay talked of her ignorance about sex and her feelings of guilt about engaging in some sex play with her first boyfriend just before she began to lose weight. Hypothesizing that gaining control over her sexuality might aid Kay in her struggle to become an adult and enhance her self-esteem, they developed a pro-gram of sexual education and behavior modification based on Masters and Johnson's (1970) treatment of orgasmic dysfunction. Desensitiza-tion was done *in vivo*. Initially, Kay was desensitized to body touching, viewing her genitals, and finally masturbating using a vibrator. She received daily instructions and education from an experienced female psychiatric nurse and practiced twice daily. When Kay experienced some anxiety this was discussed and more practice sessions were held before proceeding further. She received considerable positive reinforce-ment in the form of praise as she completed each part of the program. She began to gain weight at a rate of over three pounds a week and within two weeks had experienced her first orgasm. She gained 14 pounds in five weeks before being discharged to outpatient care. At one year follow-up she had normal menstruation, was employed, had a boyfriend, no longer felt she was fat, achieved orgasm regularly, and was planning to leave her parents' home. She had had no periods of dieting, bulimia, or depression.

One possible negative outcome of sexual behavior modification is illustrated by the case of Bea, an 18-year-old girl with anorexia nervosa who was living at home with her parents and working as a secretary. At age 16 her boyfriend began to pressure her to have intercourse with him. She continued to refuse to do so but did agree to oral-genital sex "so that he would maybe leave me alone about the other." After he ejaculated in her mouth she became very nauseated and vomited. She performed fellatio several more times, and after each time she vomited.

Her boyfriend then broke up with her and within a month she decided to lose weight to become more attractive. A month later she decided that she was not losing weight fast enough so she began to vomit after eating supper, her only meal of the day. Soon she was secretly taking large quantities of ice cream, cookies, donuts, and other high caloric food up to her bedroom and rapidly eating it prior to vomiting.

In therapy she stated that she had never had an orgasm and had not masturbated since age 13 "because mother caught me doing it once and told me it was bad." She did not have any objections to masturbation on moral or religious grounds, and was curious about her body and sexual functions "because neither of my parents ever talked to me about these things." She was given a copy of a chapter on female anatomy and sexual physiology to read and was asked to mark sections she did not understand, had questions about, or felt were very important. At the next session Bea was to bring the chapter back to discuss it. The girl's mother arrived for her next appointment, having found the chapter in her daughter's room (in a desk drawer) while "straightening up a bit." She asked why her daughter had been given such material when her problem was vomiting and losing weight—not sex. The daughter had responded to her mother's questions about the material, "my doctor just asked me to read it and he said we'd talk about it." The mother stated that she did not want her daughter to return to therapy until she had talked with him.

Since the mother did not know about her daughter's vomiting after fellatio, the therapist spoke in general terms about the relationship between sexuality and anorexia nervosa with or without bulimia. The mother was not convinced of the necessity of her daughter knowing about sex and sexuality "before she's ready to get married," and announced that she would find another psychiatrist for her daughter.

Such negative outcomes may be avoided by holding a family session prior to initiating a sexual education and/or behavior modification program with all patients who are living with their parents, instead of just those who are below the age of 18. At the Carrier Foundation we try to involve the mother whenever possible by having her read sexual education material with her daughter and to discuss her feelings about the information with the patient. Usually the parents are very cooperative, and mothers are frequently relieved that the treatment team can, without embarrassment, impart to the patients sexual knowledge and attitudes which are compatible with the families' religious and moral beliefs.

In summary, sexual therapy can be a very useful component in the overall psychotherapeutic program for patients with anorexia nervosa. Major goals are to increase knowledge of sexual anatomy and physiology, to decrease guilt feelings about sexual feelings, desires, or past behavior, and perhaps to treat orgasmic dysfunction. The specific goals for each patient can be formulated only after considering the patient's age, her and her family's religious and moral beliefs, and the patient's prior fears and experiences.

Hypnosis

Charcot was probably the first to treat an anorexia nervosa patient with hypnosis. In 1883 Deniau wrote that Charcot had once given a hypnotic command to eat to a girl who was in danger of death by starvation. The girl immediately began to eat and made a full recovery from her illness. Birnie (1936) reported the case of a 16-year-old girl who had lost from 103 to 65 pounds in a 14-month interval. She had also begun to vomit after each meal. He treated her with 15 weekly outpatient hypnotic sessions and produced a weight gain of 27 pounds. In hypnosis she was given suggestions to eat more, improve her appetite, and have regular bowel movements. She was particularly given suggestions to eat those foods which she disliked.

Kroger and Fexler (1976) stated that the most significant changes in their small sample occurred when anorexia nervosa patients received hypnotherapy on an outpatient basis. Their approach was to give posthypnotic suggestions of an increase in appetite and to utilize imagery and fantasy evocation. One of their patients refused to come for therapy sessions regularly and died of malnutrition. A repetition of this negative outcome of hypnotherapy could probably best be prevented by committing such a patient to a psychiatric hospital where medical and/or behavioral interventions could be utilized.

Daves (1961) reported that he had used hypnosis to treat a 12-year-old anorexic girl. It was generally unsuccessful, so he went on to electroconvulsive therapy.

Spiegel and Spiegel (1978) administer the Hypnotic Induction Profile to all of their patients with anorexia nervosa, and then split them into two groups on the basis of their scores. Those with low scores and a "decrement" profile are not treated with hypnotherapy, because the Spiegels' experience indicates that these patients will have negative outcomes. Instead, the Spiegels recommend psychotropic medication and structured milieu therapy. The anorexic patients with medium or high hypnotic ability and an "intact" profile are given hypnotic suggestions that: "1) overeating and undereating are insults to body integrity, in effect they become a poison to the body; 2) you need your body to live; and 3) to the extent that you want to live, you owe your body this respect and protection" (p. 227). They frequently utilize antidepressant medications to facilitate the self-hypnosis exercises.

Crasilneck and Hall (1975) treated 70 cases with hypnosis, and said that over half showed marked improvement. However, it is unclear how many actually had anorexia nervosa. One of the three cases they reported in detail certainly did not. He was a man in his early fifties who had undergone surgery four times in five months for gastric bleeding and was very depressed. He did not have a distorted body image or other symptoms of anorexia nervosa. His eating disorder consisted of vomiting and refusal to eat, which was rapidly reversed by daily hypnotic sessions.

One of their fatal cases entered a deep trance on the first induction and in response to direct suggestion ate virtually all of the food offered in her next two meals. That evening she refused to reenter hypnosis and subsequent attempts at induction were also unsuccessful. She died a few days later with no clear cause of death found on autopsy.

One of the most common negative outcomes of utilizing hypnosis in the treatment of anorexics is a patient's refusal to become involved in the therapeutic modality. Gross (1981) recommends giving patients knowledge that hypnosis could be utilized in their therapeutic program and then waiting for patients to ask for the technique when they want it. He reports that 10 to 15 percent of his patients do subsequently request hypnosis and are aided by it.

The following case, similar to one of Crasilneck and Hall's discussed above, demonstrates how inadequate preparation can undermine the usefulness of hypnotic intervention.

Dee, an attractive 5 foot 7 inch 20-year-old girl, had a five-month history of weight loss from 140 to 97 pounds. She usually consumed less than 200 calories per day but would still use laxatives and self-induced vomiting "because I'm so fat and disgusting." She had very high hypnotic ability (scoring 12 on the 0–12 point Stanford Hypnotic Susceptibility Scale; Weitzenhoffer & Hilgard, 1962) and agreed to use hypnosis to help her eat. Under hypnosis the patient was able to eat a normal meal without anxiety, but posthypnotic suggestions to eat had no effect. After two therapeutic hypnotic sessions, the patient refused to enter hypnosis and also refused to utilize self-hypnosis for anxiety reduction. Behavioral techniques were subsequently employed to produce weight gain of 27 pounds up to 124. After she maintained this weight for three weeks she was discharged to continue outpatient psychotherapy. Five months later Dee revealed that she had become pregnant by her boyfriend and had had a secret abortion just prior to the onset of her illness. She told her psychiatrist, "I just feel so guilty about it—I murdered another human being and now I don't deserve to live. I didn't want anyone, even you, to know about it. I knew if I would even eat under hypnosis I would also tell you everything. I didn't want to risk telling you about the abortion so I just decided not to go into a hypnotic trance anymore."

Perhaps the refusal to enter hypnosis could have been avoided if the preparation for hypnosis had placed more emphasis on the idea that no person will say or do anything under hypnosis that she does not want to. Also, plans for a session can be discussed in advance with the patient and if there are objections to a portion of the plan, it can be modified before an unsuccessful induction attempt is made.

At the Carrier Foundation patients are informed that the hypnotic ability of all admissions to the Eating Disorders Program is routinely assessed by a series of standard hypnotic scales. If they so desire, after this assessment, a therapeutic hypnotic program based on their specific hypnotic abilities can be designed. Patients are carefully prepared for the first hypnotic scale by a comprehensive discussion of what hypnosis is and is not. It is emphasized that no one will enter hypnosis if she does not want to do so and a person in the altered state of consciousness that we call hypnosis will not respond to any hypnotic suggestion that she does not want to carry out. Thus, the person in hypnosis remains "in control" of her body and mind at all times. This discussion usually provides enough reassurance that an accurate measurement of hypnotic capacity can be made. After a discussion of the results of the standard scales, a majority of patients request the addition of this technique to their own individualized treatment plan.

Whether hypnotic ability is low, medium, or high, hypnosis can be utilized to produce relaxation and reduce tension. Patients with good imagery ability can decide, for example, to be on a beautiful warm deserted beach with high waves pounding onto the shore or to go to a shallow cold mountain stream flowing away from a restful waterfall through glistening rocks which produce small rapids. These anorexics with the ability to alter perceptions can see themselves as others see them instead of with the usual measurable 15 to 20 percent distortion they see in the waking state. Those with the highest hypnotic ability are able to utilize exploratory techniques which combine age regression and posthypnotic amnesia to recover traumatic memories of the past without having to deal consciously with these memories after awakening. Ego- and confidence-building suggestions are usually employed in all hypnotic sessions, but posthypnotic suggestions to eat are rarely requested by the patient.

In summary, the use of hypnosis may be a highly effective means of treating patients who have been previously unresponsive to other forms of psychotherapy. One of the most frequent but potentially avoidable negative outcomes of hypnotherapy is the failure to continue to utilize this treatment modality. It is especially important that the patient understand that the locus of control of the hypnotic situation always remains with the person who is in trance. When presented in this manner to the patient, hypnosis can become a powerful technique to increase self-confidence, improve self-esteem, reduce anxiety, and increase one's sense of autonomy.

Psychopharmacology

Pharmacological therapy may be a useful adjunct to psychotherapy in the treatment of anorexia nervosa, but it can also have negative outcomes, be they unresponsiveness or adverse side-effects. Chlorpromazine and other neuroleptics should be avoided in most cases because risks seem to outweigh benefits. Antidepressants show much promise for those anorexics with significant depression, especially if they have been unresponsive to psychotherapy alone. Benzodiazepines, if administered at all for reduction of anxiety, should be limited to short intervals because of the high potential for psychological dependence. Phenytoin may be useful in certain patients to help reduce episodes of bulimia. Many other medications have been suggested to treat anorexia nervosa, but their value is not yet proven.

Patient Variables

Relatively little attention has been given to the influence of patient variables in the outcome of psychotherapy for anorexia nervosa. This seems to be because few clear-cut factors have emerged from the research which has been done, as well as clinicians' fears that a patient who reads that she has one or more poor prognostic signs might become more hopeless. Crisp (1980) prefaces his discussion of factors affecting outcome with a lengthy caveat which includes "No one should despair. I have seen many exceptions in every instance" (p. 153).

Many studies (Crisp, 1980; Frazier, 1965; Halmi, Brodland, & Loney, 1973; Halmi, Brodland, & Rigas, 1975; Morgan & Russell, 1975; Pierloot, Wellens, & Houben, 1975; Rowland, 1970; Starkey & Lee, 1969; Theander, 1970) have found that the earlier the onset of anorexia nervosa following the start of puberty, the better the outcome. Other studies (Browning & Miller, 1968; Dally, 1969) have found no difference in outcome attributable to age of onset. Dally et al. (1979), in his series of 400 patients with long-term follow-up, may provide the answer for this discrepancy. If recovery of a satisfactory stable weight is utilized as a criterion for outcome, patients with an onset of illness between 11 and 14 years have a better outcome after 2 years, but patients in all age-groups continue to improve so that significant differences do not exist at 4- or 10-year follow-up periods.

Chronicity of illness prior to entering treatment has been associated with a tendency for nonresponsiveness to therapy in several studies (Crisp, 1980; Kay & Schapiro, 1965; Morgan & Russell, 1975; Pierloot et al., 1975) but was found to be unrelated to prognosis in another study (Browning & Miller, 1968). This probable factor in negative outcome is best avoided by increasing the awareness of parents, educators, and young people themselves about the seriousness of the illness. Hopefully, the recent upsurge in information about anorexia nervosa on radio and television and in newspapers, news magazines, and teen magazines will help to get young people who develop the illness to seek competent professional help quickly.

The presence of bulimia was associated with poor outcome in therapy in most studies (Crisp, 1980; Pertschuk, 1977; Selvini, 1971) but was of no significance in others (Halmi et al., 1975; Pierloot et al., 1975). Similarly, vomiting and laxative abuse may be indicative of negative outcome; several studies had this finding (Crisp, Harding, & McGuinness, 1974; Halmi et al., 1973; Selvini, 1971; Theander, 1970) while others found that it was not significant (Halmi et al., 1975; Morgan & Russell, 1975; Pierloot et al., 1975).

No other patient variables seem to have even the above level of consistency in predicting negative outcome in psychotherapy.

Summary

Anorexia nervosa is a life-threatening illness whose natural history includes a mortality of 15 to 20 percent. Optimally patients will enter psychotherapy when they are motivated to change their eating behavior instead of only in response to familial pressure. The initial focus of therapy must be weight gain. If a patient's illness is so severe and overpowering that she cannot gain weight, her environment must be changed to provide sufficient incentive. Behavior therapy can be very effective in producing weight gain so that the patient can respond to other psychotherapeutic approaches. If it is utilized alone, negative long-term outcomes are assured.

Nor can traditional psychoanalysis be utilized alone for the treatment of anorexia nervosa. Recommended modifications in technique to produce successful outcome have included providing a warm nurturant relationship, minimizing interpretations, focusing on correcting disturbances in body image and interpersonal relationships, shifting the focus of psychoanalysis from sexual drive disturbances to disorders in the mother–child relationship, utilizing behavioral techniques and pharmacology to obtain a weight gain prior to or concurrent with psychoanalysis, and producing change in the family of anorexics with simultaneous couples or family therapy.

Family therapy is especially useful if the patient is young or will be returning to the same family environment after the initial treatment. Families must be helped to improve communications among members without relying upon food as a language.

Sexual therapy techniques are often useful in helping patients to cope with problems of puberty or guilt about sexual feelings, desires, or past behavior.

Hypnosis can often be utilized effectively to increase self-confidence, improve self-esteem, reduce anxiety, and increase one's sense of autonomy. The amount of hypnotic ability a patient has must determine the specific techniques selected for incorporation into a treatment program. Relaxation, visual imagery, visual, olfactory, or gustatory hallucinations, hypnotically induced dreams, age regression, posthypnotic suggestions, or amnesia are among the hypnotic techniques that have been successfully utilized in the past.

Pharmacotherapy, particularly antidepressants, may be a useful adjunct to psychotherapy in carefully selected patients.

To successfully treat anorexia nervosa and alter the high mortality and morbidity associated with this illness, it is essential to utilize flexibility in designing a therapeutic program. Individual patients may require elements from many of the following: behavioral, psychoanalytic, family, sexual, hypnotic, or pharmacological therapies.

9

Which Obsessionals
Fail to Change?

Margaret Vaughan and Harold R. Beech

Obsessive-compulsive disorders have proved notoriously difficult to treat. Even with the relatively recent advent of behavioral procedures, many patients remain refractory (Beech & Vaughan, 1978). Such a conclusion underlines the need to consider carefully why it is that treatment of obsessive-compulsive disorders may fail. Paradoxically, even though behavioral treatments appear to have produced the greatest success rates, they also provide a useful means for examining failure, since poor results have to be contrasted with good if the variables influencing either are to be identified.

Keeping within a behavioral framework, there appear to be three contributory components to therapy: the therapist, the patient, and the form of treatment employed. Successful outcome seems to depend upon all three factors being favorable, and there is a risk of failure if any one component or any combination of them carries an unfavorable weighting.

There are no obvious *a priori* grounds for giving more weight to one component than to another, yet almost invariably it is treatment that receives research attention. Obviously, such emphasis was essential in early studies as therapeutic effect can hardly be assessed in the absence of a treatment. However, now that a viable range of approaches has been developed, attention should be properly directed to patient and therapist characteristics—and this chapter will be concerned with these variables—as well as to treatment characteristics, drawing material from current research, a small survey of case material, and clinical experience.

When considering failure, it would be useful to distinguish between those patients who merely show no change in response to treatment and those who deteriorate and become worse. Unfortunately the published results of treatment trials rarely allow such a distinction to be made and, in clinical practice, those who actually become worse seem to be too few to permit useful generalizations to be made. Hence, we have not attempted to differentiate between patients in whom no change has been observed and those who deteriorate, but have chosen rather to consider both groups together as "failures." Legitimacy is lent to this rather rough and ready grouping by the common plight of the substantial number of patients on whom no benefit has been conferred. Often behavioral intervention is the last treatment (apart perhaps from psychosurgery) open to these patients as it is often the case that all possible drug and other regimes have been tried extensively without success. The failure to respond to behavioral treatment means that the patient is left suffering from a severe and incapacitating disorder, at best for months before spontaneous remission, at worst for years or perhaps for the remainder of his or her life. The need to investigate why such patients are unresponsive to treatment is at least as pressing as the delineation of the minority who seem to become worse. A review of the evidence concerning both types of failure together may pave the way for more refined inquiry in which the two are kept distinct.

The Therapist

The question of what constitutes a bad or unsuccessful therapist has been ignored totally in the present context. Such neglect perhaps arises from the fact that, in many studies, the therapists involved are either the researchers themselves or their colleagues or students. This may well impose a degree of constraint upon the kinds of comments which might be made concerning the presence or lack of appropriate skills.

Psychologists, both postgraduate and experienced, psychiatrists, and nurses trained in the use of behavioral techniques (Marks et al., 1975) have all been used as the therapists in published research, often without appropriate evaluation of their skill in such matters, when it is self-evident that such considerations are important. A degree of skill, perhaps largely borne of experience, is often a critical factor in gaining the cooperation and active participation of obsessional patients, many of whom will be invited, in the name of treatment, to engage in behaviors which they find frightening or repugnant. We are aware, for example, that the less experienced psychologist may unwittingly become embroiled in a contest of wills with the patient in which the patient must surely always win. In one example that has come to our attention, an otherwise very sensible junior psychologist, in attempting to encourage the patient to terminate a ritual, so far allowed persuasion to develop into an inflexible attitude that an admittedly rather difficult patient "lost confidence" in her. We are surprised, too, when we learn of the extent to which physical restraint has been employed with obsessional patients in some institutions, particularly as it is in our view almost always possible, with an appropriate deployment of clinical skills, to gain the patient's effective collaboration in treatment procedures.

At the other end of the scale we think it worth noting that, in our clinical experience, the skillful therapist has a much greater chance of engaging the motivation of the obsessional patient and, additionally, we have observed that the therapeutic message provided by older psychologists is less inclined to be doubted or rejected by the patient.

It is pertinent to point out in this context that we would include among these skills both knowledge and a capacity to appreciate the application of general psychological findings to the treatment situation. In our experience one can sometimes discover a degree of subservience to technique which blinds the user to facets of the therapeutic situation that demand a more sophisticated and flexible approach. For this reason, we feel that those employing "behavioral strategies" should have been exposed to lengthy and appropriate psychological training, which may help to prevent an excessive narrowness of approach and, at the very least, confer a measure of circumspection concerning how and when to use behavioral techniques. While it may well be swimming against the tide of opinion, it is our belief that it is entirely inappropriate to train nurses and social workers in such techniques without providing extensive instruction in general psychology that allows an appropriate perspective and judicious deployment of method to develop. Enthusiasm, unbridled by such considerations, can only result in a disservice to patients.

In short, for perfectly understandable and cogent reasons, involving both professional experience and technical competence, therapist variables will influence the response of obsessional patients to treatment.

The Patient

Personality factors

It is only recently that differences between patients have been investigated as potential contributors to good and poor treatment outcome. To date, three main areas have been studied: the patient's personality, the occurrence of concomitant depression or anxiety, and the form and content of the formal obsessional symptoms.

An interest in personality factors appears to have arisen partly from the contention that about two-thirds of obsessional patients have obsessional personality traits (Pollitt, 1960) and partly because the presence of such traits is thought to be associated with a better prognosis for the disorder (Lo, 1967; Pollitt, 1969). Rabavilas, Boulougouris, Perissaki, & Stafanis (1979) sought to confirm this latter observation when investigating the effect of obsessional personality on the outcome of behavioral treatment. In their study a traditional definition of obsessional personality was adopted, the patients being assessed for the presence of characteristics such as parsimoniousness, obstinacy, and orderliness. Six patients with obsessional symptoms and with obsessional personalities were compared with six obsessionals in whom such traits were absent, both before and after a course of eight flooding sessions directed toward the obsessional symptoms. The two groups responded equally well to the treatment given, apparently disconfirming the prediction that those with obsessional personalities would show greatest improvement.

However, the obsessional personality group showed a significant reduction in anxiety over flooding sessions as well as an appreciable improvement in psychophysiological reactivity within a session, whereas the group without obsessional traits showed no such changes. These observations led the investigators to set aside the nonsignificant treatment outcome results and to conclude, albeit with a degree of caution, that patients with obsessional personality traits show a greater measure of benefit with flooding than do those without obsessional traits.

The influence of obsessional personality on the outcome of behavioral treatment has been highlighted in our own recent study of obsessional patients who were seen as routine treatment referrals in the Clinical Psychology Department at Withington Hospital, Manchester. This Department has provided a Regional Service for the treatment of obsessive-compulsive disorders and hence attracts more patients of this type than would normally be expected to accrue to a Department of this kind. The study was concerned with patients who were first seen and had completed their treatment in this Department between September 1973 and December 1978. This allowed from two to five years between the date of first treatment and that of our study, during which time relapses could (and did) take place. Excluding one or two patients with a history of frank psychosis, there were 40 patients and, with one exception, the first contact was also the patient's first experience with behavioral treatment. The obsessional symptoms presented covered a wide spectrum of contamination fears, washing and cleaning rituals, checking, repetitious behaviors, and unwanted thoughts.

Symptoms and Outcome. No relationship was found between type of symptom and the outcome of treatment. It was also the case that none of the particular treatments, which included modeling, exposure, response prevention, thought-stopping, satiation training, and occupational therapy programs were related to the degree of benefit experienced by the patient.

Twenty-nine patients were reported to have responded well to treatment, 19 of whom appeared to have remained well since no record appeared in the notes concerning further treatment or referral to another hospital. The remaining 10 patients were found to have relapsed one or more times in the two-to-five-year follow-up period. Eleven patients had either failed to respond or had shown only minimal improvement, leaving them still substantially impaired. The 11 patients who had failed to respond to treatment and the 10 who had relapsed were compared with a sample of 9 patients drawn randomly from the 19 who did well, providing a total sample of 30 patients.

Quite by chance the sexes were represented equally. Eighteen patients were married, nine were single, and three were either separated or divorced; their mean age was 35.5 years (SD 14.81). None of these variables was found to have any association with the three forms of outcome (failed to improve, improved but relapsed, good outcome).

The approximate duration of obsessive-compulsive illness prior to treatment ranged from 8 months to 20 years, but this variable also was unrelated to treatment response. Although such an outcome may seem to be surprising, it is consistent with Turner, Hersen, Bellack, & Wells' (1979) finding that two patients having histories of disturbance extending over 40 years responded well to treatment (one patient had had a leukotomy prior to behavioral treatment and was included in the failure group). This does not mean that leukotomized patients necessarily fare badly since Rachman and Marks and their colleagues (Marks et al., 1980; Rachman et al., 1979) have reported that five of their patients who had had psychosurgery did not differ from other obsessionals in their treatment response.

The remaining data from our retrospective study were taken from the *Psychology Department Notes* and *Psychiatric Case History Notes,* abstracts of which were entered on cards under the headings "Personality," "Treatment," and "Presenting Complaints".

Ratings and Classification of Obsessionals. Ratings of obsessional personality were made independently by three psychologists who were experienced in dealing with obsessionals. The ratings were made without awareness of the outcome group to which the patient belonged. In making the ratings, a broad definition of obsessional personality was adopted. The classification of obsessional personality was recorded only if such was mentioned in the notes, or if there was evidence of marked obsessional traits or isolated symptoms prior to the onset of the disorder, or if very marked neurotic or anxiety traits were present. At the same time the raters noted the presence of any other personality factors which might have interfered with the course of treatment (i.e., "abnormal" personality). In this connection, obsessional and abnormal personalities were not considered to be mutually exclusive as an individual patient could be characterized by both. Approximately 75 percent agreement was achieved between any pair of raters and this, although far from optimal, could not be improved upon with the data available. The classification of a patient as having an obsessional personality was made if two of the three judges agreed that this was the case. Insufficient information was available in one case but, of the remaining 29, 12 patients were identified as having obsessional personalities and 7 as having abnormal personality traits.

The relationship between obsessional personality and behavioral treatment outcome was investigated by comparing numbers of patients with obsessional personalities within the three outcome groups [good outcome maintained ($N = 9$), good outcome followed by relapse ($N = 10$), and poor outcome ($N = 11$)]. The single patient for whom there was insufficient information to evaluate personality was characterized by a good outcome. Six of the remaining "good outcome" group had obsessional personalities, as did six of those who relapsed. In contrast, none of the "failure" group had obsessional personalities. It is apparent that the "good outcome" and "relapse" groups were comparable in frequency and when they were combined a significant difference was observed between them and the "failure" group ($p < 0.005$, Fisher's Exact Test). It appears that a patient having an obsessional personality, as we have defined it, will respond favorably to treatment initially. However, such patients are as likely to relapse as they are to stay well. In contrast, the absence of such personality characteristics affords no useful prediction of immediate treatment outcome, since 7 patients did well while 11 failed to show improvement. In evaluating this finding, however, it is important to keep in mind the broader than usual definition of obsessional personality adopted here.

Negative Outcome and Personality

If the personalities of the "failure" patients tend not to be obsessional, then can they be identified as possessing some other characteristic? Seven out of 29 patients had been classified by the raters as having an "abnormal personality," none of whom were located in the "good outcome" group, while 2 had relapsed and 5 were classified as "failures." Since "good outcome" and "relapsed" patients were comparable, they were combined and the difference between them and those who failed to respond to treatment fell just short of achieving significance at the 5 percent level. Although not conclusive, it would seem that those patients who fail to respond to treatment may be more likely to have abnormalities of personality (other than obsessional characteristics) than those who show a good initial response. The frequency of abnormal personalities within the "good outcome" and "relapse" groups was too low to allow any prediction of relapse.

No single trait characterized all seven patients who had been rated as having "abnormal personalities." Two female patients were described as being "histrionic," one having an extraverted hysterical personality and the other with obsessional traits and a tendency to "shout, scream, and throw herself around." A third female patient was regarded as borderline subnormal in intelligence and to be overly dependent on her more competent sister. One 16-year-old boy was described as being "extroverted with psychopathic traits" and had been in trouble with the police for minor offenses, which were quite out of keeping with his professional middle-class family background. A second teenage boy had "always had problems," was a "loner," feared animals, talked to himself, and lacked appropriate social skills. One of two older male patients was said to be extroverted but to have been hypochondriacal since childhood, while the other, perhaps the least disordered of the seven, claimed always to have been very moody and a "loner." Although this conclusion requires confirmation in a larger sample, it may be that any one of several abnormalities of personality may be associated with a poor response to behavioral treatment.

Although perhaps not strictly referring to personality, some observations made by Rachman and Hodgson (1980) may be pertinent to the discussion. They have reported that five out of six patients who failed to respond significantly to modeling, flooding, and response prevention did so because they were unable to prevent themselves from performing rituals between sessions, and/or they were unable to tolerate either the exposure session or the period of response prevention that succeeded it. In short, it appeared that those patients who failed had been unable to comply with the requirements of treatment. Futhermore, Rachman and Marks and their colleagues (Marks et al., 1980; Rachman et al., 1979), using a global rating of compliance with behavioral treatment, found that patients receiving clomipramine showed much greater compliance than those taking a placebo, suggesting that clomipramine (Anafranil®) may be helpful in those patients who find it difficult to adhere to the rules of treatment. However, it may be pertinent to observe that the mechanisms by which Clomipramine® achieves this effect is probably in terms of its influence upon the mood state of the individual and it may well be that "compliance" is a quality affected by an improvement in the mood of the patient.

The findings respecting the contribution of obsessional personality traits in the present study may be said to be contrary to one of the three prognostic considerations mentioned by Beech (1979). He had indicated that frequency and intensity of mood swings (later pursued in a study by Rabavilas and Boulougouris, 1979) as well as the tendency to be "clearly oppositional in character, finding it difficult to countenance interference from authority . . . and disposed to adopt a contrary viewpoint," were both features of a poor prognosis. While the former was confirmed in the Rabavilas and Boulougouris study, that concerning the "oppositional" character is often regarded as part of the obsessional personality, which might suggest that Beech's observation was erroneous. Yet Rachman and Hodgson (1980), as stated, later drew attention to what they believed to be a lack of compliance in some of their patients, and it is tempting to suppose that this may be the same feature as that identified by Beech. Should this be so, and if one may assume the validity of the observation itself, then one must express doubts about the nature of the obsessional personality, perhaps regarding "oppositional" or "noncompliant" behavior as not being a necessary part of the definition.

Influence of depression and anxiety

Information from our study of 30 patients was used to investigate the relationship between depression and anxiety and the outcome of treatment. The case notes contained many reports from patients of depressed mood, tension, and anxiety, but it was difficult to evaluate the severity of these complaints with any accuracy. For this reason it was decided to use the prescription of antidepressants and/or the administration of ECT during the treatment period as an indication of the patient's depressed condition. Correspondingly, the prescription of either major or minor tranquilizers was taken as an indication of tension and anxiety, but reports that relaxation training had been given to the patient were not used for this purpose since such training is so often an integral part of other treatments provided, regardless of the patient's state. Relevant information was available concerning the provision of antidepressants and ECT for all but three of the patients (two "good outcome" and one "failure"). The most striking finding was a strong association between age and the presence or absence of depression. Twelve out of 18 patients over the age of 30 were regarded as depressed, whereas this quality was absent in 8 out of 9 patients under that age ($p < 0.025$). However, no association was found between the presence of depression and outcome within either of these groups.

Contrasting relationships were observed between outcome and the prescription of major and minor tranquilizers. Information on this point was available for 26 patients, there being no appropriate data for two patients from the "good outcome" group and two from the "failure" group. None of the remaining patients with "good outcome" had taken tranquilizers, whereas half of the patients who had relapsed and 6 of the 9 who "failed treatment" did so. The "good outcome" group differed significantly (Fisher's Exact Test, $p < 0.05$) from both the other groups, but the "relapsed" and "failed" patients were again comparable. It was noted that the use of tranquilizers showed no association with age.

It appears that the prescription of tranquilizing medication may be predictive of either treatment failure or relapse, but that if such medication is not prescribed this carries no implication for outcome since of the 15 patients not taking tranquilizers, 7 had a good outcome, 5 relapsed, and 3 did badly.

The finding that the use of tranquilizers (and our assumption that this denotes the presence of anxiety) may indicate that the probability of a poor treatment response could reconcile the apparent disagreement about the role of depression in the present study and in that reported by Foa (1979). Foa reported that 4 out of 10 obsessional patients who failed to respond to behavioral treatment were suffering from severe depression, one of whom showed psychomotor retardation while the other three exhibited agitated depression with high anxiety. It could be argued that it was the high anxiety loading which contributed to failure, rather than depressed mood state.

However, this speculative explanation could not account for the observation of Rabavilas and Boulougouris (1979) of a link between mood changes and poor treatment response. In their study, 25 patients were rated on a five-point scale, from 0 (no depressive mood swings) to 4 (swings more frequently than four times a year). Patients ($N = 15$) rated 0 or 1 were grouped together and compared to those ($N = 10$) rated 2 to 4. The two groups did not differ on pretreatment measures but those patients characterized by mood swings had improved significantly less at the end of treatment. Moreover, six of the patients with mood swings relapsed during the two-year follow-up period, while only 2 patients without this feature did so.

It is difficult to reconcile these results with the absence of influence of depression revealed in the study reported here, but since the means of identifying depressed patients differed and the problem of ensuring that the severity of the depression was comparable, the discrepancies between the finding may be more apparent than real. However, it is clear that the role of depression in the response to treatment requires considerable further investigation, perhaps with particular reference to the separate contribution which may be made by anxiety.

The third area of patient functioning examined in our study was the nature of the obsessive-compulsive symptoms themselves. In our patients, nearly all of the symptoms could be assigned to one of three classes: contamination fears and washing or cleansing rituals, checking and repetitive behavior, and obsessional thoughts. It was found that none of these forms of symptom was related to outcome. This finding is more difficult to interpret than at first appears since differences between symptoms and treatments were confounded. As all the patients were being seen in the course of routine clinical practice and not in the context of research, the treatments chosen may be assumed to be those which were considered to be most relevant to the present symptoms and it could be that this careful matching produced a uniformity of outcome.

Differential Treatment Responses

Washers and checkers. Perhaps a more useful way of investigating the problem would be to compare patients having different symptoms but who have been given the same treatment, as has been done informally in studies evaluating the effects of modeling, flooding, and response prevention. Rachman and Hodgson (1980), reviewing their carefully conducted series of treatment investigations (Marks, Hodgson, & Rachman, 1975; Rachman, Marks, & Hodgson, 1973), concluded that the most difficult patients to treat in their group of 20 were those with repetitive and pervasive checking rituals. The most favorable results appeared to be with patients having contamination fears and cleaning rituals that were confined to a limited number of stimulus situations.

However, the results reported by Foa and Goldstein (1978) are not consistent with this conclusion. Having treated 21 patients with therapist and self-controlled exposure and response prevention, these authors found no difference in response between patients with checking rituals and those with hand-washing rituals, with both types of patient showing marked improvement. In fact, three patients with checking rituals who were still mildly or moderately symptomatic at the end of treatment were found to continue their improvement during follow-up, whereas relapses occurred only among those with hand-washing rituals where obsessions had remained very intense. Obviously the relative responsiveness of "checkers" and "washers" to exposure, modeling, and response prevention requires clarification. But even if differences between them become evident, these may not necessarily be attributable to the symptoms since the treatment procedures appear to be much easier to apply to contamination and hand-washing than to checking.

It is a comparatively simple matter to expose patients to "contamination," and the subsequent response prevention can be applied with supervision if the patient is unable to control himself. On the other hand, the patient with checking rituals is exposed only to doubt and uncertainty (relating to *not* having checked his actions) and, quite often, patients do not experience such feelings when their behavior is being regulated by others or when they are in the protected environment of a consulting room. Furthermore, checking behavior is often fleeting and difficult for either patient or therapist to control. In short, it may well be that entirely new procedures for the treatment of checking should be available before any firm conclusions can be reached about its amenability to change.

Obsessional thinkers. Patients suffering predominantly from obsessional thoughts seem to have been excluded from most studies of exposure and response prevention, only Solyom and Sookman (1977) having investigated flooding with this group. They reported that improvements in this symptom could be obtained both with flooding and with Clomipramine®, but to a lesser extent with thought-stopping. Such a conclusion may appear to be somewhat optimistic; Beech and Vaughan (1978), in their literature review, felt that the outcome of treatment for obsessional thoughts was in doubt mainly because of the absence of appropriately rigorous research. It is at least possible that some of the failures noted by Beech and Vaughan had occurred because of the inadequacy of the treatment procedures employed. However, Stern (1978) has suggested that treatment outcome might also be related to the nature of the obsessional thought. Applying satiation training to six patients who failed to respond to thought-stopping, he found that only two patients improved, but both had experienced feelings of horror attaching to the pathological thoughts, while the remaining four had reported feelings of doubt, guilt, or pleasure. The number of patients in this study is far too small for the results to be taken as establishing the general case, but it is possible to argue that repeated exposure to a thought by repetition might affect "horror" in much the same way as has been reported in the context of anxiety or fear. The question of whether the character of the emotional experience accompanying the obsessional thought is related to treatment outcome, however, remains a question to be resolved.

Of course, in the context of this discussion the question of what constitutes "thought" is begged and it is noteworthy that descriptions of behavioral treatments fail totally to come to terms with the inherent problems in this area. It may be of passing interest to observe here that when obsessionals are asked to identify and describe their thought processes, they appear to be no more successful than the rest of us in doing so and this sometimes seems to stand in sharp contrast to the extent to which they report being involved in certain thought patterns. Indeed, while the substance of a worrying thought can be described by most patients so afflicted, the verbal symbols employed or the visual imagery conjured up by the patient to comply with the therapist's request to "think about the worrying idea" often appear fragmentary, infrequently followed through to the "logical" conclusion that the therapist may infer to be the case and, in other particulars, appear to be only tangentially related to, for example, the formulations typically employed in "thought-stopping."

Prognostic features

De Silva, Rachman, and Seligman (1977) entertained a more general interest in the nature of obsessive-compulsive symptoms, being concerned with the relationship between treatment outcome and Seligman's (1971) concept of "preparedness." In this they examined the case-notes of 82 obsessional patients who had received behavioral treatment and rated the symptoms in terms of "preparedness," but no relationship between preparedness and outcome was noted. Another attempt to look at symptoms was by Foa (1979), who observed that four out of ten treatment failures encountered were among patients characterized by overvalued ideas concerning their obsessions.

What appears to be the same observation was made by Beech (Beech & Perigault, 1974; Beech & Vaughan, 1978; Beech, 1979) as part of the three prognostic features that he considered to be of most significance among this group of patients. The first two of these (mood variations and oppositional temperament) have already been described. The third that Beech considers bears upon the degree to which the patient is able to distinguish between the "truth" of the obsessional beliefs he entertains and the need to act as if such beliefs were true. Beech has argued that patients may be arranged along a continuum from those who regard their pathological thoughts as the expression of some quite reasonable proposition, to those who recognize the foolishness of the thoughts and actions so inspired but feel compelled to behave *as if* the thoughts are a reasonable spur to action. Beech has pointed to the delusional quality of thought in the former group and also to the observation that obsessional patients appear to span the space between what are ordinarily regarded as the independent dimensions of neuroticism and psychoticism. He contends that those whose verbal expressions of belief appear to have a delusional quality are very much less responsive to treatment of any kind, behavioral or otherwise.

In this connection it is also pertinent to observe that Beech has argued that obsessional disorder is made up of two components, one of which is the faulty mechanism that may be regarded as the basic cause of the breakdown. This predisposes the individual to the acquisition of the obsessional thoughts and actions, which are therefore secondary in nature. He has suggested that the primary mechanism appears as a special potential for becoming aroused and exhibiting defensive reactions to minimal stimulation (Beech & Perigault, 1974; Vila & Beech, 1977, 1978). In short, the defect is such that minor variations in the level of incoming stimulation can precipitate major defensive reactions to cues which will come to be labeled as "distressing" and to which the organism will be compelled to respond. It is contended (Ciesielski, Beech, & Gordon, 1981) that the basic failure of the mechanism may be observed through the assessment of evoked potentials, and a further (as yet unpublished) study has confirmed the observations made in 1981.

The implication of this, as Beech has pointed out (Beech, 1974; Beech & Vaughan, 1978), is that the control of the underlying pathological state is of paramount importance and that merely dealing with the secondary symptoms may have serious limitations. However, according to this viewpoint, since the primary defect can be episodic in character, one may have only the residual secondary symptoms with which to deal and these will be amenable to behavior modification. Since the primary disturbance is probably unaffected by behavioral techniques, it is hardly surprising that relapse is commonly observed in obsessionals following successful treatment. From the point of view of satisfactory treatment procedure, it is clearly incumbent upon the therapist to carefully evaluate the factors contributing to the total disturbance and to ensure that appropriate attention has been given to both the primary and secondary components of the disturbance.

Treatment

A comprehensive review of the early research into treatment methods is found in Beech and Vaughan (1978), but a summary of the conclusions drawn about such matters may help to clarify the state of knowledge prior to 1978. At that time it was reported that *in vivo* desensitization to "contaminated" or other avoided objects was superior to imaginal treatment and appeared to work best when the avoided stimuli were relatively circumscribed. On the whole, it was felt that the flooding, modeling, and response prevention package was likely to be more beneficial when rituals were involved. These procedures appear to effect improvement in the target compulsive symptoms in the majority of patients.

Two procedures, thought-stopping and satiation training, had been developed especially to deal with recurrent unwanted and usually abhorrent thoughts. Neither had undergone full experimental validation by 1978 and, correspondingly, neither had yielded any established degree of success. In addition to these methods, there were a number of self-control procedures which were based on little more than clinical applications in a few isolated cases.

The picture respecting treatment outcome has remained essentially the same since 1978. The success of various combinations of modeling, exposure, and response prevention has been confirmed in several studies (Foa & Goldstein, 1978; Rabavilas & Boulougouris, 1979; Turner, Steketee, & Foa, 1979), the most comprehensive of which were those of Rachman and Marks and their colleagues (Marks et al.,1980; Rachman et al., 1979). A positive outcome has also been achieved with *in vivo* desensitization (Emmelkamp, Van Der Helm, Van Zanten, & Plochg, 1980). In contrast, Stern (1978) had little success in treating obsessional thoughts with either thought-stopping or satiation training, and Blue (1978) reported a failure to improve the condition of two patients who employed self-administered aversive stimulation for unwanted thoughts. On the other hand, electric shock employed as an aversive stimulus has been reported to yield favorable results, Kenny, Mowbray, & Lalani (1973) observing that four out of six patients improved considerably following extended treatment by this means. However, this was an uncontrolled trial and one cannot eliminate the possibility that the observed changes occurred through spontaneous remission.

It is appropriate to point out here that there are numerous reservations to entertain about the use of aversive stimulation (Rachman & Teasdale, 1969). Indeed, Beech has pointed out in an early paper (1960) that where the response is mediated by anxiety, electric shock appears to exacerbate rather than reduce the abnormality of function. In a recent example, Beech observed that the application of faradic stimulation had the effect of producing the sudden and spontaneous appearance of rituals in an obsessional patient.

One may conclude that modeling, exposure, and response prevention, aimed primarily at overt rituals, appear consistently to produce benefits for the obsessional, but that the various techniques directed toward the reduction of obsessional thoughts do not. It is possible to argue, and tempting to conclude, that the discrepancies in outcome merely reflect differences in the efficacy of the treatments themselves. Of course, such a conclusion cannot be drawn with any degree of confidence as the types of symptoms to which the treatments have been directed have not been comparable, and investigations in which the type of symptom is held constant over treatments are much needed.

However, it is worth noting that no differences between the two symptom groups are apparent, save in outcome. Certainly, such differences were not observed in psychophysiological reactivity (Beech & Perigault, 1974) and, more recently, in terms of the evoked potentials of obsessionals (Ciesielski et al., 1981). It is our opinion that the fundamental disturbance of function is the same in both symptom groups and it is merely the form that the disorder takes which serves to apparently differentiate them. Assuming that this is the case, then one might argue that any observed differences in outcome are attributable to the comparative ease with which externally manifested abnormalities are amenable to behavioral control, and the contrasting difficulty of securing this for internal events. However, we would reiterate the view expressed earlier, that there exists a profound lack of understanding of cognitive mechanisms, and the assumption that the laws governing such processes are identical to those that apply to externalized behaviors may be entirely erroneous.

Returning to the relationship between type of symptom and treatment approach, however, the study by Solyom and Sookman (1977) contributes to an understanding of the problem by comparing Clomipramine®, flooding, and thought-stopping. After treatment, symptoms were found to be reduced to about half of their original severity for all groups, although the various forms of symptom appeared to be differentially affected by the treatments. Clomipramine® and flooding were reported to be very much more effective in reducing ruminations than was thought-stopping, but neither thought-stopping nor flooding was as effective as Clomipramine® in reducing doubt and decision-making difficulty. However, the position was reversed with respect to overt rituals, where thought-stopping and to a lesser extent flooding were found to be the most successful. The superiority of thought-stopping in this context is rather unexpected. Additionally, those patients receiving the two behavioral treatments (but not those receiving drugs) rated themselves as improved in social adjustment.

Clearly, this and other similar studies can be regarded as only a modest beginning to what could prove to be fruitful comparisons of treatment procedures as related to symptom patterns.

Conclusion

From the findings reviewed one may offer a speculative description of the "vulnerable patient," embodying all the characteristics which militate against the success of behavioral treatments. It is not implied that such negative signs are additive (i.e., that the more vulnerable characteristics the patient has, the more likely he is to fail to respond), and we would argue that it is not known how the characteristics may combine to determine outcome. Nevertheless, it might be useful to describe the hypothetical patient who is unfortunate enough to possess them all.

Our vulnerable patient can be of any age and marital status and of either sex. The length of time that he has possessed his obsessive-compulsive symptoms seems immaterial but he is likely to have diffuse checking or repetition rituals and/or obsessional thoughts. He may well be suffering from anxiety which requires treatment with minor or major tranquilizers and could be depressed (especially if he is over the age of 30). Psychophysiologically, he will be found to be hyperresponsive to stimulation and will exhibit abnormalities in visual evoked potentials, primarily involving faster latency and reduced amplitude of the N220 component. It is unlikely that this patient will have an obsessional personality, although he may be "oppositional" in character. It is quite possible that he will be characterized by some disturbance of character or personality which, if present, will be associated with a poorer prognosis.

Taking a more positive viewpoint, the outlook for such a patient may be less dismal than it at first sight appears. In the long term, existing behavioral treatments may be modified and new ones developed. More immediately, however, great care must be taken in selecting the appropriate behavioral treatment or combination of treatments for the patient's presenting complaints. The precise description and indentification of problems, the correct choice and refinement of techniques, as well as the sensitivity of their application demand a broad-based training in psychology. Such qualities are not acquired through more technical training in behavior modification techniques.

Psychophysiological assessment can be useful in the description of the patient and may be helpful in determining the choice and level of medication to be offered. The use of medication such as clomipramine may assist the patient to cooperate more fully with treatment and alleviate any depression present. Tranquilizers may also be prescribed to combat anxiety if this is indicated. (It is unclear whether the use of tranquilizers will improve the patient's outcome, although our study of 30 patients indicated that this is not the case. However, such medication may improve the patient's sense of well-being.)

With close attention to definition of problems and selection of treatment procedures and, it is hoped, some amelioration of adverse mood state, anxiety, and arousal level, there remains the problem of the patient's personality. Clomipramine® may have helped to soften any opposition or negativism and any residual difficulties of this kind are best dealt with by a therapist who has had much previous experience of obsessional patients and their special problems.

There is no easy remedy that we can suggest to deal with other disorders of personality that the patient may possess. In any event, it is not as yet possible to predict what type of personality disorder will be damaging, but the appearance of such features in our study indicates that the personality-disordered patient may have very little chance of improving his obsessive-compulsive symptoms.

Our description of what may be done to help the vulnerable patient perhaps represents the most that may be possible in the present state of knowledge, but the systematic application of the practices which we have suggested might be advantageous in certain individual cases. Of course, we would not claim that any of these will provide a solution to what may be the fundamental problem of failure to respond. Far more knowledge of the nature of obsessive-compulsive disorders, optimal treatment strategies, and therapist training and style will be needed before cogent answers can be given on that score. Indeed, it will be evident from this review of the factors involved in the failure to respond to treatment that more questions are raised than have been answered.

Summary

The main purpose of this chapter has been to collect and review findings relevant to failure in the behavioral treatment of obsessive-compulsive disorders. Treatment was considered to have failed either if a patient showed no change after therapy or if deterioration occurred within the period of follow-up employed. Material was drawn from current research, a survey of case material, and clinical experience and was discussed in terms of three components of therapy: the therapist, the patient, and the treatment procedure.

Little or no research in this specific area has been directed toward the role of the therapist. In terms of our own clinical experience it is concluded that it is of paramount importance that the therapist should have a thorough knowledge of general psychology, and the more experienced therapist is also thought more likely to be successful.

Using data from a retrospective study of 30 obsessive-compulsive patients, it was found that those with obsessional personalities were likely to do well in treatment but that they were as likely to relapse one or more times during the next two to five years as to stay well. The absence of an obsessional personality had no predictive value respecting treatment outcome. A tendency was noted for patients with other disorders of personality to fail to respond to treatment.

Our study of the 30 patients also indicated that the presence of depression was significantly related to age but not to treatment outcome. The latter finding is at odds with some published results. Among those patients it was found that the use of tranquilizers was strongly related to a poor outcome, which may indicate that the presence of anxiety could have accounted for some of the variance which has previously been attributed to depressed mood. However, it was concluded that the separate effects of anxiety and depression on the outcome of behavioral treatment require further investigation.

It is generally agreed that patients with relatively circumscribed cleansing and washing rituals associated with fears of contamination respond well to flooding, modeling, and response prevention. Those with diffuse checking and repetition rituals do not respond so well to the same procedures, possibly in part because the treatment does not seem to be entirely appropriate to the symptoms. The evidence available respecting patients with obsessional thoughts indicates that there are many failures among this group and that the procedures used are far from optimal.

It was suggested that failure may also arise when the nature of obsessive-compulsive disorder is conceptualized inappropriately. In addition to the observable ritualistic symptoms and thoughts, there is, in our view, evidence of a basic disturbance of state revealed, for example, in the evoked potentials of such patients. Recognizing this, and its probably episodic manifestation, alerts the therapist to a more appropriate consideration of treatment requirements.

Without denying the valuable contributions made to the treatment of obsessional patients, we have tried throughout this chapter to draw attention to the complexity of the disorder, the inadequacy of existing evidence, and the need for more research.

10

Negative Outcome: Treatment of Depressive Disorders

Steven D. Hollon and Michael G. Emerson

EDITORS' NOTE: *Hollon and Emerson are referring here to* average *changes in treatment and control* groups. *This does not necessarily imply that no individual patient in any of these studies deteriorated, but only that the data are not presented in a manner which permits a determination of negative outcome in individual cases. This is a limitation of the available research base, not of Hollon and Emerson's scholarship. We examined studies which show or which had been purported to show negative outcome, and failed to locate a single instance of negative outcome pertaining specifically to depressed patients treated with psychotherapy. This is an obvious gap in the research literature. Nonetheless, depressed patients appear to present a heightened risk of suicide. Of a consecutive series of child and adolescent suicide attempters reported by Mattson, Sesse, and Hawkins (1969), 69 percent appear to have been depressed at the time of the attempt. Rennie (1942) estimates a 5 percent rate of death by suicide among severely depressed patients. Arieti and Bemporad (1978) note suicidal ideation in about 75 percent of their depressed patients, and actual attempts in at least 10 to 15 percent. However, these statistics are not necessarily relevant to patients receiving psychotherapy. As far as we know, similar statistics among such patients are unavailable.*

Even without treatment, the typical depressed outpatient is expected to return to normalcy within six months to a year from the onset of any given episode (Beck, 1967). Nonetheless, the issue of greater deterioration with treatment than without treatment is an important one, particularly in a self-limiting disorder like depression. In this chapter, we approach the issue of deterioration associated with the treatment of

Preparation of this chapter was supported in part by National Institute of Mental Health Grant IRO1-MH32209-03 to Steven D. Hollon, University of Minnesota, and the Department of Psychiatry, St. Paul-Ramsey Medical Center, and by the Medical Education and Research Foundation Grant No. 6827.

depressed clients. In so doing, we look both at the formal outcome literature and our own clinical experiences. Further, we extend our discussion to pharmacological and somatic (convulsive) therapies.

Types of Outcomes in Depression

Elsewhere (DeRubeis & Hollon, 1981; Hollon, 1981), we have described various measures of clinical outcomes. *Magnitude* refers to the absolute amount of change shown by the average patient in a given treatment. *Universality* refers to the probability that any given patient will show a particular level of response. The deterioration argument raised by Bergin is largely a universality issue, with a greater number of patients allegedly evidencing a poorer response in treatment than if not in treatment. It is not neccessarily true that deterioration must involve a worsening of the client's condition. Since spontaneous remission is a likely occurrence in depression, a negative treatment effect may simply involve a slowing of the tendency toward remission for treated relative to untreated patients.

Generality can refer either to changes across the various components of the depressive syndrome (e.g., affective versus cognitive versus vegetative symptom clusters) or changes across situational contexts. *Stability* refers to the maintenance of changes over time, either the prevention of relapses within the index episode or the recurrence of a new episode. Given that depression is not only a self-limiting disorder but also an episodic disorder, stability aspects of outcome may be particularly important.

Acceptability refers to the attractiveness of entering or staying in a treatment. When comparing two or more types of interventions, acceptability (as indexed either by refusal or premature discontinuation) can be an important differential outcome between conditions. With regard to the distinction between treatment and no treatment, acceptability indices may play a role in terms of the expectation disconfirmed in patients and the attributions made in association with discontinuation (see Duckro, Beal, & George, 1979, for a review). For example, although we know of no clear evidence proving that starting then discontinuing treatment is any worse than not starting treatment at all, we have observed patients who have had hopes dashed and who then conclude that they were untreatable (and, hence, doomed to continued dysphoria) on the basis of dissatisfaction with progress in therapy.

Finally, *safety* refers to the freedom from undesirable complications associated with treatment. Dangerous medication side effects and the increased lethality of available means of suicide attempts are two aspects of pharmacological therapy which could be argued make that approach more hazardous than its absence. Similarly, concerns over memory deficits and long-term chronic organic impairments have long plagued advocates of electroconvulsive therapy (cf. Scovern & Kilmann, 1980). Few studies exist which explicitly evaluate the long-term health and safety consequences of receiving a radical therapy, such as ECT, versus not receiving treatment (see Avery & Winokur, 1976, for an interesting exception). Finally, the various types of psychotherapies have been the focal points of various types of concerns. Critics have long suggested that dynamic approaches may only serve to exacerbate tendencies to wallow in affective misery. Critics of behavior therapies have been concerned with issues of symptom substitution. Critics of cognitive approaches have focused on concerns regarding induced obsessiveness or more frankly psychotic decompensations.

Even relatively desired changes can have undesirable consequences in an unyielding environment. The rather elegant treatment manual designed to accompany a newly streamlined variant of dynamic-eclectic therapy called Interpersonal Psychotherapy (IPT: Klerman, Rounsaville, Neu, Chevron, & Weissman, 1979) provides one example based on the authors' clinical experiences. They note that their modal client, the middle-aged housewife from a lower-middle-class, blue-collar, ethnic background, can readily be seen as the victim of rather shoddy treatment and restriction of opportunities in the conventional marriage. Efforts to ensure appropriate assertiveness and reduce passivity may help ameliorate depressive symptomatology in the short run but may also fan smoldering marital dissatisfaction into open marital conflict.

Throughout this chapter, we shall address each of these aspects of outcome, although with different emphases. Clearly, universality, stability, and safety aspects are most directly relevant to the issue of deterioration effects, and we shall concentrate our attention on these domains.

Types of Intervention

There is a rich and varied range of interventions for depression that has been shown to be more effective than no treatment, when effectiveness has been defined in terms of either the magnitude or the universality of positive outcomes. The somatic convulsive therapies were the earliest established interventions. Lehman (1977), for example, points out that the probability of response to ECT approaches 90 percent for inpatient depressives, higher than for any other treatment. Concern with the safety of the procedure, however, frequently leads to the selection of other interventions with lower probabilities of response as the first choice for treatment.

Quite frequently, that first choice involves pharmacotherapy, usually one of the tricyclics, less often lithium, and least often one of the MAO inhibitors. The tricyclics have been repeatedly shown to be more effective than no treatment or inert pill-placebos. For example, Morris and Beck (1974) reviewed over 200 studies which overwhelmingly supported the efficacy of the tricyclic antidepressants. Concerns over the safety of the approach have typically focused on the increased availability of lethal means for suicide attempts and dangerous side-effects. It is cruel irony that the tricyclics, so effective in the amelioration of depressive symptomatology, have one of the lowest active dosage to lethal dosage ratios of any of the major psychoactive medications. Further, there is evidence that at least some patients may be thrown into hypomanic episodes (cf. Akiskal, Ojenderdejian, Rosenthal, & Khani, 1977; Akiskal, Khani, & Scott-Strauss, 1979; Bunney, 1978) or psychotic decompensation (cf. Bowers & Freedman, 1975; Nelson, Bowers, & Sweeney, 1979).

Lithium, although more clearly effective in controlling the manic component of the common bipolar mood disorders, is also touted as an effective agent for at least some depressive episodes (American Psychiatric Association Task Force, 1975). But lithium is itself a poison, and appropriate management requires careful monitoring of blood plasma levels. Patients with renal disease may not be able to prevent the buildup of toxic levels in the body, and there has been some concern that long-term lithium maintenance medication may so overtax the kidneys that physical damage results (cf. Hwang & Tuason, 1980).

The MAO inhibitors were the first antidepressant agents introduced. Concerns over life-threatening side-effects led to their withdrawal in the United States. Careful dietary monitoring can prevent the bulk of these complications. Although rarely the first medication of choice, the MAO inhibitors may have an important role to play in the treatment of atypical depressions (cf. Paykel, Parker, Penrose, & Rassaby, 1979; Sargant, 1961; Tyrer, 1976) or hysteroid dysphorias (Liebowitz & Klein, 1979).

As recently as the mid-1970s, Akiskal and McKinney (1975) were forced to conclude that there was no convincing evidence that any psychosocial intervention produced desirable outcome effects with depressed patients. That conclusion seemed warranted at that time, given the apparent relative ineffectiveness of such psychological interventions relative to pharmacological approaches (cf. Cole et al., 1959; Covi Lipman, Derogatis, Smitt, & Pattison, 1974; Daneman, 1961; Friedman, 1975; Klerman, DiMascio, Weissman, Prusoff, & Paykel, 1974; Olson, 1962).

Since that time, several types of psychosocial interventions have demonstrated at least initial evidence of efficacy. Chief among these have been the cognitive-behavioral or more strictly behavioral approaches. Beck's cognitive therapy has generated some impressive evidence of efficacy in several controlled trials (cf. Beck et al., 1981; Blackburn, Bishop, Glen, Whalley, & Christie, 1981; Rush, Beck, Kovacs, & Hollon, 1977; Shaw, 1977). Similarly Rehm and colleagues have shown rather consistant superiority of a self-control approach to various controls in community volunteers (cf. Fuchs & Rehm, 1977; Rehm, Fuchs, Roth, Kornblith, & Romano, 1979). McLean and colleagues have produced two trials supporting the efficacy of a social learning approach for marital therapy (McLean & Hakstian, 1979; McLean, Ogston, & Grauer, 1973).

During this same period, the apparent efficacy of a streamlined, time-limited interpersonal dynamic approach to working with acutely depressed patients has been touted (Weissman et al., 1979). In this interpersonal psychotherapy (IPT), not only depressive symptomatology, but also interpersonal relationship problems, appear to be ameliorated.

Drug and psychotherapy combinations appear to be at least comparable, and perhaps superior, in terms of efficacy, to either modality singly employed (cf. Beck et al., 1981; Blackburn et al., 1981; Weissman et al., 1979). Earlier fears of negative interactions between drugs and psychotherapies, either in terms of "stirring up" issues that interfere with medication effects or the elicitation by the medication regime of psychological processes disruptive of psychotherapy processes, appear to have been unfounded (cf. Hollon & Beck, 1978; Klerman, 1975, 1976).

Overall, then, there appear to be a range of interventions which are either well established or show promise of becoming established as effective interventions for depression. These include somatic, pharmacological, and psychosocial approaches. Within the psychosocial interventions, several different types of cognitive-behavioral or behavioral approaches, and at least one time-limited interpersonal dynamic approach, appear promising, at least with regard to magnitude and universality parameters of outcome. Generality parameters may actually favor some types of interventions over others. For example, IPT appears to have impact on the quality of interpersonal processes in addition to depressive symptomatology (Weissman et al., 1979). It may prove that the combination of IPT with medication might be superior to, say, cognitive therapy plus medication if it turns out that the former combination has a broader band of impact.

Negative Outcome

Is there evidence for negative outcome as a consequence of treatment with depressives? With regard to the magnitude of outcomes on syndrome depression measures, there appears not to be. We have been unable to uncover even one published study in which any treatment group fared worse, on the average, than a no-treatment control.[1] There are, however, important gaps in our empirical knowledge which constrain the external validity of that statement. The available literature does not, for example, contain any methodologically adequate studies applying an uncovering, deep-psychoanalytic intervention to a homogeneously depressed population. Clinical lore clearly embraces the notion that moderately to severely depressed patients are poor candidates for an unstructured, uncovering psychoanalytic approach. The closest approximations to such an approach in the published outcome literature have been the several trials described earlier as providing little efficacy for the impact of psychotherapy with depressives (cf. Cole et al., 1959; Covi et al., 1974; Daneman, 1961; Friedman, 1975; Klerman et al., 1974; Olson, 1962). Even in these trials, psychotherapy was generally time-limited and somewhat focused, because of the constraints of the research trials.

Second, there appear to be no adequately operationalized trials involving any of the humanistic psychosocial interventions. Several of the published trials have utilized "nondirective" comparison groups (cf. Padfield, 1976; Shaw, 1977), but in such instances these interventions appear to have been approached more as controls for nonspecific treatment factors than as bona fide, carefully executed interventions consistent with Rogerian client-centered approaches. Nothing akin to the more intrusive encounter group approaches has been adequately tested with depressed populations. Given that the Lieberman, Yalom, and Miles (1973) study of "casualties" in encounter groups is one of the classic sources of support for the "deterioration" hypotheses, we must wonder how a severely depressed patient would fare in such an approach.

Third, clinical lore suggests that depressed patients frequently do not fare well in diagnostically heterogeneous group therapy situations (cf. Hollon & Shaw, 1979; Yalom, 1970). Our own experience has clearly suggested that the demands of group process may often be more than a depressed client can readily handle. This seems to be particularly troublesome either when group membership is diagnosti-

---

[1]See Editor's Note at the beginning of this chapter.

cally heterogeneous, in which case the typically passive depressed patient gets "lost in the shuffle," or when the groups are unstructured, in which case the depressed patients tend to "wallow" in dysphoric affect.

Is there evidence of greater variance in outcome for treated as opposed to untreated control groups? In some cases, there is. Such a finding has been said by Bergin and colleagues to be indicative of deterioration in some patients combined with improvement in others. However, in the absence of equivalent magnitudes of change, differential variance is difficult to interpret. Further, greater variance is not necessarily always indicative of deterioration. It is quite possible that somewhat greater improvement in an active treatment cell will result in greater variance in outcome than that exhibited by a nontreatment control. Thus, although greater variance in treatment relative to control cells is the rule in controlled treatment outcome trials, it is misleading to infer that deterioration has occurred without examining individual patient changes in status from pretreatment to posttreatment.

In our own work, we have been associated with three controlled clinical trials, with the third currently still in progress. In the first (Rush et al., 1977), 41 nonbipolar, primary depressed outpatients were randomly assigned to either imipramine pharmacotherapy or cognitive therapy in a 12-week treatment trial. Of the 19 patients assigned to cognitive therapy, one patient did not complete treatment (dropping out when her depression resolved after she and her estranged husband reconciled), while 18 patients did complete therapy. Of these 18, 15 evidenced either full or partial remission, while only 3 did not evidence a satisfying clinical remission. None of the 3 nonresponders evidenced any particular clinical worsening, with 2 showing slight improvement over pretreatment levels and 1 showing little change over the 12 treatment weeks. This last patient was subsequently placed on at least two different tricyclic medications and seen by four different therapists over the next nine months, with no appreciable change in her clinical picture. When switched to an MAO inhibitor, more than a year after her initial entry into the research clinic, the patient evidenced a complete clinical remission within three weeks.

In that same study, response to pharmacotherapy was, on the average, somewhat less satisfying, but still consistent with what one would expect from the literature. Eight of the original pharmacotherapy-assigned patients discontinued treatment prematurely, 7 because of dissatisfaction with lack of progress or treatment assignment, and 1 because of a severe allergic reaction to the medication. Of the remaining 14 treatment completers, most evidenced either a full or at least a partial response. Only 3 of the 14 patients did not evidence at least a partial clinical response. Two of those patients ended treatments in worse condition than they began. One, although scoring no more highly on measures of syndrome depression, became (or was found to be) delusional and was hospitalized shortly after termination. This patient subsequently responded to a combination of antipsychotic and antidepressant medication. The second patient experienced a major exacerbation of symptoms relative to a marital crisis near the end of treatment, an exacerbation which was relatively short-lived. This patient subsequently responded readily to the combination of medication and cognitive therapy.

Overall, there was virtually no evidence of deterioration in an absolute sense when intraindividual pretreatment–posttreatment comparisons were made. In general, our impression is that we merely failed to match the occasional patient to an appropriate intervention, rather than that we did any of the patients a disservice by treating them at all. Nonetheless, the absence of any nontreatment control in this design does not allow us to eliminate the possibility that at least some patients might have improved faster or more completely if left untreated. While almost no one got worse in either treatment cell, it might have been the case that treatment retarded spontaneous remission for a specific subsample of our population. Such a possibility quite frankly strikes us as being remote, but we do not have the data to rule it out.

The results of the Beck et al. (1981) trial were basically similar to those of Rush et al. (1977): 33 patients were assigned to either cognitive therapy or combined cognitive-pharmacotherapy (amitriptyline). Fourteen of 17 patients assigned to cognitive therapy completed treatment, while 12 of 16 patients completed the combined modality. None of the dropouts evidenced serious side-effects, and most pursued other treatments in our clinic or treatment elsewhere. None of the completers in either cell finished treatment more symptomatic than they began, but several patients in each cell did evidence only minimal improvement. Again, it would be hard to argue that deterioration had occurred when within-individual comparisons over time failed to indicate any instances of absolute worsening. However, as with Rush et al., we cannot be sure that patients might not have improved more rapidly if left untreated. This seems unlikely, but again, we did not have the necessary design to detect such a phenomenon. What is clear is that neither of the treatments involved in the two trials was comprised of a heterogeneous mix of improved and deteriorated patients at the end of treatment.

Finally, in a study currently still in progress (Hollon, Wiemer, & Tuason, 1979), we have randomly assigned nonbipolar depressed outpatients to one of four cells: (1) cognitive therapy, (2) pharmacotherapy without maintenance medication, (3) pharmacotherapy with maintenance medication for one year post treatment, and (4) combined cognitive pharmacotherapy. Pharmacotherapy again involved imipramine. Results to date, based on the first 70 patients assigned to treatment, are largely consistent with those described for the Rush et al. (1977) and the Beck et al. (1981) designs. Few if any patients have completed the 12 weeks in treatment in worse condition than they began treatment. The sole exceptions, and they are important exceptions, are as follows.

Three patients have made suicide attempts, one twice, during protocol study treatment. One of these patients died as a result of an attempt. All attempts involved the use of study medications, and all attempts were made by patients in one of the two pharmacotherapy-alone conditions. Suicide is, of course, always a tragic event, and depressed patients are at least as great a risk as any other population. Again, our design prevents us from knowing whether or not the rate of attempts or complications was lower or higher than might have been the case had the patients not been in treatment, but clearly the study medications were a moderately lethal means readily available to our dysphoric population. One patient in cognitive therapy alone also became suicidal, but, lacking any ready access to the means for carrying out the attempt, contacted his therapist and was hospitalized briefly until the immediate crisis abated.

A second class of undesirable concomitants involved the rare noxious side-effect. One patient experienced a urinary blockage and had to be removed from medication. A second patient in the combined modality experienced a brief hypomanic episode which remitted after she discontinued her medications (see Akiskal et al., 1977, 1979; Bunney, 1978).

In general, few if any patients ended treatment in worse condition clinically than they had begun, our absolute definition of attrition. The suicidal patient in cognitive therapy described above was equally, but not more, symptomatic at eight weeks, when he was hospitalized. One other cognitive therapy patient also evidenced no clear change in symptomatology, and ended treatment equally as, but not more, symptomatic as he had begun. Several of the pharmacologically treated patients also evidenced no measurable response to treatment, although none deteriorated during treatment. None of the combined cognitive-pharmacotherapy–treated patients failed to evidence at least some clinical response, with most showing a full clinical remission.

In summary, we can find little evidence supportive of treatment-induced deterioration in depressed populations, either in our cursory review of the literature or in our more intimate association with our own outcome studies. The available evidence is more suggestive of failures to match patients to approximate treatments, followed by simple nonresponse, rather than actual deterioration. Organic complications associated with ECT, infrequent but troublesome major side-effects associated with medication, and the increased availability of a lethal means of attempting suicide with pharmacotherapy appear to represent important qualifications to such a conclusion.

Predicting Response as a Means of Treatment Selection

If our contention proves to be correct and nonresponse due to an unfortunate treatment selection is more of a problem than treatment-induced deterioration, then one might hope to improve clinical practice by improving initial treatment selection. In part, of course, such efforts have already been widely instituted. Delusional depressive patients are generally thought to be refractory to either conventional antidepressants or psychosocial interventions. Antipsychotic-antidepressant combination or electroconvulsive therapy are the more likely treatments of choice with this population (Glassman, Kantor, & Shostak, 1975).

Bielski and Friedel (1976) have provided a particularly succinct review of variables predictive of response to trycyclics. Predictors of positive response to imipramine and amitriptyline included upper socioeconomic class, insidious onset, anorexia, weight loss, middle and late insomnia, and psychomotor disturbance. Predictors of poor response included neurotic, hypochondriacal, and hysterical traits, multiple prior episodes, and delusions. Others (cf. Klein, 1967; Roger & Clay, 1975) have described endogenicity as a positive predictor of response to either pharmacotherapy or ECT.

Prediction of response to the psychosocial interventions has been less thoroughly researched. Weissman, Prusoff, DiMascio, Neu, Goklaney, & Klerman (1979) have reported that the patients, endogenous or nonendogenous, with a clear-cut situational precipitant do better in IPT than do nonsituational depressives. In that same trial, endogenicity predicted response to pharmacotherapy. Cognitive therapy, on the other hand, appears to overlap with pharmacotherapy in that endogenous outpatients appear to be the better responders to either modality (Hollon, Beck, Kovacs, & Rush, 1977).

The Problem with Prediction

There remains a major conceptual problem with many efforts at prediction, both data based and impressionistic. This problem involves the failure to discriminate between predictors of response and indicators of optimal treatment. Any design which holds treatment constant while allowing individual differences to vary and then notes covariation between those individual differences and outcome will provide a prognostic index, but not a basis for selecting treatments. For example, in a reanalysis of the earlier Rush et al. data (1977), we found that patients with an acute episode (onset less than six months prior to beginning treatment) responded more favorably to cognitive therapy than did patients with a more chronic episode (onset longer than six months before beginning treatment) (Rush, Hollon, Beck, & Kovacs, 1978). Does this mean that chronic depressives are poorly served by cognitive therapy? Not at all. When we compared acute depressives in either cognitive therapy or pharmacotherapy, there was no differential treatment effect, because the acutely depressed responded well to either modality. When we compared chronic depressives in those same two modalities, the chronic depressives did far better in cognitive therapy than they did in pharmacotherapy, although they did worse than acute depressives in either modality. Thus, although chronicity was a universal predictor of poor response, it was an important indicator of differential treatment response. As this example indicates, the only sound basis for treatment selection is a design which holds individual differences constant across varied treatments.

Childhood Depression

Opinion remains divided as to whether or not prepubertal children can experience depression in a manner analogous to adults. Therefore, it comes as no surprise that opinion is divided as to whether children suspected of being depressed can or should be treated. Lefkowitz and Burton (1978) have argued that depression in children is a transitory phenomenon which remits on its own without need of intervention. In the face of such transitoriness, they argue that efforts at intervention unnecessarily risk iatrogenic treatment effects. Conversely, it is possible that even self-limiting disorders can produce relatively irreversible consequences. For example, even though depression (if it occurs) may remit spontaneously, problems generated during the depression, for example, social isolation or school problems, may become relatively fixed. The decision whether or not to intervene may actually be a rather complex issue calling for a careful cost/ benefit analysis.

Cost/Benefits Analysis

As with childhood disorders, it is often important to conduct cost/benefit analysis regarding potential iatrogenic effects versus likely benefits. Even when iatrogenic effects are troublesome, such an analysis may prove advisable. The study by Avery and Winokur (1976) illustrates this point. The authors followed a sample of patients either treated with ECT or not so treated over a several-year posttreatment period. Although the ECT-treated patients initially evidenced a higher rate of treatment-related complications, the non-ECT-treated patients evidenced a higher rate of mortality over the full follow-up period. The authors concluded that although some iatrogenic effects were clearly associated with initial ECT, the long-term effects of the intervention were less debilitating than experiencing an inadequately treated depression.

Clinical Vignettes

In the remaining sections, we describe several of our clinical experiences which have resulted in less than adequate patient outcomes. Since the bulk of our experiences have involved either cognitive therapy or pharmacotherapy, our examples of treatment failure draw heavily on patients treated in those modalities. This does not reflect any view on our part that these approaches are not effective. Indeed, we think each approach strikingly effective. Nonetheless, negative outcomes clearly do occur. As described earlier, we have little evidence that such negative outcomes involve deterioration in patient condition relative to pretreatment status. Rather, failure to obtain relief from symptom levels, perhaps due to faulty treatment selection or implementation, appears to be the more frequent occurrence.

Failure to Obtain Symptom Relief

Patient Does Not Accept Modality.   Not infrequently, the patient is unwilling to accept the preferred approach(es) of a particular therapist. One client treated by Hollon in an earlier outcome trial (Beck et al., 1981) clearly illustrated the dangers inherent in such a situation. This client, a middle-aged male, was a professional actor. His recent dysphoria had begun when he and his wife had separated several months earlier, but he had experienced multiple prior episodes throughout his adult life.

The client gave an early history of being an orphan, shuttled from one home to another. He entered therapy with a belief, not fully articulated at intake, that there was some core separation experience in his early childhood that had to be resolved if he were to be able to master his adult vulnerability to separation. His therapist in the research clinic was prepared to focus more on a here-and-now approach, preferring to explicate and remediate beliefs and actions in current life situations, rather than embarking initially on any historical reconstruction targeted at early affective experiences.

Such clear and strongly held beliefs about the optimal path to follow in therapy did not fully emerge until several weeks into therapy. The first indirect evidence involved a repeated inability on the client's part to complete agreed-upon assignments. Only over time did it emerge that the patient was unwilling, rather than unable, to comply. At that point, after consultation, the therapist attempted to arrange a referral to another therapist more adept at taking an historical reconstructive approach. The referral itself was problematic, since the patient viewed this as yet another example of rejection, the latest in a long line of such rejections stretching back to early childhood. Thus the client rejected both the therapist's treatment approach and his attempt to refer the client elsewhere.

It was not clear, even in retrospect, what could have been done to forestall the development of this situation. Routine practice in our research clinic at that time involved a careful screening by an independent clinician, extended discussions of what was involved in the preferred treatment modality, and a description of other types of therapy available elsewhere. Similarly, once it became apparent that strong differences existed in the way the therapist and the patient conceptualized proceeding, efforts were made to both facilitate compromise leading to a working consensus and to make an appropriate referral. None of these efforts was successful. Although a referral was ultimately made, the experience was a traumatic one for the patient.

Patient Does Not Respond to Modality. We have also had the experience of working intensively with clients who joined into the process enthusiastically, yet did not gain any relief from treatment. The young woman described earlier in this paper represents one of our clearest examples. This was a young woman screened into our initial trial and assigned to cognitive therapy (Rush et al., 1977).

At intake, she appeared to be a good candidate for treatment, relatively bright, non-neurotic, and with a good premorbid history. During therapy, she complied in a reasonable fashion with the requests of the therapist, charting moods and behaviors and identifying and testing dysphoric beliefs. Nonetheless, she evidenced little if any change over the three-month study treatment course.

After termination, she was started on tricyclic medication (imipramine) as an adjunct to cognitive therapy. Again, all indications were that she complied fully with the medication regime. Nine months, three tricyclics, and four therapists later, the patient was essentially unchanged. Although she was symptomatically unchanged, both she and her latest therapist (Hollon) were coming to dread the weekly sessions, which were increasingly degenerating into a fruitless (and at times personalized) search for the explanation as to why treatment was not producing change. Had treatment ended at that point, the client would clearly have been more demoralized than when she had begun treatment.

At this point, unknown to her cognitive therapist, the client's pharmacotherapist switched the client to an MAO inhibitor. Change was striking and rapid. The client's dysphoria lifted within a matter of weeks, her response initiation deficits totally reversed, and her social isolation ceased. Quite clearly, the only appropriate attribution for change was to the new medication.

We have seen similar rapid changes in longstanding clinical pictures with other changes in treatment approach. Some of the more dramatic switches have involved the use of MAO inhibitors. For example, we have seen several very positive outcomes in longstanding rapid cycling depressive disorders when those disorders corresponded to the hysteroid dysphorias described by Liebowitz and Klein (1979). Similarly, in our current outcome study, we had the experience of watching one candidate for treatment respond rapidly and completely to a tricyclic despite the fact that his clinical picture was far more consistent with that of a long-term characterological depression of the type considered to be a predictor of poor medication response. In fact, this same candidate had been evaluated on three different occasions over the previous two years, and was each time assigned to some variant of psychotherapy without medication, largely because the client was viewed as a poor candidate for medication. We have also seen numerous instances of successful response to psychotherapy following unsuccessful pharmacotherapy or in the face of low expectations regarding the likelihood of response.

Our basic impression is that our reliance on the predictive literature should be limited to providing guidance for the initial selection of treatment, not to exclude any reasonable form of treatment. If the intervention does not produce a satisfying response in a fairly brief period of time, usually within four to eight weeks, then the first thing to do is to make sure that the intervention has been skillfully or adequately executed. We have, for example, had patients referred to our research trials who were labeled treatment-nonresponsive by their therapists. Although treatment practice doubtless varies across geographic regions, one common practice, at least in the upper Midwest, is to treat depressed patients on subclinical tricyclic levels (e.g., 50–150 mg per day).

If treatment execution appears adequate, yet initial evidence of response is not evident, then we have adopted the position that a rapid change or addition to the treatment regime is called for. We have simply observed far too many instances of initial treatment failure followed by satisfying response to alternate treatment not to try an alternate treatment.

In our experience, actual iatrogenic effects are most likely to occur in the face of patient nonresponse. It is at this juncture that both patient and therapist are likely to engage in what one of our colleagues has referred to as playing "blame the patient." In the absence of response to an adequately executed intervention, it is often tempting to conclude that the patient is not improving because he or she does not want to improve or is sabotaging treatment. Closely related is the belief, again likely to develop in either patient or therapist, that the patient is essentially untreatable. In either case, the proliferation of viable interventions for depression suggests that varying interventions, rather than blaming patients, is the more reasonable approach to such problems.

Patient Sabotages Modality. Although our clinical experience and theoretical orientation lead us to deemphasize "secondary gain" theories of depression, we have occasionally encountered patients who appear to have private agendas which conflict with the therapist's agenda for therapy. One example came from a patient in group cognitive therapy with Brian Shaw and Steven Hollon in Philadelphia, who appeared to resist actively engaging in any activities which would make her less dependent on her husband. Throughout the course of therapy, she verbalized only that she thought it was a wife's role to be closely tied to her husband, and a husband's role to care for his wife. With encouragement and support from the group, she was able to begin, over time, to behave more assertively and independently. She also became less depressed. Within two weeks of her consensually negotiated termination from therapy, however, her husband announced that he was leaving her. His dissatisfaction did not stem from her increased independence and, indeed, he had already been long involved with a series of "other women" and had maintained a separate domicile (unbeknownst to his wife) in nearby New Jersey for several years. He had not, however, been willing to openly withdraw from her while she was depressed or even to inform her that he was considering doing so. In retrospect, it appeared that the dependency and depression served to hold together a troubled marriage and that early efforts to change had run counter to a dimly perceived view by the client that "improvement" entailed danger.

Symptom Relief Followed by the Emergence of Other Symptoms

This process, sometimes referred to as symptom substitution, suggests that the resolution of one set of symptoms, for instance, depression, without the resolution of underlying "causes" will lead to the emergence of new, and perhaps more primitive, symptomatology. Our experience, buttressed by our standard research practice of following all patients for at least two years post treatment, has been that such concerns are largely unfounded. We have yet to observe a client treated with a short-term, structured psychological intervention decompensate or develop other neurotic disorders of clinical magnitude (e.g., become clinically obsessive as a consequence of structured interventions). The emergence of hypomanic or minipsychotic episodes with tricyclic therapy appear to represent two exceptions to this assertion. In our experience, there is usually some indication, either in the patient's prior history or family history, of the increased probability of such occurrences. Typically, such occurrences are usually short-lived and remit when medications are withdrawn or changed.

Somewhat related, but eschewing notions of underlying dynamics, are situations in which clients may be confronted with new or unfamiliar experiences when depressive or longstanding characterological problems begin to change. The client with chronically inadequate social relationships represents a common example. Not infrequently, successful treatment of depressive and related symptomatology makes it possible for such a client to begin to engage in activities previously believed to be unattainable. Confronted with new situations, the client may experience anxiety or desires to avoid which previously were not part of the clinical picture.

Relapse Following Symptom Relief

Our clinical and research experience has led us to conclude that, in most cases, it is easier to intervene successfully in a current episode of depression than it is to forestall the emergence of subsequent episodes. Clinical pharmacological practice is increasingly shifting toward the utilization of maintenance medication strategies (Davis, 1976; Prien & Caffey, 1977). One of the primary rationales for attempting to develop powerful psychosocial interventions is the belief that such approaches may not only be able to produce but also to block the emergence of subsequent episodes (cf. Beck, Rush, Shaw, & Emery, 1979; Hollon & Beck, 1979). Initial indications are that at least cognitive therapy does appear to provide greater prophylaxis against subsequent episodes than does initial pharmacotherapy which is discontinued after symptomatic remission (Kovacs, Rush, Beck, & Hollon, 1981). At this point, there have been no clear tests of the prophylactic capacity of the other psychosocial approaches.

Concern with the stability of changes has caused us to focus on two aspects of treatment which, if left unattended to, can, we believe, produce iatrogenic effects in association with subsequent episodes. We address each of these concerns in turn.

Premature Termination. Not infrequently, we have had clients in cognitive therapy opt to discontinue after fairly brief treatment has led to symptomatic remission. In general, we have developed a preference for working with a client for an average of five to six sessions even after full clinical remission has been obtained. This interval is used primarily to focus on relapse-prevention training. Clients are encouraged to anticipate events that might lead them to become depressed again. Clients are then encouraged to rehearse in imagination what they would do to forestall or work through that imaginary episode.

Psychological Attributions for Relapse. Despite the best efforts, depressed clients frequently do relapse or experience subsequent episodes (the *lowest* rate of relapse we have yet observed is 33% over the first posttreatment year). Failure to prepare clients for the possibility of relapse can have deleterious consequences if the client attributes the relapse to a failure of his therapy. One client treated early in our work at Philadelphia showed a satisfying response to cognitive therapy and was terminated from treatment. Several months later, we received a call from the patient's wife that the former client had locked himself in the bedroom with a gun and was planning to shoot himself. After police intervention defused the immediate crisis, it still proved quite difficult to convince the former client to return to treatment. He viewed the emergence of this new episode of depression as evidence that his former therapy had not been effective. His conclusion was that he was untreatable, and, therefore, that it made little difference whether he lived or died. Once he was disabused of this notion, treatment proceeded rapidly to a successful resolution.

We learned from this instance to be careful to enquire of our clients in advance of termination what it would mean to them if they were to become depressed again. Not infrequently, we find clients hold beliefs similar to those of the client in the example above. Without predicting that any client will become depressed again (some, of course, will not), we do try to impress on them the notion that experiencing another episode need not be overwhelming. Rather like influenza, depression can be viewed as something that you would prefer not to experience, that makes you feel like you want to die when you have it, but which will generally resolve without producing permanent damage. Failure to attend to the patient's likely attributions for relapse, however, can lead to undesirable outcomes.

Conclusions

Overall, there appears to be a range of potentially effective interventions for depression. They appear to vary more in terms of the stability of changes they produce and the absolute safety with which they can be implemented than they do in terms of the magnitude of the changes they produce. Further, there appears to be little evidence of treatment-produced iatrogenic effects, although some exceptions are evident, most notably organic deterioration with ECT or iatrogenic side-effects with pharmacotherapy.

For the short-term structured interventions with which we are most familiar, we have encountered few indications of therapy-induced deterioration. The greater problem appears to be a failure to produce change stemming from either having selected the wrong treatment or having executed that therapy inadequately. Further, failure to attend to the possibility and perception of future episodes is a not uncommon problem with such approaches. We frankly are uncertain as to whether intensive, uncovering, depth analytic therapies or dramatic, provocative humanistic approaches might produce immediate deterioration. However, both clinical lore and recent clinical research suggest that, even if such approaches do not produce deterioration with depressed populations, their likelihood of producing desirable changes lags far behind those for the pharmacological, somatic, and short-term, focused psychosocial approaches.

Part IV _____

Negative Outcome: Parameters and Special Considerations

11

Assessment and Design Prerequisites for Identifying Negative Therapy Outcomes

Alan E. Kazdin

Introduction

The view that psychotherapy produces negative outcome and the evidence proffered on its behalf are a matter of considerable debate (see Chapter 1). Claims about the negative (or positive) effects of psychotherapy make presuppositions that need to be closely examined. The presuppositions pertain to the nature of therapeutic change and the manner in which conclusions are reached about treatment efficacy. Whether negative outcome can be documented depends on more than merely sifting through existing evidence. Basic issues about psychotherapy research need to be addressed before the notion of negative outcome can be treated as an empirical issue.

The purpose of the present chapter is to consider basic issues related to assessment and design of psychotherapy outcome research.

Completion of this chapter was supported in part by a Research Scientist Development Award (MH00353) and by a grant (MH35408) from the National Institute of Mental Health.

The issues are designed to convey that discussion of negative effects makes assumptions about therapeutic change that are not supported by research. This chapter considers assessment and design issues that need to be addressed before empirically based claims can be made about negative effects and before such effects can be considered to be therapeutically induced.

Multiple Outcome Effects

Criteria to Evaluate Therapy Outcome

Claims about the positive or negative effects of psychotherapy presuppose resolution of basic questions about treatment outcome and how it should be measured. Typically, treatment is evaluated by looking for statistically significant changes for a group of persons on a particular measure or set of measures. The conventional approach tends to focus on groups rather than individuals and on statistical significance of the changes, both of which might be questioned. However, an even more basic question pertains to the outcome measures that should be used to decide whether treatment has produced positive or negative effects.

   The complexity of the available outcome criteria relevant to psychotherapy evaluation is conveyed by Strupp and his colleagues (Strupp & Hadley, 1977; Strupp et al., 1977) who propose a tripartite model of psychotherapy outcome. The model proposes that the evaluation of treatment must consider three different perspectives: (1) society, (2) the individual client or patient, and (3) the mental health professional. The perspective of society refers to significant persons in the patient's life and others who make judgments about the person's problems or mental health. These persons are the consumers or partial benefactors of treatment other than the client. The perspective of the client is obviously important and frequently serves as the impetus for seeking treatment. The client's definition of the problem and whether it has been ameliorated, especially in adult treatment, usually is pivotal. Finally, the perspective of the mental health professional refers to judgments by "experts" about the well-being of the patient. The professional's evaluations usually encompass a theoretical perspective of some sort from which the client's problems are viewed.

   The different perspectives obviously can be examined with different types of measures. And one would not necessarily expect the different perspectives to be correlated (Strupp & Hadley, 1977). Indeed, as is evident later, when multiple measures of treatment are considered in more detail, even separate measures from a single perspective may not be highly correlated. The implications of the tripartite model for the evaluation of positive or negative effects of treatment are obvious. A given treatment might have positive and/or negative effects depending on the criterion that is examined. For example, a client may complete therapy with improved self-esteem and increased insight. However, family members (e.g., spouse and children) or the therapist may not believe that the problems have been resolved or may even believe they have become worse. Whether the client has shown positive or negative effects, if this can be meaningfully asked at all, in many cases may be in the eyes of the beholder.

The tripartite model is presented here, not because it represents a universally accepted or widely practiced approach toward treatment evaluation; rather, the model is presented to convey the multiple sources of judgment relevant for treatment evaluation. Because of the different perspectives, the possibility, if not strong likelihood, exists that the effects of treatment might be quite different depending on the measures and the views they reflect.

Apart from different perspectives, how the data are evaluated may make a major difference in whether treatment is considered to have produced positive, negative, or no changes. On a given set of outcome measures, the usual focus is on statistically significant change. Yet one might look to other measures such as the clinical significance of the change, the proportion of persons who attain this magnitude of change, and the breadth and durability of change (Kazdin & Wilson, 1978a). The different measures might lead to quite different conclusions about the effects of treatment. For example, two treatments might produce the same average (mean) improvement for each group as a whole. However, the treatments might differ significantly in the number of persons within each group who achieve a clinically significant change. Also, the durability of change may lead to different conclusions. The changes at posttreatment may not be the same as those reached at follow-up (e.g., Kingsley & Wilson, 1977; Schulz & Hanusa, 1978). Hence, the precise data extracted from a given set of measures, apart from different perspectives, might yield different conclusions about the positive or negative effects of treatment.

Discussion of different criteria that can be used to evaluate therapy outcome conveys the likelihood of discrepancies among alternative measures and the difficulties in reaching a simple verdict about the effects of treatment for a given individual or group of individuals. The problems are even more dramatically illustrated when the nature of therapeutic change is examined. In recent years, research has demonstrated that the nature of change is much more complex than previously conceived.

Behavioral Covariation

Recently, research has revealed that treatment may affect multiple areas of performance. Changes in one area of performance may lead to systematic changes in other areas of performance, a phenomenon referred to as *behavioral or response covariation* (Wahler, Berland, & Coe, 1979; Wahler & Fox, 1980b). Behavioral covariation refers to the relationship of two or more responses that go together, so that change in one behavior has impact on other behaviors as well. Behavior in this context is used in the broadest sense to encompass the full range of dependent measures of potential interest to evaluate change in a particular client's behavior. Thus, responses obtained through different assessment methods such as self-report, projective techniques, observations of overt behavior, and psychophysiological methods are included. Also, "behavior" encompasses measures of affect, cognitions, overt performance, and other levels of measuring personality and performance.

In the context of treatment evaluation, covariation is of interest because changes may occur in two or more responses when only one of these is focused on directly. The changes may occur concurrently or consecutively. However, for present purposes covariation at the same point in time will be highlighted.

The most extensive work on behavioral covariation has been completed in child behavior therapy (cf. Kazdin, 1981; Wahler & Fox, 1980b). Some of the initial investigations demonstrated that changes in one area of performance were associated with "positive" changes in seemingly unrelated behaviors. For example, Nordquist (1971) treated a five-year-old boy who was referred to treatment for frequent bedwetting, tantrums, and noncompliance. Successful treatment of noncompliance (using reward and mild punishment) led to systematic decreases in enuresis, as demonstrated in an ABAB design. Similarly, Wahler, Sperling, Thomas, Teeter, and Luper (1970) treated two children for stuttering. Other problems the children evinced, namely, oppositional behavior and hyperactivity, decreased with systematic decreases in stuttering. Additional data indicated that reductions in stuttering could not be accounted for by inadvertent responses to stuttering on the part of the therapist or parents. Finally, Jackson and Calhoun (1977) decreased inappropriate verbal behavior (whining, shouting, crying) of a ten-year-old retarded boy. In an ABAB design, reductions in inappropriate verbal behaviors were associated with increases in social behavior (joining in games, conversing with peers) and decreases in disruptive behaviors (being out of seat, hitting others).

The above studies suggest that direct changes in particular target behaviors may show beneficial effects on other behaviors. However, additional research with even broader assessment has suggested that behavioral covariation may involve multiple behaviors and that all of the changes might not be in one particular direction (decreases or increases) or viewed as beneficial. For example, Sajwaj, Twardosz, and Burke (1972, Exp. 1) observed multiple behaviors of a disturbed and retarded preschool child who evinced gross inattentiveness and poor academic skills in class. Reduction of excessive talking was associated with multiple changes in other behaviors. Specifically, initiation of conversations and cooperative play increased. However, disruptive behavior at other times of the day than when the program was conducted also increased. Similarly, Becker, Turner, and Sajwaj (1978) treated ruminative vomiting of a three-year-old girl. In an ABAB design, rumination was effectively controlled with the presentation and withdrawal of an aversive consequence (lemon juice) for behavior preceding vomiting. When rumination decreased, crying also decreased and smiling and spontaneous social interaction increased. However, stereotypic play with objects and head-slapping also increased. Thus both "positive" and "negative" changes were evident.

Several other studies might be cited to demonstrate behavioral covariation (Kazdin, 1981; Wahler & Fox, 1980b; Wahler et al., 1979). The theoretical basis of covariation has yet to be illuminated. However, Wahler and his colleagues have been instrumental in identifying the organization of behavior. Apparently, different classes of responses are intercorrelated within an individual's response repertoire. The clusters of responses may vary across individuals and across settings for a given individual (see Kara & Wahler, 1977; Wahler & Fox, 1980a, 1980b). Changes in one behavior in a cluster can alter the correlated behaviors even though these latter behaviors are not focused on directly. Behavior changes which are positively correlated with the altered response are likely to change in the same direction; behaviors negatively correlated with the altered response are likely to show changes in the opposite direction.[1]

Behavioral covariation illustrates the multiplicity of treatment effects. Positive changes in some behavior can be associated with changes in several other behaviors as well, some of which might be

---

[1] Behavioral covariation might be attributed to artifacts of measurement or treatment procedures. Perhaps behaviors covary as a function of the methods of scoring responses so that when one behavior occurs, other behaviors can or cannot occur merely as a function of definitions within the scoring system. This explanation has been ruled out repeatedly (Wahler, 1975; Wahler & Fox, 1980b). Alternatively, when treatment is applied to one behavior, perhaps it is unwittingly administered to other behaviors. This explanation, too, has been ruled out by showing that trainers, therapists, or parents who conduct treatment are not responding differently to concomitant behaviors during the intervention phases (e.g., Becker et al., 1978; Kara & Wahler, 1977; Wahler et al., 1970). In short, some of the more familiar notions or sources of methodological artifact do not readily account for the evidence of behavioral covariation.

viewed as positive and others which might be viewed as negative. Whether treatment is judged to produce one type of effect or another, except perhaps in rather extreme cases, represents a simplification of the nature of therapeutic change. In many ways it is premature to try to reach a decision about the overall positive or negative effects of therapy. The initial task is to examine further the complexity of therapeutic change. Performance of clients in multiple areas of functioning and across different situations needs to be assessed.

It might appear that behavioral covariation has been extensively and perhaps even routinely studied in conventional therapy outcome research because studies measure multiple areas of performance. Typically, clients and/or clinicians complete ratings of target symptoms and work, social, or sexual adjustment (e.g., Sloane, Staples, Cristol, Yorkston, & Whipple, 1975). Unfortunately, global ratings suffer several problems as a method of evaluating therapeutic changes. Such ratings are general, have poorly defined referents in actual performance, rely upon subjective impressions of functioning, are often poorly correlated with actual performance, and are particularly subject to sources of bias such as expectations on the part of raters (see Fiske, 1977; Kazdin & Wilson, 1978b).

To elaborate the nature of behavioral covariation, different assessment models from those currently employed in outcome research need to be examined.[2] Attempts to classify outcome effects simply on the basis of one measure probably reflect a move in the wrong direction in terms of understanding the multifaceted nature of change. From the standpoint of positive or negative effects, the present discussion merely highlights evidence suggesting the manifold effects of treatment and the simultaneous occurrence of positive and negative treatment effects.

Modality of Assessment

Behavioral covariation was illustrated by examining studies that used multiple measures of overt behavior. The research has only begun to elaborate the complexity of outcome effects because it is likely that

---

[2]Although suggestions for an alternative assessment model to evaluate treatment outcome are beyond the scope of the present chapter, the existence of a relevant model is worth noting in passing. Assessment probably should sample multiple areas of client functioning across different situations. The methodology for such assessment has emerged from an interactional model of personality which attempts to examine several dimensions of performance across different situations. Assessment evaluates different situation-response (S-R) units to recognize the interdependence of performance and situations (see Endler & Magnusson, 1976a, 1976b). For the individual client, one can examine performance accross different situations and the different perceptions and affect with which these are systematically associated (see Pervin, 1977). Such an analysis has revealed the interconnections of responses, affect, and perception. The interconnections suggest the likely impact of interventions directed toward circumscribed areas of performance (cf. Kazdin, 1981).

covariations encompass much more than overt behavior. Perceptions, affect, and behaviors are likely to combine in clinical problems and change over the course of treatment. The intricate interrelationships among overt behaviors only provides a preview of the complexity that awaits more comprehensive assessment.

In most outcome research, different methods of assessment are usually included to evaluate a particular construct. The different facets of performance or methods of assessment, for example, may include self-report, overt performance, informant ratings, physiological responses, and so on. Ideally, positive treatment effects would be demonstrated when several different measures all assessing the problem area (e.g., anxiety) show improvement. More commonly, the use of multiple measures has illustrated a high degree of specificity of behavior change (Kazdin, 1979a). Different methods or modalities of assessment of a given clinical problem may not necessarily be highly correlated or even correlated at all.

For example, the extensive outcome research on the treatment of anxiety illustrates the lack of correspondence among alternative measures and modalities of assessment. In one of the earliest demonstrations, Lang and Lazovik (1963) found that improvements in avoidance on a behavioral approach test were not associated with improvements on self-report measures immediately after treatment. More recently, in a review of several treatment studies, Borkovec, Weerts, and Bernstein (1977) examined intercorrelations among self-report, overt behavior, and physiological measures of anxiety. In general, the measures from different modalities produced few significant positive intercorrelations. Even within a single-response modality (e.g., self-report), intercorrelations among alternative measures were infrequently significant.

The lack of a correspondence among measures is by no means restricted to particular areas such as anxiety. For example, multiple measures of social skills frequently do not correspond following treatment (Hersen & Bellack, 1977). In outcome research, global self-ratings of social skills often have little or no correlation with changes in self-report inventories or measures of overt behavior (Kazdin, 1974).

The lack of correspondence among different modalities of a given response area has critical implications for making judgments about the positive or negative effects of treatment. For a particular area of performance, the effects of treatment may be quite different depending upon the measure. Self-ratings of global improvement may indicate marked changes, whereas overt performance may show little or no change or even a slight decrement. To judge treatment as simply showing positive or negative effects requires agreement on a single measure which takes precedence over all others or the neglect of different measures and their interrelationships.

Temporal Variation

Another difficulty in evaluating the positive or negative effects of treatment pertains to variations in the conclusions that might be reached at different points in time for a given measure or set of measures. Most claims about the effects of treatment are based on assessment immediately after treatment is completed. The question is whether the changes immediately after treatment are the appropriate or even major criteria that should be used to evaluate outcome. Conceivably, the conclusions reached about the positive or negative effects of treatment might vary at different points in time.

A few examples readily convey how the verdict about treatment may vary as a function of the particular point in time at which the data are examined. In an outcome study completed by Schulz (1976), institutionalized elderly clients received one of three different interventions that were designed to overcome some of the physical and psychological deterioration associated with aging. The interventions consisted of frequent visits by a college student but varied on the basis of whether the clients could predict and control the visits (e.g., determine the frequency and duration of the visits). Two of the interventions fostered predictability or control with the rationale that these dimensions might influence feelings of depression and helplessness. After treatment, assessment continued at different points in time (24, 30, and 42 months) to monitor the long-term effects of treatment (Schulz & Hanusa, 1978).

The two treatments which were intended to foster feelings of control led to marked changes on measures of physical and psychological status. Both were superior to a random-contact treatment where clients could not predict or control the interactions, and to no treatment. At the follow-up intervals, the results were very different from what they had been immediately after treatment. Specifically, the two major treatment groups became worse at posttreatment assessment; over the course of follow-up, indicators of physical and psychological status showed that these groups were now worse than no-treatment and random-contact subjects. In short, the immediate or short-term positive effects of treatments were compensated by long-term negative effects. In the long run (42 month follow-up), the most favorable results, given the measures used, were obtained for the no-treatment group. For present purposes, the critical point to note is that verdicts about the positive or negative effects of treatment would be very different depending on which point in time treatment effects were evaluated.

Demonstrations of the long-term deleterious effects of treatment relative to no treatment are not rare. An example that has stirred controversy is the 30-year follow-up evaluation of the well known Cambridge Sommerville Youth Study which was designed to prevent delinquency (see McCord, 1978). The results indicated that boys (5–13 years old) who received treatment were worse than no-treatment children years later in terms of crime record, alcohol abuse, mental illness, stress-related disease, and mortality, findings which have stirred controversy (Marquis & Gendreau, 1979; Sobel, 1978).

In therapy outcome studies, it is still the case that follow-up of any sort is infrequent; follow-up beyond a year is rare. Studies that have assessed follow-up of even relatively short durations suggest that the conclusions may vary at different points in time. For example, Kent and O'Leary (1976) compared a behavioral program conducted in the home and at school versus no treatment for conduct problem children. Immediately after treatment, the gains evident in various measures of overt behavior and teacher evaluations indicated marked treatment effects. However, over the course of a nine-month follow-up, the control group improved sufficiently as to make these differences no longer significant. Interestingly, academic performance measures, which were no different at termination of treatment, were significantly higher for the treatment group after the follow-up interval. Thus, the effects of treatment would be evaluated quite differently as a function of the point in time that treatment and no-treatment conditions were compared. Moreover, whether measures of problem behaviors or academic performance were examined also would influence the conclusions that are reached about the effects of treatment.

The dependence of conclusions about treatment effects on the point in time that the results are evaluated is also illustrated in a study by Kingsley and Wilson (1977), who compared alternative treatments for obesity. The treatments included individual and group behavior therapy and a social pressure comparison group. After a 2-month basic treatment period (followed for some subjects with booster sessions), follow-up assessment of weight continued at 3-month intervals for up to 12 months. At posttreatment, the results indicated that the two behavioral conditions led to significantly greater weight losses than the social pressure group. However, at the end of the 12-month follow-up, the two behavioral conditions were quite different. Individual behavior therapy was significantly less effective than group behavior therapy; the social pressure group was intermediate. The basis for the change in pattern of the results was the significant increase in weight of the individual behavior therapy group over the course of follow-up.

The above results suggest that conclusions reached about the relative effectiveness of alternative treatments might vary markedly depending on the follow-up duration. Also, conclusions about the positive or negative effects of particular treatments might vary at different points in time. Thus, unqualified claims about the effects of treatment are likely to be misleading.

General Comments

From the standpoint of assessment there are several issues that militate against simple verdicts about the positive or negative effects of treatment. The first task of research is to document these effects. The multiplicity of changes as an area of research is relatively unchartered; current evidence only argues strongly for the existence of multifaceted and multidirectional changes. Specifically, evidence suggests that within a given modality (e.g., overt behavior) multiple treatment effects occur, some of which might be viewed as positive and others which might be viewed as negative; across modalities for a given construct (e.g., anxiety, social skills), different results are likely to be evident; finally, the results for a given measure or set of measures may vary markedly depending upon the point in time over the course of treatment and follow-up that conclusions are drawn.

On the basis of these, and no doubt other complexities of outcome assessment, it is extremely difficult to discuss treatment effects as being either positive or negative. Perhaps on each specific measure at a single point in time, one might discuss the direction of effects. However, even with such a restricted focus, the meaning of "negative" or "positive" outcome is still not obvious. Presumably, global statements about simple treatment effects would require combining in some fashion information from different measures obtained at different points in time. Even if consensual decision rules could be reached about the means of combining the data from different measures and time frames, the meaningfulness of any simple conclusion might be questionable.

Inferring That Negative Effects Are Treatment Induced: Design Issues

The concern with negative effects is that they are therapeutically induced. Assume for present purposes that assessment issues, discussed earlier, were resolved. To address the design issues, consider the simplest case where a measure of outcome indicates that negative effects occurred, that is, persons showed changes in the direction of becoming worse. Several design issues remain to be resolved before one could discuss whether treatment induced these negative effects.

Instrumentation

Many assessment issues regarding negative effects, discussed earlier, raised questions about the different measures that might be used to draw conclusions about the effects of psychotherapy. For the evaluation of change from one occasion (e.g., pretest) to another (posttreatment), other assessment issues are relevant. Negative effects usually are inferred from the change from pretreatment to posttreatment. Assessment issues related to the internal validity of the investigation are relevant. For several reasons, the researcher may mistakenly conclude that negative (or positive) effects have occurred or are due to treatment.

It is possible for clients to show change from pretreatment to posttreatment as a function of changes in the measuring instrument rather than actual changes in behavior. Campbell and Stanley (1963) referred to artifacts introduced by changes in the measuring instrument as *instrumentation*. Measurement changes could partially account for conclusions about positive or negative treatment effects.

Instrumentation may be especially plausible in many situations where clinical ratings are used to evaluate improvements over the course of treatment (Sloane et al., 1975). Global clinical ratings are based on subjective impressions of assessors and are not carefully anchored to explicit descriptors of behavior. Because the assessment criteria are not tied to specific referents, the likelihood of their changing from one assessment occasion to another is high.

In studies using global ratings that purportedly show negative outcome, the possibility exists that clients have actually become worse in their problems or that they have not changed but the assessors have changed in their criteria for rating symptoms from one assessment occasion to the other. Assessors often are not informed of different treatment conditions as efforts to keep them "blind" or naive are invoked. However, assessors may be well aware of different conditions often because of client comments during posttreatment assessment. Also, at the very least assessors often are aware of which assessment is pretreatment and which is posttreatment by virtue of the time of assessment (e.g., month) or inadvertent comments by the patients during assessment.[3] In any case, changes in the assessors' criteria might well account for the direction and magnitude of pre- and posttreatment changes.

Instrumentation is not restricted to clinical global ratings. Changes

---

[3]Clinical ratings need not necessarily be subject to instrumentation. To ensure that rating criteria do not change over time or at least that changes do not differentially affect pre- and posttreatment assessment, videotaped records of different assessment interviews can be made of patients and evaluated in random order. The difficulty with ratings of live interviews is that due to the timing of assessment, raters can more readily determine whether the rating is likely to be after treatment. Hence, ratings can be systematically influenced by expectations of improvement or no improvement.

in self-report ratings or inventories might vary as a function of the criteria that clients invoke when completing the measure. For example, the threshold for clients for reporting problems might vary over the course of treatment. The specific problems (i.e., actual referents) may or may not be altered but the client's views of the problems and their insight, candor, and willingness to acknowledge them might well change. Hence, even though the measure might be a standardized instrument (e.g., MMPI), the criteria that clients invoke when answering questions may vary from one assessment occasion to another and constitute instrumentation.

If instrumentation occurs, one might expect the impact to be similar across groups. As long as a control group (e.g., no-treatment, waiting list) were included in the study, the effects of instrumentation might not be sufficient to explain differential negative effects across groups. However, it is quite possible that an investigation would show an instrumentation × treatment interaction. This interaction would refer to the fact that instrumentation might vary as a function of the condition (treatment vs. no-treatment) to which persons were assigned. An interaction would be evident if clients who completed treatment responded differently from no-treatment clients to questions related to their mental health, adjustment, or symptoms merely because of differential changes in the rating criteria in each group.

For example, a study might compare treatment with no-treatment for couples seeking counsel for marital discord. After completing treatment, several of the clients may show considerable improvement. The improvement might be due in part to instrumentation, that is, changes in the rating criteria. Perhaps the treated clients realize that their problems are relatively common and that they are not solely at fault. Their marriages may not have improved, perhaps an original goal of treatment, but their evaluation of their unchanged situations may be more positive. Other treated clients may have become worse on the outcome measures. Perhaps some of these clients evaluate their plight more negatively even though there has been no change in their marital situation. More negative evaluations may result from recognition that marriage for life may be unrealistic and that their expectations of themselves and each other were and could not be met. Thus, due to instrumentation in the treated group both positive and negative effects might be evident. That is, therapy altered the criteria that clients invoked to reevaluate their problems. In contrast, no-treatment clients may not have changed in their evaluations at the second assessment.

The conclusion reached in this hypothetical investigation is that some treated clients improved, others became worse, and control subjects did not change. The implication would be that the positive and negative changes in the treated group were therapeutically induced. In fact, treatment and control conditions might have been equally effective (or ineffective). However, the contact with treatment may have precipitated changes in the measurement devices (e.g., client or clinician ratings). The treatment may have led treated and nontreated clients to evaluate their situations and problems differently. Essentially, the plights of treated and nontreated clients may have remained unchanged after treatment although their willingness to recognize, admit, and elaborate their problems may have differentially changed.

Statistical Power Issues

Several issues related to statistical evaluation of the data are relevant to the demonstration of negative outcome. To begin with, negative outcomes usually are estimated to occur at relatively low frequencies in groups that receive treatment. Estimates have varied widely over individual studies because of the different diagnostic groups, clinical problems, and criteria for evaluating outcome. However, the estimates typically have been relatively small (e.g., 10% or under in many studies). Moreover, the differences in percentages between treatment and control groups often are quite small (Lambert et al., 1977). The fact that the proportion of treated clients who show negative outcomes is relatively small and that a small proportion of control clients also show these effects make evaluation of negative outcome rather difficult.

For example, a therapy study may include 30 patients who are assigned randomly to either treatment or no-treatment conditions. At the end of the study, assume that 5 of the 15 clients (33%) who received treatment show negative effects. Assume further that a much lower rate encompassing 2 of 15 (13%) of the control clients show negative effects. Even with such a large difference in percentage, the actual difference in the number of persons who evince negative effects would not be statistically significant ($\chi^2 = 1.68$, uncorrected). Thus, from a statistical standpoint, the low relative frequencies of negative effects in treatment and no-treatment groups make it difficult to detect group differences.

Perhaps the number of persons who show negative outcomes is not as important as the magnitude of these effects among the persons who become worse. A more relevant comparison might be made by extracting for separate analyses the data of clients in treatment and no-treatment groups who became worse. Presumably, if both treated and nontreated clients show deterioration, the deterioration of the former might be greater. To evaluate the magnitude of negative outcome, clients in each group who became worse could be compared (t or F test).

Actually in most studies it would be extremely difficult to detect a significant difference in magnitude of change, if one existed, because of the small subsample size and the commensurately large t or F required to detect change. The small proportion of persons who show negative outcomes, assuming for the moment that criteria for such effects were agreed upon, make evaluation of the statistical significance of these effects problematic.

Other issues are relevant regarding the magnitude of change. The criterion to indicate that persons show negative outcome usually consists of a change on one or more dependent measures in the direction of a worsening of symptoms.[4] However, a simple change in score is not sufficient even if in a negative direction. An increase or decrease in score would be expected by chance since measures rarely have perfect test–retest reliability and show no change in magnitude of scores from one test occasion to another. Thus, persons for whom measures are obtained on separate occasions will show some change. A change in a negative direction does not mean that the client has become worse. What is needed is a means of determining whether the amount of change is statistically significant and exceeds the magnitude that would be expected by "chance."

Whether change in an *individual's* score is statistically significant is difficult to assess. Several tests are available to evaluate change in individual subjects (see Kazdin, 1970; Kratochwill, 1978). However, most tests require continuous assessment conducted before and during (or after) treatment. With multiple data points, the likelihood of a change of a particular magnitude exceeding the changes occurring by chance can be determined. Unfortunately, research cited in support of negative effects does not provide the opportunity to estimate whether the magnitude of change for individuals is statistically significant.

The clinical significance or importance of the changes in individual patients represents an important issue as well. If persons change a few or even several points on a particular measure, they may be "worse" in the strict sense of their numerical scores. Yet it is quite another matter to evaluate whether the scores reflect a difference that has any counterpart in the person's daily performance or functioning. Whether there

---

[4]Bergin (1966,1971) has also used as evidence of deterioration an increase in variance of the treatment group's performance relative to the variance of the no-treatment group. The rationale was that an increase in variance indicates that some clients improve whereas others become worse, increasing the spread of posttreatment scores. However, the lack of necessary connection between variance increases and deterioration has been pointed out by Gottman (1973), leading to partial retraction of the claim by Bergin that variance changes entail deterioration (Bergin & Lambert, 1978). For present purposes, whether a variance change is evident or not, the concern is with those persons who are said to have become worse.

are concrete implications in performance for clients who are said to have become worse goes beyond statistical considerations. If claims are to be made about treatment producing negative effects, further attention to the clinical significance of the change is needed.

Nonspecific Treatment Factors

Evaluation of the effects of alternative treatments is complicated by the fact that clients may improve for a variety of reasons, some of which may be peculiar to the specific treatment that is applied. Several ingredients are common to most forms of psychotherapy, including meeting with the client, providing a conceptual framework to identify and explain the problem, mobilizing the client's hopes and expectancies for improvement, and so on (see Frank, 1973). These ingredients are often referred to as *nonspecific treatment factors* to denote their commonality across manifold techniques.

From the standpoint of outcome research, nonspecific treatment factors are of concern because they raise questions about the reasons why treatments produce change. When an investigator is interested in identifying why a particular technique produced change, it is important to rule out as a rival explanation that change could be explained by participation in treatment *per se*. Various control conditions or alternative treatment conditions are necessary so that group differences are not likely to be explained by nonspecific treatment factors (Jacobson & Baucom, 1977; Kazdin, 1979b; O'Leary & Borkovec, 1978).

Although researchers have been aware of the importance of nonspecific treatment factors for many years, the use of control procedures to address these factors is relatively recent. And even for many well-researched techniques, data have not completely ruled out the hypothesis that changes over the course of treatment might be due to nonspecific factors rather than to unique characteristics of treatment (see Kazdin & Wilcoxon, 1976).

Nonspecific treatment effects raise critical issues for the investigation of positive or negative treatment effects. Claims are made that negative effects are therapeutically induced. It is important to identify whether such effects are peculiar to particular forms of treatment or to treatment in general. Reviews of the evidence and case material have suggested that negative effects occur across a variety of different treatments (Lambert et al., 1977), although insufficient evidence exists to make comparisons among alternative techniques. If all or most treatments produce negative effects, then the specific ingredients associated with different treatments become less plausible as the basis for the effects. Common ingredients become more parsimonious as an explanation.

Conceivably, treated clients rather than nontreated clients may show more negative outcome because of ancillary features of treatment. For example, the effects of knowing that one is entering treatment or that one has been treated, formal acknowledgment that one needs help and cannot handle one's own problems, and reactions of others who know one is in therapy all might lead some persons in a treatment group to perform less well than those who are in a no-treatment group. In such cases, negative outcome would be more evident in a treatment group than in the no-treatment group. However, these negative outcomes can be traced to accoutrements of being in treatment. The specific treatment techniques would not be responsible for inducing negative outcomes.

Obviously, a major role of outcome research is to identify the bases of positive or negative treatment effects. Basic questions still remain about the reasons why treatments produce change. Relatively few studies have tested alternative explanations and have ruled out the potential impact of ingredients common to different techniques. Hence, in one sense, until such research increases, whether treatment effects of any sort are "therapeutically induced" will be clouded. The experience of therapy includes many facets, experiences, and procedures that are weighted and interpreted differently as a function of different conceptual positions. The contribution of specific features of treatment to client change, independent of the direction of change, remains to be elaborated.

General Comments

Whether negative outcome is therapeutically induced requires consideration of several design issues. Within a given group, either positive or negative changes occasionally might be traced to changes in assessment criteria of those who complete the outcome measures. Also, changes in assessment may not be identical across groups so that inclusion of a no-treatment group *per se* may not control all of the sources of assessment bias that operate. Assignment to and participation in treatment may sensitize some clients to posttreatment assessment in ways consistent with the pattern of data considered to reflect negative effects.

Nonspecific treatment factors also raise important considerations for negative effects. If agreement existed that negative outcome is more characteristic of treatment rather than no-treatment groups, the basis for this difference would still need to be elaborated. Because of the gamut of variables included under the rubric of nonspecific treatment factors, it is not clear that treatment or some ancillary or common feature associated with treatment produces negative effects.

Finally, the whole issue of negative outcome needs greater analysis at the level of the individual client. As yet, it is unclear whether the magnitude of change within individuals who supposedly show negative outcomes is greater than the magnitude of change expected by chance. Until additional analyses of statistical and clinical significance of change are provided for individual clients, negative outcome will be difficult to evaluate. For groups of clients, the relatively low proportion of clients who are considered to show negative outcome also raises problems. The statistical power to detect negative outcome is limited, so that general conclusions beyond the individual are also difficult to extract.

Summary and Conclusions

Discussions of negative outcome have been based primarily on sifting of the outcome evidence. Controversy has focused on whether various measures proposed to demonstrate deterioration are appropriate, and whether the evidence is sufficiently clear to support claims for therapeutically induced effects. Actually, several basic assessment issues need to be resolved in psychotherapy outcome research before one can meaningfully discuss the negative (or perhaps positive) effects of therapy. To begin with, the notion of positive or negative effects is oversimplistic. Positive and negative effects are quasi-technical terms to denote that the results are either "good" or "bad" for a given client (although the same effects may be either good or bad for different clients). The more familiar terms boldly convey the dichotomous thinking underlying current attempts to classify therapy outcome.

Existing research suggests that the effects of treatment are multifaceted and broad. Many changes may occur, some of which might be viewed as positive, others of which might be viewed as negative. Hence, the effects of treatment can be both positive and negative for the same client but of course in different ways. Also, any particular change might be viewed as positive and negative by different persons (e.g., client, spouse, therapist). When several different measures of the same construct are used, they may not correspond at outcome. Hence, negative effects on one measure may not reflect the direction of change on another measure. Finally, for a given measure or set of measures, conclusions about the effects of treatment at one point in time (e.g., posttreatment) may not reflect the conclusions that would be reached at a different point in time (e.g., one-year follow-up).

Claims for the existence of negative outcome require much more detailed consideration of the multiplicity of outcome effects and their dependence on several factors such as assessment methods, perspective, and point in time of their evaluation. It is unfair to demand, at this time, that all conclusions about treatment be based on a complete assessment battery of multiple measures of different areas of functioning. In fact, the course and range of therapeutic changes have not been elaborated sufficiently. Rather than simple classifications of circumscribed treatment outcomes, the emphasis needs to shift to elaboration of the breadth and complexity of change.

Assuming that many of the assessment problems noted above were resolved, several matters would still remain. Whether changes in clients over the course of treatment represent a statistically or clinically significant decrement in performance has yet to be addressed. Without decision rules for evaluating change for the individual client, so-called negative outcome is difficult to interpret. Further, assuming that this issue were resolved, there would still be the matter of determining that treatment induced negative effects. Alternative rival interpretations (e.g., instrumentation or instrumentation × treatment interactions) pose problems of identifying the mechanisms or bases for outcome effects, and have yet to be addressed.

The purpose of the present chapter is not to deny the existence of negative outcome following treatment. However, before the phenomenon can be meaningfully evaluated a number of issues need to be addressed. In particular, the multiple effects of treatment need to be charted more carefully so that therapeutic outcome is better understood than is currently the case. Also, design issues need to focus more squarely on the mechanisms that account for any therapeutic change.

12

Negative Outcome: The Influence of Factors Outside Therapy

Peggy Thoits

EDITORS' NOTE: *This chapter addresses research on the influence of life stressors upon psychiatric status, both in conjunction with and independent of psychotherapy. While the impact of life stressors upon the functioning of individuals who are not in therapy may at first appear tangential to the main topic of the book, we believe that including this material is important nonetheless. First, the available evidence suggests that these factors affect individuals, whether they are in therapy or not. Second, insufficient attention has been paid by psychotherapy researchers to the influence of factors outside therapy. Furthermore, the literature reviewed by Dr. Thoits, coming as it does from a sociological perspective, is not familiar to most practitioners. For these reasons material has been included in this chapter which extends beyond the issue of psychotherapy proper. Implications of factors outside therapy upon the practice of therapy are further addressed in Chapter 14.*

Psychotherapy outcome studies typically examine characteristics of the therapist, the client, or the therapist–client relationship which correlate with subsequent client functioning. Less commonly, outcome studies compare the psychological adjustment of treated clients to untreated controls. In a review of outcome research Bergin and Lambert (1978) conclude that "on the average, psychotherapy is better than no therapy, that above average therapy often yields excellent results, and that below average therapy may even be harmful" (p. 152). No particular set of client or therapist or treatment variables clearly and strongly predict therapeutic outcome (Bergin & Lambert, 1978; Garfield, 1978; Parloff, Waskown, & Wolfe, 1978).

Implicit in outcome studies is an assumption which may be unwarranted: that subsequent psychological functioning is determined largely by what has gone on in treatment between clients and therapists of certain types. Clients see therapists for extremely short periods of time at relatively infrequent intervals during the course of treatment. Outcome researchers have generally failed to investigate the possibility that occurrences outside the therapy context or occurrences independent of client, therapist, or treatment characteristics may account for deterioration or improvement in psychological functioning.

It is striking that the role of situational, or environmental, factors has been neglected in outcome research (Voth & Orth, 1973). This may be because situational factors have been assumed to be stable throughout the course of therapy, or because situational change has been treated as a dependent rather than an independent variable. Or perhaps because therapy has been assumed to be the only effective procedure for bringing about change (see Bergin & Lambert, 1978), the effects of external circumstances have been ignored.

Ironically, Bergin and Lambert's (1978) discussion of factors which promote spontaneous recovery among control subjects identifies key situational variables of some use in predicting therapeutic outcomes. They suggest that "symptomatic changes in untreated cases could easily result if the person is able to change the environment; or it changes, independent of their actions, in such a way that the conflict trigger is removed" (p. 151). "Conflict trigger" refers in their discussion to problematic parental or heterosexual relationships, yet this concept may be extended easily to other problematic situations—for instance, ongoing occupational, marital, or financial strains. Bergin and Lambert (1978) also suggest that "controls are getting better because they are getting help from persons untrained in formal psychotherapy, who practice a kind of natural therapy" (p. 150). In short, control subjects may exhibit "spontaneous recovery" because life changes reduce ongoing difficulties or because social support is available to ameliorate the effects of stressful conditions.

Interestingly, Bergin and Lambert miss an important implication which follows from these observations: if control subjects can recover due to these factors outside therapy, why cannot patients in therapy as well? Conversely, if patients in treatment deteriorate, could not this also be due to external factors? In short, both negative and positive therapy outcomes may be partially determined by negative and positive changes in the life situation of the patient.

A considerable amount of research in the past 40 years has shown that external, situational factors have major impacts upon individuals' psychological functioning. Research has centered on four sets of variables: major life events, ongoing chronic strains, available social support, and coping tactics. This chapter reviews the evidence regarding these factors and then turns to their possible effects upon therapeutic outcomes. The complex interactions of treatment factors with situational factors are also discussed in some detail.

Life Stresses: Events and Strains

Life events and life strains are used to refer to distinct subsets of a more general construct, life stress. Life events refer to "objective events that disrupt or threaten to disrupt the individual's usual activities" (Dohrenwend & Dohrenwend, 1969, p. 133). These are changes which force the individual to readjust his or her behavior substantially. Such changes are thought to be stressful as they require extensive coping efforts from the actor. Examples of life events include marriage, divorce, change of job, graduation, birth of a child, involvement in a law suit, experience of a natural disaster, and so on. As can be seen from these examples, life events include life cycle stage transitions experienced by most individuals (e.g., marriage, change of job), as well as more uncommon disruptions of daily life (e.g., natural disaster, law suit), and even positive events (e.g., birth of a child).

Life strains refer to ongoing problems that have the potential to arouse threat (Pearlin & Schooler, 1978) and that require the individual to make adjustments more or less continuously in the course of daily life. Examples of life strains include unhappy marital relations, economic deprivation, job pressures, crowded living conditions, and so on. These are problematic circumstances which endure over long periods of time. In contrast, life events represent marked discontinuities in daily life. Strains may follow from events, of course (Gersten, Langner, Eisenberg, & Simcha-Fagan, 1977; Pearlin & Lieberman, 1977; Pearlin, Lieberman, Menaghan, & Mullan, 1981). For example, a divorce may cause financial difficulties, social isolation, and perhaps even problems at work. Strains may also produce events: job pressures may cause an individual to quit work; marital conflict may result in divorce (Gersten et al., 1977). But strains may exist independent of events, as well.

For convenience here, events and strains are together termed life stresses, or stressors, because both are presumed to generate physical and/or psychological disorder. Roughly the same reasoning underlies this presumption for both life events and ongoing life strains (cf. Lazarus, 1966; Pearlin & Schooler, 1978; Scott & Howard, 1970; Selye, 1956): events and strains are thought to threaten the actor's sense of well-being or self-esteem. Efforts to cope with such threats, if unsuccessful, eventually tax the physical and emotional resources of the actor, resulting in physical and/or psychological symptoms of distress. Life stresses, then, consist of problematic social situations, both discontinuous and continuous, which if not mastered may generate disorder.

The relationship between stress and psychological disorder has been extensively studied, particularly in the case of life events. The events–disorder relationship has been examined in three major ways over the past 30 years. First, there have been studies of the psychiatric effects of particular events. During and after World War II, for example, soldiers' reactions to combat (Hastings, 1944; Star, 1949), civilian responses to air raids (Bremer, 1951), and survivors' psychiatric adjustments after concentration camp imprisonment (Eitinger, 1964) were studied. Subsequently, the psychological impact of other events were investigated; for example, the effects of natural disasters (Barton, 1969; Erikson, 1976; Lindemann, 1944; Sterling, Draybek, & Key, 1977; Tyhurst, 1951; White & Haas, 1975), residential relocation following slum clearance (Fried, 1963), job loss accompanying plant shutdowns (Cobb & Kasl, 1977; Gore, 1978), bereavement (Clayton, Desmarais, & Winokur, 1968; Clayton, Halikas, & Maurice, 1971, 1972; Lindemann, 1944), and even President Kennedy's assassination (Sheatsley & Feldman, 1964). Studies of the psychological effects of particular events have generally examined the correlation between the degree of exposure to the event and the intensity or duration of psychological reaction (cf. Church, 1974; Eitinger, 1964; Lifton, 1974; Star, 1949; Sterling et al., 1977; Tyhurst, 1951), or have examined the subjects' reactions to an event over time, with psychiatric assessments taken before, during, and after the event's occurrence (cf. Cobb & Kasl, 1977; Gore, 1978). Designs which compare the psychological adjustment of persons who have experienced a major event with matched controls who have not experienced the event have been comparatively rare (but see Thoits & Hannan, 1979; Cobb & Kasl, 1977; Sterling et al., 1977; Thoits, 1981a).

The second approach to the study of the relationship between life events and psychological disorder, the community survey, has examined the effects of multiple events. Large community samples have been surveyed; respondents were asked about life events recently experienced and about current physical and psychiatric symptoms (Coates, Moyer, & Wellman, 1969; Coates, Moyer, Kendall, & Howat, 1976; Coddington, 1972; B.P. Dohrenwend, 1974; B.S. Dohrenwend, 1973a; Gersten, Langner, Eisenberg, & Orzek, 1974; Markush & Favero, 1974; Myers, Lindenthal, & Pepper, 1971, 1972, 1974; Pearlin & Lieberman, 1977).

Finally, several studies have compared the number and types of events experienced by psychiatric patients prior to hospitalization to those experienced by nonpatient controls. Patient to nonpatient comparisons have been made for schizophrenia (Birley & Brown, 1970; Brown & Birley, 1968), depression and suicide attempts (Barrett, 1979a; Brown & Harris, 1978a; Paykel, 1974; Paykel, Myers, Dienelt, Klerman, Lindenthal, & Pepper, 1969; Paykel, Prusoff, & Myers, 1975), adolescent affective disorders (Hudgens, 1974; Hudgens, Morrison, & Barchha, 1967; Hudgens, Robins, & Delong, 1970), anxiety disorders (Barrett, 1979a), and undifferentiated disorders (Dekker & Webb, 1974).

The results of these three types of studies have yielded strikingly consistent findings over the past 40 years. Life events do increase psychiatric symptoms; the more life events experienced in a given period of time, the greater the symptomatology and the greater the likelihood of hospitalization for psychiatric disorder. However, except for the effects of extreme situations or the extension of effects due to secondary gain, psychiatric responses to events tend to be transitory (Dohrenwend & Dohrenwend, 1969). Symptoms usually disappear spontaneously within one or two years of an event's termination. Thus, there appears to be a sharp increase in distress following one or more events which gradually, with adjustment, decreases to an equilibrium level over time.

Life event researchers have attempted to identify the types of events which are most stressful; the degree of control over the events' occurrence; the degree of anticipation—or expectedness—of the occurrence; and the permanence of the event. Previous laboratory and clinical research has shown that unexpected noxious events over which a subject has little control are highly distressing and may eventually result in depressive symptoms (Glass & Singer, 1972; Schmale, 1972; Seligman, 1975). Life event studies also support this finding. Events judged to be outside the respondent's control are more often reported by depressive patients and suicide attempters than by normal persons (Paykel, 1974) and are significantly and moderately correlated with psychological distress (Dohrenwend, 1974; McFarlane, Norman, Streiner, Roy, & Scott, 1980). Unexpected events, both desirable and undesirable, appear to cause distress, with unexpected undesirable events more highly correlated with distress (McFarlane et al., 1980). Finally, undesirable long-term (permanent) events are more likely to cause depression onset than are short-term events (Brown & Harris, 1978a).

Other studies have attempted to identify events which precipitate particular disorders (schizophrenia, depression, suicide attempt, and neuorsis, Paykel, 1974, 1979; generalized anxiety and panic disorder, Barrett, 1979b; depression, Brown & Harris, 1979a).

In general, permanent undesirable events and, to some extent, uncontrollable events have been indentified as the most stressful.

These findings are consistent with the vast literature on the distressing effects of chronic life strains as well (for reviews see Bachrach, 1975; Bernard, 1972; Croog, 1970; Gross, 1970; Kasl, 1978). Persistent marital, parental, financial, and occupational problems are associated with increased symptoms of psychiatric disturbance. Particularly compelling and careful documentation of the relationships between ongoing strains and psychological distress can be found in Pearlin and Johnson (1977), Pearlin and Lieberman (1979), and Brown and Harris (1978a).

Of special note is the finding that ongoing strains intervene in the relationship between events and disorder (Gersten et al., 1977; Pearlin & Lieberman, 1977; Pearlin et al., 1981). That is, events are most likely to generate disturbance when their occurrences create persistent difficulties. Chronic strains partially explain the relationship between undesirable events and psychological disturbance, although events also have effects on disturbance independent of strains (Pearlin et al., 1981).

Methodological criticisms have resulted in improved research strategies in recent years (cf. Brown & Harris, 1978a; Dohrenwend, Krasnoff, Askenasy, & Dohrenwend, 1978). More recent and careful studies continue to affirm a significant but still modest relationship between life stress and psychological disturbance. Researchers have recently turned attention to mediating factors, focusing on two sets of mediating variables: interpersonal variables, namely the amount of social support available to stressed individuals, and intrapersonal variables, in particular, the person's repertoire of coping responses.

Factors Which Mediate the Events–Disorder Relationship: Social Supports and Coping Resources

Social Support

Numerous investigators have hypothesized that an individual's social support system may help mediate, or buffer, the effects of life events and life strains upon psychological state (Antonovsky, 1974; Caplan, 1974; Cassel, 1976; Cobb, 1976; Kaplan, Cassel, & Gore, 1977; Moss, 1973). Those with a strong social support system should be better able to cope with major life stress; those with little or no social support should be more vulnerable to life stress.

To date, few researchers have offered conceptual definitions of support, preferring to rely solely on simple operational indicators such as whether or not the respondent is married or not, lives alone or not, and so on. Because conceptual definitions of support have been rare, and systematic attempts to develop reliable and valid measuring instruments for support even rarer (but see Duncan-Jones, 1978; Lin, Dean, & Ensel, 1981; McFarlane, Neale, Norman, Roy, & Streiner, 1981, for recent attempts), operationalizations of support have been extremely crude. However, numerous studies using such crude measures suggest the importance of support as a stress-buffer (Andrews, Tennant, Hewson, & Vaillant, 1978; Brown, Bhrolchain, & Harris, 1975; Brown & Harris, 1978a; Caplan, 1972; Cobb & Kasl, 1977; Dean, Lin & Ensel, 1980; de Araujo, van Arsdel, Holmes, & Dudley, 1973; Eaton, 1978; Gore, 1978; Henderson, Byrne, Duncan-Jones, Scott, & Adcock, 1980; House, 1981; LaRocco, House, & French, 1980; Liem & Liem, 1976; Lin, Dean, & Ensel, 1979, 1981; Lowenthal & Haven, 1968; Myers, Lindenthal, & Pepper, 1975; Nuckils, Cassel, & Kaplan, 1972; Pearlin et al., 1981; Thoits, 1978; Turner, 1980; Walker, MacBride, & Vachon, 1977).

In sum, the interrelationships of life stress, social support, and psychological state require further empirical disentangling and exploration. Although the results of most studies completed thus far must be viewed with caution, when coupled with other investigations which demonstrate a substantial relationship between amount of support and psychological well-being (Brown, Davidson, Harris, MacLean, Pollack, & Prudo, 1977; Henderson, Byrne, Duncan-Jones, Adcock, Scott, & Steele, 1978; Henderson, Byrne, Duncan-Jones, Scott, & Adcock, 1980; Henderson, Duncan-Jones, McAuley, & Ritchie, 1978; Lin, Ensel, Simeone, & Kuo, 1979; Miller & Ingham, 1976; Moriwaki, 1978; Roy, 1978), this literature strongly indicates that supportive relationships play a dual role in determining the psychological vulnerability of individuals: lack of support is disturbing in itself, and is especially so in the presence of other life stresses.

Coping Repertoires

Social supports and coping repertoires are typically treated by researchers as separate and unrelated topics (Pearlin et al., 1981). Indeed, social support implies a mobilization of interpersonal resources while coping implies a mobilization of intrapersonal resources. But clearly, both function in the same way: people use these resources to modify the distressing effects of problematic life situations. Coping repertoires, then, are a second set of factors which may mediate the life stress–disorder relationship.

It is important to distinguish between two types of coping: coping as disposition, trait, or style; and coping as a process or set of tactics (Averill & Opton, 1968). A coping disposition refers to the tendency of an individual to use a particular pattern of behavior across a variety of problematic situations. Of special note is the research on "Type A" and "Type B" dispositions (see review by Jenkins, 1976). The Type A disposition—marked by intense achievement motivation, competitiveness, easily provoked impatience, time urgency, abruptness in speech and gesture, overcommitment to vocation, and excessive energetic drive—may interact significantly with work-related strains to produce serious physical and/or mental disorder. Other personality factors, such as flexibility–rigidity, also may mediate the relationship between job strains and distress (Kahn, Wolfe, Quinn, Snoek, & Rosenthal, 1964; McMichael, 1978). Most work in this area, however, is inconclusive. Although the dispositional approach implies consistency in coping behavior, there is little evidence that such consistency exists (Cohen & Lazarus, 1979). Rather, people appear to employ a myriad of coping tactics both within the same situation and across situations.

A review of the voluminous coping literature is impossible here (but see Antonovsky, 1979; Coelho, Hamburg, & Adams, 1974; Cohen & Lazarus, 1979; Haan, 1977; Lazarus, 1966; Lazarus & Launier, 1978; Sarason & Spielberger, 1975; Silver & Wortman, 1980; Spielberger & Sarason, 1975, 1978). It is sufficient to note that experimental studies clearly confirm the mediating effects of coping strategies.

Although life events, particularly undesirable events, and strains seem to be somewhat more prevalent in the lives of the poor, the female, the young, and the unmarried, a body of recent work by Kessler (Kessler, 1979a, 1979b; Kessler & Cleary, 1980) indicates that these life stresses account for little of the variance in psychological outcome within sociodemographic categories. Instead, it appears that these disadvantaged groups are more vulnerable to events and strains. That is, life stresses have more impact on these groups. These findings strongly suggest that not only are life stresses differentially distributed among social groups, but that social supports and coping resources are differentially distributed as well. The clear implication is that disadvantaged groups possess fewer supports and use inefficacious coping strategies in dealing with the life stresses to which they are more often exposed. Only one study has examined the distribution of social support by sociodemographic categories. Thoits (1981) found that lower-class persons possessed significantly less support (e.g., fewer involvements with friends, neighbors, or organizations) than middle- or upper-class persons. Only Pearlin and Schooler (1978) have explored the distributions of coping tactics. As discussed earlier, they found that lower-class individuals and women tended to underutilize efficacious coping responses. These findings support the implications of Kessler's work.

Life Stress and
Psychological Disorder:
A Summary of the Evidence

The weight of the evidence accumulated thus far strongly indicates the following:

1. Undesirable events, particularly uncontrollable and permanent undesirable events, increase the risk of psychological disturbance. The more such events experienced, the greater the risk.

2. Ongoing strains in marital, family, work, and financial activities increase the risk of psychological disturbance.

3. Social support buffers the impacts of undesirable events and ongoing strains on psychological state. Emotional support from a spouse or confidant appears especially efficacious in reducing the impacts of life strains. Support from individuals close to the source of the strain may be more efficacious than support from individuals outside the strain-producing situation.

4. Certain coping tactics buffer the impacts of events and strains. Efficacious tactics may vary by the type of event and/or strain experienced. Impersonal difficulties—such as those deriving from economic or occupational activities—may best be handled by alterations in the meaning of those difficulties (denial, minimization of their severity, etc.), while interpersonal difficulties—such as those arising from marital and parental roles—may be best handled by direct actions on the situation.

5. Personality dispositions may interact with conditions of strain to exacerbate or reduce distress. The role of personality factors as mediators of event or strain impacts has not been well established.

6. Events, strains, social support, and efficacious coping tactics are unequally distributed among social groups. Disadvantaged groups (females, the young, the unmarried, the poor, the uneducated) experience more undesirable, uncontrollable events and more ongoing strains. Women and lower-class indi-

viduals utilize less efficacious coping tactics than ad-
vantaged groups. Lower-class persons may possess
less social support than middle or upper-class persons; the distribution of social support among other
social groups requires further study.

Implications for Therapeutic Outcomes

We turn at last to the implications of life stress research for negative and
positive therapeutic outcomes. As mentioned at the outset, the effects of
external, situational factors upon therapy outcomes has not yet been
examined. The following discussion, therefore, is almost entirely speculative. Hopefully, future research on therapeutic success and failure will
test some of the hypotheses proposed in this discussion.

It seems that external factors may have an effect on outcomes
either independent of, in interaction with, or as a result of therapeutic
treatment. Consider independent effects first, as they have the most
straightforward implications.

Individuals enter treatment for a variety of stated reasons, which
include persistent somatic complaints or unpleasant emotional states,
specific performance problems in various social roles, or generalized
difficulties in relating to others (Gurin, Veroff, & Feld, 1960; Kadushin,
1969). In short, chronic physical, emotional, or social strains play a
major role in presenting complaints. Recently, Kessler, Brown, and
Browman (1981) have corroborated this: the majority of individuals
who enter treatment (over 75%) come from the 8 percent of the population who state that they have a personal problem and perceive themselves as needing help. The majority of these individuals have also
experienced one or more major life events, usually undesirable ones, in
the three weeks to six months preceding treatment (Barrett, 1979a;
Brown, 1978; Brown & Birley, 1968; Brown & Harris, 1978a; Paykel,
1974). It can easily be concluded from these data that life events and
ongoing strains play an important role in the decision to seek treatment. When individuals seek treatment, they probably are experiencing persistent strains that have followed one or more events or that
have existed in their lives for some time.

Given what we know from research on the psychological consequences of events and strains, if these stresses persist throughout the
treatment period, then negative therapy outcomes might well be expected. If a client's events and strains are accompanied by a lack of
external social support and/or inadequate coping techniques, negative

therapeutic outcomes might especially be expected. Further, if, during the period of therapy, additional life events and resultant strains are experienced by the client, negative outcomes would be even more likely, since events and strains tend to be cumulative in their effects.

Note that "therapeutic outcome" is somewhat of a misnomer here: negative psychological effects independent of and following the experience of therapy would be a more appropriate specification.

In short, persistent situational stresses in the life of an individual may lead both to treatment seeking and to continued or even increasing psychological disturbance. Conversely, events that occur during the treatment period which eliminate long-term strains may actually reduce disturbance, again independent of the influence of the treatment itself.

It is difficult to imagine that initial and subsequent life stresses (or their interactions with inadequate social supports or coping repertoires) would have strong effects on outcomes, given that these sources of disturbances are likely to be worked on during therapeutic treatment. However, to repeat an introductory remark, the vast majority of clients' hours are spent outside therapy; changing external circumstances should have at least some influence on subsequent psychological state. The extent of this influence requires examination in future outcome research. That decrements in client functioning are attributable to external circumstances must also be considered, humbling as the implications may be for therapeutic effectiveness.

Entrance into treatment has important implications in its own right, however. First, the sheer act of seeking assistance has ramifications. Kadushin (1969) suggests, "The very process of deciding to go to a psychiatrist or psychotherapist is 'therapeutic' and much that must ultimately change as a result of therapy already begins to change during the decision to seek help" (p. 15). In short, the decision to enter therapy may be a positive life event in itself, with attendant reductions in ongoing strains. Studies of "spontaneous remission" among controls who have had a single assessment interview and studies of clients who terminate early indicate that some improvement does follow from these brief treatment contacts (Bergin & Lambert, 1978; Garfield, 1978). Thus, treatment seeking itself may sponsor enhanced functioning. This is the first way in which the experience of treatment may be said to interact with, or mediate, the effects of events or strains in the client's life.

Provision of Social Support

The second way in which therapeutic treatment may mediate the effect of clients' problems is through the provision of social support. In a very real sense, psychotherapy is "the purchase of friendship" (Schofield,

1964). That is, the client obtains a confidant—someone who listens, who provides emotional acceptance, and who is on the client's side (at least in the ideal case). Here, research on the buffering effects of social support and research on therapist characteristics predictive of positive outcomes are mutually reinforcing. Recall that the possession of social support, particularly the possession of a confidant, reduces the impacts of life events and life strains on psychological disturbance. Research on positive therapist characteristics has also found supportive attitudes to be beneficial to clients. This research has been thus summarized:

> These studies taken together suggest that therapists or counselors who are accurately empathetic, nonpossessively warm in attitude, and genuine are indeed effective. Also, these findings seem to hold with a wide variety of therapists and counselors, regardless of their training or theoretic orientation, and with a wide variety of clients or patients. . . . Further, the evidence suggests that these findings hold in a variety of therapeutic contexts and in both individual and group psychotherapy or counseling (Truax & Mitchell, 1971, p. 310).

A more recent review of this research comes to more cautious conclusions: "The associations are modest and suggest that a more complex association exists between outcome and therapist 'skills' than originally hypothesized" (Parloff et al., 1978). Given that the client's external life stress has not been measured and interacted with supportive therapist attitudes in these studies, such modest associations are to be expected. But taken together, the buffering hypothesis research and the therapist characteristics research suggest strongly that treatment, as social support, may help mediate the impacts of client difficulties on psychological disturbance.

Direct Impact of Therapy

Up to this point in the discussion, the direct effects of treatment upon the client's life situation have been ignored. Clearly these direct effects are the most interesting and potentially the most powerful, since therapy, after all, is intended to cause ameliorative change. Upon consideration, therapy may have one or several of the following direct effects: it may decrease or increase the number of subsequent life events experienced by the client; it may decrease or increase the amount of external social support available to the client; and it may decrease or increase the repertoire of coping tactics used by the client. Each of these effects will be discussed in turn.

In the ideal case, therapy should reduce the number of undesirable events and augment the number of desirable events experienced by the client. When individuals enter treatment they are typically suffering from symptoms which, if persistent or intense enough, may cause deterioration of their performance in daily roles. Such deterioration could lead to undesirable changes, such as loss of job, divorce, failure in school, loss of child custody, or even, occasionally, a jail term. Effective therapy should arrest these processes, preventing the occurrence of such stressful events and possibly promoting the occurrence of desirable events as well. In these ways, treatment may alter a client's life situation so that it ceases to cause distress. On the other hand, therapeutic intervention may actually generate additional "undesirable" events: a client may decide in the course of treatment to free himself or herself from an unhappy marital or occupational situation or to obtain an abortion, for example. These events may be classified as socially or culturally undesirable, yet be perceived by the client as positive in nature. But despite their subjective desirability, such events may generate new strains (financial worries, social isolation, interpersonal conflict) which maintain or even heighten distress. Ironically, then, therapeutic interventions may alter the client's life situation in subjectively desirable ways, yet the client's psychological disturbance may continue or even be increased. (One might term this the paradox of therapeutic intervention.)

These latter comments also apply to ongoing strains. When changes are encouraged to eliminate chronic strains, a series of additional difficulties may result. For example, the spouse of a client seeking help with marital difficulties may be opposed to or threatened by the client's treatment (a not uncommon reaction in tense family situations). Marital conflicts may increase as the client attempts to alter his or her behavior or attitudes. Again, ironically, treatment seeking in response to strains may actually beget heightened stressful circumstances, regardless of the therapist's efforts.

Note that spouse or family antagonism to the client's treatment also reduces his or her externally available social support. Here is another area in which treatment may generate mixed effects. To the extent to which a client is socially isolated, or becomes so as a result of changes in his or her life brought about during the course of treatment (divorce, change of residence, quitting a job, etc.), the client may be handicapped in dealing with his or her difficulties. Therapist support may not be sufficient (e.g., in frequency of contact, in degree of warmth and acceptance) to buffer the client against the stresses of his or her life situation. On the other hand, here is an area in which therapists may encourage substantial and lasting positive change in the client's life. Practitioners and psychiatric researchers have begun to recognize that interventions in the patients' social system may be highly effective in reducing disturbance (Henderson, 1980; Pattison, 1977). That is, while it may be difficult to alter the objective stress conditions facing the client and be time consuming to alter his or her personality structure, intervention in his or her social life may quickly generate possibilities for new behaviors and for more positive interpersonal relationships. More positive interpersonal relationships in turn should augment the buffering of undesirable events and ongoing strains or reduce those strains directly. In short, therapist support in combination with enhanced relationships outside of treatment may be powerful methods for reducing psychological disturbance.

A final way in which therapy may have a direct effect on the client's life situation is in altering his or her repertoire of coping tactics. It can be assumed that the client's tactics are less than efficacious when he or she enters treatment; if the client were coping adequately, why would he or she seek treatment (unless it were simply for enhanced self-understanding)? Therapists may challenge the use of ineffective tactics and encourage the substitution of alternative modes. To the extent that new coping modes are appropriate to the situation (e.g., meaning alterations for intransigent occupational or economic difficulties, direct actions for interpersonal difficulties; Pearlin & Schooler, 1978), such alterations should reduce symptoms of distress. Interestingly, however, the use of certain forms of coping may be opposed by therapists, regardless of their empirically demonstrated or potential efficacy. In particular, selective ignoring, denial, and rationalization (all forms of meaning alteration) may be countered by therapists on the grounds that clients must face reality in order to function in a healthy manner. Ironically, stripping the client of such responses may leave him or her more vulnerable to situational stress. Thus, direct alterations of coping tactics may reduce or enhance the ability of the client to withstand his or her ongoing difficulties, depending upon the coping tactic and the situation.

Clearly, the effects of treatment on the occurrence of events, the experience of strains, the availability of external support, and the use of coping mechanisms may be multiple, complex, and even contradictory in their influences upon treatment outcome. Despite these complexities, incorporation of these factors in outcome research may greatly increase our ability to predict therapeutic success or failure.

Conclusions

Therapeutic outcome research has as its goal not only the evaluation of treatment efficacy but the identification of factors which promote positive outcomes. Although it appears that some therapy is generally more effective in reducing disturbance than no therapy at all, the factors which account for this efficacy have not been adequately identified. The purpose of this chapter has been to suggest factors which may help to explain therapeutic effectiveness (or its lack) and which have not previously been considered in outcome investigations. In particular, factors external to the treatment situation have been the focus of this chapter: clients' life events and ongoing life strains, and the mediators of these factors, social support and coping responses.

Substantial research literature indicates that undesirable events and chronic strains have deleterious psychological effects upon individuals. More recent work indicates that these negative effects may be significantly reduced when individuals possess adequate social support or utilize certain coping strategies. These bodies of research would seem to have clear implications for therapeutic outcomes. Those clients who decline in functioning following treatment might easily have experienced additional life stresses or losses of psychosocial resources, either independent of or as a result of therapy. Those clients who improve following treatment might have experienced fewer events and strains, benefited from added social support, and/or obtained more efficacious coping responses, either independent of or as a result of therapeutic intervention.

In short, incorporating measures of changes in the client's life situation, those which occur naturally and those which occur in response to treatment, might well improve our ability to predict negative and positive therapeutic outcomes. Improved prediction should also identify the conditions under which therapy is most likely to be effective. These conditions, in turn, may suggest new therapeutic techniques or focus efforts on current techniques most likely to promote client well-being in the face of a variety of situational stresses.

The focus of this literature review is restricted to psychological outcomes. The reader should be aware, however, that substantial bodies of research have documented a positive relationship between a number of events and physical illness (cf. Antonovsky & Kats, 1967; Gunderson & Rahe, 1974; Holmes & Masuda, 1974; Rabkin & Struening, 1976; Rahe, 1974; Theorell, 1974), as well as a relationship between on-going strains and physical illness (cf. Cooper & Payne, 1978; Insel & Moss, 1974). A useful bibliography for the interested reader has been compiled by the Human Behavior Research Group (1978).

For a more detailed review of these studies see Cobb, 1976; Dean & Lin, 1977; Mueller, 1980; LaRocco et al., 1980. For a review of the buffering effect of support on physical health outcomes, see House, 1981.

Part V

Negative Outcome: A Theoretical Framework

13

Negative Outcome in Psychotherapy: The Need for a Theoretical Framework

Hans J. Eysenck

On the factual basis offered, it is difficult to disagree with the comments made by Mays and Franks in Chapter 1. Bergin (1980), as intemperate in his criticism of their cautious and conservative survey of the literature (Mays & Franks, 1980) as he has been of my own suggestion that the proof for the efficacy of psychoanalysis and psychotherapy might still be lacking in persuasiveness (Bergin & Lambert, 1978), has not really answered the points made in their original studies (May, 1971; Mays & Franks, 1980). Anyone familiar with Rachman and Wilson's (1980) book *The Effects of Psychological Therapy,* and the devastating criticism it contains of Bergin's earlier reviews of the topic, will not need to be reminded that the summaries of research offered by Bergin often contain irrelevant and contradictory materials, as well as inaccuracies and faulty arguments, and cannot therefore be trusted.

We are left, therefore, with a number of empirical findings which are furiously debated and whose interpretation appears to be dependent on the individual prejudices of the person undertaking the interpretation. In this the outcome is very similar to that which has attended research on the outcome of psychotherapy in its beneficial aspects; there, Rachman and Wilson (1980), in what is undoubtedly the most erudite and scholarly attempt to evaluate the huge literature, came to the conclusion that as far as psychotherapy and psychoanalysis (other than behavior therapy) are concerned, there was still no scientifically admissible evidence for the effectiveness of psychotherapy or psychoanalysis, as compared with no therapy or placebo therapy. Mays and Franks (1980) make it clear that the position is no different as far as the negative outcome effects of psychotherapy and psychoanalysis are concerned; those who claim that positive and negative outcome effects have been demonstrated in a scientifically meaningful way still find it difficult to point to a single study adequately controlled and carried out which would stand up to strict scrutiny.

I would like to suggest that this unsatisfactory situation is in part due to the fact that few psychotherapists, psychiatrists, and clinical psychologists have shown very much interest in the theoretical understanding of the reasons why certain types of interference with the behaviors of neurotic patients should produce positive or negative outcomes. Unless we have a proper theory of this type, and until we can design experiments to test this theory, make predictions, and verify or falsify the deductions made, we will be unlikely to arrive at a satisfactory or agreed-upon conclusion regarding these very complex and difficult problems (Eysenck, 1976).

Such a theory would have to explain a number of findings which, although not universally accepted, do seem to have some empirical basis. The first finding is that neurotic disorders improve over time, even without any kind of psychiatric or psychological advice or help given by trained experts on the basis of some explicit theory. The second fact is that neurotic patients also improve on the whole when subjected to psychotherapy, psychoanalysis, or behavior therapy in any of the various forms assumed by these diverse methodologies. The third finding, regarded as less well established by some people, but to my mind now firmly established, is that patients treated by behavior therapy show improvement more frequently and more quickly than do patients treated by orthodox psychotherapy and psychoanalysis. Fourth, I consider it as proven that some patients experience negative effects or "deterioration" over the course of psychotherapy, although whether this deterioration is due to the psychotherapy itself has not yet been demonstrated. Is it possible to tie together all of these findings in terms of a single, general theory?

A General Theory
of Therapy Outcome

I have suggested a neobehavioristic conditioning theory of neurosis (Eysenck, 1968, 1979a) which claims to be "a unified theory of psycho-therapy, behaviour therapy and spontaneous remission" (Eysenck, 1980), and which, it is suggested, can predict all of these effects and also suggest the parameters, variation of which will produce different outcomes. The theory states, in brief, that neurotic disorders are pro-duced by Pavlovian conditioning, and that treatment consists of Pav-lovian extinction. This brief statement, however, needs, of course, to be complemented by a careful consideration of the particular type of Pavlovian conditioning involved, and the consequences the choice of this particular type of conditioning has for the development of the neurotic disorder and its treatment.

Most psychologists who have accepted some form of Watson's original conditioning paradigm for neurosis have opted for what Grant (1964) calls *Pavlovian A conditioning*, exemplified by the salivation experi-ments in dogs. As I have pointed out repeatedly (Eysenck, 1977), this is the incorrect choice; it is *Pavlovian B conditioning* which is relevant to neurotic disorders, and the many difficulties which beset Watson's origi-nal development of his theory are due to this misunderstanding. I will not here again go into the details of the theory, nor explain how they can help us avoid the pitfalls and criticisms of the Watsonian version of the conditioning theory. Let me merely consider in what ways the resulting theory is relevant to the argument of this book.

Pavlovian B conditioning is exemplified, for instance, by an animal being given repeated injections of morphine. The UCR to morphine involves severe nausea, profuse secretion of saliva, vomiting, and then profound sleep. After repeated daily injections Pavlov's dogs would show severe nausea and profuse secretion of saliva even at the first touch of the experiment, acting as the CS. As Grant (1964) points out: "In Pavlovian B conditioning . . . the CS appears to act as a partial substitute for the UCS. Furthermore, the UCS elicits a complete UCR in Pavlovian B conditioning, whereas in Pavlovian A conditioning the organism emits the UCR of approaching and ingesting the food. Thus in Pavlovian B conditioning stimulation by the UCS is not contingent on the subject's instrumental acts, and hence there is less dependence upon the motivational state of the organism. Furthermore, the CR in Pavlovian B conditioning is very similar to or identical with the UCR, and can hence substitute for it in the conditioning paradigm."

This has important consequences for extinction. It has long been known in experimental psychology that the law of extinction, *to wit,* that unreinforced conditioned responses extinguish, is only very partially true, and that there are many exceptions to the rule. I have suggested an amendment to the law of extinction, stating that under certain circumstances the repeated presentation of the unreinforced CS will lead to an enhancement of the CR; I have called this the *incubation of anxiety* effect, and have adduced a great deal of experimental evidence from work both with animals and with humans, to demonstrate its occurrence (Eysenck, 1979a).

We thus have a rather indeterminate prediction for the consequences of presenting the unreinforced CS; it can lead *either* to extincton *or* to incubation in situations involving Pavlovian B conditioning (it seems likely that in Pavlovian A conditioning only extinction can follow from the presentation of the unreinforced CS.) Under these circumstances it becomes necessary to specify the *parameters* which govern the consequences, and I have suggested strength of the CR and duration of the unreinforced CS presentation as the crucial variables. (Personality is another crucial variable which interacts with the other two, but a discussion of this point would not be relevant in this chapter.) Figure 13-1 illustrates the theory. On the ordinate we have the strength of the CR, while on the abscissa we have the duration of $\overline{CS}$ exposure ($\overline{CS}$ is used as a symbol to denote unreinforced CS presentation). Curve A illustrates the fate of the CR during $\overline{CS}$ presentation. (Our work with obsessive-compulsive neuroses, using "flooding" procedures which present an adequate test of this model, have shown curves very much like Curve A for both verbal and psychophysiological reactions of patients to exposure to dirt under conditions of response prevention; Rachman & Hodgson, 1980.)

The theory postulates that there is a critical strength of CR, such that termination of exposure to $\overline{CS}$ when the CR is above this strength will lead to incubation (enhancement) of anxiety, whereas termination of $\overline{CS}$ exposure when CR strength is below this point will lead to extinction. There is thus a critical point on Curve A above which incubation will take place, but below which extinction will take place.

It will be clear that there is also a *critical duration* of $\overline{CS}$ exposure, in the sense that exposure shorter that the critical period will lead to incubation, whereas exposure longer than this will lead to extinction. Clinical trials of various kinds have on the whole supported this view (Eysenck, 1977).

If the duration of $\overline{CS}$ exposure is continued long enough to produce extinction, then on the next presentation of the $\overline{CS}$ the response curve will be lower (Curve B) due to this extinction, and on each subsequent

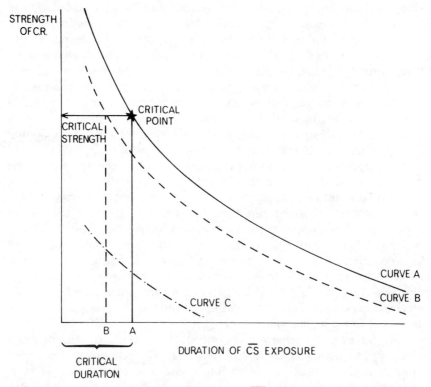

Figure 13-1: Fate of the CR after exposure to $\overline{CS}$ (unreinforced CS).

occasion the curve will be lower again. Curve C is an example of a relatively advanced stage of extinction; typically desensitization methods of treatment would be working in this area of the response space.

There is much evidence, discussed in the papers referred to already, and embracing evidence from studies in behavior therapy of human subjects, and from laboratory studies in animals, to support the theory reported in Figure 13-1. Taking this curve as our departure point, therefore, we would like to suggest that the crucial variable in all methods of treatment of neurotic illness must be *the exposure of the patient to the unreinforced CS* under conditions which either ensure that the exposure does not produce a CR strong enough to exceed the critical point, or, if the critical point is exceeded, that the exposure is continued for a long enough period of time to reduce the CR to a level below the critical point. If the theory is in fact correct, then it should be possible to explain all therapeutic successes and failures, whether achieved by behavior therapy, psychotherapy, or spontaneous remission, in these terms. Equally, we should here find an explanation of negative outcome, and a guide as to the parameters mediating it.

The major methods of behavior therapy, that is, modeling, desensitization, and flooding, clearly fall within this paradigm; what is done there is to expose the patient to the feared object or situation, either *in vivo* or in imagination, keeping his anxiety rather low in the case of desensitization by carefully working up a hierarchy, or in the case of modeling by having the model cope successfully with the object or situation, and clearly not implicating the patient directly. Flooding does produce CRs in excess of the critical point, but exposure of the $\overline{\text{CS}}$ is continued for a long enough period to reduce the CR below the critical point at termination of exposure.

Similar comments apply to Ellis's rational-emotional type of therapy, or Rogers' client-centered type of therapy. In both cases what happens is that the patient is exposed, in imagination and through a process of talking, to the feared objects or situations, thus being forced to expose himself to the unreinforced CS, which, being in a relatively weak form, prevents it from producing CRs above the critical point. The presence of the therapist encouraging the patient and generally serving to relax him acts as an additional variable reducing the strength of the CR in these situations.

As far as psychotherapy is concerned, it seems clear that something very similar is taking place there also. The patient is encouraged to discuss his difficulties, his anxieties, and to confront the objects or situations producing his fear responses. He does so against a background of a sympathetic, helpful listener who is usually supportive in his attitude, thus reducing general anxiety. The critical strength level of the CR is therefore not usually exceeded, and consequently all these encounters should be capable of being symbolized by Curve C in our diagram. It is suggested that all successful methods of psychotherapy (and by successful we do not necessarily mean that their effectiveness *exceeds* that of spontaneous remission, but merely that after therapy the patient is better than he was before therapy) follow this paradigm, and are therefore examples of Pavlovian extinction of Pavlovian B type conditioned responses.

Spontaneous remission does not, in our opinion, pose a particular difficulty to this type of explanation. It is well known that people suffering from neurotic disorders who do not consult a physician, a psychiatrist, a psychoanalyst, or a clinical psychologist will consult other people with whom to discuss their troubles, for example, priests, teachers, friends, relatives. The conditions for extinction are therefore very similar to those which obtain under psychotherapy, and an exactly similar explanation may therefore be given for the occurrence of extinction. We thus end up with a parsimonious theory which is in good accord with experimental facts ascertained in the laboratory and which explains all the phenomena of successful treatment.

It would also seem that our theory can explain the relative success of behavior therapy, and the relatively lower level of success of psychotherapy and spontaneous remission (Kazdin & Wilson, 1978b; Rachman & Wilson, 1980). The methods of behavior therapy explicitly use a mechanism of extinction and have been worked out so as to maximize the effectiveness of this mechanism. The methods of psychotherapy have been worked out on different theoretical principles, and these interfere with the quickest and most reliable methods of extinction. The same is probably true of spontaneous remission; the people to whom the neurotic turns have no explicit theory to guide them and hence their conduct will not be optimal as far as extinction of the neurotic's conditioned responses are concerned. We would therefore expect, and we do find, that the methods of behavior therapy tend to work best, followed by psychotherapy, followed or equalled by spontaneous remission.

The Theory Applied to Negative Outcome

We must now turn to the question of negative outcome, that is, the agreed fact that patients after psychotherapy or psychoanalysis (but not apparently after behavior therapy) sometimes are worse (a term which clearly has been defined in many different ways) than they were at the beginning of therapy. Psychoanalysis in particular has been implicated in this process. In terms of our theory, the explanation would of course be that during the course of treatment the critical point had been exceeded, and that consequently incubation of anxiety, or incrementation of the CR, had taken place. Before discussing this point in relation to psychotherapy and psychoanalysis, we may perhaps look at two instances in behavior therapy where an actual worsening of symptoms has been reported. Both support the explanation given above.

The first instance relates to the observation originally made by Wolpe (1958), and frequently replicated by other behavior therapists using the method of desensitization as well, to the effect that in the process of the therapy it is important to ascend the hierarchy of anxiety-producing situations or objects slowly, and in such a way that at no stage is undue anxiety produced. When an error is made by the therapist and undue anxiety is in fact produced, then it is reported that there is a serious setback in the therapy, the patient actively gets worse, and the therapist has to start all over again. It seems likely that the "excessive anxiety" referred to in these case reports can be identified with a CR in excess of the critical point, and the fact that under these conditions incubation of anxiety is observed considerably strengthens our case.

Why is it that such an exposure to a strong CS, producing a CR above the critical point, and thus resembling flooding methods of treatment, does not have the beneficial effects usually associated with flooding? The answer of course lies in the duration of $\overline{CS}$ exposure; as Figure 13-1 makes it clear, there is a critical duration of $\overline{CS}$ exposure which has to be exceeded in order to produce extinction. In the case of errors made in densensitization treatment, producing anxiety above the critical point, it is suggested by Wolpe that treatment be stopped immediately, relaxation resumed, and the patient restarted at a lower level of the hierarchy. This means, of course, that the strength of the CR is still above the critical point at termination, and the short duration makes it impossible for flooding to have the usual effect of producing extinction after a long exposure to $\overline{CS}$. It has been suggested (Eysenck, 1978) that the proper procedure, once an error has been made, is to switch over to a flooding model, and continue exposure to the CS which produced the strong anxiety for a lengthy period of time, that is, until the CR had been reduced in strength to well below the critical point. A comparison of the usual method with that here suggested would clearly test the hypothesis here used to explain the negative outcome.

Our second example comes from the work of Rachman (1966) who, in working with spider phobias, found that a flooding type of treatment, in which patients were exposed for two minutes to live spiders on a table, failed to improve their condition, and in some cases worsened it. This is a clear case of negative outcome, and may be explained in terms of our theory by the short duration of $\overline{CS}$ exposure. Clearly two minutes is not enough to reduce the CR below the critical point, and later work in our laboratories has successfully used much longer periods (Rachman & Hodgson, 1980). We may thus say that behavior therapy too, under certain specifiable conditions, produces negative outcomes, and that these negative outcomes can be explained very directly in terms of the theory outlined.

How about negative outcomes in psychotherapy and particularly in psychoanalysis? Here I think we must consider carefully the role of the therapist in reducing and keeping below the critical point the strength of the CR. The picture given in Figure 13-1 has to be expanded slightly to take into account, as far as the ordinate is concerned, not only the CR itself, but also other conditions obtaining at the moment, such as degree of (practiced) relaxation, tranquilizing drugs taken to

reduce anxiety, and most of all the attitude and behavior of the therapist, who by reassurance, helpfulness, objectivity, warmness, sympathy, and other means can reassure the patient and reduce his total
level of anxiety. (See Hull's model of drive additivity, Hull, 1943.) The
critical point is really concerned, not only with the direct conditioned
response produced by the stimulus, but with the *total level of anxiety*
reached. The CR is of course the major factor in this, but situational
and therapist-produced reactions interact critically with the CR to produce a level of anxiety above or below the critical point. The work of
Truax (1963) and Truax and Mitchell (1971), with its emphasis on the
beneficial effects of high levels of empathy, positive regard, and genuineness in therapists is very much in line with this suggestion. So of
course is the work suggesting effectiveness of relaxation-training procedures, as practiced in Wolpe's type of desensitization therapy. If these
views are at all along the right lines, it would follow that attitudes and
behaviors opposite to these adopted by a clinician may have the opposite effects, increasing the anxiety level of the patient beyond the critical point, and thus producing negative outcome rather than amelioration of the symptom. Psychoanalysts in particular often adopt an
unhelpful, pseudo-objective, interpretative attitude, which does not
help the patient to relax or encourage him or her in any way; under
these conditions anxiety may easily exceed the critical point and thus
lead to deterioration rather than to improvement. Good anecdotal examples of this effect may be found in the records of treatment published, for example, by Sutherland (1977); these documents describe
the actual behavior of a number of psychoanalysts in the treatment
situation and the effects these behaviors have on the anxiety level of
the patient. They support in every detail the suggestion made above,
and while anecdotal evidence is of course incapable of establishing a
point, it may suggest a line of research which would give us greater
insight into the parameters defining outcome of treatment.

The Theory Contrasted
with Cognitive Theories

How do explanations of this type relate to currently popular theories of
cognitive psychologists? It should be said that the conditioning paradigm here used could easily be rephrased in terms of such concepts as
Bandura's notion of self-efficacy (1979), or some other form of cognitive
expectancy theory. I have criticized such rewordings (Eysenck, 1979b)
on the grounds that (1) there is no self-contained, laboratory-based
cognitive theory which would make the kind of predictions which can

be derived from conditioning theory, and that (2) the cognitive pheno-mena associated with conditioning in humans may be regarded as epiphenomena rather than causal elements. In other words, condi-tioned responses are experienced as "expectations" by the individuals, but the causative element is the conditioning process. I do not want here to enlarge on this issue, but in broad outline my position is similar to that of Wolpe (1981).

Quite generally, it may be said that there has been a distinct failure on the part of cognitive psychologists to develop the kind of experi-mental basis for theoretical postulations which characterizes research on conditioning. Allport (1975), after examining this whole question, characterized modern cognitive psychology as showing:

> an uncritical, or selective or frankly cavalier attitude to experi-mental data; a pervasive atmosphere of special pleading; a curious parochialism in acknowledging even the existence of other workers, and other approaches, to the phenomena under discussion; interpretations of data relying on multiple, arbitrary choice point; and underlying all else a near vacuum of theoretical structure within which to interrelate different sets of experimental results, or direct the search for significant new phenomena. (p. 152)

Theories of this type are not likely to help us in gaining a scientific understanding of the phenomena of neurosis and treatment.

It is of course true to say that in human beings these cognitive phenomena do play an important part, but their relevance to the phenomena of conditioning have always been recognized, as for in-stance, by Pavlov in his notion of the "second signaling system." As he pointed out: "A word is as real a conditioned stimulus for men as all the other stimuli in common with animals, but at the same time more all-inclusive than any other stimuli." And again: "Owing to the entire preceding life of a human adult a word is connected with all the exter-nal and internal stimuli coming to the cerebral hemisphere, signals all of them, replaces all of them, and can, therefore, evoke all the actions and reactions of the organism which these stimuli produce." It is not believed, therefore, that we need go beyond the recognition factors in this connection in order to understand the processes of neurosis, suc-cessful treatment, and negative outcome.

It would, of course, be true to say that cognitive factors inevitably enter into the recognition and definition of conditioned stimuli, and the organization and structuring of conditioned responses. Critics often seem to regard stimuli in the very simple-minded way that early workers in the 1920s did, and also to regard conditioned responses as simple muscle twitches of one kind or another. Modern conditioning theory has advanced far beyond this, and if exposed to criticism it should be informed criticism which takes into account recent developments (Martin & Levey, 1979). In a similar way much of the criticism of neobehavioristic theories of neurosis and treatment in terms of inapplicable paradigms such as Pavlovian A type conditioning are to be deplored; if a theory is to be criticized then it should be criticized in its most recent and strongest form. Failure to do so has been a noticeable feature of the views put forward by cognitive psychologists in recent years.

Summary

We may now summarize our comments and point out their application to the main theme of this book. It is suggested that proper research into negative outcome (as well as positive outcome!) has to be guided by a general theory which specifies parameters to be investigated. The absence of agreement so clearly discernible in discussions of negative outcome is due in large measure to the absence of such a theory. Such disagreements are inevitable when there is a failure to relate the work done to an explicit theoretical statement from which deductions can be made, which suggests specific experiments, and which is subject to falsification. Several examples have already been given of the kind of work which would follow directly from the theoretical principles here outlined, such as contrasting two methods of dealing with errors in Wolpe's desensitization method, or manipulating duration of $\overline{CS}$ in a flooding model. Many others could be suggested, but this is not the place for such an exercise. Let us merely emphasize that the model here suggested clearly states the parameters responsible for successful or unsuccessful treatment of neurotic disorders and is eminently testable both in the animal laboratory, the human laboratory, and the clinic. The model does suggest that negative outcomes are likely to occur, as are positive outcomes, and that the causal factors can be deduced from the theory in question. It is to be hoped that future work on the problem of negative (and positive) outcome will make use of the guidelines so furnished in order to lead to better experiments and greater agreement among practitioners and experimentalists.

Part VI

Conclusions and Implications

14

Negative Outcome:
What To Do About It

Daniel T. Mays and Cyril M. Franks

One way to approach the issue of negative outcome is to formulate a theoretical framework for the investigation of its possible sources and how they interact. This structure can then be used to develop recommendations for future research into the validity of the framework, the incidence of negative outcome, and implications for clinical practice.

Summary of the Evidence to Date

The development of such a framework rests upon a definition which is free of *à priori* bias about causality. Previous definitions have tended to focus primarily upon therapist-caused deterioration, paying little attention to patient, extra-therapeutic, and other factors. The definition proposed in this volume (see Chapter 1) views negative outcome as a significant decline in one or more areas of a patient's functioning, between the onset of therapy and termination of therapy, which persists for a substantial period of time beyond termination of therapy. Thus, the term *negative outcome* is not restricted to negative changes which are therapy induced, and usage does not imply that the therapist is necessarily responsible for the negative change.

The conclusions which follow sum up current knowledge about negative outcome as documented in greater detail in the appropriate pages of this volume. For reasons detailed by the various contributors, these conclusions must be viewed with caution. Kazdin, for example, enumerates a number of possible threats to validity: clinical significance, instrumentation factors, instrumentation × treatment interactions, and statistical power issues are among the most prominent. He also notes that the magnitude of treatment effects, both positive and negative, may be more important than their frequency of occurrence. In evaluating the relevance of any effect, it is essential to consider clinical as well as statistical significance. Barbrack enumerates two possible threats to the external validity of outcome research: possible selective bias against outcome research which reveals poor overall treatment response; and possible differences between therapy conducted under research conditions and therapy practiced in clinical settings. Both would result in the number of negative outcomes which actually occur being understated in published reports. These cautions must be kept in mind when evaluating evidence pertaining to the issue of negative outcome.

There is widespread agreement that negative outcome, as defined above, occurs in psychotherapy other than behavior therapy. As far as behavior therapy is concerned, it is possible to draw firm conclusions only with respect to punishment and the withholding of positive reinforcement (see Chapters 1, 4, 8, and 9), where the risk of negative outcome appears to be greater. Apart from these treatments, evidence to date suggests that rates of negative outcome in behavior therapy are generally low, and significantly below rates among comparable controls. Excluding behavior therapy and also group therapy from consideration (Dies and Teleska conclude that adequate treatment–control comparisons of group therapy are not readily available; see Chapter 6), psychotherapy patients appear to have lower rates of negative outcome than comparable untreated controls (see Chapter 1). Marital therapy represents a qualified exception to this generalization. Provided that negative outcome is defined so as to include cases involving "a worsening of the relationship when the treated patient improves," rates of negative outcome among treated patients exceed those among untreated patients.

Patient Characteristics

In the present volume, investigation of negative outcome in nonpsychotic diagnostic groups was confined to four high-risk groups. Since nearly all patients with a psychotic disorder receive medications which are likely to exert a strong confounding effect (see, for example, May & Tuma, 1976), the issue of negative outcome with psychotic patients was not addressed in this volume. The diagnostic groups considered are: borderline personality disorder, anorexia nervosa, obsessive-compulsive disorder, and depressive disorder.

The present consensus seems to be that patients with borderline personality disorders are more prone to experience negative outcome than the patient population in general. This is especially true when the treatment is psychoanalysis or insight-oriented psychotherapy (see Chapters 2, 3, and 7; see also Aronson & Weintraub, 1968; Horwitz, 1974; Weber, Elinson, & Moss, 1965), and also group psychotherapy (see Chapter 6). It may be that patients with borderline personality disorders are at higher risk in other types of therapy as well. In group psychotherapy, patients (including those with borderline personality disorders) who fail to develop a working alliance with the rest of the group seem to be at especially high risk for negative outcome. These individuals are much more likely to assume either "scapegoat" or "defiant" roles. Thus, the maladaptive interpersonal styles of these patients, which are self-defeating elsewhere, may prove to be equally destructive in therapy (see Chapter 6).

The high mortality rate among anorexic patients (15–20% in the absence of treatment) suggests inclusion of this group in any investigation of negative outcome. Horne concludes that mortality rates among anorexic patients treated with psychoanalysis are not significantly different from those among untreated patients (see Chapter 8). Most investigators would agree that these rates are unacceptably high. He also concludes that behavior therapy is effective in promoting rapid weight gain among anorexic patients, but notes that some authors postulate that when other areas of patient difficulty are neglected, rapid weight gain can be accompanied by increased subjective distress and risk of suicide (e.g. Bruch, 1974). Of course, most contemporary behavior therapy programs address these other areas.

The inclusion of obsessive-compulsive disorders in the list of high-risk groups is based in part upon studies by Jonckheere (1965) and Kringler (1965). In their analysis of negative outcome among obsessional patients (Chapter 9), Beech and Vaughan take issue with this contention and conclude that, as far as behavior therapy is concerned, negative outcomes are "too few to permit useful generalizations to be made." Individuals with poorer prognoses generally fail to make significant improvements, but they rarely experience negative outcomes. An exception appears to be aversive conditioning with high anxiety obsessive-compulsives, which tends to be associated with higher rates of negative outcome.

Depressive disorders were included in the list of high-risk diagnostic groups because of the higher risk of suicide among these patients (see Arieti & Bemporad, 1978; Farberow & Shneidman, 1961; Mattson, Sesse, & Hawkins, 1969; and Rennie, 1942). In their review, Hollon and Emerson conclude (Chapter 10) that virtually no evidence is available to suggest that rates of negative outcome among treated depressives exceed those among comparable controls, although they properly note that the absence of adequate patient–control comparisons limits inferences about relative rates of suicide and other negative outcomes. This conclusion does not mean that depressives are a low-risk group. Rather, it suggests that they are a high-risk group without therapy, and that therapy may serve to reduce this risk. This hypothesis is buttressed by Hollon and Emerson's finding that all individuals in their own studies (encompassing 144 patients) who attempted suicide had received only drug therapy but not psychotherapy. In addition to suicide, Hollon and Emerson note another possible negative outcome among depressed patients, namely, increased patient hopelessness. They attribute this outcome to instances of the therapist explicitly or implicitly blaming the patient for lack of progress.

Therapist Characteristics

Most contributors agree that low levels of such therapist-offered facilitative conditions as empathy, positive regard, and genuineness increase the risk of negative outcome in individual psychotherapy. However, there is disagreement about whether these variables are more significant than patient variables in predicting negative outcome. Inconsistencies exist in studies of the relationship between outcome and facilitative conditions (see Garfield & Bergin, 1971).

When the treatment is psychoanalysis (and possibly for other treatments; see Chapter 2), the more disturbed the patient, the more therapist skill appears to be critical to the avoidance of negative outcome. In insight therapy, both increased therapist activity and continual attention to structuring and maintaining the treatment contract are important in avoiding negative outcome with more disturbed patients.

Therapist facilitative conditions are also important in group therapy but the presence of the group introduces additional complications. Dies and Teleska (Chapter 6) draw attention to potentially harmful effects of therapists who "push for strong emotional expression almost as an end in itself." Two leadership patterns which are particularly likely to lead to deleterious outcome are (1) a confronting and aggressive style, coupled with lack of warmth and consideration; and (2) a laissez-faire style which combines low activity with low affection. The latter produces adverse effects by permitting high levels of negative feedback in the absence of protective group norms. Similarly, in family therapy, either distant or overly confrontative therapist styles appear to be associated with increased risk of negative outcome. To avoid negative outcome, Kniskern and Gurman underline the importance of father involvement in family therapy, and spouse involvement in marital therapy. It is also important for the therapist to consider the impact of therapy on other family members even when, or perhaps especially when, the latter are not involved in the treatment.

Extratherapeutic Factors

Considering the fact that therapy rarely occupies more than a few hours a week, it is surprising how little attention has been paid by outcome researchers to events occurring outside the consulting room. Commenting from a sociological perspective, Thoits (Chapter 12) reviews the reported relationships between life events and life strains, on the one hand, and psychiatric status on the other. Life events are those events which require individuals to readjust their behavior substantially, such as life cycle stage transitions or uncommon disruptions of daily life. Life strains pertain to those potentially threatening events which require more or less continual adjustment by the individuals concerned. These variables consistently correlate at least moderately with measures of subjective distress, especially anxiety and depression. Psychiatric disorders following traumatic life events tend to be transitory, usually disappearing within one to two years following cessation of the event. In other words, an increase in the number of life events a person is dealing with can be expected to result in at least a transient increase in negative outcome on such measures. Both greater availability of social supports and a better repertoire of coping responses tend to reduce the impact of life stressors upon the level of distress.

In addition to relationships among the variables reviewed by Thoits, there are a number of potential interaction effects among various dimensions of personality and social relationship, pertaining both to patients and to family members. Colson and his co-workers note an extraordinary tendency for family members of those patients experiencing negative outcome (in the Menninger Foundation research project on psychotherapy and psychoanalysis) either to reinforce pathological behavior or to shield the "sick" family member from the consequences of his or her pathological behavior. Colson and co-workers (Chapter 3) also found a consistent pattern in which overindulgent behavior among family members alternates with harshly controlling and punitive behavior. An important point is that these family interaction patterns are reciprocally determined. That is, both the patient and the family members influence the pattern. Many of these patients would try the tolerance and patience of even the best intentioned and most psychologically stable of family members. At the same time, family members undoubtedly act at times to manipulate patient behavior in pursuit of their own pathological gratification. Gurman and Kniskern (Chapter 5) suggest that the development of alliances with key family members may reduce both deliberate and unwitting "sabotage" of therapy and the risk of negative outcome.

Toward a Theory of
Negative Outcome

As Eysenck points out in Chapter 13, psychotherapy outcome research suffers from the absence of a general theory. Given specified parameters, such a theory should be able to predict outcome, allow variables to be operationally defined, and permit testing of predictions derived from the theory. While many parameters pertaining to negative outcome require further exploration and refinement (*vide infra*), enough is currently known to permit formulation of a set of provisional postulates as a working basis for future research. These postulates are as follows.

Postulate I

The overall impact of psychotherapy is to reduce the negative outcome which would occur in the absence of treatment. This applies to individual as well as group therapy. In therapy directed at marital issues, it is hypothesized that rates of negative outcome are generally less than or equal to rates among controls, except for a greater degree of patient dissatisfaction with lack of relationship improvement among treated patients. (Consistent with this hypothesis, Kniskern and Gurman found that fewer negative outcomes occur when the couple is treated together, which would presumably permit a greater evolution of mutual expectations, than when they are treated separately.)

Postulate II

Negative outcome results from the interaction of factors which serve to reduce negative outcome with factors which serve to increase negative outcome.

Postulate III

Certain characteristics of the treatment modality, and certain therapist characteristics, are likely to increase the incidence of negative outcome. Characteristics of treatment modality include those which use punishment or the withholding of positive reinforcement, such as occur in aversive conditioning and in poorly planned behavior modification programs using punishment. In addition, it is likely that certain patients experience psychoanalysis and insight-oriented forms of therapy as involving the withholding of positive reinforcement (see below). Therapist characteristics which increase the risk of negative outcome include low levels of such therapist-facilitative conditions as empathy, positive regard, and genuineness in individual and group psychotherapy; a confronting and aggressive style coupled with lack of warmth and consideration in group and family therapy; and a style which combines low activity with low affection in group psychotherapy. Therapist characteristics which increase the risk of negative outcome appear to be separable into two categories: those which constitute a perceived threat to the patient; and those which are perceived to provide low levels of support.

Postulate IV

There are specific patient characteristics associated with higher risk for negative outcome. Four patient populations were examined in this volume. One of these, the obsessive-compulsive group, does not appear to be at high risk for negative outcome. Another, the depressed group, appears to be at increased risk without psychotherapy, but at less risk when receiving therapy. The third and fourth, the borderline disordered and the anorexic groups respectively, appear to experience increased risk in at least certain forms of therapy. An examination of the characteristics of these high-risk groups reveals a remarkable similarity from group to group.

In depressed patients, certain personality characteristics have been identified as markers for increased risk of suicide: (1) limitations in the ability to relate to others; (2) marital isolation; (3) use of distorted communications; and (4) help negation. This last characteristic encompasses (1) a belief that help is unavailable; and (2) behavior which rejects or negates offered help (Fawcett, Leff, & Bunney, 1969).

Those studies suggesting a relationship between borderline disorder and higher risk of negative outcome include features consistent with the operational criteria for borderline and schizotypal personality disorders enumerated in *DSM-III*. The distinction between borderline

and schizotypal personality disorders arose from Spitzer and co-
workers' investigation of what was then conceptualized as borderline
schizophrenia (Spitzer, Endicott, & Gibbon, 1979). Operational criteria
based on data from the Extended Family Study became the basis for
the *DSM-III* schizotypal disorder. Despite the evidence that as many as
54 percent of patients in some samples meet criteria for both schizotypal and borderline disorders, the *DSM-III* criteria have been found to
be statistically independent (Spitzer et al., 1979), and the two classifications appear to have different familial patterns. At present, both borderline and schizotypal personality features should be regarded as indicators of high risk potential in psychotherapy.

Characteristics of the borderline personality disorder include: (1)
impulsivity or unpredictability in potentially self-damaging areas (including physically self-damaging acts); (2) a pattern of unstable and
intense interpersonal relationships; (3) inappropriately intense anger or
lack of control of anger; (4) identity disturbance [uncertainty about several identity issues such as self-image, gender identity, long-term goals,
friendship patterns, values, and loyalties ("Who am I?")]; (5) marked
rapid shifts from normal mood to depression, irritability, or anxiety; (6)
physically self-damaging acts; and (7) chronic feelings of emptiness or
boredom. According to *DSM-III*, during periods of extreme stress, transient psychotic symptoms may occur in this population. Nonetheless, it
is important to emphasize again that a borderline personality disorder is
neither a neurosis, nor an antisocial personality disorder, nor a psychosis (except during these occasional transient episodes).

The schizotypal personality disorder (*DSM-III*) is characterized by:
(1) magical thinking; (2) ideas of reference; (3) social isolation; (4) recurrent illusions, depersonalization, or derealization (not associated with
panic attacks); (5) digressive, vague, overelaborate, circumstantial, or
metaphorical speech; (6) inadequate rapport in face-to-face interaction;
(7) suspiciousness or paranoid ideation; and (8) undue social anxiety or
hypersensitivity to real or imagined criticism. During periods of extreme stress, transient psychotic symptoms may be present.

The importance of the borderline personality disorder syndrome is
further underscored by the fact that according to some investigators
such patients constitute 6 to 10 percent of the total population (see
Chapter 6). Considerable research effort is currently being expended to
validate and/or refine the concept of borderline disorder (see Gunderson, Siever, & Spaulding, 1983; Koenigsberg, Kernberg, & Schomer,
1983; Soloff & Millward, 1983). While future understanding of the disorder will benefit from such research, the borderline concept and current criteria have utility today, not the least of which is that of alerting
psychotherapists to high risk potential for negative outcome.

Garfinkel and Garner (1982) conclude that a subtype of anorexics, bulimic anorexics, frequently display features of borderline personality organization. Since both patient groups appear to be at high risk for negative outcome, this finding is particularly significant. These authors note a number of features in these patients which are consistent with a borderline diagnosis: (1) poor impulse control (even in areas not related to eating, including impulsive sexual patterns); (2) misuse of drugs and alcohol; (3) stealing; (4) self-mutilation; (5) suicide attempts; (6) severely disturbed identity; (7) transient depersonalization episodes; and (8) fluctuating interpersonal relationships (between transient superficial and intense dependent ones) as the most prominent features. They suggest that problems with separation and autonomy, which occur frequently among borderline patients, may predispose some to develop anorexia.

These four high-risk patient groups (depressed, borderline, schizotypal, and bulimic anorexics) have certain general characteristics in common:

1. Impaired or conflicted social support:
   a. social isolation;
   b. unstable and intense interpersonal relationships;
   c. inadequate interpersonal rapport due to limited interpersonal skills (see 2 below);
   d. prominent conflicts between dependence and autonomy;
   e. inability to accept social support due to:
      (i) hopelessness;
      (ii) suspiciousness, ideas of reference or paranoia;
      (iii) conflicts concerning the meaning of accepting help.
2. Disturbances in the ability to communicate with others:
   a. overuse of distorted or indirect communication;
   b. digressive, vague, overelaborate, circumstantial, or metaphorical speech;
   c. undue social anxiety or hypersensitivity to criticism (real or imagined).
3. Disturbances in mood or affect:
   a. depression;
   b. inappropriately intense anger or lack of control over anger;
   c. labile affect (rapid shifts from normal mood to depression, anger, or anxiety);
   d. chronic feelings of emptiness or boredom.
4. Disturbances in identity and sense of self:
   a. disturbed identity:

       (i)   self-image (including body image);
       (ii)   gender identity;
       (iii) long-term goals.

    b. recurrent illusions, depersonalization, or derealization (not associated with panic attacks).

  5. Disturbances in impulse control:

    a. impulsive suicide attempt;
    b. behavior which is actually or potentially physically self-damaging;
    c. bulimia;
    d. impulsive sexual patterns;
    e. drug and/or alcohol abuse;
    f. stealing;
    g. self-mutilation.

Determining the relative contribution of these factors to negative outcome, as well as understanding the interrelationships among characteristics, is a matter for future study. At present, it is hypothesized that patients displaying personality features from each of the major categories above are at especially high risk for negative outcome. For convenience, such patients are categorized as high-risk patients.

Postulate V

Identifiable environmental events increase the distress of human beings whether or not they are in therapy. These events include those which require individuals to readjust their behavior substantially, such as life cycle stage transitions or uncommon disruptions of daily life (life events), and those characterized as having threat potential requiring more or less continual adjustments by the individual concerned (life strains). Individuals undergoing therapy who experience negative changes in the net impact of these events can be expected to show increased risk of negative outcome.

Postulate VI

Psychotherapy has the potential to reduce the impact of life stresses by increasing the individual's ability (1) to improve his or her social support system; and (2) to increase the effectiveness of his or her coping skills. While space does not permit discussion of the entire realm of those variables contributing to positive outcome, several will be mentioned here. Obviously, the availability of a supportive, empathic therapist immediately adds to the individual's support system. In addition to this direct contribution, there are aspects of therapy which enhance the individual's ability to improve his or her own support system. Training in improved social skills, whether directly through such techniques as behavior rehearsal, or indirectly through modeling influences and the extinction of socially conditioned anxiety (see Chapter 13), allow the individual to improve his or her support system. Certain behavior manifested by patients serves to "distance" them from others. Aspects of psychotherapy which, directly or indirectly, reduce "distancing" behavior are likely to result in the patient being able to improve his or her own social support system.

In addition to enabling the patient to improve his or her social support system, there are aspects of therapy which serve to improve coping ability. Therapy can teach the individual to modify interpersonal stressors (for example, by training in increased assertion); change maladaptive attitudes which mediate emotional behavior (for example, through techniques such as cognitive restructuring); increase the ability to control emotional behavior (for example, through techniques such as relaxation, anxiety and anger management training or biofeedback); become more effective in achieving desired goals (through training in problem-solving); and so on. The concepts employed here relate most directly to social learning theory and behavior therapy. Those employing other conceptual models would formulate the effective ingredients of therapy somewhat differently.

Postulate VII

Except with high-risk patients, negative outcomes produced by increased life stressors are temporary. Typically, the impact of therapy is to reduce negative outcome to rates which are lower than those which occur in the absence of treatment. Since high-risk patients tend to possess tenuous social supports and repertoires of coping responses, their abilities to respond effectively to life stressors are correspondingly less effective. Unless the therapist is successful in improving the individual's coping resources and ability to establish stable social supports, life stressors may precipitate a long-term worsening in overall condition that persists for years (see Chapter 2).

Postulate VIII

Except in the therapy of high-risk patients, antitherapeutic therapist styles, while contributing to the overall incidence of negative outcome as measured cross-sectionally, are likely to be transitory or to produce premature termination from therapy, rather than producing enduring negative outcomes. This derives from the fact that treated patients generally show lower rates of negative outcome than comparable controls, as well as from evidence that, except for those manifesting high-risk characteristics, even without therapy individuals generally recover from a major life stressor within one to two years. It can be argued that the impact of antitherapeutic therapist behavior would not exceed the impact of another major life stressor in these individuals.

Postulate IX

A definable subgroup of patients, namely high-risk patients who experience increased life stressors and/or who are exposed to "antitherapeutic" therapist behavior (*vide infra*), represent the major group for whom rates of enduring negative outcome in therapy exceed rates among controls. These patients tend to be interpersonally reactive, volatile, and prone to misinterpret the intentions and behavior of others. Thus, any significant or intense relationship may enhance the potential risk of negative outcome, unless that relationship is handled with care. High-risk patients lack the coping skills to tolerate the stress of the situation as well as the interpersonal skill to confront the therapist when (1) the therapist appears to be unempathic, cold, or lacking in genuineness; (2) when his style is confronting and aggressive; or (3) when therapist inactivity and lack of affection in the group situation is perceived as rejecting by the patient or allows other group members to attack.

What To Do About Negative Outcome

If substantiated, these postulates could serve as the basis for recommendations for changes in clinical practice leading to reduced negative outcome. The most significant implication is that, for the most part, negative outcome is a specific rather than a general problem. It involves identifiable high-risk patients.

Early Identification of High-Risk Patients

The process of reducing negative outcome among high-risk patients must begin with early and accurate identification of such patients. Several researchers have noted a high rate of misdiagnosis of such patients in the direction of underestimating the degree of pathology. A high educational and/or occupational level among patients later diagnosed as borderline tends to be associated with misdiagnosis, a possibility to which clinicians should be alert (see Chapters 2 and 6).

Psychological testing and structured clinical interviewing appear to be useful tools for increasing initial diagnostic accuracy among high-risk patients. Psychological testing has been shown to be more accurate than "any other single or combined source of clinical data" in the identification of patients with borderline personality disorders (Applebaum, 1972; see also Maltas Berg, 1978). The Diagnostic Interview for Borderlines has been shown to be an effective tool with inpatients (Gunderson, 1977; Gunderson & Kolb, 1978; Kolb & Gunderson, 1980), but less so with outpatients (Koenigsberg et al., 1983).

In addition to the increased use of such diagnostic techniques in identifying suspected high-risk cases, the deployment of more experienced therapists in the initial assessment process also appears to be warranted. Studies show that relatively ineffective therapists tend to underestimate the severity of patient pathology as well as the degree of psychological distress (Beutler, 1983; Beutler, Dunbar, & Baer, 1980). Thus, the very therapists who are least capable of handling high-risk cases appear most likely to fail to recognize them. In addition, once a relationship has been established problems of transferring cases to other therapists are particularly difficult with borderline personality disordered patients (and probably with other high-risk patients). One method of reducing initial diagnostic errors and therapist–patient mismatches is to conduct the initial interview with the prospective therapist in conjunction with a more senior therapist. This permits the senior therapist to alert his colleague to potential danger areas in working with that patient and facilitates reassignment if need be. The consulting therapist is a member of the original assessment team, and therefore recommendations for reassignment appear to be part of the assessment routine. Participation of the senior therapist from the outset also allows patient transfer to be effected before a significant relationship has been developed with the therapist.

Improving the Treatment of
High-Risk Patients

Recommendations for improving treatment of high-risk patients involve two main areas: improving patient–therapy and patient–therapist matching; and improving the quality of therapy for high-risk patients.

Recommendations for patient–therapy matching involve: (1) avoiding psychoanalysis as a treatment for high-risk patients; and (2) proceeding with extreme caution in treating high-risk patients with punishment or the withholding of reinforcement. Given the present state of knowledge, it would appear that psychoanalysis, and possibly all intensive forms of insight therapy, are contraindicated in the treatment of borderline personality disorders, anorexics, and certain patients with psychosomatic disorders. When the treatment is psychoanalysis (and possibly for other treatments; see Chapter 2), the more disturbed the patient, the more therapist skill appears to be critical to the avoidance of negative outcome. If insight therapy is conducted with high-risk patients, it is important both to increase therapist activity and to attend continually to structuring and maintaining the treatment contract. Therapists involved in treatment programs using punishment or the contingent withholding of reinforcement should carefully monitor all patients for the possible emergence of deleterious effects. Furthermore, these methods should be employed only after stringent consideration of alternative treatment approaches (preferably with peer review), and then only when it is concluded that potential benefits outweigh potential risks. Given the risks involved in these forms of treatment, the advisability of paraprofessionals and technician-level therapists using either punishment or negative reinforcement techniques without a fully trained professional being present or nearby and readily available is usually contraindicated.

Recommendations for improving patient–therapist matching include assigning high-risk cases to therapists who are able to sustain the highest levels of empathy, warmth, and genuineness with those patients, and who have greatest knowledge of the potential pitfalls involved in their treatment. As with all therapies, practitioners are more successful in treating some patients than others. There are patients who are likely to be particularly difficult to treat, perhaps even too difficult for any therapist. It behooves those involved in case assignment to know the limitations of staff members. A particularly distressing conclusion from studies of therapist style variables is that there are few "high functioning" psychotherapists (Mitchell, Bozarth, & Krauft, 1977). Direct observation of therapy in progress is perhaps the best means for supervisors to become aware of the stylistic limitations of staff therapists. It is enlightening to find studies which indicate that even untrained observers are able to identify antitherapeutic behaviors with a fair degree of accuracy (see Chapter 11). It is particularly important for individual therapists in private practice, where patients are generally self-assigned, to become aware of their limitations. One way to improve sensitivity to personal limitations is to maintain an ongoing assessment of all cases. Follow-up evaluations, at least via questionnaires sent to patients inquiring about patient satisfaction with the therapy, are a simple way to obtain feedback from patients. Obviously, practice should be restricted to those cases the therapist is able to manage successfully.

The practice in some mental health centers of assigning high-risk cases to inexperienced therapists is also questionable on a different account. Many high-risk patients require fairly long-term treatment. Given the skill required to work with these patients and the difficulties such patients often have in adjusting to change, it is usually undesirable to expose these patients to multiple changes of therapist determined by training requirements rather than the needs of the patient.

Those who are successful in treating high-risk patients must be alert to a different problem. These patients are taxing to treat, and those with demonstrated skill in working with such patients tend to receive numerous additional referrals. There is therefore a risk of overtaxing these therapists; this could lead to therapist burn-out. When this happens, there is a tendency for the therapist concerned to distance himself or herself emotionally from the patient as a self-protective mechanism. The result is a reduction in the therapist's effectiveness. There is a maximum number of patients, especially difficult, high-risk patients, with which any therapist can successfully contend at one time. Thus, too great a patient load may indirectly contribute to negative outcome.

Recommendations for improving the quality of therapy with high-risk patients are directed at three main areas: (1) use of formal and informal peer review; (2) improving selection and training of therapists; and (3) issues pertaining to the therapy itself.

Perhaps the best antidote to therapist myopia is the discussion of difficult cases with peers. Peers can frequently detect and alert the therapist to the development of antitherapeutic responses. Two main difficulties are common in the treatment of high-risk cases. The first derives from the ability of some of these patients to provoke anger in the therapist. The most common therapist manifestations seem to be (1) avoiding dealing with issues of anger because of fear or concern about losing control; or (2) responding defensively to patient expressions of anger by attempting to justify personal positions or behavior, rather than helping the patient to examine the reasonableness or unreasonableness of the anger. Furthermore, therapists are frequently loath to admit to other therapists their own anger reactions toward patients, perhaps because such reactions might be considered unprofessional. Nonetheless, peer consultation can be helpful in sorting out the sources of one's anger and placing it in manageable perspective.

The second area involves difficulty on the part of the therapist in maintaining the structure of the treatment process. In these instances, the therapist is frequently unwittingly reinforcing maladaptive patient behavior or failing to intervene when the patient oversteps the agreed-on limits of the treatment contract (for example, by phoning incessantly, canceling appointments without notification when angry, and so on). Again, peer consultation is frequently helpful in regaining perspective. Peer consultation is helpful in those instances where the therapy is not going well, to assist the therapist in detecting patterns which have been overlooked, in gaining detachment from the current mental set, and in arriving at new treatment strategies.

Finally, the treatment of certain types of patients, such as anorexics, requires special skills and experience. Peer review can be essential in working with these cases. In this context, the efforts of professional associations such as the Association for Advancement of Behavior Therapy to institute formal peer review programs is commendable.

As noted above, relatively few therapists can sustain a warm and empathic climate when working with high-risk patients (see Mitchell et al., 1977). In view of the fact that the level of these conditions is tremendously affected by patient characteristics, this is not surprising (Gurman, 1973). Many of these patients have succeeded in alienating nearly everyone with whom they have come in contact. Nonetheless, there continues to be a need to emphasize stylistic as well as intellectual strengths in the selection of therapists-in-training. Given the available evidence that even untrained observers can recognize antitherapeutic behavior with a fair degree of accuracy (see Chapter 11), it may be that incorporating analogue therapy sessions into the process of selecting candidates for advanced degree programs will aid in increasing the number of professionals who have already acquired a high degree of interpersonal skills prior to beginning advanced training.

In addition, there is considerable evidence that these stylistic skills can be taught (Carkhuff, 1972; Mitchell et al., 1977; Oksaner, 1973; Perlman, 1973; Truax & Mitchell, 1971). Greater emphasis upon formal training in these skills should be incorporated into graduate school and psychiatric residency curricula. Given the complexity of the skills involved, acquisition of them may be enhanced through observational learning. Students in training should be encouraged to observe experienced and talented practitioners conducting sessions. Co-therapy also offers an excellent opportunity both for observing an experienced role-model, and for receiving constructive feedback. Providing therapists in training with role-playing experiences with low-frequency but difficult-to-manage patient behavior is another useful device.

In addition to recommendations designed to maximize the quality of stylistic variables to which high-risk patients are exposed, there are two other implications of the postulates enumerated above. First, the therapist should be alert to increased life stressors among high-risk patients as an indicator of increased risk potential for negative outcome. Second, these postulates suggest that interventions designed to enhance the coping skills and social supports among high-risk patients might be especially helpful in reducing negative outcome. Behavior therapists particularly emphasize the development and refinement of techniques for enhancing stress management skills, as well as the development of behavioral competencies, including more effective interpersonal behavior. If it is correct that enhancing coping skills and social supports is crucial to avoiding negative outcome among high-risk patients, then behavior therapy may be particularly effective in treating these patients. Behavioral treatment of both anorexia and depression has received considerable attention, and the preliminary indications are that, on the whole, such treatment is safe and effective. The treatment of borderline personality disordered patients has received scant attention in the behavior therapy literature, presumably because of a preference among most behavior therapists for emphasizing specific target problem areas rather than broader personality variables. Behavior therapy is particularly promising in improving coping skills and training patients in the skills needed to develop a more solid social support system. In addition, behavior therapists have long been treating patients who qualify for the diagnosis of borderline personality disorder, without necessarily labeling these patients as such. Improved treatment effectiveness is a core issue in the reduction of negative outcome among these patients and, in this respect, the potential benefits of behavior therapy appear promising. A discussion of behavior therapy in the treatment of borderline personality disorders is included as an Appendix to this volume.

Additional Recommendations

Postulate V, based upon research reviewed in Chapter 12, indicates that unexpected, unpleasant life changes, particularly those which are outside an individual's control, are likely to result in a worsening in psychological status, with an increase in depressive symptomatology in particular. This appears to be especially true if the life changes also result in persistent life strains, such as chronic conflict or financial difficulty. Both social support and a personal repertoire of coping resources appear to mediate the impact of stressors upon psychological status. This contention has important implications for reducing negative outcome. First, it suggests which individuals are most likely to develop psychological distress: those who are experiencing life cycle transitions and major losses, and those who are experiencing chronic life strains. Mental health professionals may help prevent the development of the psychological distress through preventive programs to enhance the coping skills needed to foster broader social supports in individuals at risk.

Among those who are already in psychotherapy, the occurrence of a life event should alert the therapist to the possibility of a worsening in level of functioning. One might expect the patient to inform the therapist of such a change in functioning. But frequently this is not the case, especially where the main focus of therapy has been upon issues other than distress symptoms. Patients are often paralyzed following a major life event to an extent where they fail to act constructively to forestall ensuing consequences, including alerting their therapists to what is going on in their lives. For example, a female patient going through a difficult divorce became so despondent that she busied herself with minor household details rather than seek an additional loan to prevent foreclosure on her house when her husband defaulted on payment of the mortgage. (Her house had ample equity to permit obtaining such a loan). She also neglected to inform her therapist of the situation until the day before the foreclosure. In reviewing recent events in the patient's life, the therapist became aware of the situation quite by accident. Once aware of the situation, he had the patient construct a list of things she needed to do, and had her assign time priorities to each. She obtained a loan the next day and, as a result, was able to sell the house on her own without major financial loss. One must not assume that patients who are feeling overwhelmed will necessarily alert the therapist to crisis situations. Being alert to the occurrence of a life event and the frequent consequences of such an event permits the therapist to assist the patient in taking constructive action.

Patients who have gone through recent major life stressors do not automatically associate their increased distress with the life changes which have occurred. Consequently, they experience their distress as more frightening because it is unexplained. Here, the therapist can help reduce distress by assisting the patient in making this association. Otherwise, patients tend to become frightened by the worsening in status, thus compounding the distress and further impairing the ability to respond constructively.

In group therapy, recommendations include carefully selecting potential group members, preparing clients for therapy, continual monitoring of emotional expression within the group, and viewing emotional expression as a means to an end rather than as an end in itself. Both distant and overly confrontative therapist styles should be avoided or moderated. Dies and Teleska recommend that, early in the group life, the interaction should be built on positive group experiences. Feedback should be sequenced positive to negative. Therapist behaviors involving the attribution of meaning to patient behavior, clarifying, interpreting, explaining, and providing frameworks for understanding and change are all associated with enhanced positive outcome and reduced negative outcome.

Implications for Further Research

Certain implications for outcome research in general and for negative outcome in particular emerge from the foregoing postulates. First, it is important to recognize that much of the data generated in outcome research are reported in a fashion which makes investigation of negative outcome difficult. Negative outcome can easily be overlooked when group data are combined. Perhaps the single most important step in improving the sensitivity of researchers to the occurrence of negative outcome involves simple scrutiny of pre and post data on a case-by-case basis.

To date, the greatest limitation to systematic investigation of negative outcome has been the inability to structure prospective studies of negative outcome. The postulates outlined above permit just such an investigation. Each postulate neatly leads to a set of testable hypotheses. Each concept can be operationally defined. Collectively, the model could permit investigators to identify high-risk patients in advance. Patients could be followed over the course of therapy, permitting analysis of contributing factors in a fashion hitherto much less possible (primarily because the relatively infrequent cases of negative outcome were spread over a number of studies). Aggregating high-risk patients in one study permits testing of the hypothesized causative variables. Identifying high-risk patients would also permit explicit investigation of the relative safety and effectiveness of various treatment approaches. For example, the impact of psychoanalytic supportive-expressive therapy upon borderline personality disorders could be compared with that of behavior therapy or time-limited dynamic psychotherapy. Within such a project, it would be possible to investigate the effects of various therapist variables and the impact of life stresses upon outcome. It may be, for example, that therapists with certain styles have lower rates of negative outcome with one therapeutic modality, whereas others fare better using another approach. Such research would provide a necessary corrective to what Kiesler (1966) calls the "patient uniformity myth." Much of the controversy surrounding the issue of negative outcome stems from the failure of previous investigators to make distinctions among differences among patients and to explore the effects of patient–therapist–treatment interactions. This failure could also be responsible in part for the lack of attention to high-risk potential among borderline personality disordered patients, and to the lack of recognition of common behavioral features among high-risk patients. Investigation of the postulates outlined in this chapter is needed to guide effective treatment decision making. In the long run, effective research holds the most promise for systematic refinement of clinical practice. Such research is an indispensable component of any set of recommendations for how to reduce negative outcome.

Conclusion

As the evidence presented in this volume demonstrates, it is incorrect and overly simplistic to view therapist characteristics as the sole or even primary causative factors in negative outcome. Potentially identifiable patient characteristics, extratherapeutic events, therapeutic modality, and therapist characteristics interact in ways which we are only beginning to understand. Identification of these factors and their interactions would facilitate identification of patients at high risk, and the development of more effective treatments for them. If this can be achieved, then the practice of psychotherapy will be a stride closer to honoring that principal dictum for health service providers: "Above all, do not harm."

APPENDIX

Behavior Therapy with Borderline Personality Disorders: One Clinician's Perspective

Daniel T. Mays

Perhaps the most consistent trend to emerge in this volume is the high risk for negative outcome among borderline personality disorders. The term borderline is a misnomer. It arose from psychoanalytic speculations about a nebulous group of patients whose pathology lay in the borderline between neurosis and psychosis. More searching examination leads to quite a different formulation. For example, following intensive investigation of phenomenology, family history, treatment response, and long-term outcome, Pope and co-workers conclude that:

> "borderlines" do not appear to lie on the border of anything; they do not appear to have "borderline affective disorder" or "borderline schizophrenia . . ." As a group they have a rather stable form of serious psychopathologic disorder with a morbidity as severe as schizophrenia in our sample. (Pope, Jonas, & Hudson, et al., 1983)

Specific diagnostic criteria for the borderline personality disorder are addressed in Chapter 14.

The potential hazards of treating borderline personality disordered patients with psychoanalysis have been discussed in previous chapters (see Chapters 2, 6, and 14; also Grinker, Werble, & Drye, 1968). This is understandable when one considers that the "neutral" posture of the therapist is apt to be misinterpreted as a withholding and punitive one by the borderline patient, who in turn is at high risk to respond with self-destructive behavior (*vide infra*). A psychoanalytically oriented approach termed supportive-expressive psychotherapy has been reported to be effective. The interested reader is encouraged to see Horwitz (1974); Kernberg (1967, 1977); and Kernberg, Burstein, et al. (1972) for a more detailed description of this approach. Unfortunately, evaluations of this approach to date have addressed its effectiveness only in comparison with psychoanalysis and with purely supportive therapy. Borderline patients do not function well in group therapy, at least until significant progress has been made in individual psychotherapy. Their tendencies for histrionics (such as becoming angry and storming out of the room), exaggerated attention-seeking, and indirect expression of affect are all difficult to address in a group setting. The behavior of these patients frequently exerts a disruptive influence upon other group members as well. It is perhaps best to defer group therapy treatment of borderline disordered patients at least until the major disruptive behaviors noted above have been addressed in individual therapy. Even if group therapy treatment is delayed until this time, it is best to establish an explicit contract with the patient concerning acceptable behavior in the group, so that this agreement can be referred to if disruptive behavior emerges later.

Evidence of a relationship between borderline personality disorder, on the one hand, and a family history of bipolar or major depressive disorder (Loranger, Oldham, & Tulis, 1982; Pope et al., 1983; Soloff & Millward, 1983) on the other, suggests a possible role for medication in the treatment of borderline patients. Schizotypal disordered patients have been shown to obtain some benefit from tricyclic antidepressants or monoamine oxidase inhibitors (Hedberg, Houck, & Glueck, 1971; Klein, 1968). More recently, Pope and and his co-workers (1983) investigated response to medication of two groups of borderline personality disordered patients: those with a family history of major affective disorder (51.5%); and patients with no such family history (48.5%). None of those in the latter group showed more than an "equivocal" response to medication, whereas in the group with a positive family history, 46.2 percent showed a "definite" positive response. Medication regimens showing a definite response in the group with a positive family history included neuroleptics, tricyclics, and lithium carbonate (regimens had been individualized). Note, however, that overall only 23.8 percent of the borderline patients in this study showed a definite positive response to medication.

The literature on behavior therapy with borderline personality disorders is exceedingly sparse, and empirically based investigations of treatment response of borderline patients to behavior therapy do not, to my knowledge, exist. Lack of attention to the problem of treatment of borderline disordered patients results from a preference among most behavior therapists for molecular functional analysis of behavior rather than syndrome analysis. For this reason, and perhaps because the concept of the borderline personality disorder was developed by psychoanalytic writers (beginning with Stern in 1938; see Millon, 1981, pp. 340ff.), few behavior therapists have addressed this syndrome. Given the limited treatment effectiveness of other therapies, along with the evidence for high risk of negative outcome among these patients, and considering the advantages of behavior therapy for specific focus upon training patients in social skills and enhanced coping skills, the application of behavior therapy to this patient population warrants further investigation.

What follows here is (1) a description of the phenomenology of the borderline disorder; (2) a description of some of the problems encountered in straightforward application of behavior therapy techniques to these patients and some strategies for managing them; and (3) some of the behavior therapy techniques which may be relevant for treating borderline patients. The treatment techniques described have been adapted from standard cognitive and behavior therapy techniques, based upon frequently observed problems emerging in treatment of these patients. While there is considerable support for these techniques in general, their effectiveness with borderline patients has not been established. The lack of empirical support for the views to follow should be kept in mind.

Clinical Phenomenology

The general description which follows identifies the behavior patterns, affective features, and cognitive distortions which one frequently observes in treatment of patients with borderline personality disorders. The cognitions described are those which patients frequently verbalize, either during the therapy or following clinical improvement. Despite many similarities, there is a great diversity among patients meeting the criteria for a diagnosis of borderline personality disorder, and not all of the comments below will apply to any individual case. It is important that therapists avoid overgeneralizing about the individual case based upon a diagnostic label. Nevertheless, the generalizations which follow can serve as a set of hypotheses for therapists working with borderline patients, which subsequent observation of each patient will either confirm or refute.

Patients with borderline personality disorders have adopted rather extreme styles in order to maintain psychological equilibrium. While frequently highly skilled in manipulating others to comply with their wishes, they are also remarkably inflexible in adapting to the environment. They often persist in relying upon a few basic strategies, even when these are manifestly inappropriate to a situation. Typically, they are preoccupied with receiving attention, and they experience anxiety when they feel even temporarily cut off from support, because they see themselves as incapable of functioning independently. They frequently also experience rage toward others for failing to gratify their exaggerated needs. Thus, a frequent cognitive distortion of these patients is the placing of unreasonable expectations upon others. This distortion is frequently compounded by deficits in the appropriate verbalization of expectations and requests, which prevents the feedback from others which would allow the patient to correct the cognitive distortions.

The most characteristic feature of borderline patients is the intensity and rapidity of fluctuation in affect, leading frequently to self-destructive behavior. They have difficulty maintaining a stable identity, possibly as a result of their affective instability. Lacking a stable identity, they often become incredibly dependent upon others, a dependency which is all the more intense when others are regarded as the repositories of who they are and because they see themselves as incapable of surviving without support. A belief in the inability to function independently is reinforced by separation anxiety when support is withdrawn. Finally, they regard the support of others as exceedingly tenuous, likely to be withdrawn at any moment. The self-damaging behavior and the manipulative threats of borderline personality disordered patients are frightening to others. Often, friends and family members mobilize considerable support for these patients initially, in an effort to help them through what is often perceived as a crisis situation, and these individuals frequently remain involved for some time despite the strain of dealing with the patient. Ultimately, however, others frequently distance themselves from these patients when they lose tolerance for these patients' extremely demanding and manipulative behavior. This only serves to reinforce future fears of abandonment. However, borderline personality disordered patients rarely recognize the role that their behavior plays in the abandonment cycle.

Instead, borderline personality disordered patients may become even more clinging and demanding after rejection, thus intensifying and perpetuating the cycle.

Most borderline personality disordered patients consciously recognize their manipulative behavior as such (though they rarely admit it), and this recognition only serves to reinforce cognitions about being unworthy and unlovable. They frequently communicate fears of this sort to the therapist in the form of comments such as, "If you really knew what I'm like, you would hate me the way I hate myself." Praise as a social reinforcer may thus produce the paradoxical effect of heightened anxiety (presumably linked to the cognition "When he finds out what I'm like, he'll leave") combined with verbalizations of unworthiness and self-abnegation. These verbalizations may serve the function of eliciting reassurance against abandonment. When the reassurance is not forthcoming, a gesture of self-destruction frequently results. For example, one borderline patient frequently resorted to banging her head on the office door following a compliment from the therapist.

Anger plays a key role in the behavior of these patients. They often carry over massive residual anger from childhood. Furthermore, they are frequently trapped in an ambivalent posture with those upon whom they depend. They generally resent the power others hold over them (at times amounting to the power to define their very identity), yet see no way to become independent of that power, because they believe they cannot function without it. Thus, (1) control over affect is tenuous; (2) anger is primitive and massive; (3) these patients typically lack the skills for modulated assertion; (4) their anger is frequently based upon unwarranted and unverbalized expectations of others; and (5) they view expressions of anger as likely to lead to the very abandonment they most fear. The result is that these patients frequently resort to indirect expression of anger, or to unmodulated expression. Another frequent response to the experience of anger is self-punishment. For example, one borderline patient used to hide in the corner of the closet when angry with her husband, in order to shave the skin from the backs of her hands with razor blades. Another slowly and carefully burned herself with the end of a lit cigarette. A third frequently called her therapist, reporting fear while rhythmically banging her head on a metal bedpost as she talked. These patients frequently report that such behavior relieves what is otherwise an intolerable inner experience. The challenge to the therapist is that of detecting unexpressed anger and of dealing with this anger in a fashion which is not experienced by the patient as rejection (all of the while coping with his or her own exasperation, because work with these patients can be very frustrating). If the therapist fails to do this, there is in many instances a high probability that the patient will resort to self-punishment or even, at times, to a suicide attempt.

Diagnostic Issues

The value of two diagnostic techniques, psychological testing and the structured clinical interview, is addressed in Chapter 14. There are also aspects of patient behavior whose emergence may alert the therapist to the possibility of a borderline personality disorder.

A history of self-mutilation, especially in conjunction with excessive guilt or rage, may particularly alert the therapist to the presence of a borderline personality disorder. Other clinical "tipoffs" include indirect or nonverbal expressions of anger or inordinate expressions of rage directed at others but not at the therapist. Excessive telephone calls are frequently significant, especially when tied to fear of being alone (although this may not be verbalized initially by the client). Bleak dysphoria when childhood events are explored is another clue (but caution should be exercised since this occurs frequently with other patient groups). According to Stone, the occurrence of grotesque dreams during psychoanalysis is another clue. Colson and his co-workers note a greater tendency among high-risk borderlines to abuse drugs and alcohol and then to lie about it.

Treatment Goals

Straightforward application of behavior therapy techniques is less effective with borderline patients than with other patients unless relationship crises are effectively dealt with. Nonetheless, once one is acquainted with the typical cognitive distortions these patients are prone to, a solid grounding in social learning theory allows the therapist to adapt techniques to the patient. The essential difference in behavior therapy with borderlines is that application of technique is not as straightforward as it is in therapy with most other patient groups. The therapist must to a far greater extent rely on use of the therapeutic relationship as a prototype for other healthy relationships.

In general terms, the goals of therapy with borderline patients include: (1) the establishment and maintenance of a therapeutic relationship; (2) reduction and eventual elimination of self-destructive behavior; (3) assisting the patient to develop an adequate social support system; and (4) teaching the patient more effective coping skills.

In establishing a therapeutic relationship with the borderline patient, it is important to recognize the ambivalence these patients feel toward improvement. For many such patients, fear of "becoming well" is connected with leaving therapy, with all the attendant fears of abandonment. Yet they fear that if they do not make progress in therapy, they will be asked to leave. A frequent compromise is to comply with the directions of the therapist just enough to avoid fears of being expelled from therapy, while attributing their progress to the superior powers of the therapist ("I'm able to do this only because you're helping me."). This is an issue which must be dealt with in therapy with other types of patients as well. Many patients initially strive to function more effectively in order to please the therapist, but these patients tend to maintain gains which produce a better response from the environment, while gradually transferring their sources of important support and gratification to significant others outside the therapy. Borderline patients, in contrast, frequently do only well enough to avoid the perceived possibility of being expelled from therapy. They tend to become worse as the emphasis in therapy is shifted to functioning without therapy. Helping borderline patients shift their sources of support and gratification to persons in the natural environment is the major long-term approach to overcoming this problem. As an intermediate step, one can emphasize to the patient that the therapy will take quite a long time, and that the therapist will be available as long as needed. Periodically during the therapy, it pays to remind the patient of the goal of eventually functioning independently, in order to desensitize the patient to this idea. One should, however, expect an increase in anxiety when this is done, and as a result these interventions should be carefully timed.

Another feature of the behavior of many borderline patients is their tendency to violate the conventions of the therapy contract, such as paying fees, attending scheduled sessions, arriving for sessions on time, leaving when the session is over, etc. This occurs most often as a means of communicating anger. It seems impossible for the therapist to avoid provoking anger with these patients. Such minor incidents as the therapist having left a dictation unit out at the start of a session may provoke fantasies of distrust coupled with rage. As discussed in Chapter 2, it is utterly essential to deal with these violations as they occur. Recognizing that anger is frequently the underlying motive will aid the therapist in understanding why the violations occur when they do. Most often in the beginning phases of therapy, it is necessary for the therapist to specifically encourage the patient to communicate the anger. Explicitly asking, "Are you angry or upset with me?" may allow the patient to bring up the issue provoking the anger. More often, it is necessary for the therapist to illustrate to the patient that expressions of irritation can and will be tolerated by the therapist. It is essential that the therapist avoid attacking the patient, even indirectly, for expressing anger. Once the issue provoking the anger is verbalized by the patient, two strategies can be employed to diffuse it. First, the therapist can use the issue as an opportunity to clarify his or her intent in behaving as he or she has. Second, the therapist can engage in mutual problem solving of the options involved in his or her choice of behavior. In this way the real consequences of the various choices of the therapist can be seen by the patient as motivating the therapist's behavior, and the patient can be assisted in taking the event less personally. Eventually, patterns of overreaction will become apparent, and the therapist can use these to illustrate to the patient his or her tendency to generate excessive expectations toward others.

In the initial phase of treatment, the foremost goal beyond that of relationship-building must be the reduction of self-destructive behavior. A sufficient relationship bond must be developed so that the patient will call the therapist rather than harm him- or herself. It is best to explicitly instruct the patient to call in a situation of imminent self-harm. When such a call is received, the patient often needs to be calmed. Then the events which have recently transpired in his or her life can be reviewed. Since, as noted above, such actions are most often related to unexpressed anger, the therapist can be alert to this type of incident and can point out to the patient the possibility that the anger may be related to the self-destructive urge, while simultaneously explaining to the patient that it is normal to feel anger (to forestall the patient's misinterpretation of the therapist's comment as a criticism). Over time, just as is the case with violations of the conventions of treatment, a pattern typically emerges of unexpressed anger leading to self-destructive impulses, and the patient becomes aware of it because the therapist has repeatedly pointed it out. At this point, the therapist can explicitly formulate a treatment goal involving the direct expression of anger. These incidents allow the therapist to work through what may be conceptualized as *in vivo* desensitization to the expression of anger. The therapist initially articulates the patient's angry feelings to him or her, while reassuring the patient that no harm has been done to the relationship. This reassurance, coupled with the fact that the catastrophic response the patient fears fails to materialize, allows the patient to become desensitized to anger expression. Over time, the patient is encouraged to verbalize these feelings him- or herself, first to the therapist, and gradually to significant others. Since the anger is frequently inappropriate, this latter aspect of desensitization must be coupled with cognitive restructuring of dysfunctional beliefs leading to anger, along with training in self-talk of dialogue questioning whether anger is justified at that time. This approach is similar to, although less structured than, that of Novaco (1974). Once direct expression of anger has emerged consistently, self-destructive behavior almost invariably decreases or disappears entirely, unless maintained by operant features of reinforcement from the environment. If this appears to be the case, training the patient in more adaptive attention-seeking behavior coupled with anger management frequently eliminates the self-destructive behavior.

The third major goal of therapy is that of assisting the patient to develop or expand his or her social support system. The work done by the patient and therapist assists considerably in this area, by becoming the prototype for mature interaction. As patients become less manipulative and dramatic, first with the therapist and then with others outside the therapy, mature reciprocally rewarding relationships have an opportunity to develop. Most frequently, however, the patient's relationships need to be dealt with explicitly. This involves correcting the patient's misinterpretations of others' behavior by pointing out alternative interpretations. It is important to encourage impersonal conceptions of blame, since most of these patients believe that someone must always be at fault. This cognition must be challenged and replaced with the recognition that sometimes no one is at fault. (This intervention frequently reduces self-blame as well). Borderline patients often benefit from explicit assignments to make contact with potential friends, relatives, and others in addition to the therapist. While they frequently do so initially to please the therapist, they gradually benefit from a broader base of social support. The improvements in assertive expression discussed above also facilitate improved interpersonal relationships, as does fostering greater awareness in the patient of his or her contribution to others' behavior. Both learning how to express one's needs and coping with the guilt which such expression provokes must be dealt with in therapy. In addition, borderline patients frequently need to be encouraged to become more aware of others' needs, and to respond to those needs, since the behavior of these patients is often incredibly egocentric. Finally, it is frequently necessary to help these patients to reduce pathological interactions with significant others (especially around issues related to dependency).

The final goal of therapy with borderlines concerns the development of better coping skills. Once relationship issues have been dealt with satisfactorily, this aspect of treatment often proceeds in fairly straightforward fashion, and standard behavior therapy techniques can be employed effectively. There are some aspects of these techniques toward which borderline patients respond somewhat idiosyncratically, however.

A frequent major goal of treatment is that of reducing anxiety and fear of being alone. While relaxation training, biofeedback, and/or anxiety management training may facilitate this goal, one must be alert to possible differences in how borderline patients may respond to these techniques. One important difference is that these patients frequently regard being given a relaxation tape as a symbolic gesture of caring, and the calming influence of the tape results from the patient's feeling closer to the therapist while listening to it, particularly if the tape is recorded in the therapist's voice. Several patients have literally worn out three or four tapes using them in this manner. Another important difference is the possibility of a paradoxical increase in anxiety, and sometimes a transient psychosis-like decompensation. One patient jumped up during a relaxation training session, screaming, "My God! It's a crypt!" Once he was calmed down he explained that his relaxation imagery had suddenly changed, and he was confronted with an image of himself trapped in an underground vault with his mother's casket. It may be that the reduction in stimuli which occurs during relaxation training may facilitate malignant associations in susceptible patients. Specific task assignments while alone at home may help the patient deal with the fear of being alone early in treatment. Frequently, this fear results from fear of self-harm. Once the patient's self-destructive impulses have been reduced, and his or her sense of self-worth and self-efficacy have improved, one can explicitly define reducing fear of being alone as a treatment goal, using *in vivo* desensitization, by gradually increasing the length of time alone while gradually decreasing access to therapist support.

Another major coping skill is that of independent decision making. This can be promoted through a blend of problem-solving training and cognitive restructuring. Generally, rather than attempt to teach these skills step-by-step as one would do with a more functional patient, issues which emerge in ongoing conversation can be used as the basis for training. Once a maladaptive cognitive pattern has been identified in several contexts, the patient can be instructed to substitute an alternative cognition when a maladaptive one has been detected. A short-hand slogan can be written on a card which the patient then carries around. For example, one patient tended to respond to emerging difficulties in her life with panic, linked to the cognition "My life is falling apart; I'll never be able to handle this." She was given a card upon which was written "There's always another way!", which she learned to use as a cue to generate possible alternative responses. This simple strategy had a major impact for this patient upon reducing panic and increasing constructive responses to different incidents. Areas in which these strategies can be used include the following: reducing erroneous assumptions about self-efficacy; enhancing ability to predict others' behavior; reducing cognitions about the need to be perfect or to be liked by everyone; encouraging a more internal locus of control (that is, challenging cognitions that the patient is incapable of influencing external events); reducing "black-and-white" thinking; and reducing impulsive actions based upon limited decision making. In the later stages of therapy, it is necessary to correct patient illusions of therapist omnipotence and omniscience.

Space limitations prevent extensive discussion of how to perform specific behavior therapy and cognitive therapy techniques. Many excellent references are available elsewhere (see especially Goldfried and Davison, 1976; O'Leary & Wilson, 1975; Beck, 1976; Walen, Hauserman, & Lavin, 1977; Emery, Hollon, & Bedrosian, 1982; and the *Annual Review of Behavior Therapy* series by Franks, Wilson, Kendall, & Brownell, e.g., 1982). The emphasis here has been upon the context within which these techniques are applied, and upon the often idiosyncratic responses of borderline patients to certain techniques.

References and Bibliography _____

Abramowitz, C.V., Abramowitz, S.I., Roback, H.B., & Jackson, C. Differential effectiveness of directive and nondirective group therapies as a function of client internal-external control. *Journal of Consulting and Clinical Psychology*, 1974, 42, 849–853.

*Aderman, D. Elation, depression, and helping behavior. *Journal of Personality and Social Psychology*, 1972, 24, 91–101.

*Agras, W.S., Barlow, D.H., Chapin, H.N., Abel, G.G., & Leitenberg, H. Behavior modification of anorexia nervosa. *Archives of General Psychiatry*, 1974, 30, 279–286.

Agras, S., Chapin, H. & Oliveau, P. The natural history of phobia. *Archives of General Psychiatry*, 1972, 26, 315–317.

Agras, S., & Werne, J. Behavior modification in anorexia nervosa: Research foundations. In R.A. Vigersky (Ed.), *Anorexia nervosa*. New York: Raven Press, 1977.

Akiskal, H.S., Khani, M., & Scott-Straus, A. Cyclothymic temperamental disorders. *Psychiatric Clinics of North America*, 1979, 2, 527–554.

Akiskal, H.S., & McKinney, W.T. Overview of recent research in depression: Ten conceptual models. *Archives of General Psychiatry*, 1975, 32, 285–305.

Akiskal, H.S., Ojenderdejian, A.H., Rosenthal, R.H., & Khani, M.K. Cyclothymic disorder: Validating criteria for inclusion in the bipolar affective group. *American Journal of Psychiatry*, 1977, 134, 1227–1233.

Alexander, F. & French, T.M. *Psychoanalytic therapy*. New York: Ronald Press, 1946.

Allport, D.A. The state of cognitive psychology. *Quarterly Journal of Experimental Psychology*, 1975, 27, 141–152.

American Psychiatric Association Task Force: The current status of lithium therapy: Report of an APA Task force. *American Journal of Psychiatry*, 1975, 132, 997–1001.

*Amrein, P.C., Friedman, R.F., Kosinski, K., & Ellman, L. Hematologic changes in anorexia nervosa. *Journal of the American Medical Association*, 1979, 241, 2190–2191.

Andrews, G., Tennant, D., Hewson, M., & Vaillant, G.E. Life event stress,

---

*These sources are not cited in the text, but are provided here as suggested supplementary readings.

social support, coping style, and risk of psychological impairment. *Journal of Nervous and Mental Disease*, 1978, *166* (5), 307–316.

Antonovsky, A. Conceptual and methodological problems in the study of resistance resources and stressful life events. In B.S. Dohrenwend and B.P. Dohrenwend (Eds.), *Stressful life events: Their nature and effects.* New York: Wiley, 1974, pp. 245–258.

Antonovsky, A. *Health, stress, and coping.* San Francisco: Jossey-Bass, 1979.

Antonovsky, A., & Kats, R. The life crisis history as a tool in epidemiologic research. *Journal of Health and Social Behavior*, 1967, *8*, 15–29.

Appelbaum, A. A critical-examination of the concept of 'motivation for change' in psychoanalytic treatment. *International Journal of Psychoanalysis*, 1972, *53*, 51–59.

Arieti, S., & Bemporad, J. *Severe and mild depression: The psychotherapeutic approach.* New York: Basic Books, 1978.

Aronson, H. & Weintraub, W. Patient changes during classical psychoanalyses as a function of initial status and duration of treatment. *Psychiatry*, 1968, *31*, 369–379.

*Asch, S. Varieties of negative therapeutic reaction and problems of technique. *Journal of the American Psychoanalytic Association*, 1976, 24, 283–308.

Atkinson, D.R., Furlong, M.J. & Wampold, B.E. Statistical significance, reviewer evaluations, and the scientific process: Is there a (statistically) significant relationship? *Journal of Counseling Psychology*, 1982, *29*, 189–194.

Averill, J.R., & Opton, E.M., Jr. Psychophysiological assessment: Rationale and problems. In P. McReynolds (Ed.), *Advances in psychological assessment (Vol.1)*. Palo Alto, CA: Science and Behavior Books, 1968.

Avery, D., & Winokur, G. Mortality in depressed outpatients treated with electroconvulsive therapy. *Archives of General Psychiatry*, 1976, *33*, 1029–1037.

Babad, E.Y., & Amir, L. Trainers' liking, Bion's emotional modalities, and t-group effect. *Journal of Applied Behavioral Science*, 1978, *14*, 511–522.

Bachrach, L.L. Marital status and mental disorder: An analytical review. *U.S. Department of Health, Education and Welfare No 75-217 (ADAMHA), publication No. 75-217.* Washington, D.C.: U.S. Government Printing Office, 1975.

Bachrach, A.J., Erwin, W.J. & Mohr, J.P. The control of eating behavior in an anorexic by operant conditioning techniques. In L.P. Ullman & I. Krasner (Eds.), *Case Studies in Behavior Modification.* New York: Holt, Rinehart, & Winston, 1965.

Bachrach, H.M., & Leaff, L.A. 'Analyzability': A systematic review of the clinical and quantitative literature. *Journal of American Psycho-Analytic Association*, 1978, *26*, 881–920.

*Bandura, A. *Principles of behavior modification.* New York: Holt, Rinehart & Winston, 1969.

Bandura, A.A. *Social Learning Theory.* Englewood Cliffs, N.J.: Prentice-Hall, 1977.

Bandura, A. Self-efficacy: Toward a unifying theory of behavioral change. *Advances in Behaviour Research and Therapy*, 1979, *1*, 139–162.

*Barcai, A. Family therapy in the treatment of anorexia nervosa. *American Journal of Psychiatry*, 1971, *128* (3), 286–290.

Barbrack, C.R. *What's the meta? Meta-analysis data in search of an information audience (that's what)*. Submitted for publication.

Barlow, D.H. Behavior therapy: The next decade. *Behavior Therapy*, 1980, *11*, 315–328.

Barlow, D.H. On the relation of clinical research to clinical practice: Current issues, new directions. *Journal of Consulting and Clinical Psychology*, 1981, *49*, 147–155.

Barlow, D.H. & Mavissakalian, M. Directions in the assessment and treatment of phobia: The next decade. In M. Mavissakalian & D.H. Barlow (Eds.), *Phobia: Psychological and Pharmacological Treatment*. New York: Guilford Press, 1981.

Barlow, D.H. & Wolfe, B.E. Behavioral approaches to anxiety disorders: A report on the NIMH-SUNY, Albany, research conference. *Journal of Consulting and Clinical Psychology*, 1981, *49*, 448–454.

*Barnett, M.A., & Bryan, J.H. Effects of competition with outcome feedback on children's helping behavior. *Developmental Psychology*, 1974, *10*, 838–842.

*Barnett, M.A., King, L.M., & Howard, J.A. Inducing affect about self or other: Effects on generosity in children. *Developmental Psychology*, 1979, *15*, 164–167.

Barrett, J.E. (Ed.). The relationship of life events to the onset of neurotic disorders. In J.E. Barrett (Ed.), *Stress and mental disorder*. New York: Raven Press, 1979, pp. 87–109. (a)

*Barrett, J.E. (Ed.). *Stress and mental disorder*. New York: Raven Press, 1979.(b)

Barron, F., & Leary, T. Changes in psychoneurotic patients with and without psychotherapy. *Journal of Counseling Psychology*, 1955, *19*, 239–245.

Barton, A. *Communities in disaster: A sociological analysis of collective stress situations*. Garden City, N.Y.: Doubleday, 1969.

Baum, C.G. & Forehand, R. Long-term follow-up assessment of parent training by use of multiple outcome measures. *Behavior Therapy*, 1981, *12*, 643–652.

Beck, A.T. *Depression: Clinical, experimental and theorectical aspects*. New York: Harper and Row, 1967.

Beck, A.T. Phases in the development of structure in therapy and encounter groups. In D.A. Wexler & L.N. Rice (Eds.), *Innovations in client-centered therapy*. New York: Wiley, 1974.

Beck, A.T. *Cognitive therapy and the emotional disorders*. New York: International Universities Press, 1976.

Beck, A.T., Hollon, S.D., Bedrosian, R.C., & Young, J. *Combined Cognitive Pharmacotherapy Versus Cognitive Therapy in the Treatment of Depression*. Unpublished manuscript, University of Pennsylvania, 1981.

Beck, A.T., Rush, A.J., Shaw, B.F., & Emery, G. *Cognitive therapy for depression: A treatment manual*. New York: Guilford Press, 1979.

Becker, J.V., Turner, S.M., & Sajwaj, T.E. Multiple behavioral effects of the use of lemon juice with a ruminating toddler-age child. *Behavior Modification*, 1978, *2*, 267–278.

Bednar, R.L., & Kaul, T.J. Experiential group research: Current perspectives. In S.L. Garfield & A.E. Bergin (Eds.), *Handbook of psychotherapy and behavior change: An empirical analysis* (2nd ed.). New York: Wiley, 1978

Bednar, R.L., & Lawlis, G.F. *Empirical research in group psychotherapy and behavior change*. New York: Wiley, 1971.

Bednar, R.L., Melnick, J., & Kaul, T.J. Risk, responsibility, and structure: A conceptual framework for initiating group counseling and psychotherapy. *Journal of Counseling Psychology*, 1974, *21*, 31–37.

Beech, H.R. The symptomatic treatment of writer's cramp. In H.J. Eysenck (Ed.), *Behavior therapy and the neuroses*. Oxford: Pergamon, 1960.

Beech, H.R. Advances in the treatment of obsessional neurosis. *British Journal of Hospital Medicine*, 1979, Jan., 54–59.

Beech, H.R., & Perigault, J. *Toward a theory of obsessional states*. Methuen & Co. Ltd., 1974, pp. 114–141.

Beech, H.R., & Vaughan, M. *Behavioral treatments of obsessional states*. New York: Wiley, 1978.

Bennis, W.G., & Shepard, H.A. A theory of group development. *Human Relations*, 1956, *9*, 415–438.

*Bemis, K.M. Current approaches to the etiology and treatment of anorexia nervosa. *Psychological Bulletin*, 1978, *85*, 593–617.

Bergin, A.E. The empirical emphasis in psychotherapy: A symposium. The effects of psychotherapy: Negative results revisited. *Journal of Counseling Psychology*, 1963, *10*, 244–250.

Bergin, A.E. Some implications of psychotherapy research for therapeutic practice. *Journal of Abnormal Psychology*, 1966, *71*, 235–246.

Bergin, A.E. Some implications of psychotherapy research for therapeutic practice. *International Journal of Psychiatry*, 1967, *3*, 136–160.

Bergin, A.E. The deterioration effect: A reply to Braucht. *Journal of Abnormal Psychology*, 1970, *75*, 300–302.

Bergin, A.E. The evaluation of therapeutic outcomes. In A.E. Bergin & S.L. Garfield (Eds.), *Handbook of psychotherapy and behavior change: An empirical analysis*. New York: Wiley, 1971.

Bergin, A.E. Psychotherapy can be dangerous. *Psychology Today*, 1975, *11*, 96–103.

Bergin, A.E. Negative effects revisited: A reply. *Professional Psychology*, 1980, *11*, 93–100

Bergin, A.E., & Lambert, M.J. The evaluation of therapeutic outcomes. In S.L. Garfield & A.E. Bergin (Eds.), *Handbook of psychotherapy and behavior change: An empirical analysis* (2nd ed.). New York: Wiley, 1978.

*Berkowitz, L. Social norms, feelings, and other factors affecting helping and altruism. In L. Berkowitz (Ed.), *Advances in experimental social psychology (Vol. 6)*. New York: Academic Press, 1972.

Bernard, J. *The future of marriage*. New York: World Book, 1972.

*Berscheid, E., & Walster, E. When does a harm-doer compensate a victim? *Journal of Personality and Social Psychology*, 1967, *6*, 435–441.

Betz, B.J. Experiences in research in psychotherapy with schizophrenic patients. In H. H. Strupp and L. Luborsky (Eds.), *Research in Psychotherapy (Vol. II)*. Washington D.C.: American Psychological Association, 1962.

Beumont, P.J.B., Abraham, S.F., & Simson, K.G. The psychosocial histories of adolescent girls and young women with anorexia nervosa. *Psychological Medicine*, 1981, *11*, 131–140.

Beutler, L.E. *Eclectic psychotherapy: A systematic approach*. Elmsford, N.Y.: Pergamon Press, 1983.

Beutler, L.E., Dunbar, P.W., & Baer, P.E. Individual variation among therapists' perceptions of patients, therapy process and outcome. *Psychiatry*, 1980, *43*, 205–210.

Bhanji, S., & Thompson, J. Operant conditioning in the treatment of anorexia nervosa: A review and retrospective study of 11 cases. *British Journal of Psychiatry*, 1974, *124*, 166–172.

Bielski, R.J., & Friedel, R.O. Prediction of tricyclic antidepressant response. *Archives of General Psychiatry*, 1976, *33*, 1479–1489.

*Birley, J.L.T., & Brown, G.W. Crises and life changes preceding the onset or relapse of acute schizophrenia: Clinical aspects. *British Journal of Psychiatry*, 1970, *116*, 327–333.

Birnie, C.R. Anorexia Nervosa treated by hypnosis. *Lancet*, 1936, *2*, 1331–1332.

Bitgood, S. C., Crowe, M. J., Suarez, Y. & Peters, R. D. Effects and side effects of stereotyped behavior in children. *Behavior Modification*, 1980, *4*, 187–208.

Blackburn, I., Bishop, S., Glen, A. I. M., Whalley, L. H., & Christie, J. E. The efficacy of cognitive therapy in depression: A treatment trial using cognitive therapy and pharmacotherapy, each alone and in combination. *British Journal of Psychiatry*, 1981, *139*, 181–189.

*Blanco, R.F. *Prescriptions for children with learning and adjustment problems*. Springfield, IL: Charles C. Thomas, 1972.

Blinder, B.J., Freeman, D.M.A., & Stunkard, A.J. Behavior therapy of anorexia nervosa: Effectiveness of activity as a reinforcer of weight gain. *American Journal of Psychiatry*, 1970, *126*, 77–82.

Blue, R. Ineffectiveness of an aversion therapy technique in treatment of obsessional thinking. *Psychological Reports*, 1978, *43*, 181–182.

Blum, R.H., Garfield, E.F., Johnstone, J.L. & Magistad, J.G. Drug education: Further results and recommendations. *Journal of Drug Issues*, 1978, *8*, 379–426.

Bolman, L. Some effects of trainers on their T groups. *Journal of Applied Behavioral Science*, 1971, *7*, 309–325.

Boren, J.J. & Coleman, A.D. Some experiments in reinforcement principles within a psychiatric ward for delinquent soldiers. *Journal of Applied Behavior Analysis*, 1970, *3*, 29–37.

Borkovec, T.D., Weerts, T.C., & Bernstein, D.A. Assessment of anxiety. In A.R. Ciminero, K.S. Calhoun, & H.E. Adams (Eds.), *Handbook of behavioral assessment*. New York: Wiley, 1977.

Boruch, R.F. & Gomez, H. Sensitivity, bias and theory in impact evaluations. *Professional Psychology*, 1977, *8*, 411–439.

Bowers, M.B., Jr., & Freedman, D.X. Psychosis associated with drug use. In S. Arieti (Ed.), *American handbook of psychiatry* (Vol. 4, 2nd ed.). New York: Basic Books, 1975.

*Branch, C.H.H., & Eurman, L.J. Social attitudes toward patients with anorexia nervosa. *American Journal of Psychiatry*, 1980, *137*, 631–632.

Braucht, G.N. The deterioration effect: A reply to Bergin. *Journal of Consulting Psychology*, 1970, *75*, 293–299.

Bremer, J. A social psychiatric investigation of a small community in northern Norway. *Acta Psychiatrica et Neurologica Scandinavica*, 1951, *62*, Supplementum.

Brown, B.B. Social and psychological correlates of help-seeking behavior among urban adults. *American Journal of Community Psychology*, 1978, *6*, 425–439.

*Brown, G.W. Meaning, measurement, and stress of life events. In B.S. Dohrenwend & B.P. Dohrenwend (Eds.), *Stressful life events: Their nature and effects*. New York, Wiley, 1974, pp. 217–243.

Brown, G.W., Bhrolchain, M.N., & Harris, T. Social class and psychiatric disturbance among women in an urban population. *Sociology*, 1975, *9*, 225–254.

Brown, G.W., & Birley, J.L.T. Crises and life changes and the onset of schizophrenia. *Journal of Health and Social Behavior*, 1968, *9*, 203–214.

Brown, G.W., Davidson, S., Harris, T., MacLean, U., Pollack, S., & Prudo, R. Psychiatric disorder in London and North Uist. *Social Science and Medicine*, 1977, *11*, 367–377.

Brown, G.W., & Harris, T. *Social origins of depression: A study of psychiatric disorder in women*. New York: Free Press, 1978.(a)

*Brown, G.W., & Harris, T. Social origins of depression: A reply. *Psychological Medicine*, 1978, *8*, 577–588.(b)

*Brown, G.W., Harris, T.O., & Peto, J. Life events and psychiatric disorders (Part 2): Nature of causal link. *Psychological Medicine*, 1973, *3*, 159–176.

Brownell, K.D., Heckerman, C.L., Westlake, R.J., Hayes, S.C. & Monti, P.M. The effect of couples training and partner cooperation in the behavioral treatment of obesity. *Behavior Research and Therapy*, 1978, *16*, 323–333.

Brownell, K.D. & Stunkard, A.J. Behavior therapy and behavior change: Uncertainties in programs for weight control. *Behavior Research and Therapy*, 1978, *16*, 301.

Browning, C.H. & Miller, S.I. Anorexia Nervosa: A study in prognosis and management. *American Journal of Psychiatry*, 1968, *124*, 1128–1132.

Bruch, H. *Eating disorders: Obesity, anorexia nervosa and the person within*. New York: Basic Books, 1973.

Bruch, H. Perils of behavior modification in treatment of anorexia nervosa. *Journal of the American Medical Association*, 1974, *230*, 1419–1427.

Bruch, H. How to treat anorexia nervosa. *Roche Report: Frontiers of Psychiatry*, 1975, *5*(8), 1–8.

Bruch, H. Psychological antecedents of anorexia nervosa. In R. Vigersky (Ed.), *Anorexia Nervosa*. New York: Raven Press, 1977.

Bruch, H. *The golden cage: The enigma of anorexia nervosa*. Cambridge, MA: Harvard University Press, 1978.

Bunney, W.E., Jr. Psychopharmacology of the switch process in affective illness. In M.A. Lipton, A. DiMascio, & K.F. Killam (Eds.), *Psychopharmacology: A generation of progress.* New York: Raven Press, 1978.

Butler, T., & Fuhrinam, A. Patient perspective on the curative process: A comparison of day treatment and outpatient psychotherapy groups. *Small Group Behavior,* 1980, *11,* 371–388.

Campbell, D.T., & Stanley, J.C. Experimental and quasi-experimental designs for research and teaching. In N.L. Gage (Ed.), *Handbook of research on teaching.* Chicago: Rand McNally, 1963.

*Campbell, K. The psychotherapy relationship with borderline personality disorders. *Psychotherapy: Theory, Research and Practice,* 1982, *19,* 166–193.

Caplan, G. *Support systems and community mental health.* New York: Behavioral Publications, 1974.

Caplan, R.D. *Organizational stress and individual strain: A social-psychological study of risk factors in coronary heart disease among administrators, engineers, and scientists.* Doctoral Dissertation, Department of Sociology, University of Michigan, 1972.

Carkhuff, R.R. New directions in training for the helping professions: Toward a technology for human and community resource development. *The Counseling Psychologist,* 1972, *3,* 12–30.

Cartwright, D.S. Note on "changes of psychoneurotic with and without psychotherapy." *Journal of Consulting Psychology,* 1956, *20,* 403–404.

Casper, R.C., & Davis, J.M. On the course of anorexia nervosa. *American Journal of Psychiatry,* 1977, *134,* 974–978.

Cassel, J. The contribution of the social environment to host resistance. *American Journal of Epidemiology,* 1976, *104* (2), 107–122.

*Cheshire, N.M. A big hand for Little Hans. *Bulletin of British Psychological Society,* 1979, *32,* 320–323.

*Cheshire, N.M. *The nature of psychodynamic interpretation.* London: Wiley, 1974.

Church, J. The Buffalo Creek disaster: Extent and range of emotional and/or behavioral problems. *Omega,* 1974, *5,* 61–63.

*Cialdini, R., Darby, B., & Vincent, J. Transgressions and altruism: A case for hedonism. *Journal of Experimental Social Psychology,* 1973, *9,* 502–516.

Ciesielski, K.T., Beech, H.R., & Gordon, P.K. Some electrophysiological observations in obsessional states. *British Journal of Psychiatry,* 1981, *138,* 479–484.

*Ciseaux, A. Anorexia nervosa: A view from the mirror. *American Journal of Nursing,* August 1980.

*Claggett, M.S. Anorexia nervosa: A behavioral approach. *American Journal of Nursing,* April 1980.

Clayton, P.J., Desmarais, L., & Winokur, G. A study of normal bereavement. *American Journal of Psychiatry,* 1968, *125,* 168–178.

Clayton, P.J., Halikas, J.A., & Maurice, W.L. The bereavement of the widowed. *Diseases of the Nervous System,* 1971, *32,* 597–604.

Clayton, P.J., Halikas, J.A., & Maurice, W.L. The depression of widowhood. *British Journal of Psychiatry,* 1972, *120,* 71–77.

Coates, D.B., Moyer, S., Kendall, L., & Howat, M.G. Life event changes and mental health. In I.G. Sarason & C.D. Spielberger (Eds.), *Stress and anxiety* (Vol. 3). New York: Wiley, 1976, pp. 225–250.

Coates, D.B., Moyer, S., & Wellman, B. Yorklea study: Symptoms, problems and life events. *Canadian Journal of Public Health*, 1969, *69*, 471–481.

Cobb, S. Social support as a moderator of life stress. *Psychosomatic Medicine*, 1976, *38*, 300–314.

Cobb, S., & Kasl, S.V. Termination: The consequences of job loss. *U.S. Department of Health, Education, and Welfare (NIOSH) Publication No. 77-224*. Washington D.C.: U.S. Government Printing Office, 1977.

Coche, E., & Dies, R.R. Integrating research findings into the practice of group psychotherapy. *Psychotherapy: Theory, research and practice*. 1981, *18*(4), 410–416.

Coddington, R.D. The significance of life events as etiologic factors in the diseases of children. II. A study of a normal population. *Journal of Psychosomatic Research*, 1972, *16*, 205–213.

Coelho, G.V., Hamburg, D.A., & Adams, J.E. *Coping and adaptation*. New York: Basic Books, 1974.

Cohen, F., & Lazarus, R.S. Coping with the stresses of illness. In G.C. Stone, F. Cohen, & N.E. Adler (Eds), *Health psychology: A handbook*. San Francisco: Jossey–Bass, 1979, pp. 217–254.

*Cohen, J.H., & Pope, B. Concurrent use of insight and desensitization therapy. *Psychiatry*, 1980, *43*, 146–154.

Cole, C.E., Patterson, R.M., Craig, J.B., Thomas, W.E., Ristine, L.P., Stahly, M., & Pasamanick, B. A controlled study of iproniazid in the treatment of depression. *Archives of General Psychiatry*, 1959, *1*, 513–518.

Colson, D. *Protectiveness in the borderline patient: A neglected object relations paradigm*. Unpublished manuscript, 1981.

Cone, J.D. Confounded comparisons in triple response mode assessment research. *Behavior Assessment*, 1979, *1*, 85–96.

Cooper, C.L. Adverse and growful effects of experiential learning groups: The role of the trainer, participant, and group characteristics. *Human Relations*, 1977, *30*, 1103–1129.

Cooper, C.L., & Payne, R. (Eds.). *Stress at work*. New York: Wiley, 1978.

Covi, L., Lipman, R.S., Derogatis, L.R., Smith, J.E., & Pattison, J.H. Drugs and group psychotherapy in neurotic depression. *American Journal of Psychiatry*, 1974, *131*, 191–197.

Crasilneck, H.B. & Hall, J.A. *Clinical Hypnosis: Principles and Applications*. New York: Grune & Stratton, 1975.

*Crisp, A.H. Clinical and therapeutic aspects of anorexia nervosa: A study of 30 cases. *Journal of Psychosomatic Research*, 1965, *9*, 67–78.

*Crisp, A.H. A treatment regime for anorexia nervosa. *British Journal of Psychiatry*, 1965, *112*, 505–512.

Crisp, A.H. Anorexia nervosa. *Hospital Medicine*, May 1967, 713–718.

*Crisp, A.H. Primary anorexia nervosa or adolescent weight phobia. *Practitioner*, 1974, *212*, 525–535.

*Crisp, A.H. The differential diagnosis of anorexia nervosa. *Proceeding of the Royal Society of Medicine*, 1977, *70*, 686–690.

Crisp, A.H. *Anorexia nervosa: Let me be*. London: Academic Press, 1980.

*Crisp, A.H. Therapeutic outcome in anorexia nervosa. *Canadian Journal of Psychiatry*, 1981, *26*, 232–235.

Crisp, A.H., Harding, B. & McGuinness, B. Anorexia nervosa: Psychoneurotic characteristics of parents: Relationships to prognosis. *Journal of Psychosomatic Research*, 1974, *18*, 167–173.

*Crisp, A.H., Hsu, L.K.G., & Harding, B. The starving hoarder and voracious spender: Stealing in anorexia nervosa. *Journal of Psychosomatic Research*, 1980, *24*, 225–231.

*Crisp, A.H., Hsu, L.K.G., Harding, B., & Hartshorn, J. Clinical features of anorexia nervosa: A study of a consecutive series of 102 female patients. *Journal of Psychosomatic Research*, 1980, *24*, 179–191.

*Crisp, A.H., Palmer, R.L., & Kalucy, R.S. How common is anorexia nervosa? A prevalence study. *British Journal of Psychiatry*, 1976, *128*, 549–554.

Croog, S.H. The family as a source of stress. In S. Levine & N.A. Scotch (Eds.), *Social Stress*. Chicago: Aldine, 1970, pp. 19–53.

Dally, P.J. *Anorexia nervosa*. New York: Grune & Stratton, 1969.

Dally, P.J., Gomez, J., & Isaacs, A.J. *Anorexia nervosa*. London: William Heinemann Medical Books Ltd., 1979.

Dally, P.J., & Sargant, W. A new treatment of anorexia nervosa. *British Medical Journal*, 1960, *1*, 1770–1773.

Dally, P.J., & Sargant, W. Treatment and outcome of anorexia nervosa. *British Medical Journal*, 1966, *2*, 793–795.

Daneman, E.A. Imipramine in office management of depressive reactions (a double-blind study). *Diseases of the Nervous System*, 1961, *22*, 213–217.

Davanloo, H. *Basic principles and techniques in short-term dynamic psychotherapy*. New York: Wiley, 1971.

Daves, H.K. Anorexia Nervosa: Treatment with hypnosis and ECT. *Diseases of the Nervous System*, 1961, *22*, 627–631.

Davis, J.M. Overview: Maintenance therapy in psychiatry. II. Affective disorders. *American Journal of Psychiatry*, 1976, *133*, 1–14.

Dean, A., & Lin, N. The stress-buffering role of social support: Problems and prospects for systematic investigation. *Journal of Nervous and Mental Disease*, 1977, *165* (6), 403–417.

Dean, A., Lin, N., & Ensel, W.M. The epidemiological significance of social support systems in depression. In R.G. Simmons (Ed.), *Research in Community and Mental Health* (Vol. 2). Greenwich: JAI Press, 1980.

de Araujo, G., van Arsdel, P.P., Jr., Holmes, T.H., & Dudley, D.L. Life change, coping ability, and chronic asthma. *Journal of Psychosomatic Research*, 1973, *17*, 359–363.

Dekker, D.J., & Webb, J.T. Relationships of the Social Readjustment Rating Scale to psychiatric patient status, anxiety and social desirability. *Journal of Psychosomatic Research*, 1974, *18*, 125–130.

Deniau, L. *L'hystérie gastrique*. Paris, 1883.

DeRubeis, R.J., & Hollon, S.D. Behavioral treatment of affective disorders. In L. Michelson, M. Hersen, & S. M. Turner (Eds.), *Future perspectives in behavior therapy*. New York: Plenum Press, 1981.

De Silva, P., Rachman, S., & Seligman, M.E.P. Prepared phobias and obsessions: Therapeutic outcome. *Behavioral Research and Therapy*, 1977, *15*, 65–77.

Diagnostic and Statistical Manual of Mental Disorders (Third Edition). Washington, D.C.: American Psychiatric Association, 1980.

Dies, R.R. Attitudes toward the training of group psychotherapists: Some interprofessional and experience-associated differences. *Small Group Behavior*, 1974, *5*, 65–79.

Dies, R. R. Leadership in group psychotherapy: Manipulation = facilitation? In W. Gruen (Chair), *Relevance of outcome research to clinical group practice*. Symposium presented at the meeting of the American Group Psychotherapy Association, Boston, 1976.

Dies, R.R. Group therapist transparency: A critique of theory and research. *International Journal of Group Psychotherapy*, 1977, *27*, 177–200.(a)

*Dies, R.R. Pragmatics of leadership in psychotherapy and encounter group research. *Small Group Behavior*, 1977, *8*, 229–248.(b)

Dies, R.R. The human factor in group psychotherapy research. In L.R. Wolberg, M.L. Anderson, & A.R. Wolberg (Eds.), *Group therapy 1978: An overview*. New York: Stratton Intercontinental Medical Book Corporation, 1978.

Dies, R.R. Group psychotherapy: Reflections on three decades of research. *Journal of Applied Behavioral Science*, 1979, *15*, 361–373.

Dies, R.R. Current practice in the training of group psychotherapists. *International Journal of Group Psychotherapy*, 1980, *30*, 169–185.(a)

Dies, R.R. Group psychotherapy training and supervision. In A.K. Hess (Ed.), *Psychotherapy supervision: Theory, research, and practice*. New York: Wiley, 1980.(b)

Dies, R.R., Mallet, J., & Johnson, F. Openness in the coleader relationship: Its effect on group process and outcome. *Small Group Behavior*, 1979, *10*, 523–546.

*Digersky, R., & Loriaux, D.L. The effect of cyproheptadine in anorexia nervosa: A double blind trial. In R.A. Digersky (Ed.), *Anorexia nervosa*. New York: Raven Press, 1977, pp. 349–356.

Dohrenwend, B.P. Problems in defining and sampling the relevant population of stressful life events. In B.S. Dohrenwend & B.P. Dohrenwend (Eds.), *Stressful life events: Their nature and effects*. New York: Wiley, 1974, pp. 275–310.

*Dohrenwend, B.P. Stressful life events and psychopathology: Some issues of theory and method. In J.E. Barrett (Ed.), *Stress and mental disorder*. New York: Raven Press, 1979, pp. 1–15.

*Dohrenwend, B.P., & Dohrenwend, B.S. Sex differences in psychiatric disorders. *American Journal of Sociology*, 1976, *81* (May), 1447–1459.

Dohrenwend, B.P., & Dohrenwend, B.S. *Social status and psychological disorder*. New York: Wiley, 1969.

*Dohrenwend, B.P., Dohrenwend, B.S., Gould, M.S., Link, B., Neugebauer,

R., & Wunsch-Hitzig, R. *Mental illness in the United States: Epidemiological estimates.* New York: Praeger, 1980.

*Dohrenwend, B.S. Social class and stressful events. In E.H. Hare & J.K. Wing (Eds.), *Psychiatric epidemiology.* London: Oxford University Press, 1970, pp. 313–319.

Dohrenwend, B.S. Life events as stressors: A methodological inquiry. *Journal of Health and Social Behavior,* 1973, *14,* 167–175.(a)

*Dohrenwend, B.S. Social status and stressful life events. *Journal of Personality and Social Psychology,* 1973, *78,* 225–235.(b)

*Dohrenwend, B.S., & Dohrenwend, B.P. Class and race as status-related sources of stress. In S. Levine & N.A. Scotch (Eds.), *Social stress.* New York: Aldine, 1970, pp. 111–140.

*Dohrenwend, B.S., & Dohrenwend, B.P. *Stressful life events: Their nature and effects.* New York: Wiley, 1974.

Dohrenwend, B.S., Krasnoff, L., Askenasy, A.R., & Dohrenwend, B.P. Exemplification of a method for scaling life events: The PERI life events scale. *Journal of Health and Social Behavior,* 1978, *19,* 205–229.

*Dollard, J., & Miller, N.E. *Personality and psychotherapy.* New York: McGraw-Hill, 1950.

Dubbert, P.M. & Wilson, G.T. Treatment failures in behavior therapy for obesity: Causes, correlates, and consequences. In E.B. Foa & P.M.G. Emmelkamp (Eds.), *Treatment Failures in Behavior Therapy.* New York: Wiley, 1983.

Duckro, P., Beal, D., & George, C. Research on the effects of disconfirmed client role expectations in psychotherapy: A critical review. *Psychological Bulletin,* 1979, *86,* 260–275.

*Dull, W.W. Anorexia nervosa. *Lancet,* 1:516, 1888.

Duncan, J.W. & Laird, J.D. Positive and reverse placebo effects as a function of differences in cues used in self-perception. *Journal of Personality and Social Psychology,* 1980, *39,* 1024–1036.

Duncan-Jones, P. The Interview Measurement of Social Interaction. *Proceedings of the Research Committee on the Sociology of Mental Health, Ninth World Congress of Sociology, Uppsala.* August, 1978.

Eaton, W.W. Life events, social supports, and psychiatric symptoms: A reanalysis of the New Haven data. *Journal of Health and Social Behavior,* 1978 (June), *19,* 230–234.

*Eckenrode, J., & Gore, S. Stressful events and social supports: The significance of context. In B.H. Gottlieb (Ed.), *Social networks and social support in community mental health.* Beverly Hills, CA.: Sage, 1981.

*Eckert, E.D., Goldberg, S.C., Halmi, K.A., Casper, R.C., & Davis, J.M. Behavior therapy in anorexia nervosa. *British Journal of Psychiatry,* 1979, *134,* 55–59.

Ehrenkranz, S.M. A study of joint interviewing in the treatment of marital problems. *Social Casework,* 1967, *48,* 570–574.

Ehrensing, R.H., & Weitzman, E.L. The mother–daughter relationship in anorexia nervosa. *Psychosomatic Medicine,* 1970, *32,* 201–208.

Eissler, K.R. Some psychiatric aspects of anorexia nervosa demonstrated by a case report. *Psychoanalytic Review*, 1943, *30*, 121–145.

Eitinger, Leo. *Concentration camp survivors in Norway and Israel*. London: Allen and Unwin, 1964.

Emery, G., Hollon, S.D., & Bedrosian, R.C. (Eds.). *New directions in cognitive therapy*. New York: Guilford Press, 1981.

Emmelkamp, P.M.G., Van Der Helm, M., Van Zanten, B.L., & Plochg, I. The treatment of obsessive-compulsive patients: The contribution of self-instructional training to the effectiveness of exposure. *Behavior Research and Therapy*, 1980, *18*, 61–66.

Endicott, N.A. & Endicott, J. "Improvement" in untreated psychiatric patients. *Archives of General Psychiatry*, 1963, *9*, 575–585.

Endler, N.S., & Magnusson, D. (Eds.). *Interactional psychology and personality*. Washington, D.C.: Hemisphere, 1976.(a)

Endler, N.S., & Magnusson, D. Toward an interactional psychology of personality. *Psychological Bulletin*, 1976, *83*, 956–974.(b)

Epstein, L.H., Doke, L.A., Sajwaj, T.E., Sorrell, S. & Rimmer, B. Generality and side effects of overcorrection. *Journal of Applied Behavior Analysis*, 1974, *7*, 385–390.

Erikson, K.T. *Everything in its path: Destruction of community in the Buffalo Creek flood*. New York: Simon and Schuster, 1976.

*Erman, M.K., & Murray, G.B. A case report of anorexia and Gaucher's disease. *American Journal of Psychiatry*, 1980, *137*, 858–859.

Etringer, B.D., Cash, T.F. & Rimm, D.C. Behavioral, affective, and cognitive effects of participant modeling and an equally credible placebo. *Behavior Therapy*, 1982, *13*, 476–485.

Evans, I. *Response interrelationships: Implications for method and theory in child behavior theory*. Colloquium presented at Rutgers, The State University of New Jersey, Department of Psychology, October, 1982.

Eysenck, H.J. The effects of psychotherapy, an evaluation. *Journal of Consulting Psychology*, 1952, *16*, 319–324.

Eysenck, H.J. *Experiments in Behavior Therapy*. Oxford: Pergamon Press, 1964.

Eysenck, H.J. The effects of psychotherapy. *International Journal of Psychiatry*, 1965, *1*, 322–328.

Eysenck, H.J. *The effects of psychotherapy*. New York: International Science Press, 1966.

Eysenck, H.J. A theory of the incubation of anxiety/fear response. *Behavior Research and Therapy*, 1968, *6*, 309–321.

Eysenck, H.J. Behaviour therapy—dogma or applied science? In M.P. Feldman & A. Broadhurst (Eds.), *Theoretical and experimental bases of the behaviour therapies*. London: Wiley, 1976.

Eysensck, H.J. *You and neurosis*. London: Temple Smith, Los Angeles: Sage, 1977.

Eysenck, H.J. What to do when desensitization goes wrong? *Australian Behaviour Therapist*, 1978, *5*, 15–16.

Eysenck, H.J. The conditioning model of neurosis. *Behavioral and Brain Sciences*, 1979, 2, 155–199.(a)

Eysenck, H.J. Expectations as causal elements in behavioral change. *Advances in Behaviour Research and Therapy*, 1979, 1, 171–186.(b)

Eysenck, H.J. A unified theory of psychotherapy, behaviour therapy, and spontaneous remission. *Zeitschrift fur Psychologie*, 1980, 188, 43–56.

Eysenck, H.J. Neobehavioristic (S–R) theory. In G.T. Wilson & C.M. Franks (eds.), *Contemporary Behavior Therapy*. New York: Guilford, 1982.

Eysenck, H.J. Meta-analysis: An abuse of research integration. *Journal of Special Education*, in press.

Eysenck, H.J., & Wilson, G.D. *The Experimental Study of Freudian Theories*. London: Methuen, 1973.

Fairweather, G.W., Simon, R., Gebhard, M.E., Weingarten, E., Holland, J.L., Sanders, R., Stone, G.B., & Reahl, J.E. Relative effectiveness of psychotherapeutic programs: a multi-criteria comparison of four programs for three different patient groups. *Psychology Monograph*, 1960, 74(5), Whole No. 492.

Farberow, N.L., & Shneidman, E.S. *The cry for help*. New York: McGraw-Hill, 1961.

Farkas, G.M. An ontological analysis of behavior therapy. *American Psychologist*, 1980, 35, 364–374.

Farquharson, R.F., & Hyland, H.H. Anorexia nervosa: The course of 15 patients treated from 20–30 years previously. *Canadian Medical Association Journal*, 1966, 94, 411–419.

Fawcett, J., Leff, M., & Bunney, W.E. Suicide. *Archives of General Psychiatry*, 1969, 21, 129–137.

Feifel, H., & Eells, J. Patients and therapists assess the same psychotherapy. *Journal of Consulting Psychology*, 1963, 27, 310–318.

Feighner, J.P., Robins, E., Guze, S.V., Woodruff, R.A., Winokur, G., & Munoz, R. Diagnostic criteria for use in psychiatric research. *Archives of General Psychiatry*, 1972, 26, 57–63.

*Fischer, C. *Networks and places*. New York: Free Press, 1977.

Fisher, S., & Mendell, D. The spread of psychotherapeutic effects from the patient to his family group. *Psychiatry*, 1959, 21, 133–140.

Fishman, D.B. Increasing the adoption of applied behavior activities in human services: A systems and functional analysis. Invited address, Association for Behavior Analysis, Dearborn, Michigan, May, 1982.

Fiske, D.W. Methodological issues in research on the psychotherapist. In A.S. Gurman & A.M. Razin (Eds.), *Effective psychotherapy: A handbook of research*. Oxford: Pergamon, 1977.

Fleishman, M.J. Social learning intervention for aggressive children: From the laboratory to the real world. *Behavior Therapy*, 1982, 5, 55–58.

Fo, W.S.O., & O'Donnell, C.R. The buddy system: Effects of community intervention on delinquent offenses. *Behavior Therapy*, 1975, 6, 522–524.

Foa, E. Failure in treating obsessive-compulsives. *Behavioral Therapy*, 1979, 17, 169–176.

Foa, E.B. *The behavioral treatment of obsessive-compulsive disorders. Conceptual and practical issues.* Colloquium presented at Rutgers, The State University of New Jersey, Department of Psychology, November, 1982.

Foa, E.B., & Emmelkamp, P.M.G. *Failures in behavior therapy.* New York: Wiley, 1983.

Foa, E.B., & Goldstein, A.J. Continuous exposure and complete response prevention in the treatment of obsessive-compulsive neurosis. *Behavior Therapy,* 1978, *9,* 821–829.

Ford, J.D. & Kendall, P.C. Behavior therapists' professional behaviors: A survey study. *Professional Psychology,* 1979, *10,* 772–773.

Fox, R.E. The effect of psychotherapy on the spouse. *Family Process,* 1968, *7,* 7–16.

Framo, J.L. The integration of marital therapy with sessions with family of origin. In A.S. Gurman & D.P. Kniskern (Eds.), *Handbook of family therapy.* New York: Brunner/Mazel, 1981.

Frank, J.D. *Persuasion and healing: A comparative study of psychotherapy* (2nd ed.). Baltimore: Johns Hopkins University Press, 1973.

*Franks, C.M. On behaviourism and behaviour therapy—not necessarily synonymous and becoming less so. *Australian Behaviour Therapist,* 1980, *7,* 14–23.

Franks, C.M. Behavior therapy: An overview. In C.M. Franks, G.T. Wilson, P. Kendall, & K. Brownell, *Annual review of behavior therapy: Theory and practice* (Vol. 8). New York: Guilford Press, 1982.

Franks, C.M., & Barbrack, C.R. Behavior therapy with adults: An integrative approach. In M. Hersen, A.E. Kazdin, & A.J. Bellack (Eds.), *The clinical psychology handbook.* New York: Pergamon, 1983.

Franks, C.M., & Mays, D.T. Negative effects revisited: A rejoinder. *Professional Psychology,* 1980, *11,* 101–105.

Franks, C.M., Wilson, G.T., Kendall, P.C., & Brownell, K.D. *Annual review of behavior therapy* (Vol. 8). New York: Guilford Press, 1982.

Frazier, S.H. Anorexia nervosa. *Diseases of the nervous system,* 1965, *26,* 155–159.

Freud, S. *Introductory lectures on psychoanalysis.* London: Allen & Unwin, 1922.

*Freud, S. *The ego and the id* (standard edition). 1923, Vol. 19.

Freud, S. *Analysis terminable and interminable* (standard edition). 1937, Vol. 23, pp. 216–253.

Freud, S. From a history of an infantile neurosis. In *Collected papers* (Vol. 3). New York: Basic Books, 1959 (originally published in 1918).

Freud, S. *The origins of psychoanalysis. Letters to Wilhem Fliess, Drafts and notes.* New York: Hogarth Press, 1954 (originally published in 1902).

Fried, M. Grieving for a lost home. In L.J. Duhl (Ed.), *The urban condition.* New York: Basic Books, 1963, pp. 151–171.

Friedman, A.S. Interaction of drug therapy with marital therapy in depressed patients. *Archives of General Psychiatry,* 1975, *32,* 619–637.

Fuchs, C.Z, & Rehm, L.P. A self-control behavior therapy program for depression. *Journal of Consulting and Clinical Psychology,* 1977, *45,* 206–215.

Gardner, R.A. *Treatment of the children of divorce*. Presentation at the Ninth Annual Spring Conference of the Chicago Family Institute, "Separation, Divorce, and Beyond", Chicago, April, 1982.

Garfield, S.L. Research on client variables in psychotherapy. In S.L. Garfield & A.E. Bergin (Eds.), *Handbook of psychotherapy and behavior change* (2nd ed.). New York: Wiley, 1978, pp. 191–232.

Garfield, S.L. Evaluating the psychotherapies. *Behavior Therapy*, 1981, *12*, 295–307.

Garfield, S.L., & Bergin, A.E. Therapeutic conditions and outcome. *Journal of Abnormal Psychology*, 1971, *77*, 108–114.

Garfield, S.L., & Bergin, A.E. *Handbook of psychotherapy and behavior change* (2nd ed.). New York: Wiley, 1978.

Garfinkel, P.E. Some recent observations on the pathogenesis of anorexia nervosa. *Canadian Journal of Psychiatry*, 1981, *26*, 218–223.

Garfinkel, P.E., & Garner, D.M. *Anorexia nervosa: A multidimensional perspective*. New York: Brunner/Mazel, 1982.

*Garfinkel, P.E., Moldofsky, H., & Garner, D.M. The outcome of anorexia nervosa: Significance of clinical features, body image, and behavior modification. In R.A. Vigersky (Ed.), *Anorexia nervosa*. New York: Raven Press, 1977.

*Geller, J.L. Treatment of anorexia nervosa by the integration of behavior therapy and psychotherapy. *Psychotherapy Psychosomatic*, 1975, *26*, 167–177.

Gersten, J.C., Langner, T.S., Eisenberg, J.G., & Orzek, L. Child behavior and life events: Undesirable change or change per se? In B.S. Dohrenwend & B.P. Dohrenwend, *Stressful life events: Their nature and effects*. New York: Wiley, 1974, pp. 159–170.

Gersten, J.C., Langner, T.S., Eisenberg, J.G., & Simcha-Fagan, O. An evaluation of the etiologic role of stressful life-change events in psychological disorders. *Journal of Health and Social Behavior*, 1977, *18*(3), 3 228–244.

Gifford, S., Murawski, B.J., & Pilot, M. Anorexia nervosa in one of identical twins. *International Psychiatric Clinics*, 1970, *7*, 139–228.

Giovacchini, P.L. Further theoretical and clinical aspects: countertransference reactions can be clinically useful. In L. Bryce-Boyer & P.L. Giovacchini (Eds.), *Psychoanalytic treatment of schizophrenic borderline and characterological disorders* (2nd ed.). New York: J. Aronson, 1980, pp. 269–298.

Glass, D.C., & Singer, J.E. *Urban stress: Experiments on noise and social stressors*. New York: Academic Press, 1972.

Glassman, A., Kantor, S., & Shostak, M. Depression, delusions, and drug response. *American Journal of Psychiatry*, 1975, *132*, 716–719.

*Goldberg, S.C., Eckert, E.D., Casper, R.C., Halmi, K.A., Davis, J.M., & Roper, M.T. Factors influencing hospital differences in weight gain in anorexia nervosa. *The Journal of Nervous and Mental Disease*, 1980, *168*, 181–183.

*Goldfried, M.R. Toward the delineation of therapeutic change. *American Psychologist*, 1980, *35*, 991–999.

Goldfried, M.R., & Davison, G.C. *Clinical behavior therapy*. New York: Holt, Rinehart and Winston, 1976.

Goldstein, A.P., Heller, K., & Sechrest, L.B. *Psychotherapy and the psychology of behavior change.* New York: Wiley, 1966.

Gomes-Schwartz, B. Effective ingredients in psychotherapy: Prediction of outcome from process variables. *Journal of Consulting and Clinical Psychology,* 1978, *46,* 1023–1035.

Gore, S. The effect of social support in moderating the health consequences of unemployment. *Journal of Health and Social Behavior,* 1978, *19,* 157–165.

*Gore, S. Stress-buffering functions of social supports: An appraisal and clarification of research models. In B.S. Dohrenwend & B.P. Dohrenwend (Eds.), *Life stress and illness.* New York: Neale Watson, 1981.

Gottman, J.M. N-of-one and N-of-two research in psychotherapy. *Psychological Bulletin,* 1973, *80,* 93–105.

*Gove, W. The relationship between sex roles, mental illness, and marital status. *Social Forces,* 1972, *51,* 34–44.

*Gove, W., & Geerken, M.R. Response bias in surveys of mental health: An empirical investigation. *American Journal of Sociology,* 1977, *82* (6), 1289–1317.

*Gove, W., & Tudor, J.F. Adult sex roles and mental illness. *American Journal of Sociology,* 1973, *78,* 50–73.

Grant, D. Classical and operant conditioning. In A. Melton (Ed.), *Categories of human learning.* New York: Academic Press, 1964.

*Grant, I., Gerst, M., & Yager, J. Scaling of life events by psychiatric patients and normals. *Journal of Psychosomatic Research,* 1976, *20,* 141–149.

Graziano, A.M. Failures in child behavior therapy. In E.B. Foa & P.M.G. Emmelkamp (Eds.), *Treatment Failures in Behavior Therapy.* New York: Wiley, 1983.

Greenburg, D. You are what you EST. *Playboy,* January 1977, pp. 210–223.

Greenwald, A.G. Consequences of prejudices against the null hypothesis. *Psychological Bulletin,* 1975, *82,* 1–20.

Grinker, R.R., Werble, B., & Drye, R. *The borderline syndrome: A behavioral study of ego functions.* New York: Basic Books, 1968.

Groen, J.J., & Feldman-Toledano, A. Educative treatment of patients and parents in anorexia nervosa. *British Journal of Psychiatry,* 1966, *112,* 671–681.

Gross, E. Work, organization, and stress. In S. Levine and N.A. Scotch (Eds.), *Social stress.* Chicago: Aldine, 1970, pp. 54–110.

Gross, M. *Hypnotherapeutic strategies in anorexia nervosa.* Paper presented at the Annual Meeting of the American Psychiatric Association, New Orleans, May 1981.

*Gruber, L.H., & Wood, A.M. Negative treatment response in psychiatry. *Journal of Clinical Psychiatry,* 1978, *39,* 279.

Grunebaum, H., & Chasin, R. Relabeling and reframing reconsidered: The beneficial effects of a pathological label. *Family Process,* 1978, *17,* 449–456.

Guile, L., Horne, M., & Dunston, R. Anorexia nervosa, sexual behavior modification as an adjunct to an integrated treatment program: A case report. *Australian and New Zealand Journal of Psychiatry,* 1978, *12,* 165–167.

Gunderson, E.K.E., & Rahe, R.H. (Eds.) *Life stress and illness.* Springfield, IL: Charles C. Thomas, 1974.

Gunderson, J.G. Characteristics of borderlines. In P. Hartocollis (Ed.), *Border-line personality disorders: The concept, the syndrome, the patient.* New York: International Universities Press, 1977, pp. 173–192.

Gunderson, J.G. *Self-destructiveness in borderline patients.* Presented at the 13th Annual Meeting of the American Psychiatric Association, New Orleans, May 1981.

Gunderson, J.G., & Kolb, J.E. Discriminating features of borderline patients. *American Journal of Psychiatry,* 1978, *135,* 792–796.

Gunderson, J.G., Siever, L.J., & Spaulding, E. The search for a schizotype. *Archives of General Psychiatry,* 1983, *40,* 15–22.

*Gunderson, J.G., & Singer, M.T. Defining borderline patients: An overview. *American Journal of Psychiatry,* 1975, *132,* 1–10.

Gurin, G., Veroff, J., & Feld, S. *Americans view their mental health.* New York: Basic Books, 1960.

Gurman, A.S. The effects and effectiveness of marital therapy: A review of outcome research. *Family Process,* 1973, *12,* 145–170.

Gurman, A.S., & Gustafson, J.P. Patients' perceptions of the therapeutic relationship and group therapy outcome. *American Journal of Psychiatry,* 1976, *133,* 1290–1294.

Gurman, A.S., & Kniskern, D.P. Deterioration in marital and family therapy: Empirical, clinical and conceptual issues. *Family Process,* 1978, *17,* 3–20.

Gurman, A.S., & Kniskern, D.P. Family therapy outcome research: Knowns and unknowns. In A.S. Gurman & D.P. Kniskern (Eds.), *Handbook of family therapy.* New York: Brunner/Mazel, 1981.

*Gurman, A.S., & Razin, A.M. (Eds.). *Effective psychotherapy: A handbook of research.* Elmsford, NY: Pergamon Press, 1977.

*Guttentag, M., Salasin, S., & Belle, D. *The mental health of women.* New York: Academic Press, 1980.

Guttman, H.A. A contra-indication for family therapy: The pre-psychotic or post-psychotic young adult and his parents. *Archives of General Psychiatry,* 1973, *29,* 352–355.

Haan, N. *Coping and defending: Processes of self–environment organization.* New York: Academic Press, 1977.

*Hall, J.A., & Crasilneck, H.B. *Clinical hypnosis: Principles and applications.* New York: Grune & Stratton, 1975.

*Halmi, K.A. Comparison of demographic and clinical features in patient groups with different ages and weights at onset of anorexia nervosa. *The Journal of Nervous and Mental Disease,* 1974, *158,* 222–225.

*Halmi, K.A. Pretreatment predictors of outcome in anorexia nervosa. *Psychiatry Digest,* October, 1979, p. 43.

Halmi, K.A., Brodland, G., & Loney, J. Prognosis in anorexia nervosa. *Annals of Internal Medicine,* 1973, *78,* 907–909.

Halmi, K.A., Brodland, G., & Rigas, C. A follow-up study of 79 patients with anorexia nervosa: An evaluation of prognostic factors and diagnostic criteria. In R.D. Wirt, G. Winokur, & M. Rott (Eds.), *Life history research in psychopathology* (Vol. 14). Minneapolis: University of Minnesota Press, 1975.

*Halmi, K.A., Goldberg, S.C., Casper, R.C., Eckert, E.D., & Davis, J.M. Pretreatment predictors of outcome in anorexia nervosa. *British Journal of Psychiatry*, 1979, *134*, 71–78.

Halmi, K.A., Powers, P., & Cunningham, S. Treatment of anorexia nervosa with behavior modification. *Archives of General Psychiatry*, 1975, *32*, 93–96.

*Hammer, M. Social supports, social networks and schizophrenia. *Schizophrenia Bulletin*, 1981, *7* (1), 45–57.

Hartley, D., Roback, H.B., & Abramowitz, S.I. Deterioration effects in encounter groups. *American Psychologist*, 1976, *31*, 247–255.

Hastings, D.W. Psychiatry in Eighth Air Force. *Air Surgeon's Bulletin*, 1944, *I*, 4–5.

Hedberg, D.L., Houck, J.H., & Glueck, B.C. Tranylcypromine-trifluoperazine combination in the treatment of schizophrenia. *American Journal of Psychiatry*, 1971, *127*, 1141–1146.

Henderson, S. A development in social psychiatry: the systematic study of social bonds. *Journal of Nervous and Mental Disease*, 1980, *168* (2), 63–69.

Henderson, S., Byrne, D.G., Duncan-Jones, P., Adcock, S., Scott, R., & Steele, G.P. Social bonds in the epidemiology of neurosis: A preliminary communication. *British Journal of Psychiatry*, 1978, *132*, 463–466.

Henderson, S., Byrne, D.G., Duncan-Jones, P., Scott, R., & Adcock, S. Social relationships, adversity and neurosis: A study of associations in a general population sample. *British Journal of Psychiatry*, 1980, *136*, 574–583.

Henderson, S., Duncan-Jones, P., McAuley, H., & Ritchie, K. The patients' primary group. *British Journal of Psychiatry*, 1978, *132*, 74–86.

Herbert, E.W., Pinkston, E.M., Hayden, M.L., Sajwaj, T.E., Pinkston, S., Cordua, G. & Jackson, C. Adverse effects of differential parental attention. *Journal of Applied Behavior Analysis*, 1973, *6*, 15–30.

Hersen, M. Complex problems require complex solutions. *Behavior Therapy*, 1981, *12*, 15–29.

Hersen, M., & Bellack, A.S. Assessment of social skills. In A.R. Ciminero, K.S. Calhoun, & H.E. Adams (Eds.), *Handbook of behavioral assessment*. New York: Wiley, 1977.

*Hersenberg, W. *Physics and philosophy*. New York: Harper & Row, 1958.

*Hinkle, L., Jr. The effect of exposure to culture change, social change, and changes in interpersonal relationships on health. In B.S. Dohrenwend & B.P. Dohrenwend, *Stressful life events: Their nature and effects*. New York: Wiley, 1974, pp. 9–44.

Hinsie, L.E., & Campbell, R.J. *Psychiatric dictionary* (4th ed.). London: Oxford, 1970.

Hoch, P.H., & Polatin, P. Pseudoneurotic forms of schizophrenia. *Psychiatric Quarterly*, 1949, *23*, 248–276.

Hoch, P.H., & Zubin, J. *The evaluation of psychiatric treatment*. New York: Grune & Stratton, 1964.

*Hoffman, M.L. Sex differences in empathy and related behaviors. *Psychological Bulletin*, 1977, *34*, 712–722.

*Hoffman, P.G. Amenorrhea and weight loss in young women—anorexia nervosa? *Journal of the American Medical Association,* 1976, *235*, 308.

Hollon, S.D. Behavior therapy for depression: Comparisons and combinations with alternative approaches. In L.P. Rehm (Ed.), *Behavior therapy for depression: Present status and future directions.* New York: Academic Press, 1981.

Hollon, S.D., & Beck, A.T. Psychotherapy and drug therapy: Comparisons and combinations. In S.L. Garfield & A.E. Bergin (Eds.), *Handbook of psychotherapy and behavior change: An empirical analysis* (2nd ed.). New York: Wiley, 1978.

Hollon, S.D., & Beck, A.T. Cognitive therapy of depression. In P.C. Kendall & S.D. Hollon (Eds.), *Cognitive-behavioral interventions: Theory, research, and procedures.* New York: Academic Press, 1979.

Hollon, S.D., Beck, A.T., Kovacs, M., & Rush, A.J. *Cognitive therapy of depression: An outcome study with six-month follow-up.* Paper presented at The Annual Meeting of the Society for Psychotherapy Research, Madison, Wisconsin, June 1977.

Hollon, S.D., & Shaw, B.F. Group cognitive therapy for depressed patients. In A.T. Beck, A.J. Rush, B.F. Shaw, & G. Emery, *Cognitive therapy for depression: A treatment manual.* New York: Guilford Press, 1979.

Hollon, S., Wiemer, M.J. & Tuason, V.B. Cognitive therapy in relation to drugs in depression. Unpublished Grant Perspectives. Minneapolis-St. Paul, Minn.: University of Minnesota-St. Paul-Ramsey Medical Center, 1979.

Holmes, T.H., & Masuda, M. Life change and illness susceptibility. In B.S. Dohrenwend & B.P. Dohrenwend (Eds.), *Stressful life events.* New York: Wiley, 1974, pp. 45–72.

*Holmes, T.H., & Rahe, R.H. The Social Readjustment Rating Scale. *Journal of Psychosomatic Research,* 1967, *11*, 213–218.

*Horne, R.L. Anorexia nervosa. *Carrier Foundation Letter,* 1980 (58).

Horner, A.J. The roots of anxiety, character structure, and psychoanalytic treatment. *Journal of the American Academy of Psychoanalysis,* 1980, *8*, 565.

Horwitz, L. *Therapist's personality and levels of competence.* Unpublished manuscript, January 1969.

Horwitz, L. *Clinical prediction in psychotherapy.* New York: Aronson, 1974.

*Hough, R.L., Fairbank, D.T., & Garcia, A.M. Problems in the ratio measurement of life stress. *Journal of Health and Social Behavior,* 1976, *17*, 70–82.

House, J.S. *Work stress and social support.* Reading, MA.: Addison-Wesley, 1981.

*House, J.S., & Wells, J.A. Occupational stress, social support, and health. In A. McLean, G. Black, & M. Colligan (Eds.), *Reducing occupational stress: Proceedings of a conference.* U.S. Department of Health, Education, and Welfare (NIOSH), Publication No. 78-140. Washington, D.C.: U.S. Government Printing Office, 1978, pp. 8–29.

Hull, C.L. *Principles of behavior.* N.Y.: Appleton-Century-Crofts, 1943.

*Hsu, L.K.G., Crisp, A.H., & Harding, B. Outcome of anorexia nervosa. *Lancet,* 1979, *61*, i.

*Hsu, L.K.G., Meltzer, E.S., & Crisp, A.H. Schizophrenia and anorexia nervosa. *The Journal of Nervous and Mental Disease,* 1981, *169,* 273–276.

Hudgens, R.W. Personal catastrophe and depression: A consideration of the subject with respect to medically ill adolescents, and a requiem for retrospective life-events studies. In B.S. Dohrenwend & B.P. Dohrenwend (Eds.), *Stressful life events: Their nature and effects.* New York: Wiley, 1974, pp. 119–134.

Hudgens, R.W., Morrison, J.R., & Barchha, R.G. Life events and onset of primary affective disorders: a study of 40 hospitalized patients and 40 controls. *Archives of General Psychiatry,* 1967, *16,* 134–145.

Hudgens, R.W., Robins, E., & Delong, W.B. The reporting of recent stress in the lives of psychiatric patients. *British Journal of Psychiatry,* 1970, *117,* 635–643.

Human Behavior Research Group, Inc. *Stress and physical health: A bibliography.* (Compiled by R. Friis.) Box 17122, Irvine, CA., 1978.

Hurst, A.G., Stein, K.B., Korchin, S.J., & Soskin, W.F. Leadership style determinants of cohesiveness in group therapy. *International Journal of Group Psychotherapy,* 1978, *28,* 263–277.

Hurvitz, N. Marital problems following psychotherapy with one spouse. *Journal of Consulting and Clinical Psychology,* 1967, *31,* 38–74.

Hwang, S., & Tuason, V.B. Long-term maintenance lithium therapy and possible irreversible damage. *Journal of Clinical Psychiatry,* 1980, *41,* 11–19.

*In-hospital constraints curb anorexia. *Medical Tribune,* September 1979, p. 18.

Insel, P., & Moos, R.H. (Eds.). *Health and the social environment.* Lexington, MA: D.C. Heath, 1974.

Jackson, J.L., & Calhoun, K.S. Effects of two variable-ratio schedules of time-out: Changes in target and non-target behaviors. *Journal of Behavior Therapy and Experimental Psychiatry,* 1977, *8,* 195–199.

Jacobs, A. The use of feedback in groups. In A. Jacobs & W. Spradlin (Eds.), *The group as agent of change.* New York: Behavioral Publications, 1974.

*Jacobs, S. The housewife with anorexia nervosa. *Resident and Staff Physician,* August 1975, pp. 53–59.

Jacobson, N.S., & Baucom, D.H. Design and assessment of nonspecific control groups in behavior modification research. *Behavior Therapy,* 1977, *8,* 709–719.

Janet, P. *The major symptoms of hysteria.* New York: MacMillan, 1929.

Jenkins, C.D. Recent evidence supporting psychologic and social risk factors for coronary disease. *New England Journal of Medicine,* 1976, *294,* 1033–1038.

Jonckheere, P. Consideration sur la psychotherapie: A propos de 72 nevroses. *Acta Neurologica et Psychiatrica Belgica,* 1965, *65,* 667–684.

Kadushin, C. *Why people go to psychiatrists.* New York: Atherton Press, 1969.

Kahn, R.L., Wolfe, D.M., Quinn, R.P., Snoek, J.D., & Rosenthal, R.A. *Organizational stress: Studies in role conflicts and ambiguity.* New York: Wiley, 1964.

Kaplan, B.H., Cassel, J.C., & Gore, S. Social support and health. *Medical Care,* 1977, *15,* 5 (Supplement), 47–58.

Kara, A., & Wahler, R.G. Organizational features of a young child's behaviors. *Journal of Experimental Child Psychology*, 1977, *24*, 24–39.

*Karasu, T.B. Toward unification of psychotherapies: A complementary model. *American Journal of Psychotherapy*, 1979, *33*, 555–563.

*Kasl, S. Epidemiological contributions to the study of work stress. In C.L. Cooper & R. Payne (Eds.), *Stress at work*. New York: Wiley, 1978, pp. 3–48.

*Katz, J.L. Anorexia nervosa. *Journal of the American Medical Association*, 1976, *236*, 1114.

Kaufman, M.R., & Heiman, M. (Eds.). *Evolution of psychosomatic concepts: Anorexia nervosa. A paradigm*. New York: International University Press, 1964.

Kaul, T.J., & Bednar, R.L. Conceptualizing group research: A preliminary analysis. *Small Group Behavior*, 1978, *9*, 173–191.

Kay, D.W.K., & Leigh, D. The natural history, treatment and prognosis of anorexia nervosa based on a study of 38 patients. *Journal of Mental Science (British Journal of Psychiatry)*, 1954, *100*, 411–431.

Kay, D.W.K. & Shapiro, K. The prognosis in anorexia nervosa. In J.E. Meyer & H. Feldman (Eds.), *Anorexia Nervosa*. Symposium 24/25, April, 1965 in Gottingen. Stuttgart, West Germany: Georg Thieme Verlag, 1965.

Kazdin, A.E. *Single-case research designs: Methods for clinical and applied settings*. New York: Oxford University Press, 1970.

Kazdin, A.E. Effects of covert modeling and model reinforcement on assertive behavior. *Journal of Abnormal Psychology*, 1974, *83*, 240–252.

Kazdin, A.E. Nonspecific treatment factors in psychotherapy outcome research. *Journal of Consulting and Clinical Psychology*, 1979, *47*, 846–851.(a)

Kazdin, A.E. Situational specificity: The two-edged sword of behavioral assessment. *Behavioral Assessment*, 1979, *1*, 57–75.(b)

Kazdin, A.E. Therapy outcome questions requiring control of credibility and treatment-generated expectancies. *Behavior Therapy*, 1979, *10*, 81–93.(c)

Kazdin, A.E. Nonspecific treatment factors in psychotherapy outcome research. *Journal of Consulting and Clinical Psychology*, 1979, *47*, 846–851.(a)

Kazdin, A.E. *Symptom substitution, generalization, and response covariation: Implications for psychotherapy research*. Unpublished manuscript. University of Pittsburgh School of Medicine, 1981.

Kazdin, A.E. Symptom substitution, generalization, and response covariation: Implications for psychotherapy outcome. *Psychological Bulletin*, 1982, *91*, 349–365. (a)

Kazdin, A.E. Methodology of psychotherapy outcome research: Recent developments and remaining limitations. In J.H. Harvey & M.M. Parks (Eds.) *Psychotherapy research and behavior change: The master lecture series* (Vol. I). Washington, D.C.: American Psychological Association, 1982.(b)

Kazdin, A.E., & Wilcoxon, L.A. Systematic desensitization and nonspecific treatment effects: A methodological evaluation. *Psychological Bulletin*, 1976, *83*, 729–758.

Kazdin, A.E., & Wilson, G.T. Criteria for evaluating psychotherapy. *Archives of General Psychiatry*, 1978, *35*, 407–416.(a)

Kazdin, A.E., & Wilson, G.T. *Evaluation of behavior therapy: Issues, evaluation, and research strategies*. Cambridge, MA: Ballinger, 1978.(b)

*Kellam, S.G. Stressful life events and illness: A research area in need of conceptual development. In B.S. Dohrenwend & B.P. Dohrenwend (Eds.), *Stressful life events: Their nature and effects*. New York: Wiley, 1974, pp. 207–214.

Kendall, P.C., Plous, S. & Kratchowill, T.R. Science and behavior therapy: A survey of research in the 1970s. *Behavior Research and Therapy*, 1981, *19*, 517–524.

Kenny, F.T., Mowbray, R.M., & Lalani, S. Faradic disruption of obsessive ideation in the treatment of obsessive neurosis: A controlled study. *Behavior Therapy*, 1978, *9*, 209–221.

Kent, R.N., & O'Leary, K.D. A controlled evaluation of behavior modification with conduct problem children. *Journal of Consulting and Clinical Psychology*, 1976, *44*, 586–596.

Kernberg, O.F. Borderline personality organization. *Journal of the American Psychoanalytical Association*, 1967, *15*, 641–685.

Kernberg, O. *Borderline Conditions and Pathological Narcissism*. New York: Jason Aronson, 1975.

Kernberg, O. Structural change and its impediments. In P. Hartocollis (Ed.), *Borderline personality disorders*. New York: International University Press, 1977.

Kernberg, O., Burstein, E., Coyne, L., Applebaum, A., Horwitz, L., & Voth, H. Psychotherapy and psychoanalysis. Final report of the Menninger Foundation's Psychotherapy Research Project. *Bulletin of the Menninger Clinic*, Vol. 36, Nos. 1/2, 1972.

Kessler, R.C. A strategy for studying differential vulnerability to the psychological consequences of stress. *Journal of Health and Social Behavior*, 1979, *20*, 100–108.(a)

Kessler, R.C. Stress, social status, and psychological distress. *Journal of Health and Social Behavior*, 1979, *20*, 259–272.(b)

Kessler, R.C., Brown, R.L., & Browman, C.L. Sex differences in psychiatric help-seeking: evidence from four large-scale surveys. *Journal of Health and Social Behavior*, 1981, *22*, 49–64.

Kessler, R.C., & Cleary, P.D. Social class and psychological distress. *American Sociological Review*, 1980, *45*, 463–478.

Kety, S.S., Rosenthal, D., Wender, P.H., & Schulsinger, F. Mental illness in the biological and adoptive families of adopted schizophrenics. In D. Rosenthal & S. Kety (Eds.), *Transmission of schizophrenia*. Oxford: Pergamon Press, 1968, pp. 345–362.

Kibel, H.D. The importance of a comprehensive clinical diagnosis for group psychotherapy of borderline and narcissistic patients. *International Journal of Group Psychotherapy*, 1980, *30*, 427–440.

*Kiely, W.F., & Procci, W.R. Anorexia nervosa: A group case conference. *General Hospital Psychiatry*, 1980, *3*, 238–246.

Kiesler, D.J. Some myths of psychotherapy research and the search for a paradigm. *Psychological Bulletin*, 1966, *64*, 110–136.

Kilman, P.R. Direct and nondirect marathon group therapy and internal–external control. *Journal of Counseling Psychology*, 1974, *21*, 380–384.

Kingsley, R.G., & Wilson, G.T. Behavior therapy for obesity: A comparative investigation of long-term efficacy. *Journal of Consulting and Clinical Psychology*, 1977, *45*, 288–298.

Klein, D.F. Importance of psychiatric diagnosis in prediction of clinical drug effects. *Archives of General Psychiatry*, 1967, *16*, 118–126.

Klein, D.F. Psychiatric diagnosis and a typology of clinical drug effects. *Psychopharmacology*, 1968, *13*, 359–386.

*Kleiner, R.J., & Parker, S. Social structure and psychological factors in mental disorder: A research review. In H. Wechsler, L. Solomon, & B.M. Kramer (Eds.), *Social psychology and mental health*. New York: Holt, Rinehart and Winston, 1970, pp. 203–218.

Klerman, G.L. Combining drugs and psychotherapy in the treatment of depression. In M. Greenblatt (Ed.), *Drugs in combination with other therapies*. New York: Grune & Stratton, 1975.

Klerman, G. Psychoneurosis: Integrating pharmacotherapy and psychotherapy. In P. Claghorn (Ed.), *Successful psychotherapy*. New York: Brunner/Mazel, 1976.

Klerman, G.L., DiMascio, A., Weissman, M.M., Prusoff, B.A., & Paykel, E.S. Treatment of depression by drugs and psychotherapy. *American Journal of Psychiatry*, 1974, *131*, 186–191.

Klerman, G., Rounsaville, B., Chevron, E., Neu, C. & Weissman, M. Manual for short-term interpersonal psychotherapy (IPT) for depression. 4th draft. Mimeo. New Haven, Conn.: Yale University, 1979.

Kniskern, D.P. *Research prospects and perspectives in family therapy*. Paper presented at the Annual Meeting to the Society for Psychotherapy Research, Boston, June 1975.

Koenigsberg, H.W., Kernberg, O.F., & Schomer, J. Diagnosing borderline conditions in an outpatient setting. *Archives of General Psychiatry*, 1983, *40*, 49–53.

Kogel, R.L., Firestone, P.B., Kramme, K.W. & Dunlap, G. Increasing spontaneous play by suppressing self-stimulation in autistic children. *Journal of Applied Behavior Analysis*, 1974, *7*, 521–528.

Kohl, R.N. Pathologic reactions of marital partners to improvement of patients. *American Journal of Psychiatry*, 1962, *118*, 1036–1041.

Kohn, M.L. Social class and schizophrenia: A critical review and a reformulation. *Schizophrenia Bulletin*, 1973, *7*, 60–79.

Kolb, J.E., & Gunderson, J.G. Diagnosing borderline patients with a semistructured interview. *Archives of General Psychiatry*, 1980, *37*, 37–41.

Kovacs, M., Rush, A.J., Beck, A.T., & Hollon, S.D. Depressed outpatients treated with cognitive therapy or pharmacotherapy: A one-year follow-up. *Archives of General Psychiatry*, 1981, *38*, 33–39.

Kraepelin, E. *Manic-depressive insanity and paranoia*. Edinburgh: E. and S. Livingstone, 1921.

Kratochwill, T.R. (Ed.). *Single-subject research: Strategies for evaluating change*. New York: Academic Press, 1978.

Kringler, E. Obsessional neurotics: A long-term follow-up. *British Journal of Psychiatry*, 1965, *111*, 709–722.

*Kron, L., Katz, J.L., Gorzynski, G., & Weiner, H. Anorexia nervosa and gonadal dysgenesis. *Archives of General Psychiatry*, 1977, *34*, 332–335.

Kroger, W.S. & Fezler, W.D. *Hypnosis and Behavior Modification: Imagery Conditioning*. Philadelphia: J.B. Lippincott, 1976.

*Kuhn, T.S. *The structure of scientific revolutions* (2nd ed.). Chicago: University of Chicago Press, 1970.

Lambert, M.J., Bergin, A.E., & Collins, J.L. Therapist-induced deterioration in psychotherapy. In A.S. Gurman & A.M. Razin (Eds.), *Effective psychotherapy: A handbook of research*. Oxford: Pergamon, 1977.

Lancioni, G.E. Teaching independent toileting to profoundly retarded deaf-blind children. *Behavior Therapy*, 1980, *11*, 234–244.

Lang, P. The mechanics of desensitization and the laboratory study of fear. In C.M. Franks (Ed), *Behavior Therapy: Appraisal and Status*. New York: McGraw-Hill, 1969.

Lang, P.J., & Lazovik, A.D. Experimental desensitization of a phobia. *Journal of Abnormal and Social Psychology*, 1963, *66*, 519–525.

*Langner, T.S. A twenty-two item screening score of psychiatric symptoms indicating impairment. *Journal of Health and Human Behavior*, 1962, *3*, 269–276.

*Langner, T.S., & Michael, S.T. *Life stress and mental health*. New York: Free Press of Glencoe, 1963.

LaPorte, D.J., McLellan, A.T., Erdler, F.R. & Parente, R.J. Treatment outcome as a function of follow-up difficulty in substance abusers. *Journal of Consulting and Clinical Psychology*, 1981, *49*, 112–119.

LaRocco, J.M., House, J.S., & French, R.P., Jr. Social support, occupational stress, and health. *Journal of Health and Social Behavior*, 1980, *21*, 202–218.

*LaRocco, J.M., & Jones, A.P. Coworker and leader support as moderators of stress-strain relationships in work situations. *Journal of Applied Psychology*, 1978, *63*, 629–634.

Lasegue, E.C. (1873) De l'anorexie hystérique. *Archives of General Medicine*, Vol. I. Translated in M.R. Kaufman & M. Heiman (Eds.), *Evolution of Psychosomatic Concepts: Anorexia Nervosa, a Paradigm*. London: Hogarth Press, 1965, 141–155.

*Lavenstein, A.F., et al. Effect of cyproheptadine on asthmatic children. *Journal of the American Medical Association*, 1962, *180*, 912–916.

*Lazarus, A.A. In support of technical eclecticism. *Psychological Reports*, 1967, *21*, 415–416.

Lazarus, A.A. *The practice of multimodal therapy*. New York: McGraw-Hill, 1981.

Lazarus, R.S. *Psychological stress and the coping process*. New York: McGraw-Hill, 1966.

*Lazarus, R.S. Cognitive behavior therapy as psychodynamics rendered. In M.J. Mahoney (Ed.), *Psychotherapy process: Current issues and future directions*. New York: Plenum, 1980.

*Lazarus, R.S., Averill, J.R., & Opton, E.M., Jr. The psychology of coping: Some issues of research and assessment. In G.V. Coelho, D.A. Hamburg, & J.E. Adams (Eds.), *Coping and adaptation*. New York: Basic Books, 1974.

Lazarus, R.S., & Launier, R. Stress-related transactions between person and environment. In L.A. Pervin & M. Lewis (Eds.), *Perspectives in interactional psychology*. New York: Plenum Press, 1978.

Lefkowitz, M.M., & Burton, N. Childhood depression: A critique of the concept. *Psychological Bulletin*, 1978, *85*, 716–726.

Lehman, E. Feeding problems of psychogenic origins: A survey of the literature. *Psychoanalytic Study of the Child*, 1949, *3*, 461.

Lehman, H.E. Depression: Somatic treatment methods, complications, failures. In G. Usdin (Ed.), *Depression: Clinical, biological, and psychological perspectives*. New York: Brunner/Mazel, 1977.

*Leighton, D.C., Harding, J.S., Macklin, D.B., MacMillan, A.M., & Leighton, A.H. *The character of danger: Psychiatric symptoms in selected communities*. New York: Basic Books, 1963.

*Levine, F.M. Behavior modification in anorexia nervosa—good or bad? *Resident & Staff Physician*, February, 1977, p. 17.

Levis, D.J. A reconsideration of Eysenck's conditioning model of neurosis. *The Behavioral and Brain Sciences*, 1979, *2*, 172–174.

Levis, D.J. & Malloy, P.F. Research in infrahuman and human conditioning. In G.T. Wilson & C.M. Franks (Eds.), *Contemporary Behavior Therapy*. New York: Guilford, 1982.

Lieberman, M.A., Yalom, I., & Miles, M.B. *Encounter groups: First facts*. New York: Basic Books, 1973.

*Liebman, R., Salvador, M., & Baker, L. An integrated treatment program of anorexia nervosa. *American Journal of Psychiatry*, 1974, *131*, 432–436.

Liebowitz, M.A., & Klein, D.F. Hysteroid dysphoria. *Psychiatric Clinics of North America*, 1979, *2*, 555–575.

Liem, J.H., & Liem, R. *Life events, social supports and physical and psychological well-being*. Presented at the American Psychological Association, Washington, DC, 1976.

Liff, Z.A. A general systems approach to group leadership of borderline and narcissistic patients. In L.R. Wolberg & M.L. Aronson (Eds.), *Group therapy 1979: An overview*. New York: Stratton Intercontinental Medical Book Corporation, 1979.

*Lifton, R. Psychological effects of the atomic bomb in Hiroshima: The theme of death. In G. Grosser, H. Weschester, & M. Greenblatt (Eds.), *The threat of impending disaster*. Cambridge, MA: MIT Press, 1974, pp. 152–193.

Lin, N., Dean, A., & Ensel, W.M. *Constructing social support scales: A methodological note*. Paper presented at the Conference on Stress, Social Support, and Schizophrenia. Burlington, Vermont, September 1979.

Lin, N., Dean, A., & Ensel, W.M. Social support scales: A methodological note. *Schizophrenia Bulletin*, 1981, *7*(1), 73–89.

Lin, N., Ensel, W., Simeone, R.S., & Kuo, W. Social support, stressful life events, and illness: A model and empirical test. *Journal of Health and Social Behavior*, 1979, *20*, 108–119.

Lindemann, E. Symptomatology and management of acute grief. *American Journal of Psychiatry*, 1944, *101*, 141–148.

Lo, W.H. A follow-up study of obsessional neurotics in Hong Kong Chinese. *British Journal of Psychiatry*, 1967, *113*, 823–832.

Loewald, H. Freud's conception of the negative therapeutic reaction, with comments on instinct theory. *Journal of the American Psychoanalytic Association*, 1972, *202*, 335–345.

London, P. & Klerman, G.L. Evaluating psychotherapy. *American Journal of Psychiatry*, 1982, *139*, 709–717.

Lorand, S. Anorexia nervosa: Report of a case. *Psychosomatic Medicine*, 1943, *5*, 282–292.

Loranger, A., Oldham, J., & Tulis, E. Familial transmission of DSM III borderline personality disorder. *Archives of General Psychiatry*, 1982, *39*, 795–799.

Lowenthal, M.F., & Haven, C. Interaction and adaptation: Intimacy as a critical variable. *American Sociological Review*, 1968, *33*, 20–30.

*Luborsky, L., & Singer, L. Comparative studies of psychotherapies: Is it true that everyone has won and all must have prizes? *Archives of General Psychiatry*, 1975, *32*, 995–1008.

Luborsky, L., & Spence, D.P. Quantitative research on psychoanalytic therapy. In S.L. Garfield & A.E. Bergin (Eds.), *Handbook of psychotherapy and behavior change: An empirical analysis* (2nd ed.). New York: Wiley, 1978.

Luke, R.A. The internal normative structure of sensitivity training groups. *Journal of Applied Behavioral Science*, 1972, *8*, 421–437.

Lundgren, D.C. Attitudinal and behavioral correlates of emergent status in training groups. *Journal of Social Psychology*, 1973, *90*, 141–153.

Lundgren, D.C. Developmental trends in the emergence of interpersonal issues in T groups. *Small Group Behavior*, 1977, *8*, 179–200.

Lundgren, D.C. Authority and group formation. *Journal of Applied Behavioral Science*, 1979, *15*, 330–345.

MacKenzie, K.R. The concept of role as a boundary structure in small groups. In J. Durkin (Ed.), *General systems theory and group psychotherapy*. New York: Brunner/Mazel, in press.

MacKenzie, K.R., & Dies, R.R. *The CORE battery: Clinical outcome results*. New York: American Group Psychotherapy Association, 1981.

MacKenzie, K.R., & Livesley, W.J. *Living Groups: Group Psychotherapy and General Systems Theory*. New York: Brunner/Mazel, 1981.

*MacMillan, A.M. The Health Opinion Survey: Technique for estimating prevalence of psycho-neurotic and related types of disorder in communities. *Psychological Reports*, 1957, *3*, 325–339.

Mahoney, M.J. Publication prejudices: An experimental study of confirmatory bias in the peer review system. *Cognitive Therapy and Research*, 1977, *1*, 161–175.

*Mahoney, M.J. Psychotherapy and the structure of personal revolutions. In M.J. Mahoney (Ed.), *Psychotherapy process: Current issues and future directions*. New York: Plenum, 1980.

*Mainguet, P. Effect of cyproheptadine on anorexia and loss of weight in adults. *Practitioner*, 1972, *208*, 797–800.

*Makosky, V.P. Stress and the mental health of women: A discussion of research and issues. In M. Guttentag, S. Salasin, & D. Belle (Eds.), *The mental health of women.* New York: Academic Press, 1980, pp. 111–127.

Malan, D.H. The outcome problem in psychotherapy research. *Archives of General Psychiatry,* 1973, *29,* 719–729.

Malan, D.H. *The frontier of brief psychotherapy.* New York: Plenum Press, 1976.

Maletsky, B.M. Assisted covert sensitization. In D.J. Cox & R. Daitzman (Eds.), *Exhibitionism: Description, Assessment, and Treatment.* New York: Garland Press, 1980.

Maltas, C.P. Therapeutic uses of psychological testing of borderline adolescents. *Journal of Adolescence,* 1978, *1,* 259–272.

*Manis, J., Brawer, M.L., Hunt, C.L., & Kercher, L.C. Validating a mental health scale. *American Sociological Review,* 1963, *28,* 108–116.

Mann, J. *Time-limited psychotherapy.* Cambridge, MA: Harvard University Press, 1973.

Marcovitz, R.J., & Smith, J.E. Patients' perceptions of curative factors in short-term group psychotherapy. *International Journal of Group Psychotherapy,* in press.

Margolis, P.M., & Jernberg, A. Anaclictic therapy in a case of anorexia nervosa. *British Journal of Medical Psychology,* 1960, *33,* 291–300.

Marks, I.M. Phobia disorders four years after treatment: a prospective follow-up. *British Journal of Psychiatry,* 1971, *118,* 683, 688.

Marks, I.M. Toward an empirical clinical science: Behavior psychotherapy in the 1980s. *Behavior Therapy,* 1982, *13,* 63–81.

Marks, I.M., Hodgson, R. & Rachman, S. Treatment of chronic obsessive-compulsive neurosis by in-vivo exposure. A two-year follow-up and issues in treatment. *British Journal of Psychiatry,* 1975, *127,* 349–364.

Marks, I.M., Stern, R.S., Mawson, D., Cobb, J., & McDonald, R. Climipramine and exposure for obsessive-compulsive rituals: I. *British Journal of Psychiatry,* 1980, *136,* 1–25.

Markush, R.E., & Favero, R.V. Epidemiologic assessment of stressful life event, depressed mood, and psychophysiological symptoms—a preliminary report. In B.S. Dohrenwend & B.P. Dohrenwend (Eds.), *Stressful life events: Their nature and effects.* New York: Wiley, 1974, pp. 171–190.

Marquis, H.A., & Gendreau, P. Letting the baby drown in the bathwater: Fear of facts. *American Psychologist,* 1979, *34,* 180–181.

Marshall, J.M., & Neill, J. The removal of a psychosomatic symptom: Effects on the marriage. *Family Process,* 1977, *16,* 273–280.

Martin, I., & Levey, A.B. Evaluative conditioning. *Advances in Behavior Research and Therapy,* 1979, *1,* 57–102.

Masters, W.H., & Johnson, V. *Human sexual inadequacy.* Boston: Little, Brown, 1970.

Mathews, A.M., Gelder, M.G. & Johnson, D.W. *Agoraphobia: Nature and Treatments.* New York: Guilford Press, 1981.

Mattson, A., Sesse, L.R., & Hawkins, J.W. Suicidal behavior as a child psychiatric emergency. *Archives of General Psychiatry,* 1969, *20,* 100–109.

Mavissakalian, M. & Barlow, D.H. (Eds). *Phobia: Psychological and Pharmacological Treatment.* New York: Guilford Press, 1981.

Maxmen, J. Group therapy as viewed by hospitalized patients. *Archives of General Psychiatry,* 1973, *28,* 404–408.

*Maxmen, J.S., Silberfarb, P.M., & Ferrell, R.B. Anorexia nervosa: Practical initial management in a general hospital. *Journal of the American Medical Association,* 1974, *229,* 801–809.

May, P.R. For better or for worse? Psychotherapy and variance change: A critical review of the literature. *Journal of Nervous and Mental Disease,* 1971, *152,* 184–192.

May, P.R., & Tuma, A.H. The Paul Hoch Award Lecture: A follow-up study of the results of treatment of schizophrenia. In R.L. Spitzer & D.F. Klein (Eds.), *Evaluation of psychological therapies.* Baltimore: The Johns Hopkins University Press, 1976.

Mays, D.T. *Negative effects in psychotherapy: Prevalence and causality reconsidered.* Doctoral dissertation, Rutgers University, 1979.

Mays, D.T., & Franks, C.M. Getting worse: Psychotherapy or no treatment— The jury should still be out. *Professional Psychology,* 1980, *11,* 78–92.

McCord, J. A thirty-year follow-up of treatment effects. *American Psychologist,* 1978, *33,* 284–289.

*McFall, P.M. Effects of self-monitoring on normal smoking behavior. *Journal of Consulting and Clinical Psychology,* 1970, *35,* 135–142.

McFarlane, A.H., Neale, K.A., Norman, G.R., Roy, R.C., & Streiner, D.L. Methodological issues in developing a scale to measure social support. *Schizophrenia Bulletin,* 1981, *7*(1), 90–100.

McFarlane, A.H., Norman, G.R., Streiner, D.L., Roy, R., & Scott, D.J. A longitudinal study of the influence of the psychosocial environment on health status: A preliminary report. *Journal of Health and Social Behavior,* 1980, *21,* 124–133.

McLachlan, J.F.C. Benefit from group therapy as a function of patient–therapist match on conceptual level. *Psychotherapy: Theory, Research and Practice,* 1972, *9,* 317–323.

McLean, P.D., & Hakstian, A.R. Clinical depression: Comparative efficacy of outpatient treatments. *Journal of Consulting and Clinical Psychology,* 1979, *43,* 818–836.

McLean, P.D., Ogston, K., & Grauer, L. A behavioral approach to the treatment of depression. *Journal of Behavior Therapy and Experimental Psychiatry,* 1973, *4,* 323–330.

McMichael, A.J. Personality, behavioral, and situational modifiers of work stressors. In C.L. Cooper & R. Payne (Eds.), *Stress at work.* New York: Wiley, 1978, pp. 127–147.

Melnick, J., & Woods, M. Analysis of group composition research and theory for psychotherapeutic and growth-oriented groups. *Journal of Applied Behavioral Science,* 1976, *12,* 493–512.

*Messer, S.B., & Winokur, M. Some limits to the integration of psychoanalytic and behavior therapy. *American Psychologist,* 1980, *35,* 818–827.

*Messer, S.B., & Winokur, M. Therapeutic change principles: Are commonalities more apparent than real? *American Psychologist*, 1981, 36, 1547–1548.

Meuyer, B.C., & Weinroth, L.A. Observations on psychological aspects of anorexia nervosa. *Psychosomatic Medicine*, 1957, 19, 389–398.

Michel, W. On the interface of cognition and personality: Beyond the person-situation debate. Distinguished Scientist Award Address, Division 12, Section III, American Psychological Association, Toronto, August 30, 1978.

*Miller, F.T., Bentz, W.K., Aponte, J.F., & Brogan, D.R. Perception of life crisis events: A comparative study of rural and urban samples. In B.S. Dohrenwend & B.P. Dohrenwend (Eds.), *Stressful life events: Their nature and effects*. New York: Wiley, 1974, pp. 259–273.

Miller, J.G. *Living Systems*. New York: McGraw-Hill, 1979.

Miller, P.M., & Ingham, J.G. Friends, confidants, and symptoms. *Social Psychiatry*, 1976, 11, 51.

Millon, T. *Disorders of personality*. New York: Wiley, 1981.

Mintz, I.L. Anorexia Nervosa: The Clinical Syndrome and its Dynamic Implications. *Journal of the Medical Society of New Jersey*, 1980, 77, 5, 333–339.

Minuchin, S., Rosman, B.L., & Baker, L. *Psychosomatic families: Anorexia nervosa in context*. Cambridge, MA: Harvard University Press, 1978.

*Mischel, T. The concept of mental health and disease: An analysis of the controversy between behavioral and psychodynamic approaches. *The Journal of Medicine and Philosophy*, 1977, 2, 197–219.

*Mischel, W. On the future of personality measurement. *American Psychologist*, 1977, 32, 246–254.

*Mitchell, J.C. The concept and use of social networks. In J.C. Mitchel (Ed.), *Social networks in urban situations*. Manchester: Manchester University Press, 1969.

Mitchell, K.M., Bozarth, J.D., & Krauft, C.C. A reappraisal of the therapeutic effectiveness of accurate empathy, nonpossessive warmth and genuineness. In A.S. Gurman & A.M. Razdin (Eds.), *Effective psychotherapy: A handbook of research*. Elmsford, NY: Pergamon Press, 1977, pp. 482–502.

Modell, A. The origin of certain forms of pre-oedipal guilt and the implications for a psychoanalytic theory of affects. *International Journal of Psychoanalysis*, 1971, 52, 337–346.

Moldofsky, H., & Garfinkel, P.E. Problems of treatment of anorexia nervosa. *Canadian Psychiatric Association Journal*, 1974, 19, 169–175.

*Moore, B.S., Underwood, B., & Rosenhan, D.L. Affect and altruism. *Developmental Psychology*, 1973, 8, 99–104.

*Moos, R.H. (Ed.). *Coping with physical illness*. New York: Plenum, 1977.

*Moran, E., & Beatty, J. *Anorexia nervosa*. Nursing IV term paper. November 1979.

Morgan, H.G. & Russell, G.F.M. Value of family background and clinical features as predictors of long-term outcome in anorexia nervosa: four year follow-up study of 41 patients. *Psychological Medicine*, 1975, 5, 355–371.

Moriwaki, S.Y. Self-disclosure, significant others, and psychological well-being in old age. *Journal of Health and Social Behavior*, 1973, 14 (3), 226–232.

Morris, J.B., & Beck, A.T. The efficacy of anti-depressant drugs: A review of research, 1958–1972. *Archives of General Psychiatry*, 1974, *30*, 667–674.

Moss, G.E. *Illness, immunity, and social interaction*. New York: Wiley, 1973.

Mueller, D.P. Social networks: A promising direction for research on the relationship of the social environment to psychiatric disorder. *Social Science and Medicine*, 1980, *14A*, 147–161.

*Mueller, D., Edwards, D.W., & Yarvis, R.M. Stressful life events and psychiatric symptomatology: Change or undesirability. *Journal of Health and Social Behavior*, 1977, *18*, 307–316.

*Multifactoral approach can help anorexia. *Clinical Psychiatry News*, 1980, *8*, 7.

Myers, J., Lindenthal, J.J., & Pepper, M. Life events and psychiatric impairment. *Journal of Nervous and Mental Disease*, 1971, *152* (3), 149–157.

Myers, J., Lindenthal, J.J., & Pepper, M. Life events and mental status: A longitudinal study. *Journal of Health and Social Behavior*, 1972, *13*, 398–406.

Myers, J., Lindenthal, J.J., & Pepper, M. Social class, life events, and psychiatric symptoms: A longitudinal study. In B.S. Dohrenwend & B.P. Dohrenwend (Eds.), *Stressful life events: Their nature and effects*. New York: Wiley, 1974, pp. 191–205.

Myers, J., Lindenthal, J.J., & Pepper, M. Life events, social integration and psychiatric symptomatology. *Journal of Health and Social Behavior*, 1975, *16* (4), 421–427.

*Nagel, E. Methodological issues in psychoanalytic theory. In S. Hook (Ed.), *Psychoanalysis, scientific method and philosophy*. New York: New York University Press, 1959.

*Napier, A.Y., & Whitaker, C.A. *The family crucible*. New York: Harper & Row, 1978.

Nathan, P.E. Symptomatic diagnosis and behavioral assessment: A synthesis? In D.H. Barlow (Ed), *Behavioral Assessment of Adult Disorders*. New York: Guilford, 1980.

Nelson, J.C., Bowers, M.B., & Sweeney, D.R. Exacerbation of psychosis by tricyclic antidepressants in delusional depression. *American Journal of Psychiatry*, 1979, *136*, 574–576.

Nelson, R.O. Realistic dependent measures for clinical use. *Journal of Clinical and Consulting Psychology*, 1981, *49*, 168–181.

*Noboe, R.E. Effect of cyproheptadine on appetite and weight gain in adults. *Journal of the American Medical Association*, 1969, *209*, 2054–2055.

Nordquist, V.M. The modification of a child's enuresis: Some response–response relationships. *Journal of Applied Behavior Analysis*, 1971, *4*, 241–247.

*Norris, D.L. Clinical diagnostic criteria for primary anorexia nervosa. *South Africa Medical Journal*, 1979, *56*, 987–993.

Novaco, R. A treatment program for the management of anger through cognitive and relaxation controls. Unpublished doctoral dissertation. Indiana University, Bloomington, Indiana, 1974.

Nuckolls, K.B., Cassel, J., & Kaplan, B.H. Psychosocial aspects, life crises, and the prognosis of pregnancy. *American Journal of Epidemiology*, 1972, *95*, 431–441.

Obesity/Bariatric Medicine, 1981, *10*, 51–52.

Oksaner, I.A. *The influence of training in the dimensions of empathy, respect, concreteness, and genuineness on counselor effectiveness.* Doctoral dissertation, Wayne State University, 1973. Dissertation Abstracts International, 1973, *34*, 3067A (University Microfilms No: 73-31, 762).

O'Donnell, C.R., Lydgate, T. & Fo, W.S.D. The buddy system: Review and follow-up. *Cognitive Behavior Therapy*, 1979, *1*, 161–169.

O'Leary, K.D., & Borkovec, T.D. Conceptual, methodological, and ethical problems of placebo groups in psychotherapy research. *American Psychologist*, 1978, *33*, 821–830.

O'Leary, K.D., & Wilson, G.T. *Behavior therapy: Application and outcome.* Englewood Cliffs, NJ: Prentice-Hall, 1975.

Olson, G.W. Application of an objective method for measuring action of "antidepressant" medication. *American Journal of Psychiatry*, 1962, *118*, 1044–1045.

*Orr, D. Transference and countertransference: A historical survey. *Journal of the American Psychoanalytic Association*, 1954, *2*, 621–670.

*Ossofski, H.J. *Drug therapy of anorexia nervosa.* Paper presented at the Annual Meeting of the American Psychiatric Association, May 1981.

Padfield, M. The comparative effects of two counseling approaches on the intensity of depression among rural women of low socioeconomic status. *Journal of Counseling Psychology*, 1976, *23*, 209–214.

Palazolli, M.S. *The World Diennial of Psychiatry and Psychotherapy* (Vol. 1). New York: Basic Books, 1971.

Palmer, R.L. *Anorexia nervosa: A guide for sufferers and their families.* Harmondsworth, England: Penguin Books, 1980.

Parkin, A. On masochistic enthralment: A contribution to the study of moral masochism. *International Journal of Psycho-Analysis*, 1980, *61*, 307–314.

Parloff, M.B. Can psychotherapy research guide the policy maker? A little knowledge may be a dangerous thing. In M.R. Goldfried (Ed.), *Converging Themes in Psychotherapy*. New York: Springer, 1982.

Parloff, M.B., & Dies, R.R. Group psychotherapy outcome research 1966–1975. *International Journal of Group Psychotherapy*, 1977, *27*, 281–319.

Parloff, M.B., Waskown, I.E., & Wolfe, B.E. Research on therapist variables in relation to process and outcome. In S.L. Garfield & A.E. Bergin (Eds.), *Handbook of psychotherapy and behavior change* (2nd ed.). New York: Wiley, 1978, pp. 233–282.

Pattison, E.M. A theoretical-empirical base for social system therapy. In E.F. Foulks, R.M. Wintrob, J. Westermeyer, & A.R. Favazza (Eds.), *Current perspectives in cultural psychiatry*. New York: Spectrum, 1977, pp. 217–253.

Paul, G.L. Insight versus desensitization in psychotherapy two years after termination. *Journal of Consulting Psychology*, 1967, *31*, 333–348.

Paul, G.L. & Lentz, R.J. *Psychological Treatment of Chronic Mental Patients.* Cambridge, Mass.: Harvard University Press, 1977.

*Pawlowski, G.T. Cyproheptadine: Weight gain and appetite simulation in essential anorexia patients. *Current Therapy Research*, 1975, *18*, 673–678.

Paykel, E.S. Life stress and psychiatric disorder: Applications of the clinical approach. In B.S. Dohrenwend & B.P. Dohrenwend (Eds.), *Stressful life events: Their nature and effects*. New York: Wiley, 1974, pp. 135–149.

Paykel, E.S. Causal relationships between clinical depression and life events. In J.E. Barrett (Ed.), *Stress and mental disorder*. New York: Raven Press, 1979, pp. 71–86.

Paykel, E.S., Myers, J.K., Dienelt, M.N., Klerman, M.N., Lindenthal, J., & Pepper, M. Life events and depression: A controlled study. *Archives of General Psychiatry*, 1969, *21*, 753–760.

Paykel, E.S., Parker, R.R., Penrose, R.J.J., & Rassaby. Depressive clarification and prediction of response to Phenelzine. *British Journal of Psychiatry*, 1979, *134*, 572–581.

Paykel, E.S., Prusoff, B., & Myers, J.K. Suicide attempts and recent life events. *Archives of General Psychiatry*, 1975, *32*, 327–333.

*Pearlin, L. Sex roles and depression. In N. Datan & L. Ginsberg (Eds.), *Life-span development psychology: Normative life crises*. New York: Academic Press, 1975, pp. 191–207.

Pearlin, L.I., & Johnson, J.S. Marital status, life strains and depression. *American Sociological Review*, 1977, *42*, 704–715.

Pearlin, L.I., & Lieberman, M.A. Social sources of emotional distress. In R. Simmons (Ed.), *Research in community and mental health*. Greenwich: JAI Press, 1977.

Pearlin, L.I., Lieberman, M.A., Menaghan, E., & Mullan, J. The stress process. *Journal of Health and Social Behavior*, 1981, *22*, 337–356. (forthcoming).

*Pearlin, L.I., & Radabaugh, C.W. Economic strains and the coping functions of alcohol. *American Journal of Sociology*, 1980, *82* (3), 652–663.

Pearlin, L.I., & Schooler, C. The structure of coping. *Journal of Health and Social Behavior*, 1978, *19*, 2–21.

*Peer relations help reverse teen anorexia. *Clinical Psychiatry News*, 1980, *8*, p. 19.

Pendergrass, V.E. Time-out from positive reinforcement following persistent, high-rate behavior in retardates. *Journal of Applied Behavior Analysis*, 1972, *5*, 85–91.

*Penfold, J.L. Effect of cyproheptadine and a multi-vitamin preparation on appetite stimulation, weight gain and linear growth. *Medical Journal of Australia*, 1971, *1*, 307–310.

Perlman, G. Change in 'central therapeutic ingredients' of beginning psychotherapists. *Psychotherapy: Theory, Research, and Practice*, 1973, *10*, 48–51.

Pertschuk, M.J. Behavior therapy: Extended follow-up. In R.A. Vigersky (Ed.), *Anorexia nervosa*. New York: Raven Press, 1977.

Pervin, L. The representative design of person–situation research. In D. Magnusson & N.S. Endler (Eds.), *Personality at the crossroads: Current issues in interactional psychology*. Hillsdale, NJ: Erlbaum, 1977.

Peters, D.R. Identification and personal learning in T-groups. *Human Relations*, 1973, *26*, 1–21.

*Phillips, D., & Clancey, K. Response biases in field studies of mental illness. *American Sociological Review*, 1970, *35*, 503–515.

*Phillips, D., & Clancey, K. Some effects of social desirability in survey studies. *American Journal of Sociology*, 1972, 77, 921–940.

*Phillips, D., & Segal, B. Sexual status and psychiatric symptoms. *American Sociological Review*, 1969, 34 (1), 58–72.

*Phillips, E.C. *Counseling and psychotherapy: A behavioral approach.* New York: Wiley, 1977.

*Piazza, E., Piazza, N., & Rollins, N. Anorexia nervosa: Controversial aspects of therapy. *Comprehensive Psychiatry*, 1980, 21, 117–189.

Pierloot, R.A., Wellens, W. & Houben, M.E. Elements of resistance to a combined medical and psychotherapeutic program in anorexia nervosa. An overview. *Psychotherapy Psychosomatica*, 1975, 26, 101–117.

Piper, W.E., Doan, B.D., Edwards, E.M., & Jones, B.D. Co-therapy behavior, group therapy process, and treatment outcome. *Journal of Consulting and Clinical Psychology*, 1979, 47, 1081–1089.

*Planansky, K. Changes in weight in patients receiving a tranquilizing drug. *Psychiatric Quarterly*, 1958, 32, 289–303.

Pollitt, J. Natural history studies in mental illness: A discussion based on a pilot study of obsessional states. *Journal of Mental Science*, 1960, 106, 93–113.

Pollitt, J. Obsessional states. *British Journal of Hospital Medicine*, 1969, 2, 1146–1150.

Pope, H.G., Jonas, J.M., Hudson, J.I., Cohen, B.M., & Gunderson, J.G. The validity of DSM-III borderline personality disorder: A phenomenologic, family history, treatment response, and long-term follow-up study. *Archives of General Psychiatry*, 1983, 40, 23–30.

*Popper, K.R. *The logic of scientific discovery.* London: Hutchinson, 1935.

Powers, E. & Witmer, H. *An experiment of the prevention of delinquency. The Cambridge-Somerville Youth Study.* New York: Columbia University Press, 1951.

Prien, R.F., & Caffey, E.M. Long-term maintenance drug therapy in recurrent affective illness: Current status and issues. *Diseases of the Nervous System*, 1977, 164, 981–992.

Rabavilas, A.D., & Boulougouris, J.C. Mood changes and flooding outcome in obsessive-compulsive patients. Report of a 2-year follow-up. *The Journal of Nervous and Mental Disease*, 1979, 167, 495–496.

Rabavilas, A.D., Boulougouris, J.C., Perissaki, C., & Stefanis, C. Pre-morbid personality traits and responsiveness to flooding in obsessive-compulsive patients. *Behavior Research and Therapy*, 1979, 17, 575–580.

Rabkin, J., & Struening, E.L. Life events, stress and illness. *Science*, 1976, 194, 1013–1020.

Rachman, S. Studies in desensitization. II. Flooding. *Behaviour Research and Therapy*, 1966, 4, 1–6.

Rachman, S. Obstacles to the successful treatment of obsessions. In E.B. Foa & P.M.G. Emmelkamp (Eds.), *Treatment Failures in Behavior Therapy.* New York: Wiley, 1983.

Rachman, S.J. The effects of psychological treatment. In H. Eysenck (Ed.), *Handbook of abnormal psychology.* New York: Basic Books, 1973.

Rachman, S.J., Cobb, J., Grey, S., McDonald, B., Mawson, D., Sartory, G., & Stern, R. The behavioral treatment of obsessional-compulsive disorders with and without clomipramine. *Behavior Research and Therapy*, 1979, *17*, 467–478.

*Rachman, S., & Hodgson, R.J. *Obsessions and compulsions*. New York: Appleton-Century-Crofts, 1979.

Rachman, S., & Hodgson, R.J. *Obsessions and compulsions*. Prentice Hall, 1980.

Rachman, S., Marks, I.M., & Hodgson, R.J. The treatment of obsessive-compulsive neurotics by modelling and flooding in vivo. *Behavior Research and Therapy*, 1973, *11*, 463–471.

Rachman, S., & Teasdale, J.D. *Aversion therapy and behavior disorders: An analysis*. London: Routledge & Kegan, Paul, 1969.

Rachman, S.J., & Wilson, G.T. *The effects of psychological therapy* (2nd ed.). New York: Pergamon Press, 1980.

*Radloff, L. Sex differences in depression. *Sex Roles*, 1975, *1*, (3), 249–265.

Rahe, R.H. The pathway between subjects' recent life changes and their near future illness reports: Representative results and methodological issues. In B.S. Dohrenwend & B.P. Dohrenwend (Eds.), *Stressful life events: Their nature and effects*. New York: Wiley, 1974, pp. 73–86.

Reddy, W.B., & Lipert, K.M. Studies of the processes and dynamics within experiential groups. In P.B. Smith (Ed.), *Small groups and personal change*. London: Methuen, 1980.

Rehm, L.P., Fuchs, C.Z., Roth, D.M., Kronblith, S.J., & Romano, J.M. A comparison of self-control and assertion skills treatment of depression. *Behavior Therapy*, 1979, *10*, 429–442.

*Reich, W. *Character analysis*. (T.P. Wolfe trans.). New York: Orgone Institute Press, 1949. (Originally published, 1933).

Rennie, T.A.L. Prognosis in manic-depressive psychosis. *American Journal of Psychiatry*, 1942, *98*, 801.

*Richardson, T.F. Anorexia nervosa: An overview. *American Journal of Nursing*, April, 1980.

Ricks, D.F. Supershrink: Methods of a therapist judged successful on the basis of adult outcomes of adolescent patients. In D.F. Ricks, M. Roff, & A. Thomas (Eds.), *Life History Research in Psychopathology*. Minneapolis: University of Minnesota, 1974.

*Ricoeur, P. *Freud and philosophy*. New Haven, CT: Yale University Press, 1970.

Rimm, D.C. & Masters, J.C. *Behavior Therapy: Techniques and Empirical Findings*. 2nd Ed. New York: Academic Press, 1979.

Rincover, A., Cook, R., Peoples, A. & Packard, D. Sensory extinction and sensory reinforcement principles for programming multiple adaptive behavior change. *Journal of Applied Behavior Analysis*, 1979, *12*, 221–233.

Risley, T.R. The effects and side effects of punishing the autistic behaviors of a deviant child. *Journal of Applied Behavior Analysis*, 1969, *1*, 21–34.

Roger, S.C., & Clay, P.M. A statistical review of controlled trials of imipramine and placebo in the treatment of depressive illness. *British Journal of Psychiatry*, 1975, *127*, 599–603.

Rogers, C.R., & Dymond, R.F. (Eds.). *Psychotherapy and personality change.* Chicago: University of Chicago Press, 1954.

Rohrbaugh, M., & Bartels, B.D. Participants' perceptions of "curative factors" in therapy and growth groups. *Small Group Behavior,* 1975, *6,* 430–456.

Rosenbaum, M., Friedlander, J., & Kaplan, S.M. Evaluation of results of psychotherapy. *Psychosomatic Medicine,* 1956, *18,* 113–132.

Rosenfeld, H.A. Negative therapeutic reaction. In P.L. Giovacchini (Ed.), *Tactics and techniques in psychoanalytic theory,* (Vol. II): *Countertransference.* New York: Aronson, 1975.

*Rosenhan, D.L., Underwood, B., & Moore, B.S. Affect mediates self-gratification and altruism. *Journal of Personality and Social Psychology,* 1974, *20,* 546–552.

Rosman, B.L., Minuchin, S., Baker, L., & Liebman, R. A family therapy approach to anorexia nervosa: A study, treatment, and outcome. In R.A. Vigersky (Ed.), *Anorexia nervosa.* New York: Raven Press, 1977.

*Ross, C.E., & Mirowski, J. II. A comparison of life event weighting schemes: Change, undesirability, and effect-proportional indices. *Journal of Health and Social Behavior,* 1979, *20,* 166–177.

*Ross, J.L. Anorexia nervosa: An overview. *Bulletin of the Menninger Clinic,* 1977, *41,* 418–436.

*Rotter, J.B. Generalized expectancies for internal versus external control of reinforcement. *Psychological Monographs,* 1966, *80,* (1, Whole No. 609).

*Rotter, J.B., Chance, J.E., & Phares, J.E. *Applications of a social learning theory of personality.* New York: Holt, Rhinehart, and Winston, 1972.

Rowland, C.V. (Ed.). *Anorexia and obesity.* Boston: Little, Brown, 1970.

Roy, A. Vulnerability factors and depression in women. *British Journal of Psychiatry,* 1978, *133,* 106.

*Rubin, R.T., Gunderson, E.K.E., & Arthur, R.J. Life stress and illness patterns in the U.S. Navy: Prior life change and illness onset in a battleship crew. *Journal of Psychosomatic Research,* 1971, *15,* 89–94.

Rubinstein, E.A., & Parloff, M.B. (Eds.). *Research in psychotherapy.* Washington, D.C.: American Psychological Association, 1959.

Rush, A.J., Beck, A.T., Kovacs, M., & Hollon, S.D. Comparative efficacy of cognitive therapy versus pharmacotherapy in outpatient depression. *Cognitive Therapy and Research,* 1977, *1,* 17–37.

Rush, A.J., Hollon, S., Beck, A.T., & Kovacs, M. Depression: Must pharmacotherapy fail for cognitive therapy to succeed? *Cognitive Therapy and Research,* 1978, *2,* 199–206.

*Russell, G.F.M. General management of anorexia nervosa and difficulties in assessing the efficacy of treatment. In R.A. Vigersky (Ed.), *Anorexia nervosa.* New York: Raven Press, 1977.

*Russell, G. The current treatment of anorexia nervosa. *British Journal of Psychiatry,* 1981, *138,* 164–166.

Russo, D.C., Cataldo, M.F. & Cushing, P. Compliance training and behavior covariation in the treatment of multiple behavioral problems. *Journal of Applied Behavior Analysis,* 1981, *14,* 209–222.

Sager, C.J., Reiss, B.F., & Gundlach, R. Follow-up study of the results of extramural analytic psychotherapy. *American Journal of Psychotherapy*, 1964, *18*, 161–173.

Sajwaj, T., Twardosz, S., & Burke, M. Side effects of extinction procedures in a remedial preschool. *Journal of Applied Behavior Analysis*, 1972, *5*, 163–175.

*Salkind, M.R., Fincham, J., & Silverstone, T. Is anorexia nervosa a phobic disorder? A psychological enquiry. *Biological Psychiatry*, 1980, *15*, 803–808.

Sampson, E.E. Leader orientation and T-group effectiveness. *Journal of Applied Behavioral Science*, 1972, *8*, 564–575.

Sandell, J.A. *An empirical study of negative factors in brief psychotherapy.* Unpublished dissertation, Vanderbilt University, 1981.

Sarason, I.G., & Spielberger, C.D. (Eds.). *Stress and anxiety* (Vol II). New York: Halstead Press, 1975.

Sargant, W. Drugs in the treatment of depression. *British Medical Journal*, 1961, *1*, 225–227.

*Schaefer, E.C., Millman, H.E., & Levine, G.L. *Therapies for psychosomatic disorders in children.* San Francisco: Jossey-Bass, 1979.

*Schless, A.P., Schwartz, L., Goetz, C., & Mendels, J. How depressives view the significance of life events. *British Journal of Psychiatry*, 1974, *125*, 406–410.

Schmale, A.H. Giving up as a final common pathway to changes in health. *Advances in Psychosomatic Medicine*, 1972, *8*, 20–40.

Schofield, W. *Psychotherapy: The purchase of friendship.* Englewood Cliffs, NJ: Prentice-Hall, 1964.

Schulz, R. The effects of control and predictability on the psychological and physical well-being of the institutionalized aged. *Journal of Personality and Social Psychology*, 1976, *33*, 563–573.

Schulz, R., & Hanusa, B.H. Long-term effects of control and predicability-enhancing interventions: Findings and ethical issues. *Journal of Personality and Social Psychology*, 1978, *36*, 1194–1201.

*Schwabe, A.D. Anorexia nervosa. *Annals of Internal Medicine*, 1981, *94*, 371–381.

Schwartz, A.H.; Harrow, M., Anderson, C., Feinstein, A.E., & Schwartz, C.C. Influence of therapeutic task orientation on patient and therapist satisfaction in group psychotherapy. *International Journal of Group Psychotherapy*, 1970, *20*, 460–469.

Scott, R., & Howard, A. Models of stress. In S. Levine & N. Scotch, *Social stress.* Chicago: Aldine, 1970, pp. 259–278.

Scovern, A.W., & Kilmann, P.R. Status of electroconvulsive therapy: Review of the outcome literature. *Psychological Bulletin*, 1980, *87*, 260–303.

Searles, H.F. *Countertransference and related subjects.* New York: International University Press, 1979.

*Seiler, L. The 22-item scale used in field studies of mental illness: A question of method, a question of substance, and a question of theory. *Journal of Health and Social Behavior*, 1973, *14*, 252–264.

Seligman, M.E.P. Phobias and preparedness. *Behavior Therapy*, 1971, *2*, 307–321.

Seligman, M.E.P. *Helplessness: On depression, development, and death.* San Francisco: W.H. Freeman, 1975.

Selvi, M.P. Interpretation of anorexia nervosa. In J.E. Meyer & H. Feldman (Eds.), *Anorexia nervosa: Symposium AM 24/25,* April, 1965 in Gottingen. Stuttgart, Germany: Georg Thieme Verlag, 1965.

Selvi, M.P. Anorexia nervosa. In S. Arieti (Ed.), *World Biennial of Psychiatry in Psychotherapy* (Vol. I). New York: Basic Books, 1971.

Selye, H. *The stress of life.* New York: McGraw Hill, 1956.

Shapiro, R., & Budman, S. Defection, termination, and continuation in family and individual therapy. *Family Process, 1973, 12,* 55–67.

Shaw, B.F. Comparison of cognitive therapy and behavior therapy in the treatment of depression. *Journal of Consulting and Clinical Psychology, 1977, 45,* 543–551.

Sheatsley, P.B., & Feldman, J. The assassination of President Kennedy: Public reaction. *Public Opinion Quarterly, 1964, 28,* 189–215.

*Sherwood, M. *The logic of explanation in psychoanalysis.* New York: Academic Press, 1969.

*Shevrin, H., & Dickman, S. The psychological unconscious. A necessary assumption for all psychological theory? *American Psychologist, 1980, 35,* 421–434.

*Shiner, G. Anorexia nervosa: Studied at several centers. *Research Resources Reporter, 1980, 4,* 1–7.

*Silbert, M.V. The weight gain effect of Periactin in anorexic patients. *South African Medical Journal, 1971, 45,* 374–377.

Silver, R., & Wortman, C.B. Coping with undesirable life events. In J. Garber & M.E.P. Seligman (Eds.), *Human helplessness: Theory and its application.* New York: Academic Press, 1980, pp. 279–340.

*Silverman, J.A., & Wolff, J.A. Anorexia nervosa and acanthocytosis. *Journal of the American Medical Association, 1979, 242,* 2760.

*Silverstone, T., & Schuyler, D. The effect of cyproheptadine on hunger, caloric intake and body weight in man. *Psychopharmacologia, 1975, 40,* 335–340.

Skynner, A.C.R. An open-systems, group-analytic approach to family therapy. In A.S. Gurman & D.P. Kniskern (Eds.), *Handbook of family therapy.* New York: Brunner/Mazel, 1981.

Slipp, S., Ellis, S., & Kressel, K. Factors associated with engagement in family therapy. *Family Process, 1974, 13,* 413–427.

Sloane, R.B., Staples, F.R., Cristol, A.H., Yorkston, N.J., & Whipple, K. *Psychotherapy versus behavior therapy.* Cambridge, MA: Harvard University Press, 1975.

Smith, M.L., Glass, G.V. & Miller, T.I. *The Benefits of Psychotherapy.* Baltimore: The Johns Hopkins University Press, 1980.

Smith, P.B. Are there adverse effects of sensitivity training? *Journal of Humanistic Psychology, 1975, 15,* 29–47.

Smith, P.B. Sources of influence in the sensitivity training laboratory. *Small Group Behavior, 1976, 7,* 331–348.

Sobel, S.B. Throwing the baby out with the bathwater: The hazards of follow-up research. *American Psychologist*, 1978, *33*, 290–291.

*Sollard, R.N., & Wachtel, P.L. A structural and transactional approach to cognition in clinical problems. In M.J. Mahoney (Ed.), *Psychotherapy process: Current issues and future directions*. New York: Plenum, 1980.

Soloff, P.H., & Millward, J.W. Psychiatric disorders in the families of borderline patients. *Archives of General Psychiatry*, 1983, *40*, 37–44.

Solyom, L., & Sookman, D. A comparison of clomipramine hydrochloride (Anafranil) and behavior therapy in the treatment of obsessive neurosis. *Journal of International Medical Research*, 1977, *5*, Supplement 5, 49–61.

Sours, J.A. The Anorexia Nervosa Syndrome. *International Journal of Psychoanalysis*, 1974, *55*, 567–576.

Spiegel, H., & Spiegel, D. *Trance and treatment: Clinical uses of hypnosis*. New York: Basic Books, 1978.

Spielberger, C.D., & Sarason, I.G. (Eds.). *Stress and anxiety* (Vol. 1). New York: Halstead Press, 1975.

Spielberger, C.D., & Sarason, I.G. (Eds.). *Stress and anxiety* (Vol. V). New York: Halstead Press, 1978.

*Spiesman, J.C., Lazarus, R.S., Mordkoff, A., & Davidson, L. Experimental reduction of stress based on ego-defense theory. *Journal of Abnormal and Social Psychology*, 1964, *68*, 367–380.

*Spiro, H.R., Siassi, I., & Corcetti, G. What gets surveyed in a psychiatric survey? A case study of the Macmillan Index. *Journal of Nervous and Mental Disease*, 1972, *154*, 105–114.

Spitzer, R.L., Endicott, J., & Gibbon, M. Crossing the border into borderline personality and borderline schizophrenia. *Archives of General Psychiatry*, 1979, *36*, 17–24.

*Spitzer, R.L., & Fleiss, J.L. A reanalysis of the reliability of psychiatric diagnosis. *British Journal of Psychiatry*, 1974, *125*, 341–347.

*Stanton, M.D. Strategic approaches to family therapy. In A.S. Gurman & D.P. Kniskern (Eds.), *Handbook of family therapy*. New York: Brunner/Mazel, 1981.

Star, S.A. Psychoneurotic symptoms in the army. In S.A. Stouffer et al. (Eds.), *Studies in social psychology in World War II* (Vol. 2). Princeton, NJ: Princeton University Press, 1949, pp. 411–455.

Starkey, T.A. & Lee, R.A. Menstruation and fertility in anorexia nervosa. *American Journal of Obstetrics and Gynecology*, 1969, *105*, 374–379.

Sterling, M. The Clinical Effects of Parental Neurosis on the Child. In E.J. Anthony & T. Benedik (Eds.), *Parenthood: Its Psychology and Psychopathology*. Boston: Little, Brown, & Co., 1970, 539–569.

Sterling, M. *Psychosomatic Disorders in Childhood*. London: Jason Aronson, 1978, 131–173.

Sterling, J., Draybek, T.E., & Key, W.H. *The long-term impact of disaster on the health self-perceptions of victims*. Paper presented at the American Sociological Association. Chicago, Illinois, September 1977.

Stern, A. Psychoanalytic investigation of and therapy in the borderline group of neuroses. *Psychoanalytic Quarterly*, 1938, *7*, 467–489.

Stern, R.S. Obsessive thoughts: The problem of therapy. *British Journal of Psychiatry*, 1978, *132*, 200–205.

Stokes, T.F. & Baer, D.M. An implicit technology of generalization. *Journal of Applied Behavior Analysis*, 1977, *10*, 349–367.

*Stone, M.H. Therapists' personalities and unexpected success with schizophrenic patients. *American Journal of Psychotherapy*, 1971, *25*, 543–552.

Stone, M.H. A psychoanalytic approach to abnormalities of temperament. *American Journal of Psychotherapy*, 1980, *33*, 263–280. (a)

Stone, M.H. *The borderline syndromes: Constitution, adaptation and personality.* New York: McGraw-Hill, 1980. (b)

Stone, M.H. *Personality type: Impact on outcome in the psychotherapy of borderline patients.* Presented at Dialogues on Borderlines: Earl D. Bond Symposium, Institute of Pennsylvania Hospital, Philadelphia, April 1981. For chapter in Marion Solomon (Ed.) *The Borderline Syndromes*, UCLA.

*Stonehill, E., & Crisp, A.H. Psychoneurotic characteristics of patients with anorexia nervosa before and after treatment and at follow-up 4–7 years later. *Journal of Psychosomatic Research*, 1977, *21*, 187–193.

Story, I. Caricature and impersonating the other: Observations from the psychotherapy of anorexia nervosa. *Psychiatry*, 1976, *39*, 176–188.

*Strober, M. Personality and symptomatological features in young, nonchronic anorexia nervosa patients. *Journal of Psychosomatic Research*, 1980, *24*, 353–359.

Strupp, H.H. *Psychotherapists in action.* New York: Grune & Stratton, 1960.

Strupp, H.H. Success and failure in time-limited psychotherapy: A systematic comparison of two cases (Comparison 1). *Archives of General Psychiatry*, 1980, *37*, 595–603.(a)

Strupp, H.H. Success and failure in time-limited psychotherapy: A systematic comparison of two cases (Comparison 2). *Archives of General Psychiatry*, 1980, *37*, 831–841.(b)

Strupp. H.H. Success and failure in time-limited psychotherapy: With special reference to the performance of a lay counselor. *Archives of General Psychiatry*, 1980, *37*, 831–841.(c)

Strupp, H.H. Success and failure in time-limited psychotherapy: Further evidence (Comparison 4). *Archives of General Psychiatry*, 1980, *37*, 947–954.(d)

Strupp, H.H., & Bergin, A.E. Some empirical and conceptual bases for coordinated research in psychotherapy. *International Journal of Psychiatry*, 1969, *7*, 18–90.

*Strupp, H.H., Fox, R.E., & Lessler, K. *Patients view their psychotherapy.* Baltimore: Johns Hopkins Press, 1969.

Stupp, H.H., & Hadley, S.W. Contemporary views of negative effects in psychotherapy. *Archives of General Psychiatry*, 1976, *33*, 1291.

Strupp, H.H., & Hadley, S.W. A tripartite model of mental health and therapeutic outcomes. *American Psychologist*, 1977, *32*, 187–196.

Strupp, H.H., & Hadley, S.W. Specific versus nonspecific factors in psychotherapy: A controlled study of outcome. *Archives of General Psychiatry*, 1979, *36*, 1125–1136.

Strupp, H.H., Hadley, S.W., & Gomes-Schwartz, B. *Psychotherapy for better or worse: The problem of negative effects.* New York: Aronson, 1977.

Strupp, H.H., Keithly, L., Moras, K., Samples, S., Sandell, J., & Waterhouse, G. *Toward the measurement of negative effect in psychotherapy.* Paper presented at the Conference of the Society for Psychotherapy Research: Pacific Grove, California, June 1980.

Strupp, H.H., Wallach, M.S., & Wogan, M. Psychotherapy experience in retrospect: Questionnaire survey of former patients and their therapists. *Psychology Monographs,* 1964, *74,* Whole No. 588.

*Stunkard, A. New therapies for the eating disorders: Behavior modification of obesity and anorexia nervosa. *Archives of General Psychiatry,* 1972, *26,* 391–398.

Sutherland, A.S. *Breakdown.* London: Temple Smith, 1977.

Swan, S.E., & MacDonald, M.L. Behavior therapy in practice: A national survey of behavior therapists. *Behavior Therapy,* 1978, *9,* 799–807.

*Taban, C. Changes in weight during prolonged treatment with chlorpromazine. *Revue Suisse de Zoologie,* 1955, *62,* Suppl. 280–288.

Tarplay, H.D. & Schroeder, S.R. Comparison of DRO and DSI on rate of suppression of self-injurious behavior. *American Journal of Mental Deficiency,* 1979, *84,* 188–194.

Theander, S. Anorexia nervosa: A psychiatric investigation of 94 female patients. *Acta Psychiatrica Scandinavia* (suppl), 1970, *214,* 1–194.

Theorell, T. Life events before and after the onset of a premature myocardial infarction. In B.S. Dohrenwend & B.P. Dohrenwend (Eds.), *Stressful life events: Their nature and effects.* New York: Wiley, 1974, pp. 101–117.

*Thoits, P. *Conceptual, methodological, and theoretical problems in studying social support as a buffer against life stress.* Manuscript. Department of Sociology, Princeton University.

Thoits, P. *Life events, social integration, and psychological distress.* Ph.D. Dissertation, Sociology Department, Stanford University, 1978.

Thoits, P. Longitudinal effects of income maintenance on psychological distress: four waves of analysis. *Social Science Forum,* 1982, *4,* 38–57.

Thoits, P. Undesirable life events and psychophysiological distress: A problem of operational confounding. *American Sociological Review,* 1981, *46,* 97–109.(b)

Thoits, P., & Hannan, M. Income and psychological distress: The impact of an income-maintenance experiment. *Journal of Health and Social Behavior,* 1979, *20,* 120–138.

*Thoma, H. *Anorexia nervosa.* New York: International University Press, 1967.

*Thompson, W.C., Cowan, C.L., & Rosenhan, D.L. Focus of attention mediates the impact of negative affect on altruism. *Journal of Personality and Social Psychology,* 1980, *38,* 291–300.

Title, S.H. Ask the practicing physician. *Obesity and Bariatric Medicine,* 1973, *2,* 124–126.

*Tousignant, M., Denis, G., & Lachapelle, R. Some considerations concerning the validity and use of the Health Opinion Survey. *Journal of Health and Social Behavior,* 1974, *15* (3), 241–252.

*Treating anorexia nervosa and ritualism in adolescent girls. *Frontiers of Psychiatry*, November 1978, pp. 5, 10.

Truax, C.B. Effective ingredients in psychotherapy: An approach of unraveling in the patient–therapist interaction. *Journal of Counseling Psychology*, 1963, *10*, 256–263.

Truax, C.B., & Mitchell, K.M. Research on certain therapist interpersonal skills in relation to process and outcome. In A.E. Bergin & S.L. Garfield (Eds.), *Handbook of psychotherapy and behavior change: An empirical analysis.* New York: Wiley, 1971.

Tuckman, B.W. Developmental sequence in small groups. *Psychological Bulletin*, 1965, *63*, 384–399.

Turner, R.J. *Experienced social support as a contingency in emotional well-being.* Paper presented at the American Sociological Association, New York, August 1980.

Turner, R.M., Steketee, G.S., & Foa, E.B. Fear of criticism in washers, checkers and phobics. *Behavior Research and Therapy*, 1979, *17*, 79–81.

Turner, S.M., Hersen, M., Bellack, A.S., & Wells, K.C. Behavioural treatment of obsessive-compulsive neurosis. *Behavior Research and Therapy*, 1979, *17*, 95–106.

Tyhurst, J.S. Individual reactions to a community disaster: The natural history of psychiatric projective phenomena. *American Journal of Psychiatry*, 1951, *107*, 764–769.

Tyrer, P. Towards rational therapy with montamine oxidase inhibitors. *British Journal of Psychiatry*, 1976, *128*, 354–360.

*Uhlenhuth, E., & Paykel, E.S. Symptom intensity and life events. *Archives of General Psychiatry*, 1973, *28*, 473–477.

*Underwood, B., Froming, W.J., & Moore, B.S. Mood, attention, and altruism: A search for mediating variables. *Developmental Psychology*, 1977, *13*, 541–542.

Valenstein, A.F. On attachment to painful feelings and the negative therapeutic reaction. *The Psychoanalytic Study of the Child*, 1973, *28*, 365.

Vaillant, G.E. *Adaptation to life.* Boston: Little, Brown, 1977.

Venables, J.F. Anorexia nervosa. Study of the pathogenesis of 9 cases. *Guy Hospital Report*, 1930, *80*, 213.

*Vigersky, R.A. (Ed.). *Anorexia nervosa.* New York: Raven Press, 1977.

*Vigersky, R.A., & Andersen, A.E. Conclusions. In R.A. Vigersky (Ed.), *Anorexia nervosa.* New York: Raven Press, 1977.

Vila, J. & Beech, H.R. Vulnerability and conditioning in relation to the human menstrual cycle. *British Journal of Social and Clinical Psychology*, 1977, *16*, 69–75.

Vila, J., & Beech, H.R. Vulnerability and defensive reactions in relation to the human menstrual cycle. *British Journal of Social and Clinical Psychology*, 1978, *7*, 93–100.

*Vinokur, A., & Selzer, M.L. Desirable versus undesirable life events: Their relationship to stress and mental distress. *Journal of Personality and Social Psychology*, 1975, *32* (2), 329–337.

Voth, H.M., & Orth, M.H. *Psychotherapy and the role of the environment.* New York: Behavioral Press, 1973.

*Wachtel, P.L. *Psychoanalysis and behavior therapy: Toward an integration.* New York: Basic Books, 1977.

Wahler, R.G. Some structural aspects of deviant child behavior. *Journal of Applied Behavior Analysis,* 1975, *8,* 27–42.

Wahler, R.G., Berland, R.M., & Coe, T.D. Generalization processes in child behavior change. In B.B. Laney & A.E. Kazdin (Eds.), *Advances in clinical child psychology* (Vol. 2). New York: Plenum, 1979.

Wahler, R.G., & Fox, J.J. III. *Response structure in deviant child–parent relationships: Implications for family therapy.* Paper presented to the Nebraska Symposium on Motivation, University of Nebraska, Lincoln, October 1980. (a)

Wahler, R.G., & Fox, J.J. III. Solitary toy play and time out: A family treatment package for children with aggressive and oppositional behavior. *Journal of Applied Behavior Analysis,* 1980, *13,* 23–39. (b)

Wahler, R.G., Sperling, K.A., Thomas, M.R., Teeter, N.C., & Luper, H.L. The modification of childhood stuttering: Some response–response relationships. *Journal of Experimental Child Psychology,* 1970, *9,* 411–428.

Walen, S., Hauserman, N.M., & Lavin, P.J. *Clinical guide to behavior therapy.* Baltimore: Williams and Wilkins, 1977.

Walker, K.N., MacBride, A., & Vachon, M.L.S. Social support networks and the crisis of bereavement. *Social Science and Medicine,* 1977, *11,* 35–41.

*Wallace, J., & Sadalla, E. Behavior consequences of transgression: The effects of social recognition. *Journal of Experimental Research in Personality,* 1966, *1,* 187–194.

Waller, J.H., Kaufman, M.R., & Deutsch, F. Anorexia nervosa: A psychosomatic entity. *Psychosomatic Medicine,* 1940, *2,* 3.

*Warren, M.P., & Vande Wiele, R.L. Clinical and metabolic features of anorexia nervosa. *American Journal of Obstetrical Gynecology,* 1973, *117,* 435–449.

Wasserman, T.H. & Vogrin, D.J. Long-term effects of a token economy on target and off-task behaviors. *Psychology in the Schools,* 1979, *16,* 551–557.

Wattie, B. Evaluating short-term casework in a family agency. *Social Casework,* 1973, 54m, 608–616.

Weber, J.J., Elison, J., & Moss, L.M. The application of ego-strength scales to psychoanalytic clinic records. In G.S. Goldman & D. Shapiro (Eds.), *Developments in psychoanalysis at Columbia University. Proceedings of the 20th Anniversary Conference.* New York: Columbia Psychology Clinic for Training and Research, 1965, pp. 205–273.

Wells, K.C., Forehand, R.L., Hickey, K. & Green, K.D. Effects of a procedure derived from the overcorrection principle on manipulated and nonmanipulated behavior. *Journal of Applied Behavior Analysis,* 1977, *10,* 679–687.

Weissman, M.M., Prusoff, B.A., DiMascio, A., Neu, C., Goklaney, M., & Klerman, G.L. The efficacy of drugs and psychotherapy in the treatment of acute depressive episodes. *American Journal of Psychiatry,* 1979, *136,* 555–558.

Weisz, G. & Bucher, B. Involving husbands in treatment of obesity—Effects on weight loss, depression, and marital satisfaction. *Behavior Therapy,* 1980, *11,* 643–650.

Weitzenhoffer, A.M. & Hilgard, E.R. Stanford Hypnotic Susceptibility Scale, Form C. Palo Alto, CA: Consulting Psychologists Press, 1962.

White, G.F., & Haas, J.E. *Assessment of research on natural hazards.* Cambridge, MA: MIT Press, 1975.

*White, R., & Watt, N. *The abnormal personality.* New York: Ronald Press, 1973.

Wilson, C.P. The Family Psychological Profile of Anorexia Nervosa Patients. *Journal of the Medical Society of New Jersey,* 1980, 77, 5, 341–344.

Wilson, G.T. Psychotherapy process and procedures: The behavioral mandate. *Behavior Therapy,* 1982, 13, 291–312.

Wilson, G.T. Limitations of meta-analysis and the lack of evidence that psychotherapy works. *The Brain and Behavior Sciences,* in press.

Wilson, G.T. & Rachman, S.J. Meta-analysis and the evaluation of psychotherapy outcome: Limitations and liabilities. *Journal of Consulting and Clinical Psychology,* in press.

Wispe, L.G., & Parloff, M.B. Impact of psychotherapy on productivity of psychologists. *Journal of Abnormal Psychology,* 1965, 70, 188–193.

Wolberg, L.R. *The technique of psychotherapy* (2nd ed.). New York: Grune & Stratton, 1977.

Wolpe, J. *Psychotherapy for reciprocal inhibition.* Stanford: University Press, 1958.

Wolpe, J. Behavior therapy and anorexia nervosa. *Journal of the American Medical Association,* 1975, 233, 317–318.

Wolpe, J. The experimental model and treatment of neurotic depression. *Behavior Research and Therapy,* 1979, 17, 555–565.

Wolpe, J. The dichotomy between classical conditioned and cognitively learned anxiety. *Journal of Behavior Therapy and Experimental Psychiatry,* 1981, 12, 35–42.

Wong, N. Combined group and individual treatment of borderline and narcissistic patients: Heterogeneous versus homogeneous groups. *International Journal of Group Psychotherapy,* 1980, 30, 389–404.

Woods, M., & Melnick, J. A review of group therapy selection criteria. *Small Group Behavior,* 1979, 10, 155–175.

*Wulliemier, F. Anorexia nervosa: Gauging treatment effectiveness. *Psychosomatics,* 1978, 19, 497–499.

Yalom, I.D. *The theory and practice of group psychotherapy.* New York: Basic Books, 1970.

Yalom, I.D. *The theory and practice of group psychotherapy.* New York: Basic Books, 1975.

*Yates, A. *Behavior therapy.* New York: Wiley, 1970.

Yeaton, W.H. A critique of the effectiveness dimension in applied behavioral analysis. In S.J. Rachman & H.J. Eysenck (Eds.), *Advances in Behavior Research and Therapy.* New York: Pergamon, 1982.

Yeaton, W.H. & Sechrest, L. Critical dimensions in the choice and maintenance of successful treatments: Strength, integrity, and effectiveness. *Journal of Consulting and Clinical Psychology,* 1981, 49, 156–167.

Zitrin, C.M., Klein, D.F. & Woerner, M.G. Behavior therapy, supportive psychotherapy, imipramine, and phobias. *Archives of General Psychiatry,* 1978, 35, 307–316.

Index

Index